Issues in Religion and Theology

4

Theodicy in the Old Testament

Issues in Religion and Theology

SERIES EDITORS

DOUGLAS KNIGHT
Associate Professor of Old Testament
Vanderbilt University
The Divinity School

ROBERT MORGAN
Lecturer in New Testament
University of Oxford

ADVISORY EDITORIAL BOARD

GEORGE MACRAE SJ
Harvard University
The Divinity School

SALLIE McFAGUE
Vanderbilt University
The Divinity School

WAYNE MEEKS
Yale University

JOHN ROGERSON
University of Sheffield

STEPHEN SYKES
University of Durham

Titles in the series include:

1   The Messianic Secret   *ed. Christopher Tuckett*
2   Visionaries and their Apocalypses   *ed. Paul D. Hanson*
3   The Interpretation of Matthew   *ed. Graham Stanton*
4   Theodicy in the Old Testament   *ed. James L. Crenshaw*

Theodicy
in the Old Testament

Edited with an Introduction by

JAMES L. CRENSHAW

FORTRESS PRESS | SPCK
Philadelphia | London

First published in Great Britain 1983   First published in the USA 1983
SPCK   Fortress Press
Holy Trinity Church   2900 Queen Lane
Marylebone Road   Philadelphia
London NW1 4DU   Pennsylvania 19129

Library of Congress Cataloging in Publication Data
    Main entry under title:

Theodicy in the Old Testament.

    (Issues in religion and theology; 4)
    Bibliography: p.
    1. Theodicy—Biblical teaching.   2. Bible. O.T.—Criticism, inter-
pretation, etc.   I. Crenshaw, James L.   II. Series.
BS1199.T44T48   1983   231′.8   83–8885
ISBN 0–8006–1764–9

British Library Cataloguing in Publication Data

Theodicy in the Old Testament—(Issues in religion and theology; 4)
    1. Theodicy—Biblical teaching
    I. Title   II. Crenshaw, James L.   III. Series
    231′8   BS1199.T/

ISBN 0–281–04067–2

Filmset in Monophoto Times by Northumberland Press Ltd, Gateshead
Printed in Great Britain by Richard Clay (The Chaucer Press) Ltd, Bungay, Suffolk

Contents

The Contributors

WALTHER EICHRODT (1890–1978) was Professor of Old Testament and History of Religion at the University of Basel. He is best known for his *Theology of the Old Testament*.

RONALD J. WILLIAMS, Emeritus Professor at the University of Toronto, specialized in Egyptology and ancient Near Eastern wisdom literature. He is the author of *Hebrew Syntax*, as well as numerous scholarly works on demotic literature from Egypt.

KLAUS KOCH is Professor of Old Testament and History of Ancient Near Eastern Religions at the University of Hamburg. Among his many works are *The Growth of the Biblical Tradition*, *The Prophets*, and *The Rediscovery of Apocalyptic*.

GERHARD VON RAD (1901–1971) was Professor of Old Testament at the University of Heidelberg. There he wrote his classic work, *Old Testament Theology*, commentaries on *Genesis* and *Deuteronomy*, and *Wisdom in Israel*.

A. S. PEAKE (1865–1929) edited what became the most admired one-volume commentary on the Bible in this century, *Peake's Commentary* (1919). He also wrote *The Problem of Suffering in the Old Testament* and commentaries on *Job* and *Lamentations*.

MARTIN BUBER (1878–1965) is best known for his interest in Hasidism. Out of this interest evolved his dialogical philosophy, articulated especially in *I and Thou*. He taught philosophy from 1938 to 1951 at the Hebrew University of Jerusalem.

JAMES L. CRENSHAW, Professor of Old Testament at Vanderbilt University Divinity School and editor of the Society of Biblical Literature Monograph Series, has published widely on wisdom literature. Among his many works are *Old Testament Wisdom*, *Hymnic Affirmation of Divine Justice*, and *Prophetic Conflict*.

HARTMUT GESE is Professor of Old Testament at the University of Tübingen. His published works include *Lehre und Wirklichkeit in der alten Weisheit*, *Vom Sinai zum Zion*, and *Essays on Biblical Theology*.

Acknowledgements

Walter Eichrodt, "Faith in Providence and Theodicy in the Old Testament" was first published as "Vorsehungsglaube und Theodizee im Alten Testament" in *Festschrift Otto Procksch* (Leipzig: J. C. Hinrichs, 1934) 45–70.

Ronald J. Williams, "Theodicy in the Ancient Near East" is reprinted by permission of the author from *Canadian Journal of Theology* 2 (1956) 14–26.

Klaus Koch, "Is There a Doctrine of Retribution in the Old Testament?" was first published as "Gibt es ein Vergeltungsdogma im Alten Testament?" in *Zeitschrift für Theologie und Kirche* 52 (1955) 1–42. It is translated by permission of the author. Copyright © 1972 by Klaus Koch.

Gerhard von Rad, "The Confessions of Jeremiah" was first published as "Die Konfessionen Jeremias" in *Evangelische Theologie* 3 (1936) 265–76. It is translated by permission from *Gesammelte Studien zum Alten Testament II* (TBü 48; Munich: Chr. Kaiser, 1973) 224–35. Copyright © 1973 by Chr. Kaiser.

A. S. Peake, "Job: The Problem of the Book" was first published in *Job* (Century Bible; New York: Henry Frowde; Edinburgh: T. C. & E. C. Jack, 1905) 9–21.

Martin Buber, "The Heart Determines: Psalm 73" was first published in Hebrew in *Ha-Zadek veha-Avel* (Jerusalem, 1950). This English translation is reprinted by permission of Schocken Books Inc. from *On the Bible* by Martin Buber, 199–210. Copyright © 1968 by Schocken Books Inc.

James L. Crenshaw, "The Problem of Theodicy in Sirach" is reprinted by permission from *Journal of Biblical Literature* 94 (1975) 47–64. Copyright © 1975 by Society of Biblical Literature.

Hartmut Gese, "The Crisis of Wisdom in Koheleth" was first published as "Die Krisis der Weisheit bei Koheleth." It is translated by permission from *Les sagesses du Proche-Orient ancien*, Colloque de Strasbourg 1962 (Paris: Presses Universitaires de France, 1963) 139–51. Copyright © 1963 by Presses Universitaires de France.

The editor and the publishers gratefully acknowledge the help of the translators: Laurence L. Welborn (ch. 1), Thomas H. Trapp (ch. 3), Arlis John Ehlin (ch. 4), and Lester L. Grabbe (ch. 8).

Series Foreword

The Issues in Religion and Theology series intends to encompass a variety of topics within the general disciplines of religious and theological studies. Subjects are drawn from any of the component fields, such as biblical studies, systematic theology, ethics, history of Christian thought, and history of religion. The issues have all proved to be highly significant for their respective areas, and they are of similar interest to students, teachers, clergy, and general readers.

The series aims to address these issues by collecting and reproducing key studies, all previously published, which have contributed significantly to our present understandings. In each case, the volume editor introduces the discussion with an original essay which describes the subject and its treatment in religious and theological studies. To this editor has also fallen the responsibility of selecting items for inclusion – no easy task when one considers the vast number of possibilities. Together the essays are intended to present a balanced overview of the problem and various approaches to it. Each piece is important in the current debate, and any older publication included normally stands as a "classical" or seminal work which is still worth careful study. Readers unfamiliar with the issue should find that these discussions provide a good entrée, while more advanced students will appreciate having studies by some of the best specialists on the subject gathered together in one volume. The editor has, of course, faced certain constraints: analyses too lengthy or too technical could not be included, except perhaps in excerpt form; the bibliography is not exhaustive; and the volumes in this series are being kept to a reasonable, uniform length. On the other hand, the editor is able to overcome the real problem of inaccessibility. Much of the best literature on a subject is often not readily available to readers, whether because it was first published in journals or books not widely circulated or because it was originally written in a language not read by all who would benefit from it. By bringing these and other studies together in this series, we hope to contribute to the general understanding of these key topics.

The series editors and the publishers wish to express their gratitude to the authors and their original publishers whose works are reprinted or translated here, often with corrections from living authors.

We are also conscious of our debt to members of the editorial advisory board. They have shared our belief that the series will be useful on a wide scale, and they have therefore been prepared to spare much time and thought for the project.

DOUGLAS A. KNIGHT
ROBERT MORGAN

Abbreviations

AnBib	Analecta Biblica
ANET	J. B. Pritchard, *Ancient Near Eastern Texts* (1955², 1969³)
APOT	R. H. Charles (ed.), *Apocrypha and Pseudepigrapha of the Old Testament*
ATANT	Abhandlungen zur Theologie des Alten und Neuen Testaments
ATD	Das Alte Testament Deutsch
ATLA	American Theological Library Association
BBB	Bonner biblische Beiträge
BH	*Biblia hebraica*
Bib	*Biblica*
BKAT	Biblischer Kommentar: Altes Testament
BZAW	Beihefte zur *ZAW*
CBQ	*Catholic Biblical Quarterly*
CJT	*Canadian Journal of Theology*
EHAT	Exegetisches Handbuch zum Alten Testament
ET	English translation/English translator
EvT	*Evangelische Theologie*
FzB	Forschungen zur Bibel
HAT	Handbuch zum Alten Testament
HK	Handkommentar zum Alten Testament (=HKAT)
HKAT	Handkommentar zum Alten Testament
HUCA	*Hebrew Union College Annual*
IB	*Interpreter's Bible*
IDBSup	Supplementary volume to *Interpreter's Dictionary of the Bible*
JAOS	*Journal of the American Oriental Society*
JBC	R. E. Brown et al. (ed.), *The Jerome Biblical Commentary*
JBL	*Journal of Biblical Literature*
JCS	*Journal of Cuneiform Studies*
JEOL	*Jaarbericht ... ex oriente lux*
JR	*Journal of Religion*

JSJ	*Journal for the Study of Judaism in the Persian, Hellenistic, and Roman Period*
KAT	Kommentar zum Alten Testament
KHC	Kurzer Handkommentar zum Alten Testament, Tübingen
KEK	Kritisch-exegetischer Kommentar über das Neue Testament (Meyer)
LXX	Septuagint
MDOG	Mitteilungen der deutschen Orient-Gesellschaft
MT	Massoretic Text
OBT	Overtures to Biblical Theology
OT	Old Testament
RB	*Revue biblique*
RevExp	*Review and Expositor*
RHPR	*Revue d'histoire et de philosophie religieuses*
RHR	*Revue de l'histoire des religions*
RSV	Revised Standard Version of the Bible
SÄK	*Studien zur altägyptischen Kultur*
SAT	*Die Schriften des Alten Testaments*, 3 vols, Göttingen 1920–25
SBL	Society of Biblical Literature
SBLDS	Society of Biblical Literature Dissertation Series
SBLMS	Society of Biblical Literature Monograph Series
SchTU	*Schweizerische Theologische Umschau*
SUNT	Studien zur Umwelt des Neuen Testaments
TBü	Theologische Bücherei
TDNT	G. W. Bromiley, (ET and ed.), *Theological Dictionary of the New Testament* (= *ThWNT*)
ThWNT	G. Kittel and G. Friedrich (ed.), *Theologisches Worterbuch zum Neuen Testament* (= ET: *TDNT*)
TLZ	*Theologische Literaturzeitung*
VTSup	Vetus Testamentum, Supplements
WdF	Wege der Forschung
WUNT	Wissenschaftliche Monographien zum Alten und Neuen Testament
ZÄS	*Zeitschrift für ägyptische Sprache und Altertumskunde*
ZAW	*Zeitschrift für die alttestamentliche Wissenschaft*
ZTK	*Zeitschrift für Theologie und Kirche*

Introduction: The Shift from Theodicy to Anthropodicy

JAMES L. CRENSHAW

The human compulsion to deny death[1] is exceeded only by a desire to absolve the deity of responsiblity for injustice.[2] In truth, the two motivating forces are integrally related to one another, for death stands as the ultimate question mark attached to any defense of God.[3] Why, one asks, were we fashioned from such stuff that we shall eventually become food for worms (Sir. 10:11)? If, however, death does not constitute the last word, the dark shadow cast over the deity becomes somewhat less ominous. Only gradually did ancient Israel choose to walk along this path as a means towards resolving the enigmas of human existence,[4] and even when she did haltingly profess belief in life after death (Dan. 12:2; Isa. 26:19) that new-found conviction did not altogether alleviate the misery brought on by the phenomena of evil, suffering, and death. It follows that a study of Israel's attempts to come to terms with death and its minions will introduce us to the pathos of her faith, for both agony and ecstasy characterize that struggle to understand the universal decree, "You must die."[5]

While the problem of theodicy achieves focus in death, especially premature wasting away, the issue is much broader than that. Indeed, every phenomenon that brings into question an assumption of harmony undergirding human existence presents additional evidence for the case against God. We may thus define theodicy loosely as the attempt to pronounce a verdict of "Not Guilty" over God for whatever seems to destroy the order of society and the universe. That wish to protect the deity's honor surfaced in the very first recorded utterance by a woman in the Hebrew Bible (Gen. 3:2–3). Here the serpent's accusing question cast suspicion upon divine goodness; such doubt on the serpent's part evoked a response that

1

further restricted human freedom. A subtle shift occurs in the prohibition, one from *eating* to *touching* the forbidden fruit. We shall
see that theodicy invariably gnawed away at the integrity[6] and dignity
of those who felt constrained to come to the defense of the creator.
In short, God's reputation was salvaged at immense cost.[7]

The Search for Meaning

In order to render life bearable the ancients posited a belief in order,
both in the macrocosm and the microcosm.[8] The universe was pre-
dictable, within limits, for it was subject to the wishes of the creator.
When this assumption threatened to disintegrate from the impact
of the flood waters, the Yahwist took special care to restore faith
in nature's rhythm. The so-called Noachic covenant constitutes the
divine assurance to all peoples that life could go on under changed
circumstances brought about by the Deluge (Gen. 9:8–17). Such an
assault from the forces of chaos would never again threaten the
world; the rainbow exists as a reminder of this promise, a sign that
is visible both to the one freely giving it and to those joyfully receiving
its benefits. To be sure, individuals were thereafter subject to attack
from evil in its various manifestations. Therefore, it follows that
meaning and not happiness was basic to survival. Isolated individuals
could endure sporadic irruptions of undeserved distress in the knowledge that the belief system was not threatened. So long as that
conviction of order held firm in the universe, essential meaning
remained intact despite occasional disturbances that made happiness
an elusive goal.

What was the precise nature of these disturbances? We may speak
of three basic phenomena: evil, suffering and death. The first of
these unwelcome visitors consists of moral evil, natural evil, and
religious evil. Since nature's destructive forces were unleashed by
the creator, the distinction between moral and natural evil becomes
somewhat vague in ethical monotheism. Naturally, the situation is
different where a pantheon of gods exists, for certain deities
are responsible for life's disturbing aspects, while others share no
responsibility for these vexing phenomena.[9] In Israelite thought one
God "kills and brings to life, he brings down to Sheol and raises up"
(1 Sam. 2:6), to quote a significant declaration in the Song of Hannah.
Similarly, Deutero-Isaiah announces the divine word that "I form
light and create darkness, I make weal and create woe, I am the
Lord, who do all these things" (Isa. 45:7). The consequence of
emphasis upon God's incomparability,[10] nay sole existence, was
intensified distress about undeserved suffering. Famine, pestilence,

2

and earthquake struck human society without discriminating between the innocent and the guilty.

One way to diffuse the situation was to assert that natural forces merely functioned as instruments of divine punishment for sin. While such a claim came to God's defense by reasserting the familiar theme that even Behemoth and Leviathan have been subdued by their creator,[11] this explanation failed to take into account the terrible misery inflicted upon innocent persons who happened to be caught up in the suffering occasioned by nature's fury. A case can even be made for the essential connection between belief in creation and divine justice. Although the rise of creation theology is often associated with saving history, the allusions to God as creator in wisdom literature reinforce belief in divine justice. In short, the one who brought the world into being possesses sufficient power to ensure a balance of order and equity. That is why again and again sages brought together the concepts of creation and justice.[12]

Moral evil is a relational category, but is not necessarily limited to the human sphere. On the vertical dimension issues of morality surface, for individuals seem always eager to subject the deity to norms of justice and virtue that operate among human beings. Base and inhumane treatment of others, as well as manipulation for personal ends, comprises moral evil, regardless of its source. The assumption of order on the societal level may permit moral evil to flourish unrecognized and unchallenged, for it enables rulers to justify their position and policies just as it secures a place in the overall scheme of things for those who are governed. This strange circumstance encourages two vastly different kinds of theodicies, one for the oppressor and another for the oppressed. The ensuing situation may explain the emphasis upon God as sustainer of kings and champion of widows and orphans. Each group, the powerful and the powerless, rushed to God's defense where its interests were concerned.

What, then, does the third category of evil entail? Religious evil signifies an inner disposition that perverts authentic response to the holy. That perversion may assume the form of idolatry,[13] where worship is directed away from God to a pale reflection of the ultimate. This type of evil operates wholly on the vertical plane; it concerns human relationship with God and thus extends to the innermost recesses of the imagination.[14] In this respect, religious evil is by its very nature more hidden than the other two, moral and natural evil. It is therefore all the more pernicious since its presence can be easily concealed from human eyes. In fact, some individuals dared to stretch the cloak of secrecy into the heavens, denying God's clarity of vision on grounds of remoteness or indifference.[15] "How can God see through the dark clouds?" they reasoned, whenever they did not actually suggest that the creator lacked interest in terrestrial happenings.

Does not the assumption of order carry in its train a conviction that life has some discernible purpose? Teleology, it would seem, accompanies belief in the harmony of existence. Order implies a goal whereas chaos lacks movement towards some final meaningful destination. Incursions of anomy[16] can at best momentarily divert the march towards a distant goal, but in the last resort such disturbances only hasten progress in the direction of the desired end. They do so by sharpening one's resolve and by shaping character, for adversity does not necessarily weaken individuals.

That brings us to the problem of undeserved suffering, a subject that frequently occupied the thoughts of the ancients as it continues to do in the modern world which has seen the issue present itself definitively and paradigmatically in the great Lisbon earthquake of 1755 and more recently in the nightmares of Auschwitz and Hiroshima.[17] What possible response to such puzzling nightmares exists? Space permits us to do no more than name the several approaches to this problem in ancient Israel. These consist of at least seven means of reconciling undeserved suffering with belief in order and purpose. They understand suffering as retributive, disciplinary, revelational, probative, illusory, transitory, or mysterious.[18] Admittedly, an eighth response to this problem achieves prominence in Qoheleth, who denies the possibility of discovering any meaning behind innocent suffering. In this respect such denial resembles the previous response that appeals to the unknown and unknowable (and thus constitutes something approaching an anti-theodicy), but it goes one step further and asserts that life under such conditions has no meaning, for no comforter can be found (Eccl. 4:1).

In many cases such suffering results in death; we have thus arrived at the third manifestation of anomy mentioned earlier. Now the occurrence of death does not always introduce an element of disturbance requiring explanation. In proper time and manner death resembled the gathering of golden shocks of grain at the season of harvest.[19] Lacking a view of life beyond the grave, save in some ghost-like semblance of existence, Israelites accepted death as inevitable, sometimes, to be sure, with slight tinges of resignation.[20] Entirely different, however, were those instances when death came out of season and violently. How could one believe in God's justice when the ugly dimension of death gained ascendancy?

The issue becomes more perplexing when one pauses to reflect

4

upon the character of the Israelite Lord. Lying at the very heart of her faith is the conviction that Yahweh chose the Israelites and set them apart for special promise and mission. Her sacred narrative and poetry extol God as redeemer of an oppressed people, one who subsequently experienced remarkable demonstrations of divine presence and power. Before this sovereign all earthly rulers must acquiesce, for not even Egypt's might could withstand Yahweh's initiative. Israel's sacred story abounds in divine promises to accompany the chosen ones and assurances that she need not fear enemies from without. Still, circumstances managed to transform such positive words into hollow promises devoid of substance. In a word, the covenant relationship exacerbated the problem of theodicy,[21] for the Lord confessed a personal interest in Israel's destiny. In the absence of visible proof that God continues to direct the history of Israel towards a distant goal, what was she supposed to think? Surely that question pressed itself upon the religious leaders in 722 and 587 B.C.E., for the collapse of the northern kingdom and the destruction of Jerusalem were events of no small consequence. The latter calamity was particularly troubling, for Zion had come to represent God's very presence and power, and in fact Josiah's religious reform stood under divine promise articulated in Deuteronomy.[22] The violence which stilled Josiah forever made mockery of God's assurances that success would attend faithful conduct.[23]

The notion of reward and punishment which permeates the Deuteronomistic history and most of the Hebrew Bible presented a ready defense of God: the people are merely reaping what they sowed. In some cases the claim may actually have accorded with reality, especially where "doxologies of judgement" rang forth. In such texts a guilty person or persons confessed God's goodness in pronouncing a sentence of death (see Josh. 7:19; Amos 4:13; 5:8–9; 9:5–6, and related passages). But who would contend that all instances of suffering were occasioned by the victims' wickedness? The resulting tension between divine and human culpability was nearly always eased by stressing the latter's sinfulness. In short, defense of God occurred at human expense. As a consequence theodicy was given up, and anthropodicy became the fundamental problem claiming the attention of religious thinkers.[24]

Theodicy in the Old Testament

"It is arrogant to attempt to defend God's justice; it is still more arrogant to assail the deity."[25] Whoever makes such a claim participates minimally in the spirit of the Hebrew Bible, where complaint rises to the God who has revealed the divine nature as merciful.[26] Nevertheless, even in the Old Testament all rational efforts at theodicy abort, for humans cannot possess firm knowledge of Transcendence.[27] That is why such "rational" theodicies as Job eventually cross over into the realm of feeling and will. Human beings are more than rational creatures; they also possess deep feelings and wishes, which any authentic theodicy must address.

Even those theodicies which sufficiently take feelings and desires into account fail in one important respect: they sacrifice human integrity. In a real sense, Job's silent submission before an awesome display of power amounts to loss of integrity, hence may rightly be termed an argument against humanity.[28]

It may actually be the case that self-abnegation lies at the heart of all theodicy. Only as the individual fades into nothingness can the deity achieve absolute pardon. That loss of individuality may occur in some mystical union wherein one's true selfhood is thought to come to full expression, or it may take place in abject groveling upon the ground before the mighty God. In either case the really human is denigrated, and therein lurks a fatal flaw. Such a condition gives rise to utterances like the following:

> The Lord saw that the wickedness of man was great in the earth, and that every imagination of the thoughts of his heart was only evil continually.
>
> Gen. 6:5

In this thinker's view, the flood was wholly justified because humans constituted a *massa perditiones*. The same sort of reasoning occurs to justify the later calamity that befell the southern kingdom in 587.

> Run to and fro through the streets of Jerusalem, look and take note! Search her squares to see if you can find a man, one who does justice and seeks truth; that I may pardon her.
>
> Jer. 5:1

The prophet goes first to the poor people and finds no virtue. Such results are expected, since the poorer classes are ill informed about divine law. So he turns to the upper classes, from whom he expects greater obedience to torah, and makes an astonishing discovery. The elite citizens have also rebelled against decency and have become wholly wanton. In effect, knowledge is not tantamount to obedience, and humans require a new heart (Jer. 31:31–34).

In one respect, this text contrasts with another which endeavours to justify wholesale slaughter of the inhabitants of Sodom and Gomorrah. The presence of a single righteous person suffices to spare the holy city, whereas Abraham stopped at ten when bargaining with God over the fate of the doomed cities. To be sure, the narrative in Gen. 18:16–33 depicts a responsive deity, and one could argue that the failure was Abraham's, not God's inasmuch as the absence of a single virtuous person in Sodom and Gomorrah is demonstrated by the unfolding story. Since the cities lacked a saving individual, the Judge of the whole earth acted properly, and the patriarch's stunning question, "Shall not the Judge of all the earth do right?" (18:25), loses something of its force. [29]

Such salvaging of God's honor at the expense of human integrity eventuated in a grandiose interpretation of history that amounts to a monumental theodicy. This Deuteronomistic theology justifies national setbacks and political oppression as divine punishment for sin. The portrayal of Israel and Judah as corrupt to the core suffices to justify divine abandonment of the chosen people, but such rescuing of God's sovereignty and freedom was purchased at a high price, the self-esteem of humans.

This tendency to save God's honor by sacrificing human integrity seems to have caught on in ancient Israel, for every effort at theodicy represents a substantial loss of human dignity. The various attempts at theodicy constitute immense sacrifice: of the present, of reality itself, of personal honor, and of the will.

Perhaps the most natural response to the incursion of evil into unexpected circumstances is the surrender of the present moment in favor of future rectification. Without a tiny ray of hope life would become intolerable. The eschatological dimension speaks to this fundamental need by promising that the present calamity will soon pass away, and in its place will come clear signs of God's favor. The further into the future, or indeed into a hidden realm, this expected deliverance is projected, the safer the theodicy, since it becomes less vulnerable to empirical disconfirmation. [30] On the other hand, because the anticipated event is relegated to the remote future, its credibility is likely to fade as generation after generation long for the saving event and experience no fulfilment of that wish. Habakkuk's agonizing cry, "O Lord, how long shall I cry for help, and thou wilt not hear? Or cry to thee, 'Violence!' and thou wilt not save?" (1:2), cannot be sustained indefinitely unless some indication of divine action presents itself. [31]

One means of dealing with delay in deliverance is to remove the hoped-for event from the realm of experience altogether. That can be achieved in two quite different ways. One can deny the reality of the evil, relegating it to illusion, as the author of Psalm 73 does, or one can shift the arena of God's action to the inner

7

spirit or onto a hidden dimension of reality.[32] This hidden realm may be simultaneous in time, or it may be projected into the next world. Either way, the present experience fades into the shadow cast by anticipated bliss.

Sometimes theodicy seeks to excuse this delay in restoration by interpreting adversity as discipline.[33] Such an explanation for suffering takes many forms, but invariably it assumes that true character cannot emerge apart from testing. This argument pervades the Book of Job, finding frequent expression in the speeches of the three friends as well as in Elihu's angry remarks. As everyone knows, loving parents discipline wayward children, so it should occasion no surprise that God chastens sinful Israel and Judah. From this experience of suffering emerge new insights into selfhood, just as the initial act of disobedience in the garden bestowed valuable knowledge upon the first couple.[34] Often this kind of reasoning is reinforced by the assertion that beauty needs ugliness in order to come to full fruition.

A serious flaw is present in such thinking, specifically the assumption that the universe had to be constituted in such a way that evil is indispensable to goodness. One can readily imagine that a good creator could have made the world differently. What conceivable argument exists for God to enter into a bargain with the Satan to test the faithful servant Job? Or how can one even imagine God demanding that Abraham sacrifice his own son as a test of obedience?[35] No acquisition of fresh insight seems sufficiently precious to justify the private hell initiated by the words: "Take your son, your only son Isaac, whom you love, and go to the land of Moriah, and offer him there as a burnt offering upon one of the mountains of which I shall tell you" (Gen. 22:2). Even less persuasive is Ezekiel's unthinkable declaration to the effect that God gave laws demanding human sacrifice in order to horrify the people (Ezek. 20:25–26).[36]

Another sacrifice of human integrity occurs when individuals give up every right to question God's ways. Jeremiah admits at the outset that he must be in the wrong and God in the right, for that is the nature of things.[37]

> Righteous art thou, O Lord,
> when I complain to thee;
> Yet I would plead my case before thee.
> Why does the way of the wicked prosper?
> Why do all who are treacherous thrive?

Jer. 12:1

An innocent Job smarts from God's challenge, "Will you even put me in the wrong? Will you condemn me that you may be justified?" (Job 40:8), and proceeds to reverse the offense by putting himself in the wrong. Standing before this blustering deity, such a one can only repent in dust and ashes. Where then is his integrity? Has not peace been purchased at too great a cost?

Later attempts to come to grips with human suffering at the hands of cruel oppressors seized this clue and salvaged belief in divine goodness. But that traditional conviction survived at the expense of human dignity, so that it becomes customary to describe society as a *massa damnationis*. The extent to which such thinking can go is manifest in 2 Esdras, where the hero alone is assured divine forgiveness. For the remainder of the people an awful punishment awaited. The seeds sown by Job have found fertile soil in the mind of this tormented individual.[38] Where now is the Lord of covenant love?

Earlier thinkers experienced less consternation over such negative understandings of human virtue, for they believed in something approximating an ontological link which connected an individual genealogically with others in the social group. Here the loss of the self occurs on the level of clan relations, and actual suffering poses no lasting argument against divine goodness, inasmuch as the individual survives in the life of the group. This sacrificing of the self for the welfare of the larger entity has its correlate in subsequent self-denial for the sake of the community or for God.[39]

The powerful idea of a suffering servant who voluntarily endures the afflictions of the larger society and becomes a means of redemption has been called the most profound solution offered by religion to the problem of evil.[40] This chosen one in Deutero-Isaiah takes upon himself the punishment that should have befallen the guilty, and thus spares both God and humans. The picture is not quite so clear, however, for the voluntary nature of his suffering remains uncertain. Both human acquiescence and divine intention combine in the description of the faithful servant.

> Yet it was the will of the Lord to bruise him;
> he has put him to grief;
> when he makes himself an offering for sin,
> he shall see his offspring, he shall prolong his days;
> the will of the Lord shall prosper in his hand.

Isa. 53:10

One almost gains the impression that the servant had little choice, like the lamb to which he is compared. Beyond that, the vicarious nature of suffering poses an additional problem if it is understood in a manner other than exemplary. How can someone else's suffering remove my guilt?

The preceding discussion has concentrated on the loss of human dignity that accompanies theodicy as it manifests itself in the Hebrew Bible. There is yet another dimension which calls for discussion, namely the loss of essential divine characteristics. These defenses of God's justice strike a compromise in several important respects: they place in jeopardy God's sovereign freedom and self-disclosure, and they imply that another deity exists in opposition to the Lord. One way to justify the presence of human suffering is to associate God directly with that agony. This emphasis upon the divine pathos,[41] which certain prophets stress to the limit, insists that God suffers from the effects of human rebellion.

> How can I give you up, O Ephraim!
>   How can I hand you over, O Israel!
> How can I make you like Admah!
>   How can I treat you like Zeboim!
> My heart recoils within me,
>   My compassion grows warm and tender.
> I will not execute my fierce anger,
>   I will not again destroy Ephraim;
> For I am God and not man,
>   the Holy One in your midst,
>   and I will not come to destroy.[42]
>
> Hos. 11:8–9

While some would argue that this loss of perfection in the deity is grievous, others celebrate the limitless potential of a God in process of becoming. This way of speaking about God accords well with the Hebrew Bible's tendency to highlight God's changeability. To be sure, the divine inconstancy arises from human response to prior divine action, but the Bible seems content to describe God as learning through experience.

Without question the greatest threat to the idea of God concerns freedom. The central theological question posed by the suffering Job is whether God is free or not.[43] Are human notions of justice the ultimate arbiter of God's actions? Must God succumb to the magical assumption that lies at the heart of religion as it expresses itself? Or is disinterested righteousness more than an illusion? An affirmative answer to the latter question signifies victory over bondage to magic. Now and then a rare human being will be good for the sake of the good act, not for reward or from fear of punishment.

Insistence upon God's bondage to justice takes a peculiar shape in Jonah's mind, for he objected to merciful actions when they were directed towards foreigners who had occasioned untold suffering in Israel. The ancient creed associated with God's self-revelation to a persistent Moses (Exod. 34:6–7) proclaimed the compassionate nature of the Lord in unforgettable fashion, while at the same time cautioning against presuming that sin would go unnoticed. Other texts, particularly Deuteronomy and Hosea, carried the emphasis upon Yahweh's graciousness to considerable extreme, arguing that God had chosen Israel through no worth of her own and that wanton conduct could not nullify a profound bond uniting the two. Jonah's anger towards God arose from a conviction that inhumane treatment of others should not be forgiven so readily, particularly when the prophet's reputation for truthfulness was also at stake. A peculiar irony lurks within Jonah's protest[44] since he was himself a recipient of divine compassion for a wayward sinner. How ludicrous, therefore, is the stated basis for Jonah's fury: "For I knew that thou art a gracious God and Merciful, slow to anger, and abounding in steadfast love, and repentest of evil" (4:2b).

The authors of numerous proverbs [45] and Psalm 37 come perilously close to enslaving God, who according to their view *must* reward the good deed and punish the bad one. Indeed, a break with reality has already occurred in Ps. 37:25: "I have been young, and now am old; yet I have not seen the righteous forsaken or his children begging bread." That attitude in Job's friends and in Elihu impels them to heap untold misery upon the victim of God's withdrawal.

In Job's case the divine retreat into silence was temporary, and consequently gave way to torrential rebuke. Other theodicies resort to the idea of a chasm separating humans from the divine realm. In this case appeal is made to the *deus absconditus*, the God who hides.[46] Since God is by nature unknowable, this argument is particularly persuasive – except that it is combined with belief in revelation. The self-disclosing one is also the hidden one, and therein lies the problem. Admittedly, withholding of essential nature protects the deity's sovereignty, but why must the mystery begin when injustice raises its ugly head?

Another means of protecting God's honor comes from compromising ethical monotheism, as happens in the old folk tale upon which the story of Job depends. Here the Satan confronts the deity and challenges him to a contest to ascertain the disinterested character of Job's goodness. Since the adversary is designated as a child of God in the employ of the divine court, the shift in responsibility for ensuing atrocities is slight. Ultimately, God is still at fault. A much greater step is therefore taken in Chronicles, where objectionable conduct on God's part in 2 Samuel 24 is attributed to Satan. This understanding of divine action is a great distance from later developments where Satan functions in a quasi-dualistic manner. In such apocalyptic theodicies reality fades to the extent that history is demeaned and world-denial championed. Perhaps the personification of wisdom deserves mention, inasmuch as this intriguing figure functions in God's stead, thus ensuring divine presence and power to an age that saw no visible evidence of such. Echoes within this hymnic material approach a compromise in the area of a female associate,[47] but she is not seen as the source of evil.

Conclusion

The preceding discussion of theodicy in the Hebrew Bible has endeavored to present the central theological issues and the basic biblical resources relating to defense of God. Care has been taken to avoid duplication, insofar as possible, of treatments selected for inclusion in this volume. The aim has been to be provocative; in ancient Israel defense of God was no idle chatter but was purchased at great cost, as we have seen. Was the gain worth the loss? In their own way, the ensuing essays will address this important question.

The essays chosen for reproduction in this volume introduce the reader to the scope of the dilemma ancient Israelites faced in coming to grips with phenomena that seemed to deny the force of the claim that justice prevailed on high. The first three articles address the general problem of theodicy, the initial one against the backdrop of a theological theme that organizes Israelite religious thought, specifically that of the covenant, and the following essay against the larger geographical setting of ancient Egypt and Mesopotamia. The third isolates a single issue, whether a dogma of retribution existed in biblical religion, and endeavors to clarify the implications of belief in a sphere of act-consequence. These three essays which present the problem in its broader context are then complemented by special examinations of the theological issue of theodicy in representative texts within the Hebrew canon and in one instance, within the Apocrypha. Those biblical texts are the confessions of Jeremiah, Job, Psalm 73, Sirach (Ecclesiasticus) and Qoheleth (Ecclesiastes). The focus of the entire collection, whether specific or comprehensive, serves as a faithful witness to the earnestness that has characterized investigations ancient or modern into the harrowing questions associated with belief in divine justice.

NOTES

1 Ernest Becker (*The Denial of Death* [New York: The Free Press, 1973]), has demonstrated our obsession with death and has examined in great detail heroic attempts to deny death's reality.

2 J. L. Crenshaw, s.v. "Theodicy," IDBSup.

3 "Every human order is a community in the face of death. Theodicy represents the attempt to make a pact with death." (P. L. Berger, *The Sacred Canopy* [Garden City, N.Y.: Doubleday & Co., 1969] 80).

4 Gese, *Zur biblischen Theologie: Alttestamentliche Vorträge* (Munich: Chr. Kaiser, 1977) 31–54 [=ET: 34–59].

5 See Sir. 14:11; 41:3. See J. L. Crenshaw, "The Shadow of Death in Ecclesiastes," in *Israelite Wisdom: Theological and Literary Essays in Honor of Samuel Terrien* (ed. J. G. Gammie, et al.; Missoula, Mont.: Scholars Press, 1978) 205–16.

6 Note the manner in which the first man isolates himself, accusing his newly acquired wife and God, the generous fashioner of the woman who earlier elicited an ecstatic shout of satisfaction.

7 That fact has not escaped C. G. Jung, who suspects that God needed constant reassurance that he was just, even at the expense of the truth. (*Answer to Job* [Cleveland and New York: World Publishing Co., 1960] 32). One may also consult Ernst Bloch (*Atheism in Christianity* [New York: Herder and Herder, 1972]).

8 H. H. Schmid, *Wesen und Geschichte der Weisheit* (BZAW 101; Berlin: Töpelmann, 1966).

9 G. Buccellati ("Wisdom and Not: The Case of Mesopotamia," *JAOS* 101 [1981] 36) writes that the texts dealing with theodicy "present a descriptive reflection about the pervasiveness of laws which in their absolute value transcend both the individual gods and the unresolved questions of human life. Thus the Theodicy is not a vindication of a given god or of the open polytheistic system, but rather a statement about the ultimate value of the absolute, both in the divine (or supernatural) and in the human (or political) sphere."

10 C. J. Labuschagne, *The Incomparability of Yahweh in the Old Testament* (Leiden: Brill, 1966). J. L. Crenshaw (*Prophetic Conflict* [BZAW 124; Berlin and New York: Walter de Gruyter, 1971]), emphasizes the consequences for prophecy of belief in one God as giver of good and evil.

11 J. G. Gammie, "Behemoth and Leviathan: On the Didactic and Theological Significance of Job 40:15—41:26," in *Israelite Wisdom*, 217–31.

12 J. L. Crenshaw, *Studies in Ancient Israelite Wisdom* (New York: KTAV, 1976) 26–35, esp. 31–3. For a different view, see H. J. Hermisson, "Observations on the Creation Theology in Wisdom," in *Israelite Wisdom*, 43–57. The association of creation and redemption is usually based on a conviction that as creator God possesses sufficient power to save.

13 M. Gilbert, *La critique des dieux dans le Livre de la Sagesse (Sg. 13–15)* (AnBib 53; Rome: Biblical Institute Press, 1973).

14 Although religious evil functions on the vertical plane, it has significant consequences for moral action.

15 J. L. Crenshaw, "Popular Questioning of the Justice of God in Ancient Israel," *ZAW* 82 (1970) 380–95 (= *Studies in Ancient Israelite Wisdom*, 289–304).

16 The term, as used by Peter Berger and others, refers to absence of *nomos*, that which holds society or an individual together.

17 The impact of the Lisbon earthquake upon religious claims is well known, particularly as that conflict emerges in Leibniz and Voltaire. The term theodicy arose with Leibniz.

18 See among others, J. A. Sanders, *Suffering as Divine Discipline in the Old Testament and Post-Biblical Judaism* (Rochester, N.Y.: Colgate Rochester Divinity School, 1955); E. Gerstenberger and W. Schrage, *Leiden* (Stuttgart: Kohlhammer, 1977); and R. E. Murphy, "Biblical Insights into Suffering: Pathos and Compassion," in *Whither Creativity, Freedom, Suffering?: Humanity, Cosmos, God* (ed. F. A. Eigo; Proceedings of the Theology Institute of Villanova University 13. Villanova, Pa.: The University Press, 1981) 53–75.

19 L. R. Bailey, Sr., *Biblical Perspectives on Death* (OBT; Philadelphia: Fortress Press, 1979), emphasizes the Israelite acceptance of death.

20 2 Sam. 12:15–23, especially v. 23: "But now he is dead; why should I fast? Can I bring him back again? I shall go to him, but he will not return to me." Cf. 14:14, "We must all die, we are like water spilt on the ground, which cannot be gathered up again."

21 Gideon's sharp retort to the divine messenger's assurance of God's presence speaks volumes: "Pray, sir, if the Lord is with us, why then has all this befallen us? And where are all his wonderful deeds which our fathers recounted to us . . . ?" (Judg. 6:13).

22 S. B. Frost, "The Death of Josiah: A Conspiracy of Silence," *JBL* 87 (1968) 369–82.

23 Religious pragmatism occurs with vengeance in the thought of Jeremiah's opponents in Egypt who argue that it does not pay to serve Yahweh (Jer. 44:16–19).

24 In Job "the problem of theodicy is solved by an *argumentum ad hominem* in the most drastic sense – more accurately, an *argumentum contra hominen*. . . . The question of human sin replaces the question of divine justice" (Berger, *Sacred Canopy*, 74). See A. Jäger, "Theodizee und Anthropodizee bei Karl Marx," *SchTU* 37 (1967) 14–23, for discussion of the general problem in Marxist thought.

25 The quotation is attributed to Immanuel Kant by E. G. Kraeling, "A Theodicy – and More," in *The Dimensions of Job*, ed. Nahum N. Glatzer (New York: Schocken Books, 1969) 212. See I. Kant, "Über das Misslingen aller philosophischen Versuche in der Theodizee," in *Werke* (ed. W. Weischedel; Darmstadt: 1964) 6:103–24.

26 J. L. Crenshaw, "The Human Dilemma and Literature of Dissent," in *Tradition and Theology in the Old Testament* (ed. D. A. Knight; Philadelphia: Fortress Press, 1977) 235–58.

27 G. von Rad, *Wisdom in Israel* (Nashville: Abingdon Press; London: SCM Press, 1972) 97–110.

28 For a recent attempt to grapple with the meaning of the divine speeches and Job's response, see J. G. Williams, "Deciphering the Unspoken: The Theophany of Job," *HUCA* 49 (1978) 59–72.

29 In light of Abraham's question, the sharp accusation directed at Lot by citizens of the doomed cities assumes added significance ("This fellow came to sojourn, and he would play the judge!" Gen. 19:9). For concern over God's compassion

resembling Abraham's, see the story about Moses' intercession for a wayward people (Exodus 32).

30 Naturally, Deutero-Isaiah made grand promises that far exceeded the realities of a later generation, even one of fulfilled promises.

31 On Habakkuk and theodicy, see D. E. Gowan, *The Triumph of Faith in Habakkuk* (Atlanta: John Knox Press, 1976) 20–50.

32 Such a shift occurs in Ben Sira (Sirach) and Wisdom of Solomon, for whom the psychological and metaphysical realms achieve prominence in discussions of theodicy.

33 Buccellati ("Wisdom and Not: The Case of Mesopotamia," 42–44) discusses the rise of introspection and thus lyric poetry against the backdrop of adversity. He quotes a passage in Aeschylus' *Agamemnon*: "He has pointed man on his way to wisdom by having consciousness emerge through suffering: memory of pain, instead of sleep, he will distill into the heart, until it yields the gift of wisdom, even unwanted" (1:43).

34 P. Trible, *God and the Rhetoric of Sexuality* (OBT; Philadelphia: Fortress Press, 1978) 72–143.

35 J. L. Crenshaw, "Journey into Oblivion: A Structural Analysis of Gen. 22:1–19," *Soundings* 58 (1975) 243–56. Soren Kierkegaard's difficulty in "imagining" such a monstrous test prompts him to describe the griefstruck father as eager to protect God's honor, even at his own expense. Abraham reasons that it is better for Isaac to think him a beast than to think God one (*Fear and Trembling* [Garden City, N.Y.: Doubleday & Co., 1941] 27).

36 The poverty of rational defense of God surfaces in Ezekiel's feeble efforts to persuade his opponents that God's ways were just and the people's not just (18:19–29). Here assertion alone is deemed adequate, when claim and counter-claim exist. What makes the prophet's word more credible than theirs?

37 S. H. Blank, "The Confessions of Jeremiah and the Meaning of Prayer," *HUCA* 21 (1949) 331–54.

38 W. Harrelson, "Ezra Among the Wicked in 2 Esdras 3—10," in *The Divine Helmsman: Studies on God's Control of Human Events, Presented to Lou H. Silberman* (ed. J. L. Crenshaw and S. Sandmel; New York: KTAV, 1980) 21–40. See also A. L. Thompson, *Responsibility for Evil in the Theodicy of IV Ezra* (SBLDS 29; Missoula, Mont.: Scholars Press, 1977) esp. 330–42. This new response to the problem of theodicy in 4th Ezra (2 Esdras) is the explanation in terms of an evil *yetzer*. Such a belief in a malevolent principle within the heart came to prominence in later rabbinic speculation.

39 As is well known, both Jeremiah and Ezekiel wrestle with an emerging sense of individuality which complained of suffering for others' crimes (Jer. 31:27–30; Ezekiel 18). The Book of Chronicles applies the concept of reward and retribution on an individual basis, and the Prayer of Manasseh arises as a means of justifying God's patience in sparing this wicked king.

40 D. D. Raphael, "Tragedy and Religion," in *Twentieth Century Interpretations of the Book of Job* (ed. P. S. Sanders; Englewood Cliffs, N.J.: Prentice Hall, 1968) 51.

41 A. J. Heschel, *The Prophets* (New York: Harper & Row, 1962). In his popular treatment, *When Bad Things Happen to Good People* (New York: Schocken

Books, 1981), Harold Kushner is attracted to the idea that human anguish over the suffering of innocent people reflects God's anguish and compassion (p. 85). Kushner opts for a limited deity: "He is limited in what he can do by laws of nature and by the evolution of human nature and human moral freedom" (p. 134).

42 The final decision on God's part remains uncertain, inasmuch as the Hebrew text reads "I will not come into the city," which would probably imply divine withdrawal. A worse punishment is scarcely conceivable.

43 J. L. Crenshaw, *Old Testament Wisdom: An Introduction* (Atlanta: John Knox Press, 1981) 100–125, 251–54.

44 T. E. Fretheim, "Jonah and Theodicy," *ZAW* 90 (1978) 227–37.

45 J. A. Gladson, "Retributive Paradoxes in Proverbs 10—29," Ph.D. diss., Vanderbilt University, 1978.

46 S. Terrien, *The Elusive Presence* (New York: Harper & Row, 1978); J. L. Crenshaw, "In Search of Divine Presence: Some Remarks Preliminary to a Theology of Wisdom," *RevExp* 74 (1977) 353–69.

47 On these important texts, see B. L. Mack, *Logos und Sophia: Unterschungen zur Weisheitstheologie im hellenistischen Judentum* (SUNT 10; Göttingen: Vandenhoeck & Ruprecht, 1973); and B. Vawter, "Prov. 8:22: Wisdom and Creation," *JBL* 99 (1980) 205–16.

1

Faith in
Providence and Theodicy in
the Old Testament*

WALTHER EICHRODT

Time and again faith in providence seems to have need of theodicy, when disturbing and enigmatic upheavals in nature or human life threaten to put the orderly, divine guidance of all that takes place in question. Not only since the famous work of Leibniz has theodicy had a place in Christian theology; it was already considered part of theology in the dogmatics of the early church, and was pursued with zeal. And yet theodicy was no fruit which had grown upon the tree of biblical faith in God, but was largely derived from the Stoic-Neoplatonic world view. But even before the church Fathers had taken it over as a tool of Christian apologetics, the Diaspora Jew Philo thought he had recognized in the notion of providence in Greek philosophy a concept which was akin to and allied with that of OT faith (*On Providence*). Thus the question suggests itself: whether the distinctive character of OT faith in God necessarily leads to a concern with theodicy, or whether such a notion proves to be a foreign element which cannot be assimilated by the forces which give rise to OT faith.[1]

I

1 The meaning of the providence of God was first understood by the saints of the OT in the history of their own people. God's farsighted, caring guidance in the deliverance of the people of God from Egypt and the personal conduct of them to the land of promise constituted the earliest praise of Israel's worshipers, the favorite

* First published in *Festschrift Otto Procksch* (1934) 45–70. Translated by Laurence L. Welborn.

material of its storytellers, and the testimony on the basis of which faith in God's continued help and guidance was always rekindled. For from these fundamental experiences of the community all subsequent historical developments derived their significance as deeds of Yahweh – for the establishment of dominion. Thus a religious spirit breathes through all Israel's historical narratives, even where the religiously edifying point of view seems to recede so completely as, for example, in the greater part of the story of David (2 Samuel. 9— 20). Even there a kind of reverent amazement at the superior divine rule in history can be clearly detected throughout. Israel's storytellers were particularly fond of illustrating divine providence for their people in stories about the patriarchs. They never tire of reporting how the misfortunes, even the sins and follies, in the lives of the favorite characters of folk-legend are turned to good purpose. The story of the patriarch Abraham is full of such instances. One need only be reminded of how Sarah was taken into Pharaoh's harem in Genesis 12, and its parallels in Genesis 20 and 26, of the entire story of Jacob, with its notions of trial, chastening, and blessing, and of the story of Joseph. The perspective of the narrator certainly differs in individual instances: in the accounts of Abraham and Jacob, which occur in the Yahwist, the ethical motive often recedes, and a simple joy in the triumph of the friend of God predominates. The story of Joseph, on the other hand, is the classic expression of an ethically deepened faith in providence: "To be sure, you laid evil plans for me, but God contrived to bring good out of evil, in order to carry out what lies at hand: the preservation of the lives of many men!" But in every instance one knows that the bearer of God's history stands under the special care of the divine mandator. It is not just some divine favorite who stands under the *providentia specialis* of Yahweh, but one who has been entrusted with a great historical mission. When the Yahwist narrator determines to present the story of Abraham in the form of a tale of surprises, in which Yahweh brings human hopes and expectations to utter ruin, only in order to grant his salvation in an unhoped-for manner, it is because he wishes to depict the purposefulness of God's dealings with the bearer of his salvific decrees. We find the same thing in stories of the boyhood of Moses (Exodus 2) or Samuel (1 Samuel 1), in the account of Saul's enmity against David, and so forth. Of course the great leaders and bearers of the nation's future are also, in general, the ethical characters; yet the main emphasis does not lie here, but rather on God's purposeful action in the accomplishment of things planned.

It is of great importance for an appreciation of Israel's faith in providence as a whole to make clear the primary goal behind its conception: it is completely dependent upon the experience of Yahweh's historical dealings with his people. In keeping with such a special relation to this people, the God of the covenant establishes his power on their behalf and dominion among them. It is from this experience that the concept of divine providence receives its special stamp, in the lives of individuals as well as nations.

2   It was a serious misunderstanding of the Israelite concept of the God of the covenant to have thought that there could be no talk of personal trust in Yahweh for individual Israelites until after the time of the prophets.[2] In the oldest laws God calls the "you" of the individual to account. And by the same token, the individual is allowed to expect the defense of his rights by Yahweh.[3] And in this respect there is no distinction between man and woman, citizen and alien; all know that the way to the divine helper is open to them, and they bring their concerns to him in trusting prayer.[4] Even Abraham's servant is able to take comfort in the fact that Yahweh's care can show itself to the individual in an extraordinary situation through marvelous guidance, so that everything, as if of its own accord, unites to bring about his success.[5] The fact that the image of Yahweh as the shepherd of the people is applied to the individual at a relatively early date and used in prayer as an expression of safety and security,[6] points to a powerful conviction of the divine guidance of the individual, which is also expressed in personal names such as Jonathan, Joiada, and others. This faith in providence is reflected in three particularly vivid popular conceptions. The first is that of the "bundle of the living" (ṣĕrôr haḥayyîm) found in 1 Sam. 25:29: accordingly, the life of the righteous is kept by God as a precious jewel in a pouch, while the lives of the godless are cast out like a stone from a sling. Alongside this idea, there is the notion of the "book", or more accurately the "scroll of life" in which are written the names of all those whom Yahweh wishes to keep alive. Conversely, God's hand strikes out of the book the names of those who are appointed to die.[7] A third, frequently used image for God's care is that of the wings of God; in the Psalms, for example, protection under the shadow of God's wings is a favorite consolatory motif.[8]

What lent Israel's faith in providence, for which parallels might be found here and there in pagan cultures, its unshakeable firmness and characteristic energy was the grounding of all that takes place, without exception, in God's activity, so that even the seeming accident was excluded and evil itself was traced back to God's will.

Whenever, in an unreflective manner, an accident, or *miqreh* is spoken of,[9] it is in the sense that no human intent is involved; yet God's guiding hand is also thought of as being active here. Even in the unfortunate act of homicide, God's dispensation is present, and it is God who grants such a one the protection of asylum.[10]

And precisely this example reminds us that misfortune and evil of every sort are also regarded as God's work; these things, too, are brought about and sent by God. Indeed, the jealous exclusivity and absolute sovereignty of Yahweh leave room for neither an independent, hostile divine will, nor the arbitrary action of demons, which play so great a role in the neighboring pagan religions. For everything which happens there is only *one* divine causality. And the frank attribution of even the dark and mysterious dimensions of the world's course to one divine Lord, which finds brief and striking formulation in the well-known prophetic sayings of Amos 3:5f. and Isa. 45:7,[11] leaves no doubt that divine providence knows no bounds.

Yet in all of this, the principle of God's sovereignty over Israel, which was the basic premise of Israel's faith, long held back the full development of the application of the notion of providence to the individual. To be sure, the individual had a lively ethical relationship with Yahweh from the beginning. Nevertheless, the powerful consciousness of solidarity which characterized the early period brought about an obvious deferment of personal concerns over against the concerns of the people, and led thought away from one's own condition to that of the nation and its leaders. With the unbroken power of primitive emotions, one felt the life of the individual to be embedded in the great organism of life as a whole, apart from which the individual was nothing, a drifting leaf, and within whose expanse he could achieve his own fulfillment. Thus one's sacrifice on behalf of the greater whole was ordained by nature, one's integration into the destiny of the whole a self-evident life process. This emerges most clearly in the affirmation of collective retribution, in which the participation of the individual in the guilt of the whole and also the repercussion of the individual's deed upon the fate of the community are throughout felt to be a just order.[12]

Seen in this way, it is understandable that the old Israelite faith in providence, with all of its inner firmness and solidity, was able to conceive of divine care for humankind generally only in individual events and was not concerned to observe the embodiment of the divine plan in the course of each and every life, uniting beginning and end into a meaningful whole. One only ventured to say such great things of the leaders chosen by God, and the subtlety of individualization in the accounts of the lives of Abraham, Moses, Samuel or David remains noteworthy. But it was not possible that every individual Israelite should expect such for oneself without further ado. It can be no accident that in Jeremiah we find the first direct witness to the notion of the complete incorporation of an individual life into God's plan. It was Jeremiah who learned to regard his entire existence as a realization of the decree of Yahweh (Jer. 1:5), by which his lot in life was decided even before his birth. From this time on the presuppositions were in place for comprehending the individual life as a work of divine providence, wrought by God from beginning to end. In part through the work of the prophets themselves, in part through the dissolution of the old bonds of the decaying folk-culture, the individual began to see the self as increasingly on one's own and sought to attain a new self-understanding. Thus we now encounter at more than one point the remarkable view of God's care as ordering the lives of the great and the small in the same manner.[13] The new intimacy of the personal relationship with God which is attested in these passages is illuminated from still another side: by means of the application of the father–son relationship to God's attitude towards the individual saint.[14] What had earlier been reserved for the people as a whole or for the king became now a happy certainty for the individual. This was combined with a new view of suffering as paternal correction, intended to test and refine the righteous. Thus suffering was not merely to be regarded as an evil, but as salutary, if bitter, medicine. When it succeeded in preserving one from final destruction, such suffering could actually appear as a mark of divine favor.[15]

Here a positive side is won from evil, so that it can actually be seen as confirmation of divine providence. Thus the certainty of unmediated divine guidance and protection finds characteristic expression in the spiritual conception of this epoch. It proved possible for the same generation which had been so bitterly disappointed in its ardent expectation of the fulfillment of the prophets' promises of salvation, to make wholly new statements on the presence and efficacy of the promised spirit of God. It was not only in the community that the rule of the spirit became a certainty which transcended all difficulties;[16] the life of the individual as well witnessed to the power and guidance of the spirit in a way that was hitherto unknown. Thus the individual celebrated one's new certainty of the nearness and guidance of God.[17]

3 One learned to think through the matter of faith in divine providence in all its aspects and to apply it much earlier in the life of the

people than in the realm of individual life. Here, too, in ancient Israel consideration of the matter went no further generally than judgments from case to case. Yahweh's guidance of the destiny of foreign nations entered into the realm of faith in general only insofar as Israel had immediate dealings with them. Moreover, the thought of a united world government was still remote from the ancient period. All statements which have to do with Yahweh's rule over the nations are given shape by their own experience of his historical guidance: because Canaan is promised to Israel as a home, the Canaanites must experience Yahweh's supremacy over them and endure punishment for their godlessness (Gen. 15:16; Deut. 9:5). Because Pharaoh opposes Israel's exodus from Egypt, he is humbled by Yahweh (Exod. 7:14f, 23; 8:4ff, 24ff, etc.). Now and again the view gains prominence that a universal moral law is binding for all peoples in relation to God and places them within the domain of God's action. So it is when the sins of the Canaanites are said to be responsible for their expulsion from the land (Gen. 9:22; Lev. 18:24ff; Deut. 12:29ff; 18:12; 20:18), or when the repute of the wanton and outrageous deeds of the Sodomites reaches Yahweh and induces him to intervene. In this consciousness of moral obligation of all peoples an important element is no doubt present which effectively paved the way for a comprehensive view of the destiny of the nations. Likewise, the unreflecting extension of Yahweh's judicial authority over the entire earth in the stories of primeval history, of the flood and the tower of Babel, and the belief in the common origin of all peoples, by virtue of which they actually constitute one great family, (a conviction which led to the only existing attempt at a table of nations in antiquity in Genesis 10) point in this direction. But it goes no further at first than those rather isolated, intermittent instances in which such convictions are made applicable to the conditions of Israel's neighbors. In practice, the stage which other ancient peoples also attained in their belief in certain fundamental principles of divinity is not surpassed. This atomistic view of the exercise of divine judgment over the nations, which always arises in connection with imminent conflict with one of them but which has no regard for the context of their fate either before or after their encounter, is only broken through in a significant manner at one point – namely, where one begins to think about the goal of history. Yet even here the relation of Yahweh to other peoples sometimes remains a rather negative one. Ancient blessings (Numbers 23 and 24) know only of the overthrow of other nations, and psalms which extol the king as divine savior and as the bringer of the time of salvation speak less of Yahweh's positive guidance of the destiny of the nations than of their humiliation before God's earthly representative as they attempt to flee from judgment.[18] But alongside this there exists from the very beginning the pronouncement of blessing upon the nations, as promised emphatically in the blessing of the patriarchs,[19] and as the nations are included in a limited sense in Israel's messianic hopes.[20] It is at this point that Israel's faith in this special divine guidance of its history gives rise to the boldest statements. Here a firm bond is established between Israel's fate and that of the rest of humankind, by which the nations, or in the final analysis their history, can also appear as the object of divine providence. For the present, to be sure, God lets the nations go their own way. The stars have been appointed to them as gods, it once says, and they have been given up to them.[21]

Only under the influence of the prophetic movement did Israel come to understand that Yahweh also makes use of the nations in the present. Close connection with the Syrian alliance which had dictated Israel's politics since the days of the Omrides and Ahab prepared the way for this insight. The international movement of that period not only resulted in increasing economic and cultural exchange; it also cleared the way for religious influences and responses.[22] Thus the positive value of foreign cultures was able to appear in a new light. But what was decisive was the prophetic recognition that Israel had not accomplished its task as bearer of the dominion of Yahweh, that it had failed to realize the universal conception of God. For this reason other peoples will be summoned by God into his service. In the circles of Elijah and Elisha the Aramaeans came to be recognized no longer merely as national enemies but as the rod prepared by Yahweh for chastening this degenerate people.[23] Thereafter Amos went on to place Israel's history in the midst of the history of other peoples, and he pointed out emphatically that they were guided by the will of Yahweh in the same fashion as Israel. Here Israel is placed on the same level as the pagans, not only with respect to divine judgment, which hands both over to punishment (Amos 1 and 2), but also as an object of divine care. Israel and the heathen are valued alike: "'Are you not like the Ethiopians to me, O people of Israel?' says the Lord. 'Did I not bring up Israel from the Land of Egypt, and the Philistines from Caphtor, and the Syrians from Kir?'" (Amos 9:7).

Like no other, Isaiah, from his elevated perspective, caught a glimpse of the complete universality of divine providence. At that moment in world history when the conquering Assyrians smashed the old structures of statehood in the Near East in order to build their own empire, it was granted this prophet to see in the terrible work of destruction a far-reaching blueprint of his God. For it was not God's wish to lead the nations to the slave quarters of the Assyrian taskmasters, but to the paternal house of the divine world ruler. It was not Israel alone which had a special task; a commission had also been envisioned for Assyria, which assigned it a place in the great *oikonomia tou kosmou* (Isa. 10:5ff). Both nations refused service. Yet the wisdom of God was able to use even those who were reluctant and rebellious as tools in order to achieve its purpose. [24] What the prophet encountered in concrete instances disclosed itself to him as the meaning of the entire course of world events. All was penetrated by a purposeful movement which integrated all peoples in order to build the *basileia theou*, the kingdom of righteousness and peace, [25] described in the majestic vision of Isa. 2:2–4. Jerusalem has its importance in this world-encompassing reorganization of things only as the place where the foundation of the great building will be laid; for it is here that the community of faith comes together to form the precious cornerstone which bears what Yahweh has established. Here the Israelite faith in providence is filled with universal content, and a positive evaluation of history is made possible, by means of which even terrible catastrophes can be endured, and even valued, as constructive elements in world events.

Isaiah's successors also see the divine guidance of history in this broad perspective. For Jeremiah it was possible to proclaim the downfall of his people as Yahweh's commission to his servant Nebuchadnezzar that he destroy Jerusalem (Jer. 25:9; 27:6; 43:10). The heathen king bears the honored title Ebed which is otherwise used of the Israelite king as the trusted friend of God, as Yahweh's fully authorized minister. Ezekiel sees the foreign nations approaching in his vision as the angels of Yahweh who at his command enter the holy city with their instruments of destruction (Ezek. 9:1ff). In the great picture of the last judgment (Ezek. 38f [26]), he presents Gog of Magog as a wild beast which lets itself be led by Yahweh with a bridle, reviving an image used by Isaiah. [27] The world power which is opposed to God can achieve nothing else with all its undertakings than the furtherance of God's kingdom. Likewise Deutero-Isaiah sees how the holy one of Israel guides world history to its goal. He allows Cyrus to blaze out like a meteor on the heaven of the nations, spreading Yahweh's glory to the farthest island by his unparalleled triumphal procession. Through the overthrow of the Babylonian kingdom, he opened the gates to the new age for the exiled people of Israel. [28]

This bold and unprecedented faith in providence underwent significant modification in Daniel and the apocalypticists through the addition of world periods.[29] We are ignorant of the influences under which this modification was undertaken.[30] What is clear, in any case, is that here an element of the ancient world view, the concept of history as periods which follow one upon another, superceding each other in regular fashion, has found its way into the prophetic view and has fused with it. But what is really important here lies not in the origin of these elements, but in the manner in which they are combined with the traditional body of Israelite conceptions. At the most decisive point the apocalypticist overturns the ancient period-reckoning: where at the end of the age of iron the golden age should come again, resuming the entire cycle, he introduces something completely new, the eternal kingdom, which descends from heaven – bringing earthly history to its final conclusion. Thus he remains true to the basic prophetic view, but enriches it out of the experience of the centuries. The prophets saw themselves standing immediately before the threshold of the new aeon; the old aeon possessed no interest in and of itself. But it is given greater significance by the apocalypticist by the way in which he carefully divides and arranges its end. The necessity of a proper history of the mundane world, with its own character and form, enters forcefully upon the field of vision: the earth, too, must complete its creations and bring them to maturity before God can bring about completion and perfection.

Alongside the form of faith in providence created by prophecy, which derived its power from its certainty that this aeon was hastening to its close and from the revelation of the coming God, Israel's trust in God's guidance over human history created still another form of faith whose distinctive character is usually too little considered – namely, that which is grounded in the priestly view of the world. Of course it did not grow up without contact with the prophetic proclamation. But it bears throughout its own character, and it succeeded in turning all the impulses which it may have received from the prophetic movement to the service of its own, consciously preserved point of view.[31] Its basis consisted of the regulation of relations between God and the world by means of the law which brings about the subjugation of all that exists to the sovereign will of the other-worldly God. By nature the law is an order established once and for all by the God who is exalted above the world. Thus the unchangeable validity of the world order which it has established receives strong emphasis. No historical event can disrupt this framework. Rather, all that takes place is only conceivable within it as the unfolding of basic relationships given once and for all. That is only possible because in his farsighted wisdom the creator and lawgiver has ordered all in a wonderfully expedient way. Furthermore, the creator has instructed humanity – made in the divine image and likeness and lord over the other creatures – in such a way that humans can complete the purpose of their lives in fulfilment of the task that has been assigned them. God's relationship to Israel and to the nations also has the character of an eternally valid order of life. It is given form in the covenant with Noah, which is binding for all humans, and in the covenant with Abraham, which is only binding upon Israel. Here the goal of the divine government of the world can be seen to consist in nothing else than the preservation and restoration of an eternal order which has been assaulted by humankind estranged from God. It is not the inbreaking of the kingdom of God into an ungodly world which through terrible struggles must be brought to its knees before the sole Lord of the universe, nor the vision of the future age of perfect divine rule; whose organic structure constitutes the hidden meaning of the present aeon, condemned to be abolished, which here provides the form of expression for the action of divine providence. Rather it is the perpetual execution of Yahweh's judgement by means of which Yahweh establishes the pillars of the earth (Psalm 75) and proves again and again, despite every eclipse, to be the Lord of this eternal kingdom and the king of the world.[32] The meaning of history is to be found, as the priestly writers of history attempt to show,[33] in the regular succession of sin and punishment, and the restoration of the state sought by God which it is intended to bring about. And the answer of humanity to God's action should consist in grateful obeisance before the divine Lord of the world, who already in the present affords to Israel and to the nations access to the divine and who allows them to rejoice in the fulfillment of their tasks under such government.[34]

II

It cannot be denied that, expressed in this manner, belief in providence recalls the Platonic-Stoic world view with its strong emphasis on divine providence. But parallels – to old Israelite prophetic utterances on the divine guidance of the world can, without difficulty, be found in the views of any philosophical system which presupposes a single divine principle as the basis of all things, provided that one abstracts from its concrete background. Like OT prophecy, such a philosophy holds that it is able to demonstrate the rule of the divine in a perfect world order directed towards a kingdom of ethical ends. Despite these parallels, it is possible to make quite clear how different

OT expressions of God's careful guidance of the world really are from what may be properly regarded as the principal element in the Greek view of divine providence – theodicy.

1   This is immediately evident with respect to prophetic faith in providence, a faith which is aimed at the nation and humankind. Insofar as it is clearly conceived,[35] theodicy is an express attempt to balance the present state of the world, with its physical and moral evils, with the all-inclusive government of a just and beneficent God, and thus to comprehend it as a rational and expedient order. Thus emphasis lies mainly upon the comprehension of the world as such, by which its contradictions can be mastered and its phenomena integrated into a coherent system. That such an endeavor must have been meaningless for the prophets is obvious, since it contradicted their fundamental convictions. The prophetic proclamation of the coming God is ultimately grounded in the fact that this world has departed from God's rule. Its contradictions are of such an incurable nature that they threaten to bring about a final, radical confrontation between God and humanity in a judgment of annihilation. In view of this situation, it is obvious that there is no other solution to the conflict between God's claim to authority and the present world than the dissolution of this earthly frame and the establishment of a new world order in which God's will for the world rules supreme.

But an eschatological solution of this sort obviously affords no means by which to integrate the world into a satisfactory system of thought. Indeed it did not arise from rational reflection, but is derived directly from an immediate, divine communication, and is felt to be a secret contradictory to human thought and inaccessible.[36] When historical developments appeared to discredit the prophets' message and to give easy play to the scorn of their contemporaries,[37] it never occurred to them to look for a rational theory capable of making the incomprehensible more comprehensible and the improbable more accessible to thought. All that they had to set against such scorn and doubt was their uncompromising faith in the true revelation of Yahweh which must eventually be fulfilled, and the admonition to recognize the God who is manifest in their proclamation as the Lord. Such an attitude is the only one that is possible and appropriate in response to a direct divine communication which is hidden from human eyes. This attitude emerges with particular force in Isaiah's activity. Here all attempts to fashion a god in one's own likeness are brought face to face with the holy God who is revealed in words of judgment and promise, and judgment is passed upon

27

them.[38] Such a faith is not just the interminable, hopeless waiting which it might have seemed to the realist of the following century under the weight of uninterrupted pagan world government. But it releases a fountain of inexhaustible vitality, because it affirms the claim of the living God. Such a faith is recognized by God as righteous, that is, as corresponding to the covenantal relationship. Habakkuk gave startlingly pregnant formulation to these thoughts: "The one who is puffed up cannot hold fast his life, but the righteous will have life through his faith" (2:4).[39] Here the doubting questions which arise from the incongruities in existence and become a source of temptation are answered by a resolute retreat to God who as Lord of the world is the master of its mysteries. Nevertheless God allows those who trust in the divine word to share such power; upon such trusting ones God bestows the gift of the "preservation and development of all the forces which are present in them".[40] And the same conviction of the life-giving power of faithful perseverance resounds as a joyful, dominant theme through the booklet of consolation in Deutero-Isaiah,[41] and finds its most profound expression in the figure of the servant of God. All appearances to the contrary, the servant holds fast to the word of his God in unbroken trust and through deepest sorrow is allowed to enter into the joy of victory. Malachi is likewise assailed by the doubts of the righteous. For him the eschatological renewal of the world is already on the point of passing over into a universal moral order. In keeping with this, the misfortune of the single righteous person has become a major offense. Yet the person can give no other response to these doubts than to point to the divine world rule, whose fulfillment stands at the door.[42] Thus prophecy's answer to the attack on its message is not to formulate a theory which attempts to comprehend the incongruous but to point still more earnestly to the decisive deed of the divine judge and redeemer and to call for the decision of faith, by which humans put themselves under the authority of the divine Lord and experience renewal of life through fellowship with that Lord.

2   It is more difficult to comprehend the situation, with respect to the fate of the individual, where belief in providence is put in question by the riddle of existence.[43] For the old Israelite period this did not present a particularly vexing problem, since the decisive force which the nation's destiny exercised on the thinking of the individual[44] made divine certainty largely independent of the fate of the individual member of the community. To be sure, the distress and tribulation of life could demand unspeakably difficult sacrifices and was deeply

felt.[45] But thanks to the immediate bond between the life of the individual and that of the nation, they were more easily overcome. There was no danger that the concept of God would be dragged down to the level of the demonic and arbitrary or malicious and devilish; for the incomprehensible God before whom one bowed was the one whom one experienced time and again in the destiny of the whole community as a benevolent helper. On the contrary, the breadth of such a piety, which was able to combine a reverent recognition of the freedom of divine majesty with the self-evident conviction of God's just retribution, is an important sign of its living, inner force.

This situation changed with the internal disintegration of the national federation in the seventh century, followed closely by external division. Now the life of the individual member of the community was increasingly deprived of its former supports and left to its own devices. The weighty responsibility for one's own decisions now fell upon the individual; and what is more, the fate of the individual won heightened religious significance as the principal arena in which one became conscious of the judgment and blessing of God and found confirmation for trust in God. But the more deeply prophecy impressed upon the nation that God was a just rewarder, the more burning must the need have become to experience God's requital in the life of the individual, and thus to be assured of God's living presence. The tension that thus arose was further heightened by the fact that in contrast to earlier epochs one could no longer be content with a form of collective retribution which subordinated the individual to the fate of the community. Thus this epoch perceived a difficult question where earlier generations had seen self-evident order. All of this heightened the value of the divine response to the individual in the present and made the doubts raised by the vicissitudes of existence a difficult temptation.

It is with the prophets that we first become aware of the changed spiritual situation. Yet they make no attempt to explain away the new questions by which they are troubled. In Jeremiah we find that such problems are resolutely deferred to the needs and obligations which put demands on the messenger of God (12:1ff) in the stormy present. It is here that he must stand the test, if he is to remain the mouth-piece of God. For it is this which is eventually perceived to be the noblest kind of life, far surpassing everything else (15:10–21). When one considers the approaching dissolution of the world-age and the new order of things promised by God, temptations of this sort finally become insignificant (31:29f). This vision of Yahweh's great destruction and rebuilding, at whose center stands the prophet, seems to put the question to rest. In much the same situation, Ezekiel makes use of the demand of his time for a divine response to the individual as a sturdy weapon to repel attacks against God's guidance and to awaken a new understanding of Yahweh's purpose. Ezekiel shatters that self-righteous obstinacy which maintains, in the face of the proclamation of the fall of Jerusalem, that the holy city, or at least its righteous members, will merit preferential treatment. He asserts that before God's righteous judgment there will no more be a transference of guilt, against which one would naturally rebel, than a transferal of righteousness. God may decide to make an exception in this case by preserving an entire group of those who escaped. But it is not, to be sure, because they are entitled to it but in order to present them to the exiles as living proof that the city was ripe for judgment. Such is his bitingly ironic defense of the freedom of the supreme judge (14:12ff). The cynical sceptics seek to ridicule before Yahweh the prophetic teaching on the guilt of the entire nation by making it appear to be the punishment of the guiltless for the sins of their fathers (18:2). Yet Ezekiel confronts the despairing righteous, who see nothing ahead of them but the punishment of death in exile and who have lost all strength to survive under the frightful pressure of the enormous guilt of the nation, with his God's offer of grace. God takes no pleasure in the death of the wicked, but desires that they should turn from their ways and live! (18:23, 32; 33:11) This is the rubric beneath which the oft misunderstood statements in Ezek. 18 and 33:10ff must be interpreted. When in this passage God's judgment is connected rather harshly and severely with the personal decision of the individual and any transmission of guilt from the father to the son is denied, it is not because Ezekiel intends to erect a new theory to explain God's actions in every case. Rather he only wishes to give the help of which faith is in need in the present situation, the strength to begin a new life.[46] Ezekiel does not wish to deny the connection between one's own fate and the guilt of the fathers; in the situation of the exiles this was only too obvious. In other passages the prophet speaks without hesitation of collective forgiveness which affects the entire nation (20; 21:3, 9; 16 and 23). But he denies that this is God's final word and that the plaintive cry of 33:10 is true: Because of our sins we waste away; how can we escape with our lives? To this he opposes God's will to bring about the salvation and blessing of all who let themselves be called to deeds of ethical obedience. Thus he lays great emphasis on the conscious decision to turn towards God or to depart from him, a decision in which the entire course of one's life is comprehended. He seeks to make manifest the divine

Lord, who is not concerned with the cumulative sum of one's achieve-
ments but with a personal relationship of service and loyalty. His
style may be pedantic, and his prosaic, juridical tone may be reminiscent of legal treatises; but we must not allow this to obscure the
fact that we are not dealing here with a theological theory but with
the first proclamation of salvation. Thus he tells the scoffers, as well
as those who are in despair, that God is more than inexorable,
punitive justice; God also works goodness. His proclamation gives
the individual a chance to step out of the sinful continuum of the
generations into a personal decision for the divine Lord, who is the
same here as in the great vision of dry bones (Ezekiel 37), where
those who have despaired unto death (37:11) are promised the power
of divine resurrection to new life.

Thus Ezekiel avoids the path of fruitless argumentation which
seeks to overcome the crisis of faith by devising clever theories about
God's actions, and instead brings to his contemporaries the call of
God to new, courageous activity in service to God. But the doctrine
of individual retribution constitutes the intellectual form in which
the conviction of the fruitfulness of this service is clothed. And
because it is prescribed for a period which has its fixed boundaries
in the eschatological consummation of the world, preceded by a
judgment of purification (20:35ff, 38; 13:9; 34:22), it attains its full
significance only in the preparation of the nation for the final redemption by Yahweh.[47]

3   Thus the charge that is often made against Ezekiel – that by
asserting an abstract theory of retribution he is to blame for the
unrealistic, dogmatic explanation of the world in Judaism – surely
becomes untenable. Certainly there are connections here, but they
are much more indirect than has customarily been assumed, and in
any case are not alone sufficient to explain the recent, characteristic
use of Ezekiel's lapidary statements in the sense of late Jewish dogmatics. To this must be added a new aspect of which we catch sight
in the gradual triumph after the exile of the priestly view of life and
the world. The more consistently history is subjected to the rule of
God which reveals itself in the Law, the more completely religious
thought and aspiration are directed towards obedient acts in the
present, according to the norm of the eternal divine laws of the
kingdom, and the less an explicitly eschatological attitude succeeds
in being determinative for religion. But with this change in religious
emotions the need to make the present comprehensible as the divine
government of the world in the life of the individual necessarily
awakes with undreamt-of force. As a means to this awakening, the

old belief in retribution, which spoke of the good fortune of the righteous and the misfortune of the wicked, achieved enormous importance. For through this faith alone, the reality of the living God as a world-ruling ethical power appeared to be secured. It offered a sensible explanation for the world which satisfied the demands of moral thought brought up on the Law. Thus it is no wonder that it became an indispensable statement of faith in God, in fact a dogma. To question it meant to attack the mainsprings of religious life.[48] And the more external pressure and internal strife weighed upon the Jewish community and its trust in God, the more earnestly religious thought sought to construct a secure, unassailable position from which all doubts about God's government of the world could be repulsed and refuted. In this manner the desire for an actual theodicy gained entrance into Judaism. Its disastrous effect makes itself felt in more than one way. The place of saving righteousness in faith is taken by an impartial distribution of rewards and punishments in accordance with the rule of Law, the *justitia distributiva* – a fateful narrowing of the horizon. The old historical tradition with its reverence for God's incomprehensible majesty is no longer tolerated and is thoroughly rationalized by the introduction of a mechanical system of retribution, as comparison of Chronicles with the Books of Kings clearly shows. With respect to the hope of redemption, the future consummation is secretly transformed into an ideal state attainable by human effort. Thus the idea of Israel's world rule, characterized by a wealth of natural and material goods, as conspicuous proof of God's just retribution, once again wins a special place.[49] And in prayer life the so-called psalms of innocence in particular,[50] which make God's impartial retribution into a motif of obedience, betray the detrimental effect of constantly reckoning with merit and reward on religious life. But above all, the justification of God which was sought in the dogma of retribution had an unconvincing effect where it was needed most, in the grave and inexplicable misfortunes of the righteous. One might silence many doubts by arguing that such misfortunes represent the trial and improvement of the righteous, or a final setting of accounts, or a kind of blessing, so much more certain for children. But these consolations failed when confronted with the whole weight of affliction. Instead, the temptation arose to infer the guilt of one's neighbor from that person's enigmatic fate. This tendency is depicted in exemplary fashion in Job, and also appears in several of the psalms.[51] Such experiences must have plunged the sincerely devout into the deepest temptation and threatened to confound their trust in God fully. But even here the power of genuine faith in God was preserved, in that it was able to see through the cracks of human attempts to justify God and cast away from itself the crutches of theodicy, and to seek the answer to the question of faith in God, rather than in clever theories.

The break-through which led from the God of rational abstraction to the living God of revelation took place in *three ways*: first, in conscious *relationship to the prophetic message of the coming God*. The true eschatological outlook might have survived only in small circles, but it was in these very circles that Deutero-Isaiah's message of the vicarious suffering of the servant of God was preserved and appropriated into their own life. It is not only the pericope of the vicarious suffering of the good shepherd in Deutero-Zechariah[52] that shows a lively comprehension of the fact that it is only through deep suffering that the one who stands nearest to God becomes a useful tool in God's hand for building his kingdom. One also ventured to view one's own suffering in the light of the eschatological consummation, as in Psalm 22, whose final section (v. 23–32) interprets suffering as a building-block toward the completion of God's kingdom, wholly apart from the scheme of retribution. That God would find in the suffering of the faithful the most effective means for establishing rule over humankind give this singer deep consolation in the midst of a night of affliction. This thought helped the psalmist in overcoming a feeling of abandonment by God and enabled the discovery of a victorious answer to the paralyzing doubts about the meaning of this suffering.

In the former case it was the vision of the coming God which disproved the claims of theodicy; for others who were troubled, it was *the flight to the immediate experience of the divine presence* which broke the chains of human theories. The poet of Psalm 73 movingly describes for us how the daily contradiction of an experience against the claims of God's just retribution brought suffering and how there was a struggle to solve this tormenting riddle in every conceivable way (73:16). But despite all this pondering, no theodicy brought satisfaction. The psalmist was set free from the error of attempting to calculate divine retribution in a very different manner: this person's eyes were opened to see it by direct, divine illumination.[53] For the miracle of true fellowship with God consists not in any earthly gift, however great and magnificent, but in personally opening oneself to the inconceivable greatness of God in the form of a constant faithfulness and communication of supernatural life. In this way even the poorest human life outwardly is given an incomparable inner worth which cannot itself be touched by death.

How the supposedly unimaginable good fortune of the godless pales in comparison with this costly possession, particularly when one considers that in the end one stands before the horrors of death completely forgotten by God! With a true cry of joy the singer of the psalm casts the self into the arms of God once again, sure to have found a solution to the enigma of life which far transcends all the auxiliary constructions of reason.

This experience of the present God as the real and indestructible content of life may only be compared with the confession of Jeremiah (15:15–21) and the song of thanksgiving of Psalm 16.[54] And yet we may take it as evidence for the fact that there were always people in Israel who were able to find their way by themselves back to God out of the impasse of theodicy, and thus safeguarded the regal position of the immediate reality of true faith in God hindered by no ambiguous supports.

The third protest against a theodicy based on a rational theory of retribution drew its reserves from the *belief in creation*. Religious thinkers now entered more fully into this faith, which previously had received the least consideration. The classical witness for this attempt is Job 38—41.[55] What is offered here in answer to the question of God's just government of the world, which had previously been treated with such passion, provides no rational solution. Nor should one have expected that it would turn out differently after the embittered struggle of Job against his friends' attempts at theodicy. The retreat from the moral world to the creation, and the power, greatness and wisdom of God that become visible in it, was not made with the hope of attaining to a universal reason which directs everything in nature and human life towards the achievement of rational ends, though perhaps in a manner not wholly accessible to human examination. Rather, precisely those works of creation are selected which obviously bear witness to the creator as the incomprehensible wonderworker, whose rule can no longer be embraced in a system of rational goals: the marvelous construction of the world, with its mysterious and terrible forces of blessing and annihilation, whose governance is by no means penetrable by human understanding of what is expedient; the nature and instincts of wild animals which evade all rational comprehension and yet clearly stand under divine protection. And yet one would misunderstand the view that is presented here if one did not take note of the fact that it wishes to proclaim more than the baffling incomprehensibility of God's universal plan, which strikes the questioners on the mouth and casts them into the dust.[56] The freedom of the creator, which is so strongly emphasized, is no cruel caprice, no ill-humored game, which hurls one into the feeling of one's own nothingness.[57] But it includes a mysterious inner bond between the creator and the creation, on account of which people feel themselves addressed and seized in the depths of their being by God's rule, even when they do not understand it. A vision of joyful worship and wonder permeates the entire account,[58] a vision which is only possible on the basis of the perception that there is something of eternal value in the enigma in which this human vision, as a creation of the creator, is included. This inner transport wrought by the power of the creator, which, since it is absolutely miraculous, is able to convince one of its higher right and to still all doubts, is the actual content of God's speeches and the final refutation of all rational theodicies.

But one thing must not be overlooked that does not yet appear to have been worked out clearly: something must be offered to make possible this unanimity between humanity and the wonderful melody of the works of creation. This is the word of the creator to the creation. That God speaks and instructs humankind in the proper understanding of the wonders of creation is not something that is self-evident, certainly not in the wisdom literature to which Job also belongs. To introduce God merely as a poetic device, in order to explain the view presented here, diminishes the vision in a manner that is hardly allowed. Rather, it is an essential part of the satisfaction of Job that he be allowed to see God and that his speech be found worthy (42:5f). The poet thus does not regard the meaning which he gives to the creation as an idea that any thoughtful person could come to understand by considering the greatness and beauty of nature. What is essential is that the creator does not remain dumb, but speaks to this creation. But that means that the triumph over the enigma of suffering can only come from the realm of revelation, from that which is absolutely miraculous and underived, not from rational human thought. But then every theodicy has become inherently impossible; for the idea of creation is also an expression of faith, which first becomes possible in the address of the creator. What it discloses is not a rational world order, which could be made evident to all; but it places humanity directly before the wonderful and mysterious God, to whose hidden abysses suffering also belongs. For the sake of this God the world with all its enigmas, including suffering, can be affirmed. For in the course of the speeches [in Job] God emerges from concealment and enters into an ethically positive relationship to creation. God may always be surrounded with marvels and mystery, yet as the one who invites humans into fellowship, God allows both to become palpable and visible.

Therefore these chapters of the Book of Job, which appear to depart intentionally from the proper religious heritage of Israel, point to their unexpressed but indispensable background in the revealed history of the covenant people. For only Israel knows the God – revealed in speech – who cannot be recognized from observation of the world, because this God is not a mere maker of worlds, the first cause in a series of natural events, like the primal god of paganism; nor the deepest ground of the human spirit, as in Platonic philosophy, but the sovereign Lord of the universe, who brings the creation into existence as an absolutely free act of the divine will, which carries its own norm within itself. The revelatory speeches in which God draws near to humans refer back to another speech in which they are ultimately grounded, a speech which, as the word of creation, called the world into being out of nothing. Thus Genesis 1 appears as the final basis of the statements of the Book of Job which, for their part, like a finger raised in admonition, warn against misunderstanding the account of creation as an attempt to provide an exposition of universal reason, which is rooted in human reason. While the concept of the rational purposes and plan of the cosmos plays a very different role here than in Job and betrays a different attitude towards life and the world, it is not a bridge which leads to the emergence of the idea of the creator but is wholly dependent upon faith in the absolute Lord of the universe whose rule is manifest in the absolute miracle of the word of creation, by which the world was raised out of nothing. In both accounts the statements about the creator bear witness to a theology of origins which is qualitatively different from the deistic concept of God as *prima causa*; for they see the relation of the creator to the creation as a *creatio ex nihilo*, which must not be understood as the initial founding alone, but as the immediacy of an ever new divine order and government. Both accounts present the perfect contrast to a concept of the world which infers the reasonableness of the laws which govern the cosmos and the perfection of the lawgiver from the harmony that is perceivable to the human spirit. Thus both accounts are a decisive protest against a theodicy which, by ostensibly seeking to justify the Lord of the world – placed on the same level as the world and made into an object of knowledge.

This sheds a proper light upon the expansion of the concept of the covenant here and there in late Judaism to include God's relationship to the world. In Deutero-Isaiah the relation of the creator to the creation is already transferred to the covenantal realm insofar as Yahweh's "righteousness' – covenantal graciousness, faithfulness and aid – is described as the conduct of the one who governs the world.[59] Because the people of God are gifted with God's servant as mediator of the covenant,[60] one granted absolute salvation in the form of the covenant,[61] God sheds light on the nations of the earth and leads them to voluntary subjection to the new, divine order.[62] At the same time God brings about the renewal and transfiguration of the cosmos.[63] What here remains wholly submerged in an eschatological light is powerfully related to the present in the songs in praise of the kingly majesty of Yahweh.[64] These songs see the whole of nature, along with the nations, imbued with the righteousness of God; for the natural and human orders of God's rule are intimately bound up with one another.[65] Thus the creation is capable of being taken up directly into the relationship which is the foundation for the community, insofar as divine faithfulness to the covenant (*hesed*), as universal graciousness, binds the creator and the creation together.[66] All of these expressions give evidence of a vision which embraces both the creation and history, in which the certainty of those acts in the course of history which prove Yahweh to be the true God find their strength and support in the presentation of this God's power and greatness as creator. But here as well, the inner possibility for this vision does not lie in the optimistic transposition of the lawfulness and purposefulness of natural events onto history, so as to save their teleology. Rather, it lies in the knowledge of God, whose creative word called nature into being as a whole, in relation to a particular personality. Therein God is made known to be the same one who claims to be active in history, the sovereign Lord.

Once more, and with deliberate accuracy, the struggle against theodicy was waged on the basis of faith in the creation by the author of the little Book of Koheleth (Ecclesiastes). One who was familiar with the thoughts of the wise and a member of their circle took the offensive against the self-confident wisdom teaching which had been given new life in the Hellenistic era through acquaintance with Greek philosophy, and thought itself capable of entering into God's counsels and solving the riddles of the universe.[67] By ever new paths of thought the preacher led an assault on wisdom's claim to dominance, in order to destroy its false halo and to confront it with boundaries fixed for it by a higher authority, boundaries which must not be transgressed. For even wisdom bears the stigma of all that is earthly; it neither possesses nor is able to transmit any absolute worth in itself. And measured by the highest object, it is vain. But this knowledge grows out of preoccupation with the creative power of God, whose absolute freedom makes itself felt in a predestination which is no longer perspicuous to humans (6:10; 9:1). Nevertheless this power is not an impersonal fate but a personal action which reveals itself as such to humans. The preacher has built a view of life based upon the accounts of creation in Genesis.[68] Thus the preacher knows that the creator has made everything in its own season and has placed eternity in the heart of humans, inwardly binding them to their creator. Therefore happiness can be praised as the creator's most wonderful gift,[69] and wisdom can be recognized, within its boundaries, as a lofty good,[70] and spurred on to faithful productivity.[71] The riches of the OT life of faith may no longer be accessible to this sage, but these teachings remain, nevertheless, the authentic elaboration of an OT knowledge of God. And the sage proves to be the true guardian of its otherness which cannot be assimilated by any human system. For "all" that God does "lasts forever," and "God has done it so that humans might fear before him!" (3:14).

NOTES

1 On the entire question cf. the fine overview of the history of the problem in W. Staerk, *Vorsehung und Vergeltung* (1931). Our only concern here can be to set forth the character of Old Testament faith in providence and its relation to the question of theodicy which emerges from it with the greatest possible clarity.

2 E.g. R. Smend, *Alttestamentliche Religionsgeschichte* (1899) 103; similarly B. Stade, *Biblische Theologie des Alten Testaments* (1905) 194.

3 Cf. Gen. 16:5; 20:3ff; 31:6, 50; 1 Sam. 24:13ff; 25:39; 2 Sam. 18:31; 16:12; Exod. 22:20, 26, etc.

4 Gen. 25:21; 30:24; 32:10ff; Judg. 13:8; 16:28; 1 Sam. 1:13ff, 27; 25:29; 2 Sam. 3:39; 15:8, 31; 12:16.

5 Gen. 24:12; similarly 27:20; 1 Sam. 17:37.

6 Gen. 48:15; Ps. 23:1–4; 31:4; 107:41.

7 Exod. 32:32f; Isa. 4:3; Mal. 3:16; Pss. 69:29; 139:16; Dan. 12:1.

8 Pss. 17:8; 36:8; 57:2; 63:8; 91:4. Though these psalms are predominantly later compositions, the preference which these liturgical prayers exhibit for the preservation of old stereotypical figures of speech makes the presence of older conceptions likely. But the image of the winged solar disk, for which Mal. 3:20 provides the first literary evidence, is a motif often employed on Hebrew seals of the earlier period (H. Gressmann, *Altorientalische Texte und Bilder zum Alten Testament* (2d ed.; 1927) figs. 581, 588, 595. And the use of this image *in malam partem* in Isa. 8:8; Jer. 48:40; 49:22, where the inundation of a land by enemy forces is described as a bird of prey spreading its wings over its victim, points in the same direction. We should also recall the depiction of the Egyptian pharaoh, whose head appears covered by the wings of a Horus-falcon in order to designate him as the protégé of Horus (*Altorientalische Texte und Bilder*, fig. 35). That which the Egyptians attributed to the deified pharaoh alone, the Israelites ventured to assert of every righteous person.

9 1 Sam. 6:9; Ruth 2:3, cf. 20.

10 Exod. 21:13.

11 Cf. in addition Isa. 54:16; Lam. 3:37f; Eccl. 7:14.

12 Exod. 20:5; 34:7; Num. 14:18; Deut. 5:9; Joshua. 7; 1 Sam. 14; 2 Kings 9, 26, etc.

13 Prov. 20:24; Pss. 16:5ff; 37:5, 18, 23; 73:23f; 137:16; much amplified in late Judaism, e.g., Jub. 16:3; 32:21ff; *2 Enoch* 53:2.

14 Prov. 3:12; Ps. 68:6; 103:13; Wis. 2:16ff; 5:5.

15 Thus Prov. 3:12; it is doubtful whether one can already find the first appearance of the concept of the correction and guidance of the individual in Jer. 15:11 (thus H. Schmidt, *Gott und das Leid im Alten Testament* [1926] 23) in view of the fragmentary state of the text. The idea is discussed at length in Elihu's discourse in Job 32—37; particularly in 36:5ff. In the Psalms cf. Pss. 66:20; 118:18; 119:67, 71; further Lam. 3:27. In late Judaism cf. 1 Macc. 2:52; Jdt. 8:25ff; Sir. 2:1ff; Wis. 3:5f; Jub. 17:17f.

16 Hag. 2:5; Zech. 6:4; Isa. 59:21; Neh. 9:20, 30.

17 Pss. 51:13; 143:10.

18 Pss. 2:9ff; 21:10f; 45:6; 110:5ff.

19 Gen. 12:2f and parallels.

20 Gen. 49:10.

21 Deut. 4:19, cf. 32:8f.

22 Cf., besides the invasion of Tyrian Baal, the spread of prophetic influence to Phoenicia and Damascus 1 Kgs. 17:8ff; 2 Kgs. 5 and 8:7ff.

23 1 Kgs. 19:15ff; 2 Kgs. 8:10ff.

24 Isa. 29:15f; 10:15ff, 23; 37:28f; 9:3ff.

25 Isa. 10:12; 14:26; 18:7; 22:11; 28:16ff, 22, 23—29.

26 The provenance of Ezekiel is certainly open to legitimate doubts.

27 Isa. 37:29.

28 Isa. 41:25; 43:14; 44:28; 45:1–7; 46:10f.

29 Dan. 2:31ff; 7:8.

30 It remains disputed whether Chaldaean-Iranian astral religion or Egyptian gnosis and Aion-mysticism or Greek philosophy have had an influence here; cf. H. Gressmann, *Die hellenistische Gestirnreligion* (1925) and W. Baumgartner, *Das Buch Daniel* (1926) 18ff.

31 For the following statements, which can provide no more than a brief outline, the reader is referred to my detailed presentation: W. Eichrodt, *Theologie des Alten Testaments* (1933) I: 219ff and 228ff (ET: I: 410ff and 424ff).

32 Pss. 9:12f; 48:3, 5ff; 68; 74:18ff; 85:5–8; 96:3ff; 136:23f; 145:11ff; 147:13.

33 Cf. the priestly account of history in the Pentateuch; further 1 Samuel 4—6; 2 Samuel 6; 2 Kings 12; 22; 2 Chr. 15:8–18; 17:7ff; 19:4ff; 29ff; 34f.

34 Pss. 9:5, 8f; 65:6, 9; 66; 93; 96; 97; 99; 113:3f; 145:11–13; 148:11, 13.

35 The lack of a precise definition of the concept is, as is so often the case, at fault here for much obscurity. The vague talk of theodicy, as if one could classify under this heading every statement which seeks to maintain faith in God over against the enigmas of existence, misunderstands the real meaning of the expression.

36 Isa. 29:10f, 14; 28:21, 29.

37 Isa. 5:19; 28:14; Ezek. 12:21ff; 21:5; 33:30ff.

38 Isa. 5:12f; 7:9; 8:6f, 17f; 28:16f, 22; 30:15; 31:2.

39 Textual emendation follows E. Sellin's suggestion in *Das Zwölfprophetenbuch* (KAT, 2d and 3d ed.; 1930) on this passage.

40 O. Procksch, *Die kleinen prophetischen Schriften vor dem Exil* (1916) 163.

41 Isa. 40:31; 41:17; 42:18ff; 43:8, 10; 44:21; 45:9f; 49:23; 50:2, 10; 51:5.

42 Mal. 3:1ff, 18ff.

43 Cf. on the subject E. Balla, "Das Problem des Leides in der Geschichte der israelitisch-jüdischen Religion," in *Eucharisterion, H. Gunkel zum 60. Geburtstage* (1923) 214ff.

44 Cf. above, pp. 26f.

45 On the "suppressed sighs" in the pages of the Old Testament, H. Schmidt (*Gott und Leid*, 7ff) makes some noteworthy comments.

46 Thus we leave out of account the eschatological interpretation, as represented by A. Bertholet and J. Herrmann, and find it necessary to agree with J. Köberle and others when they see here a persistent divine retribution making itself felt. But to what extent we also differ from these interpreters once again, and approach the views of the former, the following will show.

47 Here lies the element of truth in the eschatological interpretation of the passages under consideration.

48 Above all in the Proverbs (1:19, 31ff; 2:21f; 3:33ff, etc.), several Psalms (37; 39; 49; 73; 128), and in the speeches of the friends of Job.

49 Isa. 66:12; Zech. 9:11—11:3; 12:1ff; 14:1ff; Obad. 15ff; Dan. 2:44; 4:14ff; 7:27.

50 Pss. 17; 26; 59, among others; cf. Neh. 5:19; 13:14, 22, 31.

51 Pss. 7:4ff; 35:11, 19; 41:7f; 69:5, 22; 70:3f, among others.

52 Zech. 11:4–14; 13:7–9; 12:10ff. On this cf. O. Procksch, *Die kleinen prophetischen Schriften*, 107ff.

53 It is in this sense that v. 17 is to be interpreted.

54 The dialogue section of the Book of Job strives for it without being able to attain it. At the very least, Pss. 17:15 and 63:4 come near to it.

55 Here we can leave the question of whether the solution to the problem of Job originally intended by the poet is to be found in these chapters, or whether the dialogue section does not point in another direction, wholly out of account, since for our purposes it has no immediate significance.

56 The first to have put his finger on this expressly was in fact R. Otto (*Das Heilige* [10th ed.; 1923] 97ff); but B. Duhm had already pointed in this direction in his commentary. Cf. most recently W. Vischer, *Hiob, ein Zeuge Jesu Christi* (1934).

57 As it appears in the Indian conception of nature, and frequently in the modern view as well.

58 Duhm terms it rather imprecisely "enthusiasm".

59 Isa. 42:6; 45:8, 24; 51:5f. Cf. God's covenant with humankind or with the earth in Gen. 9:9ff, 13.

60 Isa. 42:6; 49:8.

61 Isa. 54:10; 55:3; 61:8.

62 Isa. 42:1–4; 45:22; 49:6; 51:5; 55:3–5.

63 Isa. 40:3f; 41:18ff; 43:19ff; 55:13; 60:13, 19f.

64 Psalms 93; 96; 97; 99.

65 Pss. 65:5ff; 89a; 135:6f; 136:4ff; 146:6f; 147; 148; cf. Jer. 33:19–26.

66 Pss. 33:5; 36:7; 89:15; 104:24; 119:64; 136:1–9; 145:9; Job 10:12.

67 Prov. 8:1ff; Wis. 7:14, 17ff; 8:8; 9:16ff.

68 This was demonstrated quite nicely in detail by H. W. Hertzberg in his commentary (*Der Prediger übers. u. erkl.* [KAT, 1932] 37ff).

69 Eccl. 2:24; 3:1–8, 22; 8:15; 9:3, 7; 10:19; 11:9.

70 Eccl. 2:13f, 26; 4:13; 7:4f, 11f; 9:16ff, etc.

71 Eccl. 9:10; 11:6.

2

Theodicy
in the Ancient Near East[*][1]

RONALD J. WILLIAMS

> Why does the way of the wicked prosper?
> Why do all who are treacherous thrive?

Jer. 12:1

These words of Jeremiah and their converse, the suffering of the innocent, together with the resultant questioning of divine justice, form the theme of this paper. It was no academic question for Jeremiah; it was wrenched from him by the mental and physical anguish which was his lot as a prophet. Although it might become a subject for learned speculation by the sages, it was nevertheless occasioned by the painful experience of men.

Long before Jeremiah directed his question to God others had posed the same problem in the literature of Mesopotamia. Until recently, only two major works dealing with the theme of theodicy were known: the poem entitled "*I Will Praise the Lord of Wisdom*", often called the *Poem of the Righteous Sufferer*, and the *Acrostic Dialogue*, known also as the *Babylonian Theodicy*. These, failing more accurate information, have been regarded as dating from the period between 1200 and 800 B.C.

Another tablet containing a poem similar in content has recently been published.[2] The text is much earlier, however, since it may be ascribed to the reign of Ammiditana (1619–1583 B.C.). Here we may have welcome confirmation of the views of von Soden, among others, who has argued that the questioning of traditional religious concepts in Mesopotamia was a result of the catastrophe which overwhelmed the Old Babylonian dynasty, ending in the domination of the land by the Kassites who first appeared about 1675 B.C.[3] In the fragmentary tablet a sufferer intercedes with his god who, moved by his plea, proceeds to heal the afflicted one, saying:

* First published in *CJT* 2 (1956) 14–26.

Having been obstructed, the way is open to you;
   The path is straight for you and mercy is granted you.
In days to come do not forget your god,
   Your creator, when you are prosperous!

rev., 17–20

Although the sufferer has declared his innocence, implicit in the words of the deity is the suggestion that he has forgotten his god in times of prosperity.

From other cuneiform sources of the same period we conclude that even before the time of Hammurabi the belief had made its appearance in Mesopotamia that sinners were punished and the righteous rewarded. This is well expressed in the following proverbial sayings culled from the literature:

> As for him who slanders and speaks evil,
> Shamash awaits him with retribution for it.[4]
> Reverence for the gods begets prosperity,
> Reverence for the Annunaki increases life.[5]

Soon there followed the corollary that suffering was evidence of sin. Only then do the facts of daily life which are at variance with the basic thesis lead to a questioning of its validity. Thence came the conclusion that the cause for suffering may often be sins committed unwittingly, as the Babylonian penitential psalms continually aver:

> The transgression which I have committed, indeed I do not know;
> The sin which I have perpetrated, indeed I do not know.[6]

In studying the literature which this problem of theodicy has created, we must bear in mind the fact that to the thought of the ancient Near East, determined as it was predominantly by motivations of religion and cult, divine justice never became a matter for philosophical speculation, but rather remained always a religious question. In contradistinction to the occidental world, the problem was stimulated, not by an abstract, speculative interest, but by the concrete circumstances of daily religious living. It was empirical observation that raised doubts as to divine justice.

The second work of Akkadian literature to be noted is the poem which the ancients knew as *"I Will Praise the Lord of Wisdom."*[7] Cast in the form of a monologue, it runs to four tablets. The central figure, originally a man of wealth and position, appears now as does Job in the Hebrew counterpart, as a man bereft of riches and power, and afflicted with a loathsome disease. Neither prayer nor sacrifice, priest nor magician can afford him relief:

Misfortune is multiplied; I cannot find justice.
I cried to the god, but he would not look at me;
  I prayed to the goddess, but she would not raise her head.
The seer could not determine my future by divination;
  The oracle-priest could not elucidate my case through sacrifice.

ii. 3–7

All his past piety has counted for nought:

  Like one who did not establish a libation for the god,
    Nor remember the goddess at meals;
  Who did not avert his face, nor was filled with humility,
    From whose mouth prayer and supplication were absent;
  Who discarded the god's day, neglected the festival,
    Who became careless, ignoring their rites;
  Who did not teach his people reverence and veneration,
  Not remembering his god, although eating his food,
    Forsaking his goddess and not bringing an offering;
  Like one who became important and forgot his master,
    Taking the weighty oath of his god lightly, I am disdained.
  Yet it was I who took thought for prayer and supplication,
    Supplication being my practice, sacrifice my rule;
  The day of reverencing the gods was my delight,
    The day of homage for the goddess was wealth and riches.

ii. 12–26

He is constrained to conclude that the will of the gods is inscrutable, and that divine justice does not parallel its human counterpart:

    What is acceptable to oneself is abominable to the god,
      What is despicable in his mind is acceptable to his god.
    Who understands the will of the gods in heaven?
      Who comprehends the counsel of the underworld gods?
    Where has mankind understood the way of a god?   ii. 34–38

The remainder of the second tablet is occupied with describing the symptoms of his disease in the most vivid detail. Then, in the third and fourth tablets, when all hope is abandoned, the god Marduk unexpectedly intervenes and in the course of three dreams health is restored to the afflicted one who then makes his way joyfully through the twelve gates of Babylon to the temple of Marduk, where he offers thanksgiving for his deliverance. Here we have no attempt to provide a solution for the problem of the inexplicable and undeserved suffering of a pious man.

The third Babylonian text is a poem of twenty-seven strophes of

44

eleven lines each, arranged in the form of an acrostic.[8] Unlike the preceding work, it is a dialogue, the two participants speaking in alternate strophes. The first speaker has experienced nothing but misfortune in his life and hence denies the existence of divine justice. He describes how he was left an orphan at an early age, to which his pious friend replies that death is the common lot of all men. Piety, however, is the guarantee of a happy life:

> He who looks on the face of the god possesses a guardian deity;
> The anxious man, who reverences the goddess, heaps up abundance.
>
> 21f.

He goes further, and suggests a reason for the suffering of his friend: the lack of piety as demonstrated by his denunciation of the just rule of the gods. This, however, does not satisfy the sufferer, for he sees no relationship between piety and material success. Drawing on the animal world as well as human society for his examples, he declares:

> The wild ass, which has uttered [defiance(?)],
>   Did it give ear [to] the ancient things, the counsel of the god?
> The fierce lion, which has repeatedly eaten the best of the flesh,
>   Did it bring its incense-offerings to appease the wrath of the goddess?
> Did the possessor of riches, who has multiplied wealth, really
>   Allot precious electron to Mami?
> Have I withheld food-offerings? I prayed to the god,
>   I dedicated the offerings of the goddess, but my word [was in vain(?)].
>
> 48–55

This, his friend asserts, is a shallow view; in the end retribution overtakes them:

> Look at the [well-]formed wild ass on the [steppe(?)],
>   He who has trampled the produce of the fields! An arrow comes back to him.
> The enemy of the beasts, the lion to which you referred, look at him now
>   (Because of) the wrong which the lion has done a pit stands open for him.
> The one who is endowed with wealth, the rich man who has heaped up possessions,
>   The prince burns him up in the fire before his appointed time.
> Did you wish to follow the course which these have pursued?
>   (Rather) seek continually the gracious mercy of the god!
>
> 59–66

The sufferer refuses to be convinced, but his friend replies by stressing the inscrutability of divine justice:

> The plans of the gods are as [inscrutable(?)] as the midst of the heavens,
> The utterance of the god or goddess is not comprehended.
>
> 82f

He further points out how zealously *he* served the gods. Now completely disillusioned, the sufferer declares that he will forsake human society and live as a vagabond and a brigand. His orthodox friend is aghast at the suggestion, but the rebel continues to point out the injustices in society:

> The son of the needy and naked (now) puts on [fine clothes(?)];
> He who used to dine on vegetables (now) [eats] a noble's banquet;
>   The son of the honoured and rich (now) [feeds on] the carob;
> The possessor of wealth is brought low ...[9]
>
> 182, 185–187

Education – all the secret lore of the scribe to which he applied himself – was of no avail to bring prosperity to the sufferer. But his pious friend still rings the changes on his conventional belief:

> As for him who bears the god's yoke, though scanty, his food is sure.
> Search continually for the favorable wind of the gods,
> And what you have lost this year you will replace in a moment.
>
> 240–242

The sceptic turns again to the theme of the prosperity of the wicked, a subject, incidentally, which is not mentioned in either of the preceding poems:

> Men extol the word of the renowned, who is experienced in murder,
>   While they despise the weakling who has done no harm;
> They justify the wicked to whom [justice (?)] is taboo,
>   While they drive out the just man who is mindful of the god's will;
> They fill the treasure-house of the violent with costly plating,
>   While the storehouse of the powerless they empty of food;
> They strengthen the mighty whose whole being is sin,
>   While they destroy the lowly and trample down the weak.
>
> 267–274

But his orthodox companion shows that conventional religion has an answer for this, too, for the gods at creation,

> Having bestowed upon men complicated speech,
>   Bestowed upon them falsehoods and untruths for ever.

As for a rich man, one speaks glowingly of his prosperity:
    "He is a king; riches accompany him!"
While the weak man one treats as if he were evil as a thief.

279–283

That is to say, with the gift of the power of speech, the gods doomed man to falsehood, to a mistaken view of life. This seems to satisfy our sceptical friend, for at this point he is moved to accept the orthodox view and, humbling himself before the gods, he cries:

    May Ninurta who cast me off establish aid!
    May the goddess who [afflicted me] have mercy!

295f

We note that in contrast to the other two poems there is here no intervention by the gods. The aim of this poet is rather to effect a psychological conversion.

When we turn to Egyptian literature, we seek in vain for any discussion of theodicy. The vivid descriptions of the social revolution of the First Intermediate Period (2280–2050 B.C.) contained in the *Admonitions of Ipuwer*[10] or the *Suicide*[11] contain no attack on the divine government, but rather accuse men of perverting *Ma'at*, the divinely ordained order. *The Tale of the Eloquent Peasant*,[12] also from the same period, deals to be sure with the subject of social justice, but no blame is attached to the gods. Most nearly akin to a discussion of the problem is the *Teaching of Amenemhet*,[13] a piece of political propaganda composed by the scribe Kheti for Senwosret I after the assassination of his father Amenemhet I, the founder of the Twelfth Dynasty. In the words placed in the mouth of the deceased king there is indeed something of a revolt against the injustice of the suffering of a righteous man. But there is a significant difference: the fault is man's, not God's! Even this document, therefore, cannot be regarded in any sense as a questioning of theodicy.

Surely there must be some reason for this strange omission in the vast body of Egyptian literary remains, especially when the theme is such a live issue in the Akkadian and Hebrew sources. Two factors may have been responsible for this state of affairs. First of all, we note the fact that in Western Asia, in the words of Jacobsen, "justice as right rather than justice as favor seems to have become the general conception."[14] It was in this area that the great law codes were produced. Now, that Egypt had laws, indeed that written formulations of law were in existence there, no one would deny. But these laws were secret, and access to them could be gained only by the proper authorities. They were the will of the king, and only as he saw fit was justice dispensed to his subjects. In Mesopotamia,

47

on the other hand, the laws were displayed in public, available to all men, that they might know their rights. Even the king must conform to them; why not, then, the gods also?

The second reason is the characteristic Egyptian belief in immortality. When rewards and punishments could be projected into a future life, the problem of seeming injustice in this life was not so vital a concern. Since in Mesopotamia and Palestine no such afterlife was envisaged, the problem remained a real one until a comparable belief arose. It is significant, for instance, that the Wisdom of Solomon, with its developed doctrine of immortality, ignores the problem, while Ben Sira, who emphatically repudiates any idea of immortality, is constrained to deal with it, emphasizing either the disciplinary value of suffering (32:14) or else affirming that the inequality is redressed at death, or at least that the reward is to be found in one's children (11:26–28).

We turn, then, to Hebrew literature. Here we find that the problem of theodicy is relatively late. It makes its appearance first as the result of Assyrian domination and the subsequent Babylonian Exile. It gained cogency from the fact that since the eighth century, accompanying the breakdown of the social organization, the clan and family groupings, in the spheres of religion and law the individual and his life step to the foreground.[15] Rewards and punishments could no longer be bestowed on the community as a whole; the consequences of piety or sin must be visited on the lives of individuals.

We can see this clearly in the prophetic literature. Here we have the doctrine of retribution for evil – doom for all, though gradually this is modified to allow the escape of a righteous remnant. Indeed, the evil may be visited upon generations yet unborn. Yahweh was a jealous God, punishing children for the sins of their fathers to the third or fourth generation of those who hate him (Deut. 5:9). The same doctrine, coupled with its obverse, the rewarding of good, is seen in the exilic historiography, governed as it was by the Deuteronomic view that divine justice may be demonstrated in the course of the nation's history. It may be, then, that the suffering of the righteous is the result of the sin of an ancestor.

It was Ezekiel who proclaimed the doctrine that rewards and punishments are apportioned justly to the individual according as he be righteous or wicked (ch. 18). This is in keeping with the rise of individualism to which we have already referred. Such a view now becomes axiomatic and is enshrined, as in Mesopotamia, in the popular speech, in the short, pithy sayings, many of which are preserved in the Book of Proverbs:

> No harm befalls the righteous,
> But the wicked are full of trouble.   12:21

> Calamity dogs sinners,
> But well-being rewards the righteous.   13:21

This view is likewise reflected in the historical writings of the later Chronicler, where retribution and reward are now seen to be meted out during the life of each king individually. It is most instructive to examine the parallel accounts in the earlier and later histories with this fact in mind.

After Jeremiah's heart-rending query with which this paper began, many voices were raised in protest at the patent falsity of such an assumption. Yet champions of the orthodox position were not lacking. Three psalms are devoted to the subject. The first is Psalm 37, an alphabetic acrostic poem of twenty-two couplets. The argument is pure orthodoxy: in spite of all appearances, the wicked who in their prosperity and power have oppressed the righteous will soon be done away with, while the pious will prosper:

> Fret not yourself because of evildoers,
> Be not incensed because of wrongdoers,
> For they will quickly wither like grass,
> And fade away like the green herb.
>
> vv. 1f

> I have been young, and now am old,
> But I have not seen the righteous forsaken;
> For those whom he blesses shall possess the land,
> But those whom he curses shall be cut off.[16]
>
> vv. 25, 22

> I saw the wicked exultant,
> Towering aloft like the cedars of Lebanon;
> I passed by and lo, he was no more!
> When I sought him he was not to be found.[17]
>
> vv. 35f

The same erroneous view is shared by the author of Psalm 49. This poem of three quatrains is a scathing denunciation of the wealthy:

> Why should I fear in days of trouble,
> When the guilt of my persecutors surrounds me—
> Those who trust in their wealth,
> And boast of the abundance of their riches?
> Alas! No man can buy himself off,
> Nor pay a ransom to God,

> That he may live for ever and ever,
>> Never seeing the pit.[18]

vv. 2–10

Note the repudiation of any idea of immortality. A later glossator penned a marginal note in prose (v. 9):

> The ransom of his life is too costly; he must cease from that for ever![19]

The poem continues:

> This is the fate of the self-confident,
>> The end of those who boast with their lips;
> Like sheep they have been appointed to Sheol,
>> Death shepherds them and rules them,
> In the grave is their resting-place,
>> In the midst of Sheol is their dwelling.
> Fear not when a man grows rich,
>> When the glory of his house increases.[20]

vv. 14–17

Again a later, pious reader, who was offended by this denial of immortality and determined to proclaim his own assurance, wrote another prose note:

> Yet God will ransom my soul from the power of Sheol, for he will take me!

v. 16

The poem concludes:

> Truly, when he dies he will take nothing away,
>> His glory will not go down after him;
> Though while he lives he congratulates himself:
>> "Men praise you because it goes well with you,"
> He will go to the generation of his fathers,
>> And will nevermore see light!
> Man is (but) an unreasoning brute,
>> He is like the beasts that perish![21]

vv. 18–21

The burden of the poet, then, is merely that the wicked "can't take it with them!"

In Psalm 73, however, we breathe a rarer atmosphere. In this poem of eight triads the writer abandons the superficiality of the other poets. He is equally convinced of the justice of God, but seeks with more success to reconcile the discordant facts of experience:

> Truly God is good to the upright,
>> The Lord to the pure in heart!

50

My feet had almost given way,
   My steps had well nigh slipped;
For I was incensed at ⟨the wealth of⟩ the boasters,
   As I beheld the prosperity of the wicked.[22]

vv. 1–3

He is driven to question the value of his piety:

Surely in vain have I kept my heart pure,
   And washed my hands in innocence!
I have been smitten all day,
   And chastening was mine every morning;
I thought, "I will thus relate,
   'Thou hast been false to the generation of thy children!' "[23]

vv. 13–15

But on entering the sanctuary the psalmist reaches a new pinnacle of faith:

As a dream after awakening, they are no more;
   When thou arousest, thou wilt disregard their forms;
But I, I am with thee continually,
   Thou hast grasped me by thy right hand,
With thy counsel thou leadest me after thee,
   Taking me by the hand.

Whom have I in the heavens ⟨but thee⟩?
   I have no delight on earth save thee;
My flesh and my heart fail,
   But God is my portion eternally;
For lo, those far from thee will perish,
   Thou destroyest all who are apostates from thee.[24]

vv. 20, 23–27

The minutiae of textual criticism have been banished to the footnotes. Suffice it to say that I do not believe that the Hebrew text supports the interpretation that our writer is putting forth a doctrine of immortality. Rather do I regard him as speaking of a spiritual fellowship with God in this life that is full compensation for all the suffering he may have encountered.

We must hasten on, finally, to the greatest of all expositions of theodicy, the Book of Job. That the book as we have it is a complete unity would be maintained by few scholars today. We recognize the existence of an old prose folk-tale, preserved in the first two chapters. With this may perhaps be associated the prose epilogue (42:7–16). Whether the author of the Dialogue was himself responsi-

51

ble for prefacing his poem with this ancient account or not, we may rest assured that he assumed on the part of his readers a knowledge of some such story. The solution of the problem which is offered by this prose tale is, of course, that the suffering which befell Job was a test of his integrity, to demonstrate the fact of disinterested piety.

The next section which is denied to the original poetic work by the majority of scholars is that containing the Speeches of Elihu (chs. 32—37). The reasons for this are well known and need not delay us now.[25] The same measure of agreement will not be found, however, with regard to the Yahweh Speeches (chs. 38—42:6). Here I must side with those scholars who regard this section too as a later addition. It presents a very different Job from the figure delineated in the Dialogue. Whereas in the latter Job maintains his integrity to the bitter end, we see him in the Yahweh Speeches repenting "in dust and ashes;" while in the Dialogue Job longs to meet God in open debate, when he does finally stand before his Maker in these speeches, there is no hint of an argument. Indeed, the central problem of the dialogue is left untouched. We are offered in these chapters nothing less than a detailed and eloquent exposition of the very point of view advanced by Job's friends: God is almighty and frail man must humbly submit to his will. Then, when all this has been said, Yahweh turns to Eliphaz and says, "My anger is kindled against you and your two friends, because you have not spoken the truth about me as my servant Job has" (42:7)! What amazing logic this is, indeed! Surely this is unworthy of so daring and skilled a poet as the author of the Dialogue.

We are left, then, with the Dialogue itself. And even here some spurious material is to be found. Chapter 28, that magnificent hymn in praise of Wisdom, is generally regarded as a later addition. But I submit that chapters 29—31, as more than one scholar has maintained, are likewise secondary. Here Job is not a desert sheikh, but a city-dweller of noble estate. The author has sought to make Job conform to traditional religious thinking and forsake completely his original position. Here "the keen and questioning seeker of the early chapters", as Dr Bovey has observed, "is presented to us as an unattractive snob, well satisfied with his own good works."[26]

Turning to the Dialogue, we find Eliphaz opening the debate (ch. 4) by describing the mystical vision by which he received a special revelation of the transcendence of God. Job reports in chapters 9 and 10 that if God be so omnipotent man is posed with a problem: "I know quite well that this is so – but how can mortal man be righteous with God?" (9:2). For Job the doctrine of God's supreme power, far from being an answer, creates a problem. If the view of the friends be right, then God is merely omnipotent Caprice:

> It is all one—therefore I say
>> He destroys both the blameless and the wicked;
> If his scourge slays instantly,
>> He mocks at the despair of the innocent;
> The earth is delivered into the power of the wicked,
>> As he covers the faces of its judges.[27]

9:22–24

It is at this point in the argument that Job hits on the bold idea that if he could meet God face to face and argue his case with him he might be vindicated. This forces him to the recognition of the necessity for an impartial third party to the debate, if god's omnipotence is not to crush him:

> If only there were an umpire between us,
>> That he might lay his hand on us both!
> That he might turn aside his rod from upon me,
>> And that fear of him might not terrify me;
> That I might speak and not fear him,
>> For I am not so with myself.[28]

9:33–35

In his next speech (chs. 12—14) Job continues to insist that God is capricious. Defiantly he challenges God:

> Only two things do not do to me—
>> Then I will not hide myself from thee:
> Remove thy hand from upon me,
>> And let not the dread of thee terrify me!
> Then call, and I will answer;
>> Or let me speak, and do thou reply to me.

13:20–23

But he is bewildered when no reply is forthcoming. His next speech, in reply to Eliphaz (chs. 16—17), returns to the concept of a third party:

> O earth, cover not my blood,
>> That there be no place for my cry!
> Even now my witness is in the heavens,
>> He who testifies for me is on high.
>
> My intermediary approaches God,
>> Before him my envoy intercedes,

53

> That he might defend a man with God,
>> Like a man for his friend.[29]

16:18–21

By a natural transition the umpire or judge has become an advocate – counsel for the defense!

So we come to the difficult passage in Job's next speech (ch. 19) in which he returns to the concept of the third party, the intermediary. Some years ago I ventured to suggest the original form of these verses, since which time I have been gratified to discover that I was anticipated in the main lines of this reconstruction by Mowinckel, who also recognizes in the *gōʾēl* the third party of chapters 9 and 16, and not God himself.[30] Job's triumphant affirmation runs:

> I know that my vindicator lives,
>> He who testifies for me will stand upon the dust;
> Afterwards he will raise me up as my witness,
>> My emancipator will see God.[31]

19:25f

To Prof. W. A. Irwin must go the credit for having observed the value of the first Elihu speech (chs. 32—33) for reconstructing the mutilated conclusion of the Dialogue.[32] Here we encounter the *mēlīṣ*, or intermediary (33:23), and we note how this figure is described as the superhuman agent of Job's subsequent restoration. We recall too that it is likewise a heavenly messenger dispatched by the god Marduk through whom comes the restoration of the afflicted one in the Babylonian *Poem of the Righteous Sufferer*.

In these words of Job we have an echo of a passage from the Ugaritic Baal epic, well known to Hebrew writers:

> In a dream, O gracious one, compassionate El,
>> In a vision, creator of creatures,
> The heavens rained oil,
>> The valleys ran with honey;
> So I know that triumphant Baal lives,
>> That the prince, lord of the earth, exists![33]

The author of the Dialogue conceives of the ancient Baal-Hadad of earlier Canaanite religion as one of the divine or semi-divine members of the heavenly conclave or council which is mentioned in Psalm 82:1:[34]

> God, taking his stand in the divine assembly,
> Gives judgment in the midst of the gods.

54

To this august body, consisting of "divine beings" (Job 1:6; 2:1) or "holy ones" (Ps. 89:6, 8), belonged the Satan of the Prologue, as well as the evil spirit referred to in 1 Kings 22:21. There is here, of course, no suggestion of polytheism. The incorporation of earlier deities into the angelic hierarchy is not without parallel elsewhere.

Who better than Baal, one who had himself suffered, but through whose passion there came fertility and life for men, could serve as the intermediary for whom Job longed? It was this message which commanded such a following in the Mystery Religions of the Greco-Roman world and which presents itself as a striking precursor of the Christian gospel of Jesus, the suffering and triumphant Savior. In the light of so heterodox a concept, it is not difficult to understand why the crucial passages in chapters 16 and 19 have been intentionally mutilated, or why the text of chapters 25—27 has been left in such hopeless disorder by the destruction of the original conclusion of the Dialogue.

Space forbids us to consider in detail one aspect of the problem which is well nigh peculiar to Hebrew literature. This is the concept of vicarious suffering which finds its noblest expression in the Servant Songs of the unknown prophet whose writings are preserved in the later chapters of the Book of Isaiah. The fact that suffering is woven into the very fabric of our universe and that it may be instrumental in bringing about God's gracious purpose for his people, reaches its ultimate manifestation in the Cross of Calvary.

NOTES

1   The Presidential Address delivered at the annual meeting of the Canadian Society of Biblical Studies on May 21, 1953, at Queen's Theological College, Kingston, Ont.

2   J. Nougayrol, "Une version ancienne du 'Juste souffrant' ", *RB* 59 (1952) 239–50.

3   W. von Soden, "Religion und Sittlichkeit nach den Anschauungen der Babylonier", *Zeitschrift der Deutschen Morgenländischen Gesellschaft* 89 (1935) 143ff. A still earlier discussion of theodicy has recently been published by S. N. Kramer, " 'Man and His God': a Sumerian Variation on the 'Job' Motif ", VTSup 3 (1955) 170ff.

4   *Proceedings of the Society of Biblical Archaeology* 38 (1916) 136, II. 29f.

5   R. F. Harper, *Assyrian and Babylonian Letters* (London, 1902) VI: No. 614, rev. 8f.

6   H. C. Rawlinson, *The Cuneiform Inscriptions of Western Aisa* (London, 1891) IV: 10, obv. 42–4.

7   *Babyloniaca* 7 (1923) 131ff; J. B. Pritchard, ed., *Ancient Near Eastern Texts Relating to the Old Testament* (Princeton, 1950) [hereafter *ANET*], 434ff; see now *Anatolian Studies* 4 (1954) 65ff.

8   B. Landsberger, "Die babylonische Theodizee", *Zeitschrift für Assyriologie* 43 (1936) 32ff; *ANET*, 439ff.

9   Cf. *JCS* 6 (1952) 3f.

10 *ANET*, 441ff.

11 *ANET*, 405ff.

12 *ANET*, 407ff.

13 *ANET*, 418f.

14 H. Frankfort et al., *The Intellectual Adventure of Ancient Man* (Chicago, 1946), 208.

15 Cf. A. Causse, *Du groupe ethnique à la communauté religieuse* (Paris, 1937).

16 Del. v. 25c as a gloss.

17 Read with Gk. *'allūṣ* and *miṯ'allê ḵĕ'ɛrɛz hal-lēḇɔnōn* and *wɔ-'ɛ'ēḇor*.

18 In v. 8 del. *pɔḏō* as dittography; for *'ɔḥ*, "alas!" cf. Ezek. 6:11; 21:20.

19 Read *napšô* with Gk.

20 In v. 14 read *'aḥărīṯɔm* with Targ.

21 In v. 20 read *yɔḇô* and *yir'ê* with Gk. and Syr.

22 In v. 1 read *yɔ̃ɔr* and del. *'ēl* (dittography); at the end read *'⟨d⟩ ny* for *wa'ănī* of v. 2. In v. 3 perhaps insert *ḥêl* after prep. (haplography).

23 In v. 14 read *wĕṯôḵaḥaṯ lī* (haplography). In v. 15 del. *'im* (dittography) which is impossible in a past unreal condition (cf. Gesenius-Kautzsch, *Hebrew Grammar* [Oxford, 1898], § 159m); read also *bɔḡaḏtɔ* with some Gk. MSS as an intentional correction to remove a blasphemous statement; read *kĕmō-hēnnɔ* with Gk. and Vulg.

24 Vv. 21f belong after v. 16. In v. 20 for *'ăḏōnɔy* read *'ēnɔm*, and for *bɔ'īr* read *bē'ūrĕḵɔ* (Gk. and Vulg. rd. suffix). In v. 24 *kɔḇōḏ* cannot mean "to glory," but only "gloriously" (as Gk. and Vulg.); however, the original text was probably *'aḥărĕḵɔ bĕyɔḏ*. In v. 25 some such word as *zūlɔṯĕḵɔ* was probably lost. In v. 26 del. *ṣūr lēḇɔḇī* as a variant or gloss.

25 For a brief and authoritative introduction to these problems see Samuel Terrien's commentary in *IB* 3 (1954) 877ff.

26 Bovey, *Hibbert Journal* 36 (1937/38) 360.

27 Del. v. 24c as a gloss.

28 In v. 33 for *lô* read *lü* with 13 MSS, Gk. and Syr.

29 The original text of vv. 20f was discussed by the writer in a paper read to the Canadian Society of Biblical Studies in May, 1946, when the following tentative reconstruction was offered for v. 20: *mēlīṣī yigga' 'ɛl-'ĕlōāh, ūlĕpɔnɔ̃w yĕpallel ṣīrī*.

30 S. Mowinckel, "Hiobs gō'ēl und Zeuge im Himmel", BZAW 41 (1925) 207ff; so also Irwin (cf. fn. 32) and most recently Terrien, *IB*.

31 The text of these vv. was examined by the writer in a paper to the same Society in May, 1952. For *'aḥărōn* in v. 25 read *śɔhāḏī* (cf. 16:19b), and in v. 26 read *'ēḏī* (cf. 16:19a) *yizqōp 'ōṯī, ūmĕśɔrī yɛḥĕzê*; note that Gk. read *ūmiššadday* for *ūmibbĕśɔrī* (κύριος is likewise a translation of *šadday* in 6:14; 22:3, 26), giving us the consonantal text for *ūmĕśɔrī*, since *d* and *r* are identical in the early script.

32 W. A. Irwin *JR* 17 (1937) 37ff; cf. also his valuable article, *JR* 13 (1933) 150ff.

33 *ANET*, 140; C. H. Gordon, *Ugaritic Handbook* (Rome, 1947) II: text 49, iii, 4–9.

34 Cf. also Ps. 89:6, 8; Jer. 23:18; Job 15:8.

3

Is There a Doctrine of Retribution in the Old Testament?[*][1]

KLAUS KOCH

The portrait of the history and religion of ancient Israel has been radically altered in the last two centuries due to the influence of the historical-critical method. Yet, remarkable as it may seem, one feature of the old portrait has not been altered in the slightest. That is the perception that, whether it is applied to Israel as a whole or its individual members, the relationship between actions and consequences is described in the OT as being determined by the retribution of Yahweh. The following statement is made in the writings of no less an authority than H. Gunkel: "From the very beginning Israelite religion maintained a belief in retribution."[2] W. Eichrodt's widely used *Theology of the Old Testament* repeats the assertion that a "deeply-rooted belief in retribution" is already to be found in pre-prophetic Israel.[3] He sees in the belief about retribution one of the characteristic peculiarities which mark Israelite religion: "Hence in Babylonia, despite a developed science of oracles and omens, we find a terrifying uncertainty about the principle of God's dealings with men; but the Israelite is certain that God in his turn will act towards him in accordance with those principles of law with which he himself is well acquainted."[4] One could assemble a list of dozens of similar references in modern studies of the OT.

It is thus rather astounding that, as far as I can determine, there has been no detailed study of this topic in the past few decades since ideas about retribution or even an explicit OT doctrine of retribution

* First published in *ZTK* 52 (1955) 1–42 [= WdF 125 (1972) 130–81]. Translated by Thomas H. Trapp. In the interest of brevity the quotations of biblical texts have usually been omitted and replaced with simple references. Several sections of the article have also been omitted, as indicated in the text.

are ordinarily used as if everyone already knows exactly what is meant.[5] A series of important questions are suggested at this time by a closer examination. These questions will be sketched out in what follows and will be answered as far as possible on the basis of specifically selected passages. Beginning with the assumption that the "Sitz im Leben" in which ancient Israel formulated its theological ideas is of crucial importance for their understanding, we will not study the OT texts which deal with "retribution" solely on the basis of chronology but will group them according to those which share a similar background.

I

The doctrine of divine retribution seems to be most obvious in the proverbs which are found in the ancient Israelite *wisdom* – at least the pertinent commentaries and monographs would lead one to this conclusion. According to B. Gemser, retribution is practically the fundamental doctrine of Israelite wisdom,[6] and P. Volz points out that the subject of retribution received major emphasis in education and was one of the chief reasons for instruction.[7] The validity of this assertion can be checked by referring to what is recognized as the oldest section of the book of Proverbs, chs. 25—29. Among the passages which are frequently cited in this connection, the following can be closely examined: 25:19; 26:27, 28; 28:1, 10, 16b, 17, 18, 25b; 29:6, 23, 25. Do these proverbs articulate a retribution teaching? They all stress that blessing follows an action which is faithful to the community but that an action which is judged ethically to be wicked will result in disaster for the one who did it. Yet, they do not say that Yahweh is the one who sets this disaster in motion. (The only exception is 25:22, to which we will return in a moment.) The question, therefore, is whether one can read these ideas into the text. These verses initially give one the impression that a *wicked action* – just like laws of nature which operate so that an action inevitably is followed by a reaction – *inevitably results in disastrous consequences*, whether it be unceasing flight (28:1, 17) or falling into the "pit" (26:28; 28:10). This observation can be seen most clearly in 29:6 where the downfall is built right into the sinning.[8] Though references to ethically good actions are not as frequent, they describe one's actions in the same terms. It is from the good actions themselves that the consequences of being blessed emerge. The faithful member of the community dwells in safety (28:1), will have a goodly inheritance (28:10), prolongs life (28:16) and will obtain honor (29:23). To speak here about a "retribution belief" is clearly a case of misunderstanding, since an essential part of the concept of *retribution* is that a *judicial process* must take place. In this process, the personal freedom and economic circumstances of the person, which up to that point have not been affected by his actions, are now indeed affected by some "alteration" in the person's circumstances relative to possessions, freedom, or maybe even life, as that person receives either a "reward" or "punishment". *In such a case, punishment and reward are not part of the person's nature, nor part of the essence of the action.* The response to one's action would be by assessment, meted out by a higher authority, and then imposed upon one from the outside. On the other hand, it seems to us that it is a special accent in these passages from Proverbs that actions and their consequences go hand in hand and are not simply to be brought into a relationship with one another at a later time. In our day, the consideration of retribution has been characterized in such a juridical fashion that it is thought to be reward or punishment *according to a previously established norm.* Yet, in the Proverbs, there is not a single word about any norm, any legal code. Corresponding to this, there is no mention of levels of severity for different types of cases. Whether it be faithlessness (25:19), a lying tongue (26:28) or the blood of another (28:17), the results are always described in general terms – at times quite picturesque terms – portraying the downfall of the one who has committed these things. The portrayal of someone who is faithful to the community also lacks elucidation of the particular consequences of certain actions. There is no differentiation in the importance of the benefits accruing to a person depending on whether that person has been true to Yahweh (28:25) or just to a fellow citizen (28:16). The only hint of a special case to be found in the verses from this section of Proverbs is the statement that the one who acts is going to experience the consequences of one's own actions (26:27; 28:10). One could possibly understand this in that, the way in which the person brought misfortune on another, that same misfortune would fall upon said person in some future time. Yet, such a remark is only one specific way of saying that, in general, certain forces are at work in the actions themselves. As the context shows, this is in no sense to be understood as meting out punishment on the basis of any pre-established norm. There are thus two concepts which challenge us not to detect overtones in the study of retribution which incorporate a Western understanding of justice. In the first place, there is in this concept a built-in and inherent connection between an action and its consequences. These consequences are not administered at a later time in a judicial process. In the second place, there is an apodictic alternative in force which very simply offers one either blessing or destruction, without further delineation based on giving special attention to how important an action is judged to be.

In the section Proverbs 25—29, there is but one solitary passage which mentions Yahweh when making an observation about a human action and its consequences, namely 25:21–22: "If your enemy is hungry, give him bread to eat; and if he is thirsty, give him water to drink; for you will heap coals of fire on his head, and the Lord will ____ you" (*yĕšallem lĕka*). The word which has been left untranslated is rendered as "reward" by most translations. If this is correct, it would cast serious doubt on the conclusions which have just been formulated. There is some evidence which leads to rejecting this rendering. In the first place, its etymology must be considered: The root *šlm* means "undamaged, be complete", and the Piel with a causative meaning would then be translated "make complete". It could only have arrived at the meaning of "reward" as a derivation from this original sense. Could Israelite thought have already come up with this transferred meaning by the time that Proverbs 25—29 was formulated? In rejecting such a conclusion, one can refer to the passages in these chapters which make it most likely that *šillēm* has still retained its ancient sense of "make complete". Yahweh "completes" the good action of the person who does it by means of the appropriate consequences which follow. This suspected use is confirmed by the use of *šillēm* in a secular, juridical sense throughout the OT. In those instances, the word carries the meaning of "provide reimbursement," so that someone fully replaced whatever belonged to the person whom the former had wronged and by that action "restored to completeness" whatever property had been damaged (Exod. 21:34; 22:2, 4, 5, 10–14 and elsewhere).[9] *Šillēm* is never used to described the specific job of a judge. Finally, linking *šillēm* with the accusative of the person in 1 Sam. 24:20 [English: v. 19]; Ps. 31:24 [23]; 35:12 provides further evidence which opposes translating this as "reward". Therefore, Prov. 25:21–22 is not speaking about Yahweh granting a "reward" by providing someone with something that would not automatically result from the interplay of that person's nature and action. Rather, just like the other verses to which reference has been made, this text presumes that an action and its consequences have to have an inherent relationship to one another, linked hand in hand as it were. In this particular instance, the concept is obviously expanded – by a good action, no less – so that in such circumstances Yahweh fulfills and completes the action. *Yahweh* is obviously described as a *higher authority* in relationship to humans, but this is not meant in the juridical sense of a higher authority who deals out reward and punishment on the basis of an established norm, but rather somewhat like a "midwife who assists at a birth" by *facilitating the completion of something which previous human action has already set in motion.*

There are numerous texts in the later collections of proverbs which could also be studied in detail, but we will not refer to all of them here. In fact, it is not necessary, seeing as how they vary little from one another. By way of example, we can consult Proverbs 11, since so many proverbs in this chapter discuss the relationship between human actions and their consequences. Particularly noteworthy are vv. 1, 3–6, 17–21, 27, 30–31. The majority of these references make the same point. An action which is performed in faithfulness to the community brings on blessed consequences. A wicked action brings with it disastrous consequences. A good action has an immediate effect in most circumstances by bringing blessing to the person for whom the favor was done – the sages also know how to speak in such terms. Yet, it is just as important to realize that there is an after-effect which benefits the one who did this too, even though it may first be recognized only at a later time (in the "day of wrath" v. 4; cf. 25:19). In some cases, in fact, such benefits are not apparent until one observes what happens to that person's descendants (v. 21 [Translator's Note: The author reads here "seed of the righteous" with the LXX]). The *action* could also be described as *having an immediate effect on the person's body and life* (vv. 17, 19; cf. 25:19; 28:16, 25). A different possibility is found in v. 4 where a comparison is made with wealth in such a way as to suggest that the good action itself is *in some sense a possession*, one that is actually of more value than material possessions. Verse 18 says the same thing: the good action, like the evil action, is something that belongs to a person from then on, just as we might say that a person's wages belong to that person even before receiving a check on payday.[10] Since Prov. 28:10, 17 presupposes similar circumstances,[11] we should really see in these descriptions more than just a figure of speech. The concept of an action and its consequences can also be developed by using the metaphor of *planting and harvesting* (v. 18) or fruit from a tree (v. 30). A third analogy which is used to help in understanding this concept emerges in the verses which describe action specifically as a *"path"*. According to wisdom, each person is on a continuous journey along one's chosen "path" and thus constantly in danger of taking a detour or getting "sidetracked", by which is meant that one finds oneself in trouble as a result of some wicked action. Prov. 11:3, 5 shows that it is within a person's power to travel along a straight and level path made smooth by continuing in actions which are faithful to the community (28:18; cf. 11:20; 28:10; 29:6, 25). The same view about the nature of things is shared in common by all these descriptions. *A person's destiny is determined by one's own actions*.

As was the case in chs. 25—29, so also in ch. 11 a few examples speak about how Yahweh takes notice of human actions. Once again, there are only a few isolated examples – obvious in only vv. 1, 20 and possibly also in v. 27 – (if it would be true that the delight which comes from good actions is not something which is there constantly, but comes instead only from time to time from Yahweh), but these verses need to be examined more closely. They do not suggest that Yahweh's divine sensitivities to human actions are only internal reactions when they speak about Yahweh's delight or outrage. They include the idea that Yahweh does something in response to how human actions affect the divine – otherwise Yahweh would be relegated to the position of a spectator.[12] Yahweh intervenes in human affairs and designates the consequences of a particular action. Is this a contradiction to what we have just described, a portrayal which says that human actions have built-in consequences? In the first place, it is noteworthy that there is not so much as a hint of juridical terminology. One does not get the impression from reading this material that Yahweh is imposing something which is not congruent with a person's nature. Instead, v. 20 shows that Yahweh's outrage affects those whose heart is already perverse and who are already in misery. Yahweh shows delight in those who are already on the "path" which is upright and therefore blessed – as we have just read in the description of those who are on this straight path. One can understand *Yahweh's activity* according to these texts and 25:22 as *setting in motion and bringing to completion the Sin-Disaster-Connection on the one hand and the Good Action-Blessings-Connection on the other*. We must deal with these texts in this way if any connections are to be made between these passages and those passages which were examined at the outset.

In order to strengthen the case against using OT wisdom literature to support the claim that retribution means that Yahweh actively administers punishment, we must still look at the most important of the remaining texts in Proverbs which connect Yahweh's activities with a person's activities and the consequences of those actions. As in chs. 25—29 and ch. 11, such passages are also in the minority elsewhere in Proverbs when compared with the numerous passages which presuppose a closed Action-Consequences-Construct. (For some examples of the latter, see 1:18, 19; 4:17, 18; 5:22, 23; 10:3, 6, 16; 12:21, 26, 28; 14:32, 34; 16:31; 21:21). It is these passages which sketch out the connections which must be explained so as to come to a satisfactory understanding. So that we do not betray any bias in our selection of passages, we will consult those passages which J. Fichtner cites as evidence for a "retribution teaching" and will omit only those passages which have already been explained.[13] The following remain: 10:29; 12:2; 15:25; 16:5; 18:10; 19:17; 20:22; 22:4, 22–23; 24:12b. Reading these will show that no explicit juridical terminology is employed. Punishment is not even mentioned. *'ēqeb* as it is used in 22:4 is usually translated "reward", but it would be better to render it "outcome, result". What is actually said is that the "path" or "name" of Yahweh is a *home and protection* for those who are faithful members of the community (10:29; 18:10). Such verses are reminiscent of some of the passages which have already been discussed, according to which those who are faithful members of the community assure themselves of protection and shelter (14:32; 28:1; 29:25). The consequences of this action and Yahweh's way of responding to their action are one and the same thing. Prov. 19:17 says it even more clearly as it shows Yahweh "completing" a person's good action. The use of the Hiphil in 12:2 is also significant. The root *rš'* means to "be(come) guilty", the Hiphil thus being used in the causative sense, that is, "treat someone as guilty and thus afflict that person". Yahweh sets in motion what the person had previously initiated. The last of these passages to which reference is made (24:12b) functions as a key to all of the passages which have been occupying our attention: Yahweh directs the exact consequences of an action back towards the person which correspond to the prior action which that person started. The last verb used in 24:12b is *hēšîb*, normally translated with "requite", the same way in which *šillēm* is usually translated. As with *šillēm, hēšîb* is etymologically very difficult – but this in itself is no insurmountable barrier. It must have been originally a causative form derived from the root *šûb* which itself means "allow to turn back, steer back towards". There is something to be said for retaining this general meaning. Just as was the case with *šillēm, hēšîb* also has a definite juridical usage, but there is no evidence that it must therefore be understood in the sense of "punish". It is rather to be rendered "make full restitution", being used when a guilty person repays a landowner or believer whatever is due in order to make up for something which the latter lost (Exod. 22:25; Num. 5:7; compare this with 2 Kgs. 3:4 Num. 18:9 and elsewhere). The phrase *"hēšîb Yahwe"* did not develop from this legal sense, for how could Yahweh be held responsible for having to compensate human actions? The sense is rather parallel to legal terminology and means: "turn (the effects of) an action back towards the person who did something". It is most closely related to other passages such as 26:27 which describe how the action in and of itself turns back towards the one who started it (*šûb* in Qal).[14] It would seem it is assumed that, for a time, an action can distance itself from the person who did it, but then Yahweh retrieves it so that it can take full effect upon the person who initiated it. Even here the passage makes clear that Yahweh does not inflict upon a person some disastrous consequences which do not even fit, but instead Yahweh does something which is intricately woven into the action itself.

Up to this point, our investigation has shown that in the book of Proverbs there is not even a single convincing reference to suggest a retribution teaching. What we do find repeated time and time again is a construct which describes human actions which have a built-in consequence. Part of this construct includes a conviction that Yahweh pays close attention to the connection between actions and destiny, hurries it along, and "completes" it when necessary.[15] The wisdom literature reflects on and articulates the close connection between the Good Action-Blessings-Construct and the Wicked Action-Disaster-Construct as this applied to individuals. Yet, there are a few passages which do speak of the nation as a whole, as a "collective-I", which characterize this connection in the same way. The well-known passage in 14:34 comes to mind here.

II

The major emphasis in the preexilic and postexilic *prophets* is on a close connection between human actions and the consequences for those humans. This inner connection does not concentrate on the destiny of an individual, however, as was the case in wisdom, but the accent is on the history of the whole nation and stresses Yahweh's intervention in this history – another marked difference when this material is compared with that in the wisdom literature. Thus, one could anticipate that the accent on a retribution motif would be more pronounced in the prophets. The huge amount of prophetic material forces us once again to focus on only a few examples. We will center our attention on the Book of Hosea, which commends itself to us both because the material in it is more ancient and because it is comprehensive in its treatment of the issues about which we have raised questions.

In a speech against the use of graven images (Hos. 8:4b–7), Hosea proclaims that fashioning them causes the anger of Yahweh to burn against the people (v. 5). Hosea's use of a proverb in v. 7 shows how this wrath works. It is obvious that there is a similarity with the way in which wisdom handles this relationship. As we have already seen,[16] it is understood that the *action is the seed*. A corresponding harvest comes out of what is planted. If the action is godless, then the consequent result is nothingness.[17] The only difference here is that the focus of attention now is on the actions of a nation. (The context is obvious. The graven images are nothing, so whoever relies on them will become a nothing in the same way. In this text, the action which they themselves initiate is circumscribed by whatever power is inherent in the action itself as the action takes effect.) Hosea thus uses this same concept of actions with built-in consequences. One might counter with the suggestion that Hosea is using a well-known expression and thus deny that this could help us to understand Hosea's own viewpoint. By consulting two other passages, this time in Hos. 12:3, 15, we will refute this argument. These two passages show that Hosea himself clearly makes use of the idea that Yahweh is active in the interplay between human actions and their consequences. In both examples, the word *hēšîb* surfaces again, meaning "turn back towards". In Prov. 24:12[18] it was plain that *hēšîb* was used to describe the construct which linked together actions and built-in consequences. There is a parallelism which can be seen in the two parts of v. 15 which strengthens still more the case for defining *hēšîb* as we have done. Whenever this word is used with Yahweh as subject, it means that a person is so handled by Yahweh that he is given over to experience the consequences of his particular actions. Hosea admittedly says that the sinning brings on Yahweh's wrath, but this itself does not introduce punishment into the situation. Instead, a person is abandoned to whatever the consequences of one's action might be, which in and of itself is damage enough (v. 15). To put it another way, Yahweh lets the action go back home to where its roots are (*pāqad*, v. 3).

The idea that the *actions of the nation bring unavoidable consequences* back on their own heads is what also furnishes the background for Hos. 5:4. Because this wickedness of a spirit of harlotry is in them, "their deeds do not permit them to return to their God." "Wickedness" is not to be taken in the limited sense of an abstract value judgment. It has an in-this-world, material, self-activating quality about it. If the people transgress, they are locked into their sins and the effect of the consequences of those sins. They cannot simply make up their mind to try to start over and thus be back on track as a faithful community just because they want to be. There is hardly another passage in Scripture where humans are so clearly portrayed as unavoidably trapped by their own past actions. After what could conceivably be understood as a decision by the people to return once again to Yahweh by presuming that He could restore them to health (6:1–3), the prophet offers an answer which is anticipatory of what Yahweh would say: "What shall I do with you, O Ephraim? What shall I do with you, O Judah? Your love is like a morning cloud, like the dew that goes early away" (6:4). The good actions offered by Israel as evidence of its faith are so minuscule and have such weak staying power that Yahweh cannot even let such actions begin to take effect; they are in fact so weak that there is no way he can reinforce them. (The background of this passage once again conceives of the actions of the nation as having an in-this-world, material quality about them. It is from this that the idea comes that they can only last so long). Worse yet, Yahweh is described in 7:1–2 *as completely perplexed* as to what to do when reaching out to heal them and is confronted with all their sins. There is no way for the people to escape from their actions since the actions have this material, spatial quality which envelops the people. Yahweh is forced to stand by helplessly and just watch.[19] And that is not all. By virtue of deity, Yahweh cannot come close to the people without this very nature triggering the consequences of the sins which are exposed by divine presence. The actions of the people have determined their destiny.

These examples show us that Hosea is not compelled by the idea that God requites sin. He is compelled, instead, by *the view that actions have built-in consequences and it is in this vein that he proclaims the onset of disasters*. There is only one place where Yahweh is seemingly described as inflicting punishment. That comes in Hosea's speech against priest and prophet in 4:4–6. He concludes: "Because you have rejected knowledge, I reject you from being a priest to me. And since you have forgotten the law of your God, I also will forget your children." If one takes this verse all by itself, one could conclude that it speaks of a retribution in the style of a *lex taliones*. If this is the case, the action would at most be conceived of as a paralegal action, certainly not like a legally binding official pronouncement of a sentence. But if we take this passage in the wider context of Hosea's proclamation, then it is obvious that it is merely one specific variation on a general theme. Hosea understands that actions have built-in consequences in the same way that the examples from Proverbs demonstrated. The one who does something will passively experience the consequences of what was actively set in motion. The present passage dovetails with the passage in Prov. 11:21 in that it also traces the destiny which will first become evident in the lives of the children, noting how the outcome was sealed by the actions of the parents. To show that this is the correct meaning and that we are on the right track, we see that Hosea says the same thing in 4:9b: "I will bring back upon him all his ways, and I will send his deeds back to him" (author's rendering). Yahweh threatens the priest with rejection, but this is no different than "sending his action back to(ward) him" or, as Hosea might otherwise put it, letting this action *home in on him* (*"Heimsuchung"*). This last term, which could also be translated "afflict", is a key concept in Hosea for describing the activity of Yahweh. The object of the activity is not the person who started it but the action itself (1:4; 2:15; 4:14; 9:9; 12:3), so that "afflict" means nothing less than to "bring to the light of day". Parallelism in 4:9b makes this quite plain. This is also obvious in 9:7 where affliction is parallel to the "completion of an action" (*šillūm*).

According to the passage we have just examined, Yahweh's action consists of the setting in motion of the consequences of a human action. To stay with Israelite vocabulary, the nation continues to broadcast the seeds of its actions and Yahweh allows the fruit of these actions to mature so that the harvest ripens. In reading 4:1–3, it would seem that Hosea says that Yahweh's appearance on the scene serves a different purpose. Hosea most likely has the wicked actions described in vv. 2, 3 in mind when he predicts that God will act. Terrible sins, which the prophet singles out and loosely connects by means of a string of infinitives, have caused the land to be "polluted" with blood. This heavy burden of bloodguilt causes grief for the land and all the forms of life which live upon it, so that they shrivel up. "Sin and suffering are inextricably interwoven."[20] It is in these circumstances that Yahweh intervenes. The battle which Yahweh instigates does not have the sole purpose of imposing upon the wicked person the corresponding consequences of one's actions. Rather, it is to protect the land from being utterly decimated by the destructive consequences of the Sin-Disaster-Connection, so that the land would not be completely ruined. Bringing the final consequences of the disaster on those who started it all is a means towards an end. Is this contradictory to what we have already seen? In these other cases we found that Yahweh becomes involved in a human action so that the proper consequences are brought to completion and thus return to the point from which they began. In this case, it does not seem to be enough for Yahweh just to stimulate the action so that the final consequences of human action are exposed. There is no real contradiction though. Hosea is convinced from the very beginning that the actions of Yahweh which will mean disaster for Israel in the immediate future are still motivated by the long-range purpose of restoring Israel to the status of being blessed. When Yahweh intervenes and smites Israel – never done before – it is with the expressed purpose of bringing out into the open a whole "bedsheet list of diseases" which were hidden until now, all of which had been spreading their infection around since the time that the wicked deeds had first been committed. They were all to be "completed" at the same time so that the territory could be prepared for a new beginning. *The disaster which Hosea announced was to be a corrective chastisement* (5:2, 7:12, 15; 10:10). It would be an extremely painful blow, but it would pass. It would take care of all past offenses by bringing on all the consequences at the same time.

Keeping in mind that the following assertion needs to be checked out by means of a detailed study of the entire text of Hosea, let us take this still further. It has been shown above that Yahweh's activity is described in both wisdom literature and Hosea in terms of the setting in motion and bringing to completion this Action-Consequences-Construct. Yahweh is not explicitly characterized as "requiting", but such statements could then be construed to mean that the OT God Yahweh merely promises to maintain an ethical order in the world. God would be keeping an eye on everything based on standards of justice, making sure humans' decisions are carried to their conclusions just as an experienced overseer is put in charge of making sure that a complicated machine runs properly and smoothly. But the concept of chastening which surfaces here in Hosea (and is also frequently mentioned in the wisdom literature) takes us still further. This may even be involved in the idea of "affliction" in Hosea's use of the verb, to show that Yahweh is not keeping some abstract principle of order fine-tuned. *Yahweh is preserving the covenant.* As has already been seen elsewhere, every action, whether faithful to the community or wicked, spreads out to affect/infect the surroundings of the person who did it and finally goes so far as to affect the whole nature of the covenant relationship between Yahweh and Israel. Whoever acts wickedly is not just hurting oneself but transgresses the covenant (6:7) and threatens the very existence of the covenant. Only after the wickedness has been completely purged from the land by being brought to its "completion" can there be a chance for Yahweh to make a new covenant for Israel (2:20).

One can hardly expect that a prophet of doom like Hosea would speak with the same frequency about a Good Action-Blessings-Construct as he does about a Wickedness-Disaster-Connection. And yet, this positive side of the concept of actions with built-in consequences can be found even in Hosea, most clearly in 10:12–13. Here he uses agricultural terminology as we have already seen in many other places. Whether the action is good or evil, it is like a seed which a person sows in the ground. The corresponding yield will eventually sprout and grow to maturity. But here Yahweh's action is described as *ṣedeq* which follows human actions of *ṣĕdāqâ*. In the final analysis, a destiny which is the outcome of human actions and Yahweh as the one who brings a person's fate to completion are no different. The relationship between these two is obvious in the description of the blessings which come from the heavens to the earth and which will bear fruit (2:23–24 [21–22]). To say here that the heavens "answer" suggests that Jezreel first "asked" for blessings. They will endure only because, as v. 21 [19] tells us, a good action initiated by Yahweh had been performed so as to conform them to the innate character of the whole realm of nature and to Yahweh. In this same sense, but in the exact opposite circumstances, disaster is the "answer" given in response to what Israel asked for with its pride (5:5; 7:10).

We must leave the discussion of Hosea at this point. The evidence demonstrated how Hosea presupposes that the concept of actions with built-in consequences is at work in the same way that wisdom understands this. When Yahweh brings disaster upon Israel, it is to be understood as a special aspect of this basic premise. It is not appropriate to speak here about a juridical concept of retribution.[21] The same concept of a relationship between actions and consequences could be demonstrated equally well in the rest of the prophetic corpus. Even the very familiar passage in Ezekiel 18 is not about "individual retribution" but about how the effect of actions with their built-in consequences will be limited so that only that individual would be affected.[22]

III

There is no place in the OT where the concept of actions with built-in consequences is so obviously at work as is the case with the Psalms. This is true for so many different sections of the Psalms but particularly in the individual laments and individual songs of thanks. We can begin by referring to Ps. 7:14–17[13–16] which is as clear an example as one would wish for to show the interrelationship between actions and consequences. Ps. 9:16[15]; 35:8[7]; 57:7[6]; 141:10 (cf. 140:10, 11) all portray the person as one who falls into the pit which that very person has dug or as one caught in the net which that individual has spread out. Two other examples can also be instructive

(38:5–6[4–5]; 40:13[12]) to show that the person who has done something carries those transgressions around with oneself, and graphic terms are employed to describe how they are affecting that individual now (cf. 34:22[21]; 37:2, 15; 54:7[5]; 59:13[11]; 106:43; 107:17). The Good Action-Blessings-Construct is found in Psalm 25, particularly vv. 12–13, 21, an acrostic psalm which probably has its roots in wisdom. Here the accent is on the absolute sense in which the word "path" is used. In reality there is only a single path of life for humankind, that being the one shaped by good actions and consequent blessings. The wicked person does not even have a "path" to follow (one "goes astray" 58:4[3]). The path of the good person is not limited to having an effect on that individual only. It will also affect the descendants of the faithful members of the community. The theme of Psalm 1 is also about the effect of faithful members of the community on their descendants. The person who stays away from sin and observes the guidance of Yahweh is "like a tree planted by streams of water, that yields its fruit in its season, and its leaf does not wither. In all that he does, he prospers" (v. 3). Here again we see the relationship between human actions and their consequences expressed, using the imagery of a plant. But now the human alone is the plant. The manner in which one will grow and bear fruit depends on one's actions. This same Good Action-Blessings-Construct is also used in Pss. 37:37; 61:8[7]; 84:6–8[5–7]; 92:13–15[12–14]. It is striking, however, that once again passages such as these are in the minority. The preponderance of the texts sketch out the Sin-Disaster-Relationship. The concept of actions with built-in consequences is not balanced equally in the Psalms with respect to positive and negative examples. Concerning the connection with actions, *the positive are much more frequently related to Yahweh's activity in blessing.* Concerning wicked actions, however, as Ps. 1:6 shows, Yahweh is not so prominent in the picture: "For the Lord knows the way of the righteous, but the way of the wicked will perish." Yahweh is mentioned in the first half of the verse, but the second half only mentions the action with its built-in consequences. The situation is similar in Ps. 125:4, 5 where Yahweh does good to the faithful member of the community but simply lets the wicked wander wherever their paths lead them (similarly 32:10; 1 Sam. 2:30).

Any mention of the actions which are determinative of the consequences must include the observation that human action is not to be seen as an event which is later assigned a value by some spiritual standard and also not as an event which continues on indefinitely in having an effect on a person's life. Instead, it is *like something which receives a charge of power* (*"machthaltigen Ding"*). It can be seen in the passages noted above, such as 38:5[4] and 40:13[12], where the heavy weight and great number of trespasses exert a power by weighing "upon a person's own head."[23] It is also seen in the fact that the Israelite does not speak of "practicing" faithfulness or "traveling down the road" of wickedness. According to the Hebrew way of expressing this, good actions or evil actions are "created". The Psalmists make use of the words *pāᶜal* and *ᶜāśāh* on the one hand for making a pit and digging it out (7:16[15]) or (Yahweh's) making the moon (104:1). Yet, on other occasions, these words can describe the "production" of a good action which is interconnected with blessings (15:2; 106:3; 119:12) or the production of an evil action which produces disastrous consequences (119:3; 31:24; 101:7). It is easy to cite other examples which describe this characteristic of an action. Wickedness sticks to the hands of the one who did it (7:4[3]; 26:10); it fills up the city (55:10–12[9–11]). The one who is praying in Psalm 69 can ask in v. 28(27) that Yahweh would "add" punishment upon punishment (*ᶜāwōn*) for his enemies. At the opposite extreme, the faithful member of the community will "stand fast" forever (112:9). But this idea conveyed by this word "thing" does not go far enough. Good actions and wickedness do not have a spatial quality like other "things" which can be held and viewed. The characteristic of the relationship between the person who does something and what that person does is highlighted by the use, throughout the OT, of the preposition *bĕ* in its original locative sense, meaning "in".[24] A person finds oneself "in(side)" one's actions. We would probably take the exact opposite view that an action would be found in(side) a person, but the OT evidence in this case is unanimous.[25] Ps. 72:3 says: "Let the mountains bear prosperity for the people, and (may) the hills (bring forth fruit) in righteousness."[26] Ps. 25:13 says that the faithful member of the community sleeps during the night "in(side) goodness". In the same way Ps. 106:38b, 39 speaks of the wicked action: "and the land was polluted *in* [RSV, *with*] blood. Thus they became unclean *in* [RSV, *by*] their acts, and played the harlot *in* their doings." Children even live inside the actions of their parents (Ps. 51:7[5]): "Behold, I was brought forth *in* iniquity, and *in* sin did my mother conceive me." In the wisdom literature (e.g. Prov. 11:5, 6) and Hosea (e.g. 5:5; 7:3) *bĕ* is used in a similar way. The many passages which describe a person surrounded by or even enveloped by one's own actions lead one to understand the preposition *bĕ* in its original locative sense, which of course does not preclude its being used in the instrumental sense which has also been mentioned (cf. Ps. 40:13[12]; Hos. 7:2 above and also Pss. 109:18–19, 29; 73:6). The same usage is found in reference to good actions in 132:9: "Let the priests be clothed in [RSV, with] righteousness." The action thus becomes a powerful sphere of influence which was created by the person who did something and is now caught by what he did.

The texts which describe *Yahweh's allowing humans to see the power in their own actions* are just as numerous as those which speak of human actions and their built-in consequences. Occasionally the first half of a verse, in *parallelismus membrorum*, will simply mention something about an action and its consequences while the second half includes a mention of Yahweh's involvement in the matter (7:10[9]; 38:4[3]; cf. Prov. 13:21). The Israelite can just as easily say that Yahweh's wrath pushes someone into a disaster as to say that a person's own action caused it (38:4–5[3–4]). The concept which wisdom and Hosea used to show human action as a *seed* and the corresponding consequences as its *fruit* is used also in Ps. 58:12[11] where Yahweh creates fruit for the faithful member of the community (cf. Psalm 1). This way of portraying an action with built-in consequences assumes that the action invisibly envelops the person and remains as long as it has not run its course. Yahweh's getting involved may trigger this action so that it appears in the *light of day*: "He will bring forth your vindication as the light, and your right as the noonday" (cf. 112:4; 97:11; Hos. 6:5b). Another passage takes this another step: "Thou hast set our iniquities before thee, our secret sins in the light of thy countenance." Here it is the light, which streams forth from Yahweh's countenance, which brings human actions forth from a "hidden" to a "visible" status. In other words, it gets them going again (cf. 51:11[9]). This *quantitative, spatial quality* of the action is also clearly seen in such passages as 41:13a[12a]: "thou hast upheld me in [RSV, because of] my integrity (*ḥesed*)" (cf. 37:17). The same is true in 32:10b: "Steadfast love surrounds him who trusts in the Lord." This is also used when considering a wicked action (5:11b[10b]): "because of their many transgressions cast them out." Ps. 68:22[21] reads: "But God will shatter the heads of his enemies, the shaggy(?; [RSV, hairy]) crown of him who walks in his guilty ways." If one searches for a technical term which conveys the sense of how God deals with good and evil, the word *šillēm*, which has been encountered already in our discussions, also keeps reappearing in the Psalms. Translating it as "complete" is also suggested by 31:24[23]: "The Lord preserves the faithful, but requites, without leaving anything [RSV, requites abundantly], him who acts haughtily" (cf. 62:13[12]; 137:8). As one would expect, *hēšîb* is used as a parallel term in 28:4; 79:12; 94:2 and is to be translated as "turn back toward", as 94:23 shows: "He will bring back on them their iniquity and will wipe them out in [RSV, for] their wickedness."[27] "Afflict" is used in 89:33[32]: "I will afflict [RSV, punish] their transgression with the rod and their iniquity with scourges" (cf. 17:3; 106 passim, where the context suggests that this affliction is to be understood as being chastised for a time).

Yahweh's *"remembering"* also plays an important role in the Psalms. Yahweh remembers (*zākar*) a human action. Yahweh is implored to remember all the hardships which the king experienced (132:1); all his offerings (20:4[3]) or even the sins of his impious enemies (74:18, 22; 137:7; Hos. 7:2[1]). What is meant here is that the Action-Consequences-Construct should take effect, as is particularly shown in these last references. When a worshiper looks at one's own sins, however, that worshipper beseeches Yahweh not to "remember" them (25:7; 79:8). On the other hand, the wicked person gets the wrong impression in being positive that "Yahweh has forgotten" (10:11). These passages are important because they demonstrate that the psalmists believe that human actions do not automatically take effect. That seems to be the impression given by wisdom. In the Psalms, however, the accent is on the active involvement of Yahweh so that an action is pushed on toward its conclusion. If Yahweh forgets, then the action does not have any effect on the present. *The correspondence between actions and consequences* where it actually takes effect *is the result of God's faithfulness at work* (*ḥesed*, 62:13[12]).[28] In such circumstances Yahweh is not functioning, as one might suppose on the basis of examples from wisdom, like a chemical catalyst which just speeds up a chemical process which has already begun its reaction. Instead, Yahweh is introduced as an element in this "process" because, without such active involvement, the process would never get started. But since Yahweh established this Action-Consequences-Construct in the human situation, the Psalms can also speak about "forgiveness". Yet, the manner in which forgiveness is described shows clearly that this construct of an action with built-in consequences and having a quantitative quality about it is in no way abandoned. It is therefore misleading to speak about "forgiveness" because this takes place in the spiritual realm and a description of such an activity is never found in the Psalms. There the Israelites talk about their sins as being "hauled away and hidden" (32:1, 5; 85:3[2]; cf. 25:18[17]; "washed thoroughly and cleansed" (51:3, 4[2, 3]); "removed" (103:12); or that they would be "healed" (103:3; cf. 107:21; Hos. 14:5[4]). When it describes the human, it says that a person is torn away from one's sins (*hiṣṣil*-39:9[8]). The in-the-world, material nature of the action's powerful sphere of influence is destroyed by Yahweh's "forgiving" intervention.[29] The worshiper can naturally express hope to Yahweh, "Hide thy face from my sins" (51:11[9]), or the psalmist can say that Yahweh "did not stir up all his wrath" (*hēšîb*, 78:38), which in no way contradicts what has already been said about the (almost substantive!)[30] wrath of Yahweh being the stimulus which sets the Action-Consequences-Construct in motion.

Of course it is common to find references in the Psalms to Yahweh's "judging" (*šāpat*). Is this possibly a different concept which tends toward a different viewpoint about retribution? A review of the pertinent passages will explain this differently. Ps. 58:12[11] explains Yahweh's role as judge by saying that fruit will be provided for those who are faithful members of the community, thus setting in motion the built-in consequences of their actions which already have a pre-determined result. Just as clearly we read in 94:2: "Rise up, O judge of the earth; turn (their) actions back toward the proud [RSV, render to the proud their deserts!]." Yahweh's judging aims thus to complete the Wickedness-Disaster-Construct. Justice is entrusted to the king by Yahweh according to Psalm 72 and is particularly to be used for the benefit of the poor (vv. 1, 4). It results in the faithful member of the community "flourishing" during one's lifetime (v. 7). Thus, when the psalmists speak of Yahweh's judgment, they are not thinking about how Yahweh applies some "objective" norm in order to assess human action so that an equivalent punishment is administered. One should not impose our Western way of thinking, which uses its own concepts of justice, and let such ideas intrude in these passages. Rather, Yahweh pays special attention to make sure that the person actually experiences the consequences which should come upon that very individual because of one's prior actions.

We can thus say that the Psalms teach essentially the same thing as the wisdom literature and Hosea; human action takes place in an arena of built-in consequences, set in motion, speeded up, and finally brought to completion by Yahweh's active involvement. But there are also differences when we compare this with wisdom. Some passages in the Psalms accentuate the fact that the consequences of an action do not automatically take place unless Yahweh is actively involved; otherwise nothing would come of these actions at all. There is, however, not the slightest hint of a theory of retribution according to which Yahweh either punishes or rewards someone for their actions according to a previously established norm. There is no evidence that a person receives, from another source, something which comes from the outside and is imposed upon the person or given as a gift.[31]

[Section IV on the ancient sagas and historical traditions has been omitted.]

V

The concept of actions which carry with them built-in consequences as has just been described has unbelievably escaped the attention of OT scholarship up to this point. The accepted conclusions have been questioned from time to time as quotations from more recent Hosea commentaries (A. Weiser, ATD; W. Rudolph, KAT) have shown, but even in these volumes it is not seen that something completely different from a theory of retribution is involved. A page from Eichrodt's *Old Testament Theology* is typical. He starts out correctly when he says "Judgment is already involved in man's spontaneous decision to separate himself from God. Guilt and punishment are not totally unrelated things, whose external connection can be brought about in any number of ways; they stand in an extremely close internal relationship." Yet, this does not stop him a few sentences later from speaking of a "deeply-rooted belief in retribution."[39]

As far as I can tell, there are only a few places in the modern literature of the OT where a differentiation is made between a concept of retribution and the concept which describes actions having built-in consequences which God simply sets in motion. One example of this is found in K. Fahlgren's study about *ṣĕdākâ.*[40] Fahlgren's "synthetic view of life" is virtually the same thing as what we would rather call a powerful sphere of influence in which the built-in consequences of an action take place. Fahlgren arrived at his conclusions from a completely different starting point, namely, as a result of lexicographical studies. He discovered that a whole series of Hebrew roots were quite remarkably used to describe both an action and its consequences. Thus *ra‘* means both "ethically depraved" and also "bringing misfortune"; [41] *rāšā‘* both "wicked person" and one who is "in the midst of misfortune";[42] the Hiphil form of this root form of the verb corresponds to this, meaning both "make oneself guilty" and "pronounce someone guilty" and also "bring a transgressor into misfortune."[43] As *ḥaṭṭā’t* means both "sin" and "disaster,"[44] so *pešā‘* means "wicked rebellion" and "one's own transgressions";[45] *‘āwōn* means "trespass" and "misfortune";[46] *ḥāmās* means "violent deed" and "destroying (oneself)."[47] This same double level of meaning is also demonstrated in the use of the word *ṣĕdāqâ* for actions which establish justice, meaning both "faithful member of the community" (Gen. 18:19; 1 Kgs. 3:6) and also the fruit of righteousness, the blessing, as is demonstrated in Prov. 21:21: "He who pursues righteousness (*ṣĕdāqâ*) and kindness will find life and righteousness (*ṣĕdāqâ*[48]) and honor"[49] [RSV omits "righteousness" but puts it in the margin]. Fahlgren explains these lexicographic findings by suggesting that in a certain time in Israel's history it could not distinguish between cause and effect and thus could not distinguish between transgression and punishment, between righteousness and reward. Israel would have thought that the person who was acting righteously would obviously live a healthy and happy life, while the godless individual would have to die an early death. Every transgression would bring its own punishment automatically, in that it cut a person off from the community. To describe this state of affairs, he coins the phrase *"synthetic view of life".*[50]

This explanation is convincing.[51] The *total of root words which share this double level of meaning* can be expanded considerably. Only a few which were discovered by chance will be added to the list at this time: *'emûnâ* usually describes the dependency of one's good actions but in Ps. 37:3 it describes the good benefits which accompany living in the land with other faithful members of the community.[52] *mîšôr* normally means "straight path" but includes the idea of blessings in Ps. 27:11.[53] *ṭohar* usually refers to "purity," but in Job 4:7[54] and Ps. 89:45[55] it includes the strength which comes from being pure. A person's "not vacillating" is connected in Ps. 17:5 with ethical conduct, but in Pss. 15:5; 16:8 it is linked to one's destiny. The verb *ḥṭ'* means both "commit sin" and "experience misfortune" (1 Kgs. 1:21). *nqh* in the Niphal means "be free of wicked deeds" in Judg. 15:3 but means "remain far from misfortune" in Exod. 21:19; Jer. 25:29; and Zech. 5:3.[56] *tōm* is completeness as it applies to a "totally pure action" as in 1 Kgs. 9:4 and "full prosperity" as used in Job 21:23.[57] The adjective *tāmîm* from the same root means "blameless" (Gen. 6:9) and "secure" in Ps. 18:33; Prov. 1:12. *ḥesed* probably also belongs here. Although it usually means "faithfulness", it seemingly has the meaning "permanence" in Isa. 40:6; cf. Pss. 52:3[1]; 32:10; 33:22.

hawwâ is a word which can include both ethically reprehensible behavior and disastrous consequences. It means both "evil" (Ps. 5:10[9]; Prov. 17:14) and "destruction" (Ps. 57:2[1]; Prov. 19:13). The verb "stumble" (*kšl*) can be used both for "commit sin" (Hos. 4:5) and "stumble and perish" (Ps. 9:4).

It is particularly noteworthy that there are also other words having this double level of meaning which do not involve ethical judgments. *yĕgîaʿ*,[58] *pĕrî*,[59] *pĕʿullâ*[60] refer both to the work itself and the wages for doing it. In Isa. 59:18, *gĕmûlâ* means "actions" (in plural), but in 2 Sam. 19:37 it means "wage" (compare Jer. 51:56). Even a word used as frequently in the OT as the word "path" for that which a person travels through life (*derek, 'ōrah*) includes both the actions and destiny of a person as their juxtaposition in Ps. 1:1, 6 shows clearly.[61] In English the meanings diverge somewhat, so that we can talk about one's "journey along life's path" but also about one's "lifestyle".

The clearest evidence for the absolute validity of the suggestion that biblical Hebrew uses this concept of actions with built-in consequences is the striking evidence that the OT *does not have a single word for "punishment"*. If one looks in the appendices of the Hebrew dictionaries like W. Gesenius-F. Buhl or E. König for the Hebrew equivalents of such a word, one will find that the closest one can come is in the word *ḥaṭṭā't* (*ḥāṭṭā'â*) which just happens to be the most specific word for "sin"! Here the Action-Consequences-Construct is plain as day. *tôkaḥat* or *mûsār* could also be cited if need be, but both of them actually mean "chastisement" and are hardly used in the sense of a punishment which ends up getting the wicked person out of the way altogether. The only word left would be *biqqōret*, a *hapax legomenon* of uncertain meaning which is only used in Lev. 19:20.[62] It is even less satisfying to look for a word which would translate the verb form "punish". After one eliminates *ykḥ* in the Hiphil, which means more nearly "chastisement" in the same sense as *tôkaḥat*, one is left only with *'nš* which means "assess a monetary payment". This does not automatically include the idea that something has been done wrong in the past (see 2 Kgs. 23:33).[63] What a frustrating development! The OT, seemingly at odds with the entire ancient Orient,[64] does not have a single expression which is an exact parallel for the most common aspect of administering justice. The gap in the lexicon suggests that even in the secular sphere of judicial terminology ancient Israel never freed itself from the concept that there was a powerful sphere of influence in which the built-in consequences of an action took place.

It is also remarkable that the word "righteousness" is never found in the OT in the sense of a *iustitia distributiva*. This assertion may take one by surprise, but the two most frequently used substantives, *ṣedeq* and *ṣědāqâ*, are never used to describe inflicting punishment,[65] but are only used in the sense of "rewarding" whenever they describe the administering of justice.[66]

These examples show that Fahlgren's idea which he labeled a "synthetic view of life" was on the right track. Unfortunately, he did not take this opportunity to expand on the consequences of this insight as they would have applied to one of the most important areas of Israelite thought. He was operating under the spell of traditional interpretation and neglected to bring his concept of the synthetic view of life together with the statements about Yahweh's involvement in the consequences of human actions. He went too far when he promulgated the questionable hypothesis that, as far as ancient Israel as a whole was concerned, whatever happened was solely in the hands of Yahweh, but that in terms of the individual's own life their own actions determined precisely what consequences came upon them. Then, when they would have seen Yahweh enter the picture, it would not have been described on the basis of a synthetic view of life in which Yahweh was also involved, but rather as an intruder who was coming to begin to administer retribution as the way to deal with actions.[67] Thus, from early on, it was assumed that, according to Fahlgren, they separated the idea of sin from the punishment which followed, separated good actions from rewards. The weakness in this theory of a synthetic view of life is that this supposed differentiation between transgressions and consequences as two separate items would have to be applied to national relationships with Yahweh as well.[68] Fahlgren found special significance in the development of the use of *pqd* to support his conclusions that there was a breakdown in this synthetic view of life in the individual sphere.[69] This is something which is hard to understand in the light of what has been demonstrated above. This word cannot be separated from the construct which describes actions with built-in consequences.[70] As further evidence, Fahlgren notes that in Deuteronomy and the Priestly Code (P) *ḥaṭṭaʾt* refers only to transgressions of the law (and the sin offering). The consequences of these transgressions, on the other hand, are described by a newly developed word, *ḥēṭ*'[71] – a fact which simply is not true. In P, *ḥaṭṭaʾt* in Num. 32:23 clearly includes the troubles which result from the sin. The use of *ḥēṭ*' in Deut. 19:15 and Num. 27:3(P) at the very least includes the meaning of a "sinful action." This section of Fahlgren's exposition was doomed from the beginning, since the study of the verbs and expressions showed already that there is always a presumed connection between Yahweh's actions and the actions and consequences for the person. There is always a presumption that there is a powerful sphere of influence in which the built-in consequences of an action take place. [A five point summary is here omitted.]

VI

This concept of a sphere of influence in which the built-in consequences of actions take effect seems strange to us *because it is so totally at odds with what lies in the realm of our experience.* The Israelites were hardly ever conscious of this contradiction. Of course, they knew that even a faithful member of the community had to suffer occasionally, since we can find "faithful member of the community" being used parallel to "poor" (Pss. 140:13, 14 [12, 13]; 146:7–9; Amos 2:6; 5:12). Ps. 34:20[19] states emphatically: "Many are the afflictions (*rāʿôt*) of the righteous." From time to time the wicked person would gain the upper hand (Ps. 37:12) and could enjoy a disproportionate happiness (Ps. 73:2, 3). Yet, the greater the wicked person's success in the short term, the greater the fall would be in the end. The faithful member of the community could be oppressed and poor only temporarily (Ps. 125:3). The wicked person could sprout like grass, but the faithful member of the community would grow perennially like the cedars of Lebanon (Ps. 92:8, 13) and would be blessed forever (Pss. 37:29; 112:3, 4, 9).

Such explanations sufficed in normal times. The concept of an action with built-in consequences was still in use to explain Israel's downfall as a nation, exile, living under external domination by foreigners, and internal social unrest. Lam. 4:13 talks about the "blood of the righteous" shed in the midst of Jerusalem (cf. Isa. 57:1, 2) – this even when individual members' lives could no longer be squared with the Good Action-Blessings-Construct. Even then, the concept of actions with built-in consequences was presumed to be in force, as in Trito-Isaiah (57:20; 58:8, 10; 59:2–8 and elsewhere). This could be explained by the predominance of the collective force of the sins of the nation.

It was when skepticism gained the upper hand that there was a *radical reassessment of the concept that there was a powerful sphere of influence in which the built-in consequences of an action took effect.* It is not surprising that this took place within wisdom, that it is here that the most radical opposition to this concept is voiced. *Qoheleth* must be mentioned here. In 7:15, there is a lament: "In my vain life I have seen everything; there is a righteous man who perishes *in* his righteousness, and there is a wicked man who prolongs his life *in* his evil-doing" (cf. 8:14). Qoh. 9:1, 2 uses a cultic catechism to assess the cultic activity of the people and determines that both pure and impure share the same fate.[73] The very fact that the whole concept of actions with built-in consequences is being re-examined at a time when it is no longer an acceptable explanation reinforces the impression that this concept was widely accepted at that time. This was true both in the wisdom sphere and also in the cultic sphere, as the observation that worship actions do not function as expected makes clear (9:1, 2). The preposition *bě* which is of such crucial importance for connecting actions and consequences is still used here in 7:15, even though it refers to the opposite of what Qoheleth has experienced. In 8:14, the verb "happen" shows that the quantitative quality of the Action-Consequences-Construct is still accepted in later times. Qoheleth does not replace the concept which is abandoned with that of a "retribution teaching" but rather sees God's actions now as incomprehensible random activity. Sometimes God showers a good fortune on one, now on another, and suspends the Action-Consequences-Construct – whenever God gets in the mood.

The *dialogues in Job* show an even more radical "shaking-to-the-foundations" of the concept that there is a powerful sphere of influence in which the built-in consequences of an action take place. There is an inexplicable contradiction between Job's conduct as a faithful member of the community and the disastrous experiences which surround him. He can no longer comfort himself with the knowledge that he is going through, at most, a temporary delay, whether of short or long duration, which would finally result in the real character of his actions becoming obvious in the corresponding consequences. Job had lost everything. According to his opinion, Yahweh had gotten the Action-Consequences-Construct backwards in his case (9:22). "It is all one; therefore I say, he destroys both the blameless and the wicked" (cf. v. 20). As v.22 demonstrates, Job discovers this perversion of the Good Action-Blessings-Construct directly in terms of his own personal misfortune, but then generalizes from this point to describe Yahweh's actions in general (cf. v. 24). In Job's case especially, God had disregarded them or had never been the least bit interested in the nature of Job's actions in the first place. Instead, God sends disasters Job's way quite arbitrarily, and so it did not matter whether he was a faithful member of the community or one who acted wickedly (cf. 10:15–16). God's indignation over against Job was seen as so severe that even if God would have let some good actions automatically take effect and bring a blessing, so that Job could "hold his head high again," God would then have come back and wrecked everything again. According to Job, God reaches back into the iniquities of his youth to find justification for sending disaster, in 13:26b: "(Thou) makest me inherit the iniquities of my youth." It is plain that these actions are God's own, having a power of their own. This is just what our study has been showing all along.

What is left for a person who is caught in such a predicament? The only solution for Job is to try to engage God in a lawsuit. It seems that Job uses cultic traditions which were used for penitential situations[74] when the people are sure of a God who still deals justly with them,[75] but the exact opposite was happening at the time they were calling to God. The man considers himself basically a more faithful member of the community than God is – at least this is the impression given to Job's three friends (4:17; 15:14; 25:4; cf. 34:17). Job starts out in this dubious undertaking by trying to demonstrate to God the Good Action-Blessings-Construct of his own life, since his heart did not reproach him for what he had done in life (cf. 27:5, 6). He treats his previous actions as a faithful member of the community as his property over which he has direct control. Such passages show us that the author of the dialogues is still using the concept of a powerful sphere of influence in which the built-in consequences of an action take place. This is also unmistakable in the speeches of Job's friends (4:8, 9). Only this commonly shared view would explain Bildad's remark that Yahweh will "rouse" himself for Job if he would ever humble himself and would "reward you with a righteous habitation (*šillēm*)" (8:6; cf. ch. 5, esp. vv. 2, 6, 7, 13; 8:4; 11:6, 20; 15:20–35; 17:9; 18:7–21).

It is this description of reality which clarifies the "solution" at the end of the dialogue, in 40:8: "Will you even put me in the wrong? Will you place me in misfortune (*taršîʿ*; [RSV, will you condemn me?]) that you (remain a faithful member of the community and) may be justified (*tiṣdāq*)?" [RSV does not read "remain ... and."] If Job wants to do this, he must have the ability to appear in theophanies just as God does (vv. 9–14). In our opinion, without having the slightest inkling of the concept of actions with built-in consequences, Budde gives the most adequate explanation: "Whoever wants to be the highest, whoever wants to exercise a lasting dominion, must be righteous. If Job is righteous in relation to God, if he is in reality more righteous than God, that must be shown by exchanging places with God and taking over the dominion of the world, since righteousness would then be best administered by Job."[76] For the poet, faithfulness to the community – what we think is a better way to say it than "righteousness" – is inseparable from dominion, and thus we see that this Good Action-Power-Construct even applies to God. Since God is the Almighty, God must also be beyond reproach as concerns a relationship with the community. If it were not so, both God and the world would have been long gone. Job is not trying to attain this level of faithfulness towards the community which God alone can perform, even though he is not aware of any wrongs within himself. In such a case, he would be trying to fashion himself as more powerful than God. This is a significant part of the answer offered by the author of the dialogue.

This answer does not invalidate the concept of a powerful sphere of influence in which the built-in consequences of an action take place.[77] It does go so far as to describe particular instances in which Yahweh's actions can operate on a different plane from that which humans would expect, based on the way the Action-Consequences-Construct normally worked. God's actions can at times suspend all dogmatic statements and theories about God's own inner workings. Thus, it is not that God is fickle, but humans can distort wisdom by trying to explain or comprehend such exceptions to the rule.

In the later documents of the OT, Qoheleth and Job show us that *the concept of actions with built-in consequences was shaken to the foundation.* At the same time, *this concept was not radically transformed by being replaced by some other basic construct.* Even less evidence for such a proposition could be found in the last book of the OT documents – the book of Daniel.[78] Even in the writings of late Judaism, it is unmistakable that a whole series of passages still operate with the principle that a person's own actions determined what would eventually happen to one.[79] This ancient concept seems to be behind what *Paul* says. H. Schlier points out repeatedly, even though he was not aware of the OT background, that this concept is at work in Romans. In commenting on Rom. 5:21, he says, "Sin carries death within it. Death is present as that wherein it 'lives' and therefore wherein its 'life' is known. ... In death sin achieves its being in a very real sense"[80] (cf. 6:21–23). The awareness that human existence is not only determined by God according to one's actions for this earthly existence, but that even at the last judgment one's actions will be determinative of whether salvation or damnation results, does not in and of itself force one to the conclusion that a doctrine of retribution is being taught, as it might seem at first glance. Rather, it can just as easily be explained in light of the concept of actions with built-in consequences (2 Cor. 5:10). According to 1 Cor. 3:10–15, the evil work (*ergon*) will be "refined out" of a Christian's nature at the time of judgment so that he will be saved "as through fire". Finally, Gal. 6:8–9 describes the relationship between actions and consequences by employing the OT description of sowing and reaping.[81]

This brief venture into the later history of this concept of a powerful sphere of influence in which the built-in consequences of an action take effect is all that can be done at this time. Within the framework of this investigation, it is merely intended to show that this unique way of describing reality did not disappear but has enjoyed a complicated and problematic history.

[Section VII on the Septuagint and Section VIII on the history-of-religions aspect have been omitted.]

We have attempted to use the broad expanse of literature to demonstrate the concept of an action with built-in consequences.[101] ... This study could leave one with the impression that we have *in nuce* a theology of the Old Testament. At the conclusion it must be repeated once again that the construct of a powerful sphere of influence in which the built-in consequences of an action take place is an important aspect, but still only one aspect, of the religious thought of ancient Israel. We have not even touched upon the important traditions of election, belief in the inherent power of Yahweh's word, covenant and theology of the law. In summary, what has been said to this point leads to asking further questions which must be answered. We have left unanswered such things as how deeply grounded one's good actions are in one's "nature", in what way they are in themselves gifts of God. On the opposite extreme, are wicked actions simply a result of the lust of a person's heart, or are they finally rooted in some supernatural power of nothingness? Finally, what relationship does the completion of actions with built-in consequences have in respect to Yahweh's cultic actions or way of handling the final judgment?

NOTES

1 I have already sketched out the main lines of argumentation, which are summarized in this article, in my dissertation: Klaus Koch, *Sdq im Alten Testament* (Heidelberg, 1953), referred to in the following as "Diss.," 85–102.

2 H. Gunkel, RGG² V: col. 1529.

3 W. Eichrodt, *Theologie des Alten Testaments*⁴ (=Eichrodt), I:191; cf. III:108, etc. (ET: I:382; cf. II:371–74).

4 Eichrodt, I:116 (ET: I:242–43).

5 W. Staerck, *Vorsehung und Vergeltung* (Furche-Studien I; 1931) is an attempt at popularization and is not a scholarly monograph. E. Würthwein, "Der Vergeltungsglaube im AT," *ThWNT* 4:710–18 (ET: IV:706–12) begins significantly: "Since the belief is found throughout the OT, there is no need to document it in detail" (711 [ET:707]). Only L. Koehler, *Theologie des Alten Testaments* (1936) 200, finds a gap: "The history of how disobedience and punishment is understood and developed in the documents and with the passage of time has not yet been written."

6 B. Gemser, *Sprüche Salomos*, HAT (1937) 6.

7 P. Volz *SAT*² [1921] III:148; cf. also J. Fichtner, *Die altorientalische Weisheit in ihrer israelitisch-jüdischen Ausprägung* (BZAW 62 [1933] = Fichtner) 62ff.

8 Because this rendering sounds so strange, Kittel's *Biblia Hebraica* (hereafter abbreviated *BH*) adopts the reading of a different text. Other "improvements" will often occupy our attention during the course of the investigation.

9 J. Pedersen, *Israel, Its Life and Culture* I/II (1926) (=Pedersen) has correctly observed how important it is to understand that *šlm* means "be complete/ make complete", p. 324.

10 When the word "reward" (*śākār*) appears from time to time as one of the many ways to describe the Action-Consequences-Connection, this cannot be taken as evidence for a retribution teaching.

11 See above, p. 58.

12 See Ezek. 18:12, 24 in connection with the description of the character of what is called *tôʿēbâ*. For *rāṣôn*, see Deut. 33:16, 23; Pss. 30:6(5); 89:18(17).

13 Fichtner, 106, notes 1–3; cf. also 2:7–8; 3:5–6, 7–8, 9–10, 31–32, 33–34; 5:21 (but note v. 22!).

14 See above, p. 58.

15 The term "destiny" sounds offensive to theological ears. And yet, this is exactly what is being discussed here. What the human sets in motion by that person's own actions continues without changing course until it reaches its "completion". This is even more apparent in Hosea than in wisdom, as we shall soon see. It is also to be seen in the institution of atonement. The complete destruction of one who acts wickedly is diverted by placing the consequences of the Wicked Action-Disaster-Connection, and thus the consequences for that person, on the head of the animal. (I hope to give further attention to this point in the near future.) *The term "destiny" includes the idea of something which is unalterable. A specific consequence is going to come upon the person who did something. That is what this is all about.* Admittedly, it is not part of our normal way of thinking to say that these consequences come right out of the action itself, but this oddity only shows how far our world is from theirs.

16 See above, p. 61.

17 A. Weiser, ATD, Hos. 8:4–7 (=Weiser) says "Hosea makes use of a proverb to show that it is impossible for a human to escape the consequence of his actions." T. H. Robinson, HAT (=Robinson) is incorrect when he comments on Hos. 8:4–7: "The law of retribution which is used here found its most detailed exposition in the Karma-teachings in India. Yet, everyone who surveys the path his life has taken will be forced to agree." He continues with a correct observation: "The human does not even have a chance to escape the consequences of his actions."

18 See above, pp. 63–64.

19 cf. Robinson, Hos. 7:1–2. It is apparent that the LXX-translator tried to get around translating 7:1 in this way. For this reason, he connected this first phrase with the previous verse. It is more difficult to understand why modern interpreters follow this reading rather than the (theologically) more difficult reading (Marti, *BH*).

20 Robinson, Hos. 4:1–3: "V. 3 is not really a threat in the narrow sense of the term, but is rather the conclusion which the prophet draws after criticizing the real nature of the nation." Weiser says that this is not a threat (as H. Gressmann [SAT] had maintained) since the person who did this is not even mentioned.

And yet, the disaster is going to come upon that person even before the others. Instead, one has the distinct impression that the "nature" of the innocent sufferer is accepted.

21 Legal terminology and forms sometimes surface in Hosea (as with the form for divorce: "She is not my wife, and I am not her husband" in 2:4[2:2]), but these examples are not the basis for understanding how Yahweh acts and are only to give emphasis to the fact that Yahweh sets these actions on their natural course or impedes them—as can be seen in the imagery from the hunt in 5:14; 7:12–13 or in the description of their wounds in 5:13; 7:1.

22 See "Diss.," 89–91.

23 See above, pp. 65–66 concerning what is said about Hosea and the way in which an action is described as a possession in Proverbs, p. 61.

24 W. Gesenius-E. Kautzsch, *Hebräische Grammatik*[27] Paragraph 119 (ET: 377–84).

25 It is also rare to find a place in the OT where it says that a sin is found "inside" a person, e.g. Ps. 140:3. Yet, this is only called sin when used to describe an idea which has been formulated into a specific plan of action. Before the person acts, the sin is in the person's heart. After one acts, the sin surrounds one with its sphere of influence.

26 This term *bṣdq(h)* is common and can only be understood in its locative sense; see "Diss.," 35ff.

27 The additional prepositional phrase in 79:12, *ʾel-ḥêqem*, would support this rendering; cf. also the passages which mention the action with built-in consequences but do not mention Yahweh. There, *šûb* in the Qal is used in 7:17[16]; 54:7[5].

28 If one tries to impose a thorough-going retribution teaching for the OT, one has to conjecture an emendation for 62:13[12] which says "almost the exact opposite" (H. Fuchs, *Christentum und Wissenschaft*, [1927] III:152).

29 One can make a connection with this construct of actions with built-in consequences also through use of the Hebrew word for "atone" (*kipper*); see above, note 15.

30 See J. Fichtner, "*Orgē*," *ThWNT* 5:399 (ET: 5:399).

31 Once more, by way of summary, it needs to be said that Yahweh's activities are not limited in the Psalms to "standing watch" and setting in motion the consequences of human actions. The Psalms, particularly the hymns, talk frequently about Yahweh's establishing the covenant or redeeming the people, but there is no mention here about human actions, which is the primary interest for this study.

39 Eichrodt, I:191 (ET: 1:381).

40 K. Fahlgren, *Ṣedaka, nahestehende und entgegengesetzte Begriffe im Alten Testament* (Uppsala, 1932 [=Fahlgren]). Fahlgren's exposition gave the first impetus to this present study.

41 Judg. 15:3; 1 Sam. 24:10; Isa. 3:11; see Fahlgren, 47ff. This evidence offered here and in the following remarks is sometimes connected only with the "evil" situation and not with the "evil" action. The evidence for this use is found without trouble in any of the lexicons. See Fahlgren for more examples of both uses.

42 Job 27:7; Fahlgren, 4.

43 1 Sam. 14:47, a passage which most modern interpreters have wrongly explained on the basis of the LXX.

44 Num. 12:11; Prov. 10:16 (often wrongly emended); Fahlgren, 16.

45 Job 8:4; Fahlgren, 24.

46 2 Kgs. 7:9; Fahlgren, 26.

47 Prov. 10:6; Judg. 9:24; Fahlgren, 45.

48 The second *ṣĕdāqâ* is omitted by the LXX because it no longer understands the concept of actions with built-in consequences.

49 Cf. 2 Sam. 19:29; Prov. 14:34; Fahlgren, 90ff.

50 Fahlgren, 50ff.

51 The only objection which one could raise is that modern languages also have similar words with a double level of meaning, without drawing the conclusion that they also teach the concept of actions with built-in consequences. We can talk about good or bad circumstances in general, good or bad health, even good or bad weather. "Wicked" can also be used in everyday speech, not only in a moral sense, but even for things connected with our body (a "wicked" cold). This objection misses the point. There was a time when our language had this double level of meaning for some of the most common everyday expressions, but they are used in Hebrew for the most important theological terminology. In addition, in our language the adjectives carry this double level of meaning, but in Hebrew it is the substantives which show this characteristic. Furthermore, in our everyday speech, each of these adjectives has only one meaning in its own special area. The fact that the Israelites often use these substantives without any explanations added shows that they already understood the context in which these words were to be used.

52 With Gunkel, HKAT, we take Ps. 37:3 to be a promise; cf. v. 29.

53 Cf. Ps. 5:9.

54 See "Diss.," 83.

55 *hišbatā miṭṭĕhārô*: "you put an end to his (from purity forthcoming) strength." If we reject this translation, then only the conjectures are left, and they alter the consonantal text radically (see F. Baethgen [HK] and Gunkel [HKAT] on Ps. 89:45). The difficulty is eliminated if purity is taken to be an action with built-in consequences and is thus describing a condition of blessing. The only other solution would be to alter this to read *'miṭṭĕhārô* since there is no noun *ṭĕhar*.

56 Numbers 5 is important here. If this accused wife, who is part of a broken marriage, is free from guilt, then she will not suffer any evil consequences (*nqh*, vv. 19, 28) and would be able to bear children (v. 28). If she is guilty, then she is standing within the sphere of her sin and made thus unable to bear children. The priest's water of bitterness would bring this sin out into the open. The husband is free from blame in this case (*nqh*, v. 31).

57 See Pedersen, 359.

58 Cf. Isa. 55:2; Ps. 78:46 with Deut. 28:33; Jer. 3:24.

59 Cf. Ps. 104:13 with Isa. 3:10.

60 Cf. Jer. 31:16 with Lev. 19:13 and Pedersen, 362.

61 See Pedersen, 361–62.

62 To this, W. Gesenius-F. Buhl adds: *mūṭṭeh*, *nĕbālâ* (Job 42:8—otherwise this is a common word for a mistake!); *negep*, *ʿāwōn* (transgression!); *pĕqūddâ* (affliction); *pešaʿ* (wickedness); *rāʿâ* (evil).

63 Gensenius-Buhl adds also: *dîn*, *zʿm*, *ʿūd pqd*, *špṭ* ptcpl. pass., *nāgûaʿ*—words which have even less in common with the idea of punishment than those listed above.

64 See the reference to Eichrodt, above, p. 57.

65 See H. Cazelles, *RB* 58 (1951) 169ff; "Diss.," 113ff.

66 The thematic statement in Ps. 18:26–27 (25–26) shows the minor importance of the idea of a *iustitia distributiva* and the great importance for Israel of this idea of a concept of actions with built-in consequences: "With the loyal thou dost show thyself loyal (Yahweh); with the blameless man thou dost show thyself blameless; with the pure thou dost show thyself pure; and *with the crooked thou dost show thyself perverse.*"

67 Fahlgren, 6, 52–53.

68 Fahlgren, 31.

69 Fahlgren, 53.

70 When the concept of actions with built-in consequences fades into the background, what is meant by *pqd* can no longer be translated with one word. See below for what happens in the LXX translation.

71 Fahlgren, 16.

    (Note 72 omitted.)

73 See K. Galling, HAT, on Qoh. 9:1–2.

74 The use of cultic traditions in the dialogues of Job is an important area of investigation which needs further study; cf. for the moment A. Weiser, *Hiob*, ATD, 11 etc.

75 See Würthwein, *ZTK* 49 (1952), 1ff.

76 K. Budde, *Hiob*, HKAT², 268–69.

77 The idea, held by Weiser, *Hiob*, 10, that the main issue in Job is that of double retribution is obviated by what has just been said; cf. G. Hölscher, *Hiob*, HAT, 6–7.

78 Cf. 9:14, 16, 24, etc. In 4:24(27), the possibility is entertained that the power of one's own sins can be "broken" by doing good actions. Sinning is still conceived in quantitative terms, even if no longer in terms of the consequences. Thus, one could, as a human, find a way to counteract one's sins.

79 E.g. *syrBaruch* 2:2; 4 Ezra 7:25,35; (cf. Rev. 14:13); 9:17; Sir. 7:1–3; 20:1–3; 20:25ff.; 27:8ff.; *Manual of Discipline* 11:17; VIII:6–7; X:18; XI:2.

80 H. Schlier, *ThWNT* 2:494 (ET: 2:498).

81 H. Schlier, *Galater*, KEK¹⁰, 204: God's kingdom is characterized by the fact that "He gives attention to the law of sowing and harvesting ... God allows humans to take care of their destiny by means of their own actions."

    (Notes 82–100 omitted.)

101 The value of this construct is not to be of interest only for the narrow discipline of OT theology. It is also of value for many text-critical questions as attested by the series of observations which are listed above.

4

*The Confessions of Jeremiah**

GERHARD VON RAD

It is his confessions that are most characteristic of Jeremiah.
Prophetic visions, oracles concerning the nations, and invectives
against the misuse of the cult are found in other prophets as well,
but his confessions – those most intimate and solitary conversations
with God – have their like in no other prophetic book.

Let us take a closer look at them and the special theological
problem that they contain for us.[1] No attempt at completeness will
be made either as to texts cited or their interpretation.

I

Jer. 15:16–20

> Thy words were found, and I ate them,
>> and thy words became to me a joy
>> and the delight of my heart;
> for I am called by thy name,
>> O Lord, God of hosts.
> I did not sit in the company of merrymakers,
>> nor did I rejoice;
> I sat alone, because thy hand was upon me,
>> for thou hadst filled me with indignation.
> Why is my pain unceasing,
>> my wound incurable,
>> refusing to be healed?
> Wilt thou be to me like a deceitful brook,
>> like waters that fail?
> Therefore thus says the Lord:
> "If you return, I will restore you,
>> and you shall stand before me.

* First published in *EvT* 3 (1936) 265–76. Translated by Arlis John Ehlin.

If you utter what is precious, and not what is worthless,
    you shall be as my mouth.
They shall turn to you,
    but you shall not turn to them.
And I will make you to this people
    a fortified wall of bronze;
they will fight against you,
    but they shall not prevail over you,
for I am with you
    to save you and deliver you,"
                        says the Lord.

In terms of form this passage falls into two parts, a prayer-speech
of Jeremiah and a divine pronouncement issued in response to it.

With v. 16 we are already in the midst of the *confessio*. For OT
sensitivities the statements are quite unusual: he "devoured"
Yahweh's words when they came to him, they were a "joy" to him,
a "heart's delight." His reaction to the revelation is very nearly
one of carnal passion. He feels a close inward connection with God,
which extends deep down into the physical roots of his being. There
can be no doubt that Jeremiah is not here voicing a typical human
reaction upon receiving a revelation, but is speaking purely out of
his own unique situation as a prophet. So an entirely spontaneous
prophetic *delectari* was indeed a possibility for him.

But being in such close alignment with God has another side to
it: anyone who is so utterly turned toward God is turned away
from humans. It is precisely his openness for God that makes him
so isolated from humans. The validity of the law that those who
are turned towards God must give up human sociability is here recognized with an unaffectedness that is quite moving; nor is there any
hint of pride over against fellow humans in this observation.

But Jeremiah elaborates further on the thought of his solitude.
It has yet another cause: Yahweh has "filled [him] with wrath."
Here Jeremiah is speaking about the content of his particular prophetic assignment. So that is the source of the breakdown in his
relationships with his fellow humans! The prophet speaks of this
wrath, whose bearer and vessel he now must be, as of a foreign
body implanted into him. Now he has no choice but to scold and
threaten; he has had to give up the freedom of his own natural
emotions. *Śaśōn* ("joy") over God and *za'am* ("indignation") over
humans – Jeremiah's life as a prophet can virtually be reduced to
this formula!

This office received from God, bestowed on him as a gift, nevertheless causes him sufferings with no end in sight, and it is this that

he rebels against; in this he sees an unfaithfulness on the part of God. The statement about the deceitful winter brook is a terrible accusation. God enticed Jeremiah the way a watercourse enticingly beckons flocks and tents. For a time it went well – but then it was like being taken in; a trust had been betrayed.

Terse and severe, the divine answer lays down the conditions under which Jeremiah can be restored to his prophetic office. In content it is closely connected with the divine word in Jer. 1:18. This immediately makes it clear that Jeremiah must go back to where God began with him. Significantly, there is no statement declaring that Jeremiah has sinned by his words, nor is there any denunciation of them; all that is already taken for granted the moment the divine response begins. In the very act of reacceptance the depth of his fall is made apparent.

He had wanted to withdraw from his prophetic office, become a citizen among citizens. That, however, he is not to do. He is not to conform to his fellow humans, but they to him, insofar as he utters what is "precious" and not what is "worthless." As to this latter expression, a curious one, we will surely not go wrong if we see it as referring to the whole foregoing statement of grievances. In God's eyes it was "vulgar," "ignoble," that Jeremiah took pleasure in his prophetic office but then wanted to divest himself of it when it led to complications and suffering.

By way of developing our theological problem, we make here but one simple observation: the only part of this passage that is divine speech, that is, prophetic proclamation in the strict sense of the term, is the answer of Yahweh. After all, it is very clearly said that the actual words of Jeremiah's confession mark the abandonment of his prophetic office! Without at this point going deeper into the question, we can nevertheless say that we do not in any way hear Jeremiah speaking as a prophet here, in the old sense of that word – insofar as one understands prophets to be humans who claim they were directly entrusted with a proclamation from God. The direction of Jeremiah's words here is not from above downward, but from below upward, and what he bears witness to here is not in the first instance a word of God but his own inner problematic, his suffering, and his despair.

II

It is no different when we read Jer. 12:1–5. The anguish behind the question that weighs so heavily upon him shows itself especially in the fact that Jeremiah discards all his trump even before he presents his case:

> Righteous art thou, O Lord, when I complain to thee;
> yet I would plead my case before thee (v. 1).

He is not an equal partner in this game but a subordinate from the moment play begins. So Jeremiah writhes and turns in an agonizing conflict. On one side is the exasperatingly unbroken chain of good fortune for the godless:

> Thou plantest them, and they take root;
> they grow and bring forth fruit (v. 2).

Yet along with this – and coming from the very same God – suffering and misery.

Once more the answer from God (v. 5) that follows has an air of brusque severity:

> If you have raced with men on foot, and they have wearied you,
> how will you compete with horses?
> And if in a safe land you fall down,
> how will you do in the jungle of the Jordan?

That is no answer at all. It totally fails to address the question that is bothering the prophet – it is itself a question! The utterance is an imposing one, ponderous and strangely obscure – almost a riddle-speech of God's, so that the broader and deeper meanings it suggests are more to be felt than understood. Little weak human, you have just barely started! Mere footracers are tiring you out already, you are already afraid while still in a peaceable land. Jeremiah had been almost overwhelmed by the question he posed, and now he must hear that he does not yet know anything about God, that he is still at the very beginning. In response to a human grievance as to riddles regarding the divine governance of the world, God momentarily pulls the veil aside and opens a perspective onto riddles and dark mysteries of an incomparably more difficult kind, without even offering the slightest beginning of an explanation! But precisely this last point is an important one: it is not a matter of theoretical problems and their solutions. By means of his question God leads Jeremiah out of the realm of theory, out of the arena of speculation, over to another question: that of the divine providence in the midst of life and of suffering. The question God is interested in is whether he will stand firm; his only concern is for obedience.

III

Jer. 8:18—9:1

18 My grief is beyond healing,
    my heart is sick within me.

19 Hark, the cry of the daughter of my people
    from the length and breadth of the land:
    "Is the Lord not in Zion?
    Is her King not in her?"
    "Why have they provoked me to anger with their graven images,
    and with their foreign idols?"

20 "The harvest is past, the summer is ended,
    and we are not saved."

21 For the wound of the daughter of my people is my heart wounded,
    I mourn, and dismay has taken hold on me.

22 Is there no balm in Gilead?
    Is there no physician there?
    Why then has the health of the daughter of my people
    not been restored?

1 O that my head were waters,
    and my eyes a fountain of tears,
    that I might weep day and night
    for the slain of the daughter of my people!

This section is filled with an eerie inner unrest. Distressing visions thrust themselves across the prophet's mind; but it does not form a cohesive presentation. A variety of pictures, perhaps even just bits of pictures, present themselves to Jeremiah's view: a cry for help rising from his people (v. 19a); he hears something like a divine response (v. 19b), then the lament resumes (vv. 20, 21); now the thought occurs to the prophet that help and healing might be obtainable from some other quarter, if not from Yahweh (v. 22). But this thought is set aside again as hopeless, and the lament dies away in inexpressible misery.

The significant fact here, however, is that these restless picture-elements, almost straining to go in different directions, are forged together into a seamless whole, held together and carried along by an unimaginably great capacity for suffering and strength in suffering. The piece begins with the expression of an intensely personal suffering, and it concludes with another such; but within the area thus bounded, as though enclosed by the walls of his heart, such pictures!

What the prophet experiences as fragmented visions crowding

together in a narrow space is in reality a tragedy that unfolds in several acts: a time of calamity; an inquiring after God, that is, a decision to seek an official ruling from him; the divine oracle with its rejection of the petition, followed by a situation for utter hopelessness. "The harvest is past, the summer is ended." The year is approaching its close, with nothing more to be expected from it.

But still there is no giving up. Thoughts now turn in another direction, and this time it is the prophet himself who seeks a way out (v. 22). But this question too fades away without an answer. Prior to this point the prophet's inner emotions were still somewhat restrained as he continued his questioning; the seeking provided an element of tension to hold him together. But now with the dying away of his last question he expresses his misery freely. The only wish he still has for himself is the possibility of completely dissolving in a flood of tears over his grief.

There can be no doubt that with this piece we have descended to a significantly deeper level of Jeremiah's suffering. Initially this suffering of his is simply an excess of sympathy, a suffering-with (an observation that almost causes a certain embarrassment for us as theologians!). The divine oracle is not, in this instance, the conceptual goal towards which the passage leads; rather, the sole and exclusive point of this confession is to describe a totally personal emotion. It does not witness to God at all, much less in the very direct manner of earlier prophetic proclamation; rather, it gives expression to a very subjective grief. So is Jeremiah still speaking as a prophet here? Before attempting an answer, we will first look at the passages that mark the lowest point in his sufferings.

IV

Jer. 20:7–9

> O Lord, thou hast deceived me,
>   and I was deceived;
> thou art stronger than I,
>   and thou hast prevailed.
> I have become a laughingstock all the day;
>   everyone mocks me.
> For whenever I speak, I cry out,
>   I shout, "Violence and destruction!"
> For the word of the Lord has become for me
>   a reproach and derision all day long.
> If I say, "I will not mention him,
>   or speak any more in his name,"

there is in my heart as it were a burning fire
  shut up in my bones,
and I am weary with holding it in,
  and I cannot.

The first verb in v. 7 [deceived] literally means to talk someone into a thing, and is used of seducing a young woman. The second one [prevailed] connotes something like a wrestling match in which Jeremiah is overpowered. How you sweet-talked me, and how strong you were![2]

This introduction is frightful. The prophet accuses himself of weakness – excusable, to be sure – over against God, as though it were even possible for him to offer resistance. Thus the accusation immediately turns against God, who has made him a laughingstock before the whole world. So as far as Jeremiah is concerned, when he was called to be a prophet the issue for him was not right or wrong, and initially not a question of inner conviction either, but a question of power pure and simple. That, therefore, is another way of seeing the relationship between God and humanity, viz., as a fearfully unequal power relationship; and this way of characterizing the relationship is probably not the most superficial.

The meaning of v. 8 is not entirely certain; Jeremiah probably does not refer here to deeds of violence happening to him, but instead is quoting key words ["Violence and destruction!"] from his own proclamation of judgment. And since he never did, after all, experience serious opposition and resistance, but only laughter and ridicule, much worse of course, Jeremiah admits to us with extraordinary candor the sort of thoughts he has actually been entertaining: God should find himself another person; he wants to be rid of the burden and sorrow of his prophetic office; yet – obviously it did not stop with mere thoughts, but an actual attempt was made to do it! – that too was unsuccessful; he would have burned up inside if he had kept the divine words to himself.

The confession fades away with a statement expressing exhaustion to the point of death (v. 9): "I wore myself down trying to hold out, but could not do it." That is certainly one of the most powerful statements the OT is capable of making in regard to the compulsion that can come from God over a human being. Once again we emphasize that God's relationship to humanity is here shifting to a level of human experience where it is definitely no longer a matter of free choices ("decision") or of intellectual agreement or persuasion. The question of the prophetic commission, and even the question of human obedience and of providence, is perceived here simply as a question of might.

V

Jer. 20:14–18

Cursed be the day
    on which I was born!
The day when my mother bore me,
    let it not be blessed!
Cursed be the man
    who brought the news to my father,
"A son is born to you,"
    making him very glad.
Let that 'day' [RSV: man] be like the cities
    which the Lord overthrew without pity;
let him hear a cry in the morning
    and an alarm at noon,
because he did not kill me in the womb;
    so my mother would have been my grave,
    and her womb for ever great.
Why did I come forth from the womb
    to see toil and sorrow,
    and spend my days in shame?

Night has now completely enveloped the prophet. Probably even in a biographical sense this section surely comes from one of the final phases in Jeremiah's sufferings. According to OT belief and that of the Near East in general, a curse like this is something more than evil, angry words. In the view of the ancients, demonic realities do in fact exist over which humans have a certain amount of control. One can call and persuade them, for they are ready and eager to deal destruction. That is how the act of providence that made the day of Jeremiah's birth into a dispensation of salvation is to be undone, nullified. Jeremiah brings out everything he has by way of curse and heaps it on this day. Thus he is, in a way, reaching back behind empirical life into the world beyond and attacking the dispensation of providence. The curse is in fact so exaggerated, so wild, that it also strikes the unsuspecting man who brought the news of the birth to the father, that fool who thought he was announcing a joyous event. This day – we have already seen that it was a day laden with destiny – should have been permitted to let Jeremiah die while he was yet in his mother's body. In fact, did he ever really have to come out of his mother's womb at all? She would instead have been perpetually pregnant with him – a grotesque thought! Yet precisely in this bizarre wish we detect the abrupt rise of a warmth of feeling for his mother: if only her womb would still enfold him, and if only she would be his grave, in which he could peacefully rest! When Jeremiah surveys his life, so far as it still lies before him, he sees it as coming to an end in toil, sorrow, and shame.

This may well be labeled the lowest point in the sufferings of Jeremiah. Everything within him is now destroyed; he even draws those nearest and dearest to him along with him into the night of his sorrow: his mother, his father, the friend of the family.[3] It is idle to speculate whether he sank even deeper. Perhaps in the hour of his final martyrdom? One may at least say, with the restraint that must be the interpreter's first commandment here, that physical death as such would probably bring not a further intensification but rather a release.

We are not making a merely esthetic judgment – though that aspect is difficult to ignore here – when we note, as the first of several fundamental observations, that the confessions of Jeremiah are unparalleled in the prophetic literature, yes in the entire OT. When we survey the content of the prophetic books from Amos to Malachi, what we find is "proclamation," and that for the most part in the directly prophetic sense of a vividly experienced revelation from God (not merely a witness to faith, as is largely the case in the historical or the poetic books). Prophetic proclamation, however, is by no means what Jeremiah's confessions are. The direction of flow in these speeches is not down from above (nor is the prophet here a two-way transfer point), but up from below. Jeremiah is not speaking about God but about himself and his inmost feelings. One could perhaps be inclined to deal with the theological problem that thereby presents itself by referring to certain of the Psalms,[4] in which the pious on occasion speak more about themselves and their situations than about God. In fact, why should Jeremiah not be permitted to speak to us once in a while apart from his prophetic office – unofficially, one might say? Would that not mean, then, that what we have here is the purest human religiosity, which simply gushes forth apart from any compulsion due to his calling as a prophet – as it were, the ultimate and most primordial example of *homo religiosus*? Anyone acquainted with the interpretation of Jeremiah in the last fifty years knows with what predilection and even reverence the exegetes have traveled this path. But it is a wrong course. Jeremiah in his confessions is definitely not speaking unofficially; rather, they come out of the very midst of his prophetic office. It simply is not true that in Jeremiah we find genuine prophetic testimonies and more general religious expressions side by side; on the contrary, it is precisely the confessions that arise out of the center of his being a prophet. That fact, however, sets before us the task of reformulating the concept of prophetic witness in Jeremiah.

A theological examination of these passages, therefore, must begin with the recognition that they spring directly *ex munere prophetico*; and on the other hand this must be brought together with the observation that in these passages it is his soul, his truly unique subjective life and experience, that stands at the focal point. One particular problem is singled out in 12:1–5, but most of these passages involve all the emotional conflicts brought on by his calling. We encounter here the whole gamut of human emotional problems: anxiety over shame, fear of failure, despair over ones ability to cope, doubts concerning articles of faith, loneliness, sympathy, disillusionment leading ultimately to hatred towards God. No feeling that can possibly come into a human heart is missing. And yet all of this suffering, disillusionment, despair has to do with the prophetic call.

Should we not be allowed to start out with an understanding of Jeremiah as very simply the last person in a historical line of prophetic figures? Did not the prophetic movement in a very real sense actually come to an end with these confessions? Unlikely as it is that an external prophetic tradition can be seen connecting Amos to Jeremiah, a strong case can nevertheless be made for the claim that Amos, Isaiah, Micah, Zephaniah are there in Jeremiah; their sense of service and responsibility, but also their silent sufferings and disillusionments, are present in him as an inherited burden, unseen but very real. Yet he differs from all his predecessors in that with him the prophetic office – which in the case of Amos was still a monolithic whole – breaks apart at a decisive point, and through that rift an ominous gloom rushes in, devoid of light. One thing is now clear: all his confessions revolve around this rift in his prophetic office.

The exegete is not called upon to make value judgments here; rather, one must simply observe that this light-expelling despair breaking into the prophet's inner being occupied Jeremiah's attention to at least the same extent as did his genuine prophetic tasks, of which we have not spoken here. In fact this desperation visibly increases in his confessions, and we see him engrossed in it to the point of exhaustion. It is not enough for us to explain this as a breaking down of the genuinely prophetic by subjective thinking, or to understand it as the outcome of his individual emotional makeup. There is something more here than subjective thinking and an individual difference in temperament. Quite the contrary, here the ultimate hopelessness of genuine prophetic service is recognized; but it is not merely recognized – it has burst into Jeremiah's life as suffering and is now something the prophet endures. Isaiah and Micah were solely proclaimers of God's word; in the case of Jeremiah something new in God's working through prophets presents itself: this man serves God not only with the bold proclamation of his mouth (his person), but his very life is unexpectedly involved in God's cause on earth. Thus the prophet (this is something new with Jeremiah) now becomes a witness to God not only by virtue of his charisma, but in his very humanity – yet not as the person who is triumphant over human sin, not as the person who is gaining the victory, but as the messenger of God going down to destruction in the midst of humanity. Therefore even the *bios* of Jeremiah now takes on the authority of a witness. His suffering soul, his life bleeding to death in God's task – all this becomes a pointer towards God. Alongside the *munus propheticum*, the *munus sacerdotale* presents itself on the scene! Jeremiah, therefore, is not only the end of a series but also a beginning. Indeed, he marks the opening of a new chapter in the stream of prophecy leading to Jesus Christ.[5]

One more point still needs to be made. The prophets preceding Jeremiah can certainly with full justification be viewed as mediator figures, also in a theological sense. But Jeremiah no longer merely has the people for whom he mediates facing himself, as did a Hosea or an Isaiah. If we truly listen to the confessions, with their despair and their rebellion, we ultimately come up against the fact that Jeremiah as mediator does not merely have the people facing himself, so as to endure suffering from them – no, he carries their entire misery inside himself. In the bottomless depths of his tribulations they are present; and along with these people whom he carries in himself Jeremiah must die in the presence of God – indeed, he dies with them many deaths all the way to his own final, physical death. At that point there is no further "nevertheless," no comforting conclusion, no ultimate victory that brings salvation. That is why Jeremiah's confessions testify to the severity of God's wrath. These self-testimonies of his give no hint of any atoning, saving power inherent in his suffering. And that is truly not because Jeremiah personally had no conception of the meaning behind his sufferings;[6]

on this point in particular we must scrupulously guard against over-interpreting. As a matter of fact, his antagonism, his rebellion, and the horrible cursing at the end show clearly the limitations on this mediatorial office of his. But also as one who is not "made perfect" in the sense of the Epistle to the Hebrews, and precisely as such, Jeremiah is a pointer towards the Coming One and teaches us to discern the full depth of Christ's office as mediator. The description here of sufferings that have their origin in the mediatorial office – from being excluded when others came together for merrymaking, all the way to the final fading away into the night of God-forsakenness – all this is a shadow and model of a future mediatorial role made perfect.

NOTES

1 This little study begins with a form-critical conclusion, specifically that of Walter Baumgartner's investigation into the "laments" of Jeremiah, *Die Klagegedichte des Jeremia* (BZAW 32[1917]). It is intended to serve as an example of how a theological interpretation can and must start with "the results of scientific criticism." The authorship of these confessions was denied to Jeremiah because they seemed incompatible with the way a prophet had come to be pictured. Baumgartner is absolutely convincing in his repudiation of this claim. But now, after what was in the first instance a purely literary-critical debate, a new situation has been created: now that the confessions have struck us as being almost a foreign body, yet without it being possible to deny their authorship to Jeremiah, a new light has come to fall on the picture of this prophet. "Laments" are, after all, totally different from "prophetic oracles." But this is only one example of the many ways in which the understanding of much that is in the Old Testament writings has recently shifted. A goodly amount of material, some of it seemingly unessential for the faith, is available as a result of the work that has been done, and it now awaits the onset of a new theological enterprise.

2 Baumgartner, *Klagegedichte*, 64.

3 Paul Volz, *Der Prophet Jeremia* (KAT, 1935) 211.

4 Cf. Gustav Hölscher, *Die Propheten* (1935) 399: "The presuppositions [of the confessions] are no other than those of most psalms of lament."

5 The Baruch narratives also belong here. They are not biography but a passion-history. For what was it that moved this man to take up his pen but the recognition that it was not only by his words that Jeremiah became a witness but that the very course of his life as it slowly turned the corner into suffering and despair was a witness in a new prophetic sense. Granted, all glorification as a martyr is lacking, but so too is all thought of an *imitatio*.

6 H. Duhm, *Jeremia* (KHC, 1935) 168: "Jeremiah is the most subjective of all the prophets. One of the ways he proves this in the confessions is that he never betrays the faintest conception of the fact that his suffering could serve to the advantage of the people. In actual fact it did turn out to benefit others."

5

*Job: The Problem of the Book**

A. S. PEAKE

Job had met the loss of wealth and children with pious recognition of Yahweh's right to take back what He had given and with blessing of His Name. When his wife's faith had failed in his second trial, the sufferer, in his excruciating pain, rebuked her temptation to blasphemy with the noble words, "Good shall we receive at the hand of God, and evil shall we not receive." But the unswerving integrity was only the continuance of the old relation into conditions ultimately incompatible with it. It was an axiom of theology that the lot of the righteous was blessed, and Job was assured of his uprightness and fidelity to God. But now the axiom, so long verified in his own felicity, had proved unequal to the strain of facts. Not all at once could the deep-rooted faith of a lifetime be plucked up, and the influence be drawn that the God, who tortured the innocent, could not Himself be moral. Yet the spirit, caged in the inexplicable, must sooner or later break from the blind alley into a clearer if unkindlier air. Even before his friends came to him he felt himself slipping from the fear of God. He craved for their sympathy to restore his fainting spirit, as the parched caravan craves for the stream in the desert. But the calamities that had made his need so desperate had dried up the springs. In the presence of his tried companions the sufferer was confident that the long-repressed complaint might find free utterance; wise and tolerant, they would not narrowly scrutinize the wild words of his despair, but soothe and reconcile him to his pain. But they failed him miserably, and, when he hungered for sympathy, offered him a flinty theology. Not, indeed, that they were callous to his suffering; they uttered their piercing lamentations, and, after demonstrations of their sorrow, sat in silent grief and compassion seven days. It is possible that their silence expressed the moral condemnation of so great a sufferer that their dogma demanded. Yet Job betrays no consciousness of this; the unrestrained complaint

*First published in *Job* by A. S. Peake (1905) 9–21.

100

with which he breaks the silence proves that he confidently cast himself on their kindness. And while the friends must have inferred his sinfulness from his disasters, the debate opens with the assumption of his fundamental integrity.

The artistic movement of the discussion has been disguised by the dislocation of the speeches in the third cycle of the debate. When they have been restored to their primitive condition the scheme followed by the author seems to have been as follows. In the first round of speeches the friends ply Job with the thought of God, Eliphaz dwelling on His transcendent purity, Bildad on His inflexible righteousness, and Zophar on His inscrutable wisdom. Failing to impress Job along this line, the friends in the second cycle of speeches paint lurid pictures of the fate of the wicked; after a life spent in torments he comes to a swift and miserable death, and his posterity is rooted out. In the third cycle Eliphaz directly charges Job with flagrant sin. But, instead of permitting the other friends as before to follow in the same strain, the poet secures variety by letting the debate double back on itself. The third speech of Bildad (25:2, 3; 26:5–14) repeats the theme of the first cycle, the incomparable greatness of God; the third speech of Zophar (27:7–10, 13–23) repeats the theme of the second cycle, the miserable fate of the wicked.

The friends have little to say beyond the general principles just mentioned. The righteousness of God is not clearly disengaged from His power and wisdom. Right and wrong are just what the Almighty decrees them to be. Hence they find it hard to conceive the distinction on which Job insists, and utterly refuse to accept it, since Job's righteousness was naturally less certain to them than God's. Nor have they suffered themselves to be disturbed by the facts which seem to Job so eloquent of God's misgovernment. But they had not had Job's experience to take the scales from their eyes and make them sensitive to the world's inexplicable pain. It is not the case, however, that they interpret suffering simply as punishment. In his first speech Eliphaz depicts for Job's encouragement the blessedness of that man whom God chastens. The friends probably saw in Job's affliction both punishment and discipline, till his rebellious words forced on them the conviction that his sin was deeper than they had surmised.

It must strike the reader as strange that the antagonists develop their arguments with such little reference to the case advanced by the other side. A Western poet would have made the speakers submit the positions maintained by the opponent to a more searching criticism. But the poet is an Oriental, with far less care for pure reasoning. The friends have their settled beliefs about God and His government;

nothing Job can say will move them. Hence in the first two cycles of the debate the three friends take substantially the same line, with very little reference to anything Job may have urged. Even the great passage 19:25–27 might just as well not have been spoken, for all the influence it has on their subsequent speeches. Similarly Job, in several of his speeches, contents himself with some words of blistering sarcasm, and then pursues his own train of thought, without reference to what his antagonists have said, though when the case has been stated by all three of the speakers he pulverizes it. He neglects them because he is wholly engaged with God.

It is this preoccupation with God which gives Job's speeches their marvellous fascination. Quite apart from all the lofty qualities that make the book a perennial delight to lovers of poetry for its own sake, there is a situation whose development is followed with breathless eagerness. Here, indeed, in the history of a soul, rather than the discussion of a problem, lies the supreme interest of the book. The detailed movement from stage to stage of the debate is exhibited in the special sections devoted to this purpose in the commentary. At present a more general sketch may suffice.

Job's problem is, in the first instance, personal. Why has God sent such undeserved calamities on His faithful servant? In his first rebellious utterance he had barely referred to God. But the reply of Eliphaz, with all its considerateness, stung him to the quick, since it took for granted his guilt and rebuked the temper he displayed. Its chief result was to drive him into open revolt against God and scornful protest against His lack of magnanimity. Yet he ends with a pathetic reminder to God that, when regrets are too late, He will long once more for fellowship with the victim He had so harshly crushed. When Bildad replies with an assertion that God cannot pervert judgement, Job bitterly assents. The Almighty sets the standard of righteousness; how can a frail mortal make good his case against omnipotence? For it is God's settled determination to make him guilty, and He who selects His victims with no moral discrimination will readily effect His purpose. If God would only release him from his pain and not paralyse him with His terror, then he would plead his cause undismayed. Resentful but wistful, he appeals to God not wantonly to destroy His creature, on whom He had lavished such pains and skill. Then with sudden revulsion, as a new light bursts in, he sees in God's care a darker design than he had guessed. All along God had planned the stroke, but He had smiled on Job to betray him, meaning to mock his confidence and make his misery extreme. And now He performs exploits of valour against His defenceless victim. Ah! why did He suffer him to be born? let him have a brief respite from torture, ere he goes for ever to Sheol's utter gloom. The reply to Zophar definitely assails the dogma of the friends. God is wise and mighty – no need to teach him such platitudes. But these qualities are displayed in destructive rather than in beneficient operations. With the friends he does not care to argue, sycophants, who would fain curry favour with God by smearing their lies over His misgovernment. As if God would tolerate such apologists, as if He dreaded to be found out! Job will fearlessly speak his whole mind, reckless though he imperils his life. Why does God refuse to answer him, and persecute him so relentlessly? Why does He bring into judgement man, so short-lived, so frail, so impure? Let him pass his brief day in such comfort as may be possible, for man dies and never wakes from the sleep of death. If only there might be a waking! if in Sheol, where there is no rememberance of God, he might wait till God's anger had ceased to burn, and then hear His voice calling him back in love, how gladly he would resume the blessed communion with Him. Vain dream of bliss! from Sheol no man can return.

Job has told all that was in his heart. He charges God outright with immorality, yet he feels that fellowship with Him is the highest good. Hence he holds together incompatible conceptions of God. The God whom he knew in the past and whom he might know again in the future, if he could still be alive to know Him, is quite other than the God of whom he has such bitter experience in the present. The hope that God might recall him from Sheol he firmly sets aside. It never establishes itself in his mind. But the feeling that his present experience of God does not reflect God's inmost character is a feeling which develops at last into the great belief, "I know that my vindicator liveth."

In the second cycle of the debate the friends simply describe the fate of the wicked. We need not assume that their main object was to hold up a mirror for Job, the allusions to his case are far less pointed than is sometimes asserted. If their descriptions fitted him, well and good; if not, they served the main purpose of establishing against Job the retributive justice of God. But while their side makes little advance, Job moves forward to a more peaceful state of mind. The very vehemence with which he paints God's hostility sends him by sharp recoil to seek his vindicator in Him. From the scorn of his friends he is driven to God, beseeching Him with tears to maintain his right. But with whom? With whom can it be but with Himself? Let the God of the future be surety for him with the God of the present. In his next speech this thought attains its climax. Two things are added. The prayer becomes an assurance, God will vindicate him. And though he has passed from this life, he will as a disembodied spirit be permitted to see God and know that his integrity is established. This lofty certainty is not without effect on Job's subsequent utterances. Yet it plays a much smaller part than we should have anticipated. This is partly due to the fact that at this point the personal gives way to the universal problem. For, as in the first, so also in the second round of the discussion, Job does not assail the friends' position till all three have stated it. Accordingly his third speech in this cycle is devoted to an attack on their dogma that the wicked suffer for their sin. Job flatly denies it, on the contrary they live a happy life in prosperity and die without lingering illness. To the suggestion that they suffer in the suffering of their children, Job answers that a penalty of which they are not conscious is no penalty at all.

In the third discussion Job ignores the direct assault of Eliphaz on his character, though in the course of his first speech he affirms his integrity. The greater part of his speech is occupied with another description of God's misgovernment. But he also comes back to his own relations to God, and strikes a less confident note than in 19:25–27. It was perhaps natural that faith should not maintain itself at such a height. But we may also trace in the relapse the influence of the indictment he has urged against the moral order of the world. Though he would fain come face to face with God, and argue his cause with Him, his inscrutable, irresponsible Judge eludes him and baffles his most earnest search. The reply to Bildad's third speech (25:2, 3, 26:5–14) seems to have been for the most part lost. Probably it contained, between 27:11 and 27:12, a criticism of God's government, so bold that it was struck out as dangerous to piety. In what remains Job once more firmly asserts his integrity. To Zophar's third speech, reaffirming the doom of the wicked, Job's final speech (29—31) constitutes the formal reply. Really it lies outside the debate. Job first describes his former happiness in the favour of God, the possession of his children, the honour of men; then sets against this the scorn and insult heaped upon him, the pain from which he is suffering, and God's cruel enmity; lastly, solemnly declares himself innocent of any such sins as might justify his calamities, and proudly declares himself ready to confront God.

So the human debate reaches a worthy close. The friends have exhausted their case and failed to vanquish Job. Their platitudes about God's greatness he feels to be irrelevant, or rather to make His immorality worse. Their assertion of His righteousness he denies, the plainest facts seem to him to refute it. Their personal accusations are shivered against his conscious integrity. In the course of his pleadings with God he has been distracted between God's persecution of him in the present and His kindness in the past. He has swung from one extreme to the other; now holding God's former goodness to have been carefully calculated to make his present suffering more intense, now feeling the old communion with Him to be the pledge that His love would reassert itself. And yet the fire of His wrath burns so fiercely that at best it will not die down till the victim has passed into the gloom of Sheol. Then when this inexplicable aberration has given place to God's normal mood, He will remember the servant whose love had been precious to Him. Once more He would call him back to renew the happy intercourse. But it will be too late. Yet not too late for some reparation. God will Himself establish his innocence, and he for one will see God as his vindicator. And there is no stranger thought in the book than that God may be surety to Himself for Job. It is as though God suffers the knowledge of His future attitude to mitigate the full sweep of His anger. He is to take sides against Himself, to secure Himself against vain regrets.

The God of the past and the future was the real God, Job's God of the present was a spectre of his morbid imagination. And when God appears, we expect that this will be plain. But He wears the spectre's mask. He speaks out of the storm, laying aside none of His terror, while Job still writhes in the grip of his unresting pains. He mocks his ignorance and limitations, plying him with questions that he cannot answer, and displaying in the marvels of the universe the wisdom and might of its Creator. Now Job had all along admitted the wisdom and power of God; he had confessed that he could not meet God on equal terms, or solve one in a thousand of the problems with which onmiscience could baffle his human understanding. Moreover, he had implored God to release him from pain when He appeared for the contest, and not to affright him with His terror; he had even expressed his confidence that God would not contend with him in the greatness of His power. Not only, then, does God seem to be forcing an open door, but to act less worthily than Job had expected of Him. The reader is also surprised that God does not explain to Job why he suffers, and especially why light is not thrown on the general problem of suffering.

These phenomena, which have led some to regard the speech of Yahweh as a later addition, have their sufficient reason. The speech is designed in the first place to widen Job's view. Maddened by his pain he had freely asserted that God's government of the world was immoral, a sweeping generalization, drawn in the first instance from his own experience, though he easily found numerous facts to support it. God convicts him of narrow outlook, and suggests in doing so the unimagined complexity of the problem. He alone, who has comprehended the vast universe that God must govern, has the full right to say whether He governs it well or ill. But Job, while he has spoken of God's power as displayed in the world, is quite unable to explain its phenomena. One by one God makes him ponder them, if each is an inscrutable mystery, what must be the mystery of that universe, whose government Job has so confidently condemned? If God is wise and strong as Job has confessed, ought there not to be much in His action that man cannot properly appraise? Further, Job is reminded that man does not constitute the whole of God's animate creation. All the incomparable pictures of the untamed creatures of the desert are meant to bring home to him the range of God's interests and the tender care He lavishes on such beings as are beyond man's everyday horizon. Thus man comes to a humbler view of his own importance, and learns that he must transcend his self-centred attitude, if he is to judge the ways of God aright.

A second lesson, which Job learns, is that it is not for him to lay down the terms on which God must meet him. He had challenged God to justify the treatment meted out to him, and God ignores his demand. He is assured that God will not contend with him in the greatness of His power, and God answers him out of the storm and makes him feel how tremendous are the resources of His energy. He concludes his proud self-vindication with the words, "as a prince I would go near unto Him," and so he quails before the vision of God and repents in dust and ashes. That this was less worthy of God the poet would not have admitted. It might indeed seem as if the majesty of God and the taunting irony of His words were calculated to bludgeon Job into submission, rather than change his opinions by convincing his reason. But Job needed a sharp lesson of this kind to chasten his presumption; he must learn the true relation of man to God. Yet this is not the chief cause why the poet chose to introduce God as he did. It was because only thus could the desired result be fully attained. For it is not what God says that is all important. It is the overwhelming impression made on Job by the vision of God that leaves him at the end of the poem contrite and subdued. All that God says he had theoretically known before, though in all its detail it had not lived to his imagination. But now he attains an experience new in quality. "I had heard of thee by the hearing of the ear, But now mine eye seeth thee; Wherefore I abhor myself and repent In dust and ashes." And we see with what subtle art the poet has introduced those very features in the poem which critics have urged to prove that the speech of Yahweh is a later addition. For it is just the fact that Job is already well aware of what God tells him which enables us to measure the impression that the vision of God makes upon him. And it is only in accordance with his practice of anticipating later developments, when he makes Job deny that God would appear as He actually appears in the sequel.

But why does he permit God to speak and yet offer no solution of the problem? Probably he had no solution, or he would surely have so constructed his poem as not simply to indicate it, but to throw it into relief. Ought he then to have kept silence, lest he should be charged with attempting a task too hard for him or reminding men of a misery he had no skill to charm away? There would be much force in such a criticism were peace to be won only in this way. But the author knows another path. And because he knows it the speech of Yahweh does not explain the origin of Job's suffering. Here his instinct was sounder than that of those who urge this silence in proof that the speech is later. It was not necessary for the reader to learn why Job suffered; he had known it all along from the Prologue. But it was necessary that Job should not be enlightened. Quite apart from the fact that the question in the Prologue is not one between Yahweh and Job but between Yahweh and the Satan, the poet, by revealing to Job what had passed in heaven, would have ruined the artistic effect and flung away the deepest teaching he had to give. It is imperative that Job should be left in ignorance at the end, since the lesson he learns is just this that he must trust God, even if he does not understand the reason for His action. And it is precisely this which constitutes the imperishable value of the book and its universal significance. For the explanation of Job's suffering would have been but the explanation of a single case, of no avail for others since the Satan would not court such discomfiture again. But Job, ignorant yet trustful, is a model and a help to all who are confronted by the insoluble mystery of their own or the world's pain. Even had the author so completely solved the problem that no problem remained, this would have been less precious than what he has actually given us. He had found another way. Job does not know now, any more than before, why he suffers. But his ignorance no longer tortures him, he does not wish to know. For he has escaped into a region where such problems exist no longer. He has attained peace and knows that all is well, though he does not know, or care to know, how it is possible. And it is most instructive to observe how the poet represents this inward rest to have been won. The caustic irony of the Divine questions, and the impressive array of the wonders of nature and Providence, above all the vision of God Himself, crush and humble the presumptuous critic of God's ways. Yet the very sense of his own ignorance and frailty, and of God's wisdom and might, is a return to the religious temper of mind. He has become a man of broken and contrite heart, penitent and self-loathing, who, because he knows himself to have nothing and deserve nothing, can most readily cast himself upon God, whose wisdom and omnipotence no longer crush but uphold and uplift him. Such is the way of peace the poet offers, a certainty of God, which rises above all the dark misgivings of His goodness, and is itself inspired by God's revelation of Himself.

Here, so far as Job was concerned, the book might have closed. He could go forward in pain and penury, still mocked by the base, still suspected by the good. He needed no outward confirmation of the assurance he had won in the vision of God. But is God to leave His loyal servant, who has won His wager with the Satan for Him, who has blessed Him in bereavement, and uttered the language of resignation in his pain, who has held fast his integrity, and refused to curry favor with Him by flattery, is He to leave him in misery, now that the cause for misery has passed away? What kind of a God would He be to do it? The writer could not represent Job as rewarded in another life, for though he turned with longing to the thought of immortality, he could not accept it with any confidence. Hence it was necessary for God to restore him in this life, if He restored Him at all. Thus the author leaves, not only his hero, but his reader reconciled to God.

6

The Heart Determines:
*Psalm 73**

MARTIN BUBER

What is remarkable about this poem – composed of descriptions, of a story, and of confessions – is that a man tells how he reached the true meaning of his experience of life, and that this meaning borders directly on the eternal.

For the most part we understand only gradually the decisive experiences we have in our relation with the world. First we accept what they seem to offer us, we express it, we weave it into a "view," and then think we are aware of our world. But we come to see that what we look on in this view is only an appearance. Not that our experiences have deceived us. But we had turned them to our use, without penetrating to their heart. What is it that teaches us to penetrate to their heart? Deeper experience.

The man who speaks in this psalm tells us how he penetrated to the heart of a weighty group of experiences – those experiences that show that the wicked prosper.

Apparently, then, the question is not what was the real question for Job – why the good do not prosper – but rather its obverse, as we find it most precisely, and probably for the first time, expressed in Jeremiah (12:1): "Why does the way of the wicked prosper?"

Nevertheless, the psalm begins with a prefatory sentence in which, rightly considered, Job's question may be found hidden.

This sentence, the foreword to the psalm, is

> Surely, God is good to Israel:
> To the pure in heart.

It is true that the Psalmist is here concerned not with the happiness or unhappiness of the person, but with the happiness or unhappiness

---

* First published in English in *On the Bible* by M. Buber (1968) 199–210.

of Israel. But the experience behind the speeches of Job, as is evident in many of them, is itself not merely personal, but is the experience of Israel's suffering both in the catastrophe that led to the Babylonian exile and in the beginning of the exile itself. Certainly only one who had plumbed the depths of personal suffering could speak in this way. But the speaker is a man of Israel in Israel's bitter hour of need, and in his personal suffering the suffering of Israel has been concentrated, so that what he now has to suffer he suffers as Israel. In the destiny of an authentic person the destiny of his people is gathered up, and only now becomes truly manifest.

Thus the Psalmist, whose theme is the fate of the person, also begins with the fate of Israel. Behind his opening sentence lies the question "Why do things go badly with Israel?" And first he answers, "Surely, God is good to Israel," and then he adds, by way of explanation, "to the pure in heart."

On first glance this seems to mean that it is only to the impure in Israel that God is not good. He is good to the pure in Israel; they are the "holy remnant," the true Israel, to whom He is good. But that would lead to the assertion that things go well with this remnant, and the questioner had taken as his starting point the experience that things went ill with Israel, not excepting indeed this part of it. The answer, understood in this way, would be no answer.

We must go deeper in this sentence. The questioner had drawn from the fact that things go ill with Israel the conclusion that therefore God is not good to Israel. But only one who is not pure in heart draws such a conclusion. One who is pure in heart, one who becomes pure in heart, cannot draw any such conclusion. For he experiences that God is good to him. But this does not mean that God rewards him with his goodness. It means, rather, that God's goodness is revealed to him who is pure in heart: he experiences this goodness. Insofar as Israel is pure in heart, becomes pure in heart, it experiences God's goodness.

Thus the essential dividing line is not between men who sin and men who do not sin, but between those who are pure in heart and those who are impure in heart. Even the sinner whose heart becomes pure experiences God's goodness as it is revealed to him. As Israel purifies its heart, it experiences that God is good to it.

It is from this standpoint that everything that is said in the psalm about "the wicked" is to be understood. The "wicked" are those who deliberately persist in impurity of heart.

The state of the heart determines whether a man lives in the truth, in which God's goodness is experienced, or in the semblance of truth, where the fact that it "goes ill" with him is confused with the illusion that God is not good to him.

The state of the heart determines. That is why "heart" is the dominant key word in this psalm, and recurs six times.

And now, after this basic theme has been stated, the speaker begins to tell of the false ways in his experience of life.

Seeing the prosperity of "the wicked" daily and hearing their braggart speech has brought him very near to the abyss of despairing unbelief, of the inability to believe any more in a living God active in life. "But I, a little more and my feet had turned aside, a mere nothing and my steps had stumbled." He goes so far as to be jealous of "the wicked" for their privileged position.

It is not envy that he feels, it is jealousy, that it is *they* who are manifestly preferred by God. That it is indeed they is proved to him by their being sheltered from destiny. For them there are not. (In what follows I read, as is almost universally accepted, *lamo tam* instead of *lemotam*.) As for all the others, those constraining and confining "bands" of destiny; "they are never in the trouble of man." And so they deem themselves superior to all, and stalk around with their "sound and fat bellies," and when one looks in their eyes, which protrude from the fatness of their faces, one sees "the paintings of the heart," the wish-images of their pride and their cruelty, flitting across. Their relation to the world of their fellow men is arrogance and cunning, craftiness and exploitation. "They speak oppression from above" and "set their mouth to the heavens." From what is uttered by this mouth set to the heavens, the Psalmist quotes two characteristic sayings which were supposed to be familiar. In the one (introduced by "therefore", meaning "therefore they say") they make merry over God's relation to "His people." Those who speak are apparently in Palestine as owners of great farms, and scoff at the prospective return of the landless people from exile, in accordance with the prophecies: the prophet of the Exile has promised them water (Isa. 41:17f), and "they may drink their fill of water," they will certainly not find much more here unless they become subject to the speakers. In the second saying they are apparently replying to the reproaches leveled against them: they were warned that God sees and knows the wrongs they have done, but the God of heaven has other things to do than to concern Himself with such earthly matters: "How does God know? Is there knowledge in the Most High?" And God's attitude confirms them, those men living in comfortable security: "they have reached power," theirs is the power.

That was the first section of the psalm, in which the speaker depicted his grievous experience, the prosperity of the wicked. But now he goes on to explain how his understanding of this experience has undergone a fundamental change.

Since he had again and again to endure, side by side, his own suffering and their "grinning" well-being, he is overcome: "It is not fitting that I should make such comparisons, as my own heart is not pure." And he proceeded to purfiy it. In vain. Even when he succeeded in being able "to wash his hands in innocence" (which does not mean an action or feeling of self-righteousness, but the genuine, second and higher purity that is won by the great struggle of the soul), the torment continued, and now it was like a leprosy to him; and as leprosy is understood in the Bible as a punishment for the disturbed relation between heaven and earth, so each morning, after each pain-torn night, it came over the Psalmist – "It is a chastisement – why am I chastised?" And once again there arose the contrast between the horrible enigma of the happiness of the wicked and his suffering.

At this point he was tempted to accuse God as Job did. He felt himself urged to "tell how it is." But he fought and conquered the temptation. The story of this conquest follows in the most vigorous form that the speaker has at his disposal, as an appeal to God. He interrupts his objectivized account and addresses God. If I had followed my inner impulse, he says to Him, "I should have betrayed the generation of Thy sons." The generation of the sons of God! Then he did not know that the pure in heart are the children of God; now he does know. He would have betrayed them if he had arisen and accused God. For they continue in suffering and do not complain. The words sound to us as though the speaker contrasted these "children of God" with Job, the complaining "servant of God."

He, the Psalmist, was silent even in the hours when the conflict of the human world burned into his purified heart. But now he summoned every energy of thought in order to "know" the meaning of this conflict. He strained the eyes of the spirit in order to penetrate the darkness that hid the meaning from him. But he always perceived only the same conflict ever anew, and this perception itself seemed to him now to be a part of that "trouble" which lies on all save those "wicked" men – even on the pure in heart. He had become one of these, yet he still did not recognize that "God is good to Israel."

"Until I came into the sanctuaries of God." Here the real turning point in this exemplary life is reached.

The man who is pure in heart, I said, experiences that God is good to him. He does not experience it as a consequence of the purification of his heart, but because only as one who is pure in heart is he able to come to the sanctuaries. This does not mean the Temple precincts in Jerusalem, but the sphere of God's holiness, the holy mysteries of God. Only to him who draws near to those is the true meaning of the conflict revealed.

But the true meaning of the conflict, which the Psalmist expresses here only for the other side, the "wicked," as he expressed it in the opening words for the right side, for the "pure in heart," is not – as the reader of the following words is only too easily misled into thinking – that the present state of affairs is replaced by a future state of affairs of a quite different kind, in which "in the end" things go well with the good and badly with the bad; in the language of modern thought the meaning is that the bad do not truly exist, and their "end" brings about only this change, that they now inescapably experience their nonexistence, the suspicion of which they had again and again succeeded in dispelling. Their life was "set in slippery places"; it was so arranged as to slide into the knowledge of their own nothingness; and when this finally happens, "in a moment," the great terror falls upon them and they are consumed with terror. Their life has been a shadow structure in a dream of God's. God awakes, shakes off the dream, and disdainfully watches the dissolving shadow image.

This insight of the Psalmist, which he obtained as he drew near to the holy mysteries of God, where the conflict is resolved, is not expressed in the context of his story, but in an address to "his Lord." And in the same address he confesses, with harsh self-criticism, that at the same time the state of error in which he had lived until then and from which he had suffered so much was revealed to him: "When my heart rose up in me, and I was pricked in my reins, brutish was I and ignorant, I have been as a beast before Thee."

With this "before Thee" the middle section of the psalm significantly concludes, and at the end of the first line of the last section (after the description and the story comes the confession) the words are significantly taken up. The words "And I am" at the beginning of the verse are to be understood emphatically: "Nevertheless I am," "Nevertheless I am continually with Thee." God does not count it against the heart that has become pure that it was earlier accustomed "to rise up." Certainly even the erring and struggling man was "with Him," for the man who struggles for God is near Him even when he imagines that he is driven far from God. That is the reality we learn from the revelation to Job out of the storm, in the hour of Job's utter despair (30:20–22) and utter readiness (31:35–39). But what the Psalmist wishes to teach us, in contrast to the Book of Job, is that the fact of his being with God is revealed to the struggling man in the hour when – not led astray by doubt and despair into treason, and become pure in heart – "he comes to the sanctuaries of God." Here he receives the revelation of the "continually." He who draws near with a pure heart to the divine mystery learns that he is continually with God.

It is a revelation. It would be a misunderstanding of the whole situation to look on this as a pious feeling. From man's side there is no continuity, only from God's side. The Psalmist has learned that God and he are continually with one another. But he cannot express his experience as a word of God. The teller of the primitive stories made God say to the fathers and to the first leaders of the people: "I am with thee," and the word "continually" was unmistakably heard as well. Thereafter, this was no longer reported, and we hear it again only in rare prophecies. A Psalmist (23:5) is still able to say to God: "Thou art with me." But when Job (29:5) speaks of God's having been with him in his youth, the fundamental word, the "continually," has disappeared. The speaker in our psalm is the first and only one to insert it expressly. He no longer says: "Thou art with me," but "I am continually with Thee." It is not, however, from his own consciousness and feeling that he can say this, for no man is able to be continually turned to the presence of God: he can say it only in the strength of the revelation that God is continually with him.

The Psalmist no longer dares to express the central experience as a word of God; but he expresses it by a gesture of God. God has taken his right hand – as a father, so we may add, in harmony with that expression "the generation of Thy children," takes his little son by the hand in order to lead him. More precisely, as in the dark a father takes his little son by the hand, certainly in order to lead him, but primarily in order to make present to him, in the warm touch of coursing blood, the fact that he, the father, is continually with him.

It is true that immediately after this the leading itself is expressed: "Thou dost guide me with Thy counsel." But ought this to be understood as meaning that the speaker expects God to recommend to him in the changing situations of his life what he should do and what he should refrain from doing? That would mean that the Psalmist believes that he now possesses a constant oracle, who would exonerate him from the duty of weighing up and deciding what he must do. Just because I take this man so seriously I cannot understand the matter in this way. The guiding counsel of God seems to me to be simply the divine Presence communicating itself direct to the pure in heart. He who is aware of this Presence acts in the changing situations of his life differently from him who does not perceive this Presence. The Presence acts as counsel: God counsels by making known that He is present. He has led His son out of darkness into the light, and now he can walk in the light. He is not relieved of taking and directing his own steps.

The revealing insight has changed life itself, as well as the meaning of the experience of life. It also changes the perspective of death. For the "oppressed" man death was only the mouth towards which the sluggish stream of suffering and trouble flows. But now it has become the event in which God – the continually Present One, the One who grasps the man's hand, the Good One – "takes" a man.

The tellers of the legends had described the translation of the living Enoch and the living Elijah to heaven as "a being taken," a being taken away by God Himself. The Psalmists transferred the description from the realm of miracle to that of personal piety and its most personal expression. In a psalm that is related to our psalm not only in language and style but also in content and feeling, the forty-ninth, there are these words: "But God will redeem my soul from the power of Sheol, when He takes me." There is nothing left here of the mythical idea of a translation. But not only that – there is nothing left of heaven either. There is nothing here about being able to go after death into heaven. And, so far as I see, there is nowhere in the "Old Testament" anything about this.

It is true that the sentence in our psalm that follows the words "Thou shalt guide me with Thy counsel" seems to contradict this. It once seemed to me to be indeed so, when I translated it as "And afterwards Thou dost take me up to glory." But I can no longer maintain this interpretation. In the original text there are three words. The first, "afterwards," is unambiguous – "After Thou hast guided me with Thy counsel through the remainder of my life," that is, "at the end of my life." The second word needs more careful examination. For us who have grown up in the conceptual world of a later doctrine of immortality, it is almost self-evident that we should understand "Thou shalt take me" as "Thou shalt take me up." The hearer or reader of that time understood simply, "Thou shalt take me away." But does the third word, *kabod*, not contradict this interpretation? Does it not say *whither* I shall be taken, namely, to "honor" or "glory"? No, it does not say this. We are led astray into this reading by understanding "taking up" instead of "taking."

This is not the only passage in the Scriptures where death and *kabod* meet. In the song of Isaiah on the dead king of Babylon, who once wanted to ascend into heaven like the day star, there are these words (14:18): "All the kings of the nations, all of them, lie in *kabod*, in glory, every one in his own house, but thou wert cast forth away from thy sepulcher." He is refused an honorable grave because he has destroyed his land and slain his people. *Kabod* in death is granted to the others, because they have uprightly fulfilled the task of their life. *Kabod*, whose root meaning is the radiation of the inner "weight" of a person, belongs to the earthly side of death. When I have lived my life, says our Psalmist to God, I shall die in *kabod*, in the fulfillment of my existence. In my death the coils of Sheol will not embrace me, but Thy hand will grasp me. "For," as is said in another psalm related in kind to this one, the sixteenth, "Thou wilt not leave my soul to Sheol."

Sheol, the realm of nothingness, in which, as a later text explains (Eccl. 9:10), there is neither activity nor consciousness, is not contrasted with a kingdom of heavenly bliss. But over against the realm of nothing there is God. The "wicked" have in the end a direct experience of their non-being; the "pure in heart" have in the end a direct experience of the Being of God.

This sense of *being taken* is now expressed by the Psalmist in the unsurpassably clear cry, "Whom have I in heaven!" He does not aspire to enter heaven after death, for God's home is not in heaven, so that heaven is empty. But he knows that in death he will cherish no desire to remain on earth, for now he will soon be wholly "with Thee" – here the word recurs for the third time – with Him who "has taken" him. But he does not mean by this what we are accustomed to call personal immortality, that is, continuation in the dimension of time so familiar to us in this our mortal life. He knows that after death "being with Him" will no longer mean, as it does in this life, "being separated from Him." The Psalmist now says with the strictest clarity what must now be said: it is not merely his flesh that vanishes in death, but also his heart, that inmost personal organ of the soul, which formerly "rose up" in rebellion against the human fate and which he then "purified" till he became pure in heart – this personal soul also vanishes. But He who was the true part and true fate of this person, the "rock" of this heart, God, is eternal. It is into His eternity that he who is pure in heart moves in death, and this eternity is something absolutely different from any kind of time.

Once again the Psalmist looks back at the "wicked," the thought of whom had once so stirred him. Now he does not call them the wicked, but "they that are far from Thee."

In the simplest manner he expresses what he has learned: since they are far from God, from Being, they are lost. And once more the positive follows the negative, once more, for the third and last time, that "and I," "and for me," which here means "nevertheless for me." "Nevertheless for me the good is to draw near to God." Here, in this conception of the good, the circle is closed. To him who may draw near to God, the good is given. To an Israel that is pure in heart the good is given, because it may draw near to God. Surely, God is good to Israel.

The speaker here ends his confession. But he does not yet break off. He gathers everything together. He has made his refuge, his "safety," "in his Lord" – he is sheltered in Him. And now, still turned to God, he speaks his last word about the task which is joined to all this, and which he has set himself, which God has set him – "To tell of all Thy works." Formerly he was provoked to tell of the *appearance*, and he resisted. Now he knows, he has the *reality* to tell of: the works of God. The first of his telling, the tale of the work that God has performed with him, is this psalm.

In this pslam two kinds of men seem to be contrasted with each other, the "pure in heart" and "the wicked." But that is not so. The "wicked," it is true, are clearly one kind of men, but the others are not. A man is as a "beast" and purifies his heart, and behold, God holds him by the hand. That is not a kind of men. Purity of heart is a state of being. A man is not pure in kind, but he is able to be or become pure – rather he is only essentially pure when he has become pure, and even then he does not thereby belong to a kind of men. The "wicked," that is, the bad, are not contrasted with good men. The good, says the Psalmist, is "to draw near to God." He does not say that those near to God are good. But he does call the bad "those who are far from God." In the language of modern thought that means that there are men who have no share in existence, but there are no men who possess existence. Existence cannot be possessed, but only shared in. One does not rest in the lap of existence, but one draws near to it. "Nearness" is nothing but such a drawing and coming near continually and as long as the human person lives.

The dynamic of farness and nearness is broken by death when it breaks the life of the person. With death there vanishes the heart, that inwardness of man, out of which arise the "pictures" of the imagination, and which rises up in defiance, but which can also be purified.

Separate souls vanish, separation vanishes. Time that has been lived by the soul vanishes with the soul; we know of no duration in time. Only the "rock" in which the heart is concealed, only the rock of human hearts, does not vanish. For it does not stand in time. The time of the world disappears before eternity, but existing man dies into eternity as into the perfect existence.

7

The Problem
of Theodicy in Sirach:
On Human Bondage*

JAMES L. CRENSHAW

The race of man stoops in bondage to a heavy yoke. As if the
universal decree writ large upon the human heart, "You must surely
die" (Sir. 14:17), were not sufficient burden for man to bear,
another sentence claims absolute sovereignty over humanity. It
reads: "You will *fear* death." None escapes the crippling effect of
this command, as no one successfully flees from death. Sociological
distinctions become meaningless in the face of the prospect of dying;
slave and king alike suffer *Angst*. Day and night anxiety reigns; even
sleep is turned into an occasion for further consternation when
imagined harm exceeds the horrors of actual reality. While anxiety
is the lot of every man, it is multiplied sevenfold for the wicked,
upon whom fall in good measure such calamities as defy description.
Death alone releases a good man from this yoke of bondage; the
sinner does not find rest on the day he returns to the mother of
all. Instead, he inherits a curse (Sir. 40:1–11).

Such reflection upon the human situation, which we have para-
phrased rather loosely, is no momentary lapse into Qoheleth-like
preoccupation with approaching night on the part of a tired teacher.
On the contrary, it joins hands with a host of texts in which Sirach
wrestles with the problem of divine injustice. In one and all Sirach
takes his point of departure from a set of premises pressed upon him
by a vocal group bent on attacking divine justice. While we cannot
identify these antagonists, we can discern the basic thrust of their
attack. In essence they argue that God's boundless mercy bestows
upon his devotees license to sin, that his blessings in material wealth
give security, that his power robs man of the freedom to act decisively

* First published in *JBL* 94 (1975) 47–64.

to avoid sinful conduct, and that his blindness makes evil profitable especially when the perfidious deed can be concealed from human eyes as well.[1]

The impact of such doubting cries can be discerned in 2:7–11. The thrice-used refrain "You who fear the Lord" suggests that Sirach addresses himself in this instance to the faithful who have begun to feel the cogency of the arguments advanced by Sirach's opponents. The ultimate seriousness of the situation is reflected in the refrain, as well as in the urgency of the exhortations to wait, trust, and hope. In addition, Sirach resorts to an appeal to the past,[2] which constitutes an attempt to enlarge the scope of vision beyond the mere present.

> Consider the ancient generations and see:
> who ever trusted in the Lord and was put to shame?
> Or who ever persevered in the fear of the Lord and was forsaken?
> Or who ever called upon him and was overlooked?
>
> 2:10

In short, Sirach's agonizing reflection and polemical thrusts ought to alert us to the disputatious nature of his writing. The latter invites us to penetrate beneath the surface to the central issue at stake in the disputes. That issue can be described in a single word, theodicy. We shall attempt, therefore, in this essay to clarify Sirach's response to his antagonists by examining his use of an ancient debate-form and by studying hymnic contexts in the light of the controversy in which Sirach found himself. To anticipate the results of our study: Sirach availed himself of the entire arsenal of debate forged by earlier figures who wrestled with the issue of theodicy, but he also introduced two new weapons that were deemed most useful by the author of the Wisdom of Solomon. We turn first to the debate-form.

Theodicy as a Problem in Sirach

In nine instances Sirach's response to his antagonists makes use of an ancient debate-form.[3] The simple prohibition formula *'al-tō'mar* can be traced back as far as the Egyptian *Instruction of Ani* and continues in use as late as the *Instructions of 'Onchsheshonqy*. In OT wisdom literature it barely finds expression in Qoheleth and Proverbs. The relative frequency of its appearance in Sirach is therefore noteworthy. So far it has escaped scholarly notice that there is a remarkable similarity of content in the texts where *'al-tō'mar* appears. The overwhelming majority of instances in which this debate-form occurs fall within the discussion of divine justice.

Do not say, "I am (too) young for thee [thy messenger: Death] to take," for thou knowest not thy death. When death comes, he steals away the infant which is on its mother's lap like him who has reached old age....

Ani, ANET, 420

God is (always) in his success,
Whereas man is in his failure;
One thing are the words which men say,
Another is that which the god does.
Say not: "I have no wrongdoing,"
Nor (yet) strain to seek quarreling.

Amen-em-opet, ANET, 423

Do not say: "I have ploughed the field but it has not paid";
Plough again, it is good to plough.
Do not say: (Now that) I have this wealth
I will serve neither God nor man,"
Wealth is perfected in the service of God, the one who causes it to happen.
Do not say, "The sinner against God lives today,"
But look to the end.
Say (rather): "A fortunate fate is at the end of old age."[4]

'Onchsheshonqy

Say not: "Why were the former days better than these?"
For it is not from wisdom that you ask this ...
Consider the work of God;
Who can make straight what he has made crooked?[5]

Qoh. 7:10, 13

Resting behind each of these prohibitions is the painful dilemma of premature death, the inscrutability of the gods that permits the idea of divine caprice to surface, the prosperity of the wicked and delayed rewards of the virtuous, or the divine inactivity after having established a pattern of benevolent deeds. In every instance the debate-form warns against a type of free thinking based on actual experience. The prohibition seldom stands alone, but offers the evidence of broader experience.[6]

Sirach's use of this ancient debate-form throbs with the intensity of agonizing soul searching. From the tone of these contexts in which *'al-tōʾmar* occurs we can conclude that Sirach felt the threat posed by his antagonists most acutely.

Do not say: "Because of the Lord I left the right way";
For he will not do what he hates.

121

Do not say: "It was he who led me astray";
For he has no need of a sinful man.[7]

15:11–12

Do not say: "I shall be hidden from the Lord,
And who from on high will remember me?
Among so many people I shall not be known,
For what is my soul in the boundless creation?"

16:17

Do not set your heart upon your wealth,
Nor say: "I have enough." (cf. Mic. 2:1; Gen. 31:29)
Do not follow your inclination and strength,
walking according to the desires of your heart.
Do not say: "Who will have power over me?"
For the Lord will surely punish you.
Do not say: "I sinned, and what happened to me?"
For the Lord is slow to anger.
Do not be so confident of atonement
that you add sin to sin.
Do not say: "His mercy is great,
He will forgive the multitude of my sins,"
for both mercy and wrath are with him.[8]

5:1–6

Do not say: "What do I need, and what prosperity could be mine in the future?"
Do not say: "I have enough, and what calamity could happen to me in the future?"[9]

11:23–24

Seven times in Sirach the prohibition formula (*'al-tō'mar*) stands in the initial position.[10] Twice it occurs in the second half of a verse (5:1) or in a parallel verse connected by means of a copula (5:6). In most instances we have an initial prohibition formula, a direct quotation, and a refutation introduced by *kî*. Once the *kî* appears in the second of two verses functioning as a refutation (11:23–26), and in still another instance the refutation with *kî* follows the prohibition when it is not in an initial position (5:6).

In sum, the ancient debate-form appears to have functioned primarily, but not exclusively, in contexts dealing with theodicy, both in Egypt and Israel. The precise setting of this form is uncertain, but its presence in early pedagogy seems established. Moreover, the form is relatively fixed, consisting of three elements: (1) the prohibition-formula *'al-tō'mar*, (2) the direct quotation, and (3) the refutation introduced by *kî*. Finally, Sirach enlists the debate-form to refute antagonists who used the delay in retribution as an excuse to multiply transgression.

Thus far we have said nothing about the great didactic poems (hymns?)[11] that bear the major force of Sirach's refutation of his opponents whose faith has been shattered by the vicissitudes of history. It is here that we discover Sirach's unique contribution to the resolution of the problem before which a groping humanity stands (Kant). There is, furthermore, a definite link between these poems and the polemical texts already cited. This connection is made by the twice-employed refrain, "No one can say, 'What is this?' 'Why is that?' " (39:17, 21; cf. 39:34). It is precisely in these texts that Sirach's distinctive answers to the problem of theodicy lie. While these three great didactic compositions (16:24—17:14; 39:12–35; 42:15—43:33) have recently been the subject of thorough analysis,[12] they were not examined for the light they throw upon the problem of theodicy. Such a probing of the texts is both timely and absolutely essential, now that Burton Mack has taught us to consider the possibility that theodicy was the formative influence upon the "hypostatization" of wisdom.[13]

The didactic poem in 16:24—17:14 belongs to a larger composition that treats the subject of God's punishment of the sinner (15:11—18:14). The unspoken question of the greater unit is, "Does God observe sin?" An affirmative answer is given in no uncertain terms (17:15–20). The poem supplies a basis for this answer. It meditates upon the vast implications of the creation narrative (Genesis 1—2), the Noachic covenant (Gen. 9:2), and the account of the fall of man (Genesis 3). With almost mathematical precision the poet sings of divine allocation, a setting of limits, an arranging and a dividing of the eternal created order. Appropriately such rational language is introduced by the instructor's appeal for a hearing, together with a promise that he "will impart instruction by *weight*, and declare knowledge *accurately*." The dominant spirit, however, is not abstract philosophy but a testimony to a vital experience with the living God who made his will known in grace and demand.[14] Here is no cold dogma of an indifferent universe, but a "hymn" of gratitude for the covenant, for knowledge, and for the law of life that the creator has bestowed upon his creatures. In this "hymn" we meet for the first time in wisdom literature the old idea that man was created in the image of God,[15] interpreted in this setting as a token of sovereignty over all creatures. The purpose of this concept, as of all other ideas in the "hymn," is to emphasize the harmony of the created order.

In short, the passage argues that nothing is out of place in all of creation.

But the emphasis upon the fitness of everything raises a question as to natural catastrophes and the like. That is, it leaves unresolved, and indeed intensifies, the issue of natural evil. The second didactic poem alluded to above (39:12–35) wrestles mightily with this difficult problem. The "hymn" opens with an eloquent appeal for a hearing and for others to participate in the singing of praise (39:12–15), and it concludes with a school teacher's personal testimony to the truth of the hymnic declaration that the works of the Lord are all good ... for all things will prove good in their season" (39:32–34). Thereupon Sirach urges everyone to take up the song of praise (39:35). The "hymn" proper affirms the divine assessment of the finished creative work, viz., that every single thing is very good, and suggests that the secret to such a positive appraisal lies in recognizing the proper time for everything. In decidedly polemical tones the poet affirms God's power and visibility: God sees everything, and his power is unlimited. In infinite wisdom he created good things for the virtuous and evil things for sinners. But even good things are perverted by wicked men and become occasions of stumbling. Thus Sirach claims that evil is attitudinal; faith and obedience are presuppositions for understanding God's ways,[16] and much that goes under the name of evil only appears that way. *In its time* everything will be revealed for what it is, and evil will function punitively in behalf of its creator. Consequently, no man can say one thing is absolutely superior to another.

With this startling conclusion we have stumbled upon a key concept for understanding much of Sirach's thought. This basic idea occurs most clearly, however, in 33:7–15 (Greek, 36:7–15). Here one encounters a concept of opposites or complementary pairs. When God created all things he made them in pairs: "Good is the opposite of evil, and life the opposite of death; so the sinner is the opposite of the godly. Look upon all the works of the Most High; they likewise are in pairs, one the opposite of the other" (33:14–15). In short, the structure of the universe itself is complementary.[17] This does not rule out a decision as to what is better; on the contrary, the wise man can discern what stands under the divine sign of blessing, which is the result of an arbitrary decision on God's part (some he blessed, others he cursed). Nevertheless, the decision as to what is better is really a discerning of the appropriate time, which Sirach, in contrast to Qoheleth, thinks is open to man.

Both this great hymn in 39:12–35 and the text we have used to illuminate it may imply that even God's actions fall under the rubric of ambivalence.[18] This much Sirach appears to concede to his opponents. The terrible effects of such ambivalence are spelled out in the brief passage with which we began this study (40:1–11). Inasmuch as even the direct intervention of God in the world of men is characterized by ambivalence, a heavy cloud of uneasiness hovers over the human race. At the same time Sirach is convinced that God has really created all things good and that everything has a purpose. Therefore, behind the dark cloud one can discern a smile inclined toward those who please God and a threatening frown turned toward those whose conduct earns his disapproval.

The final didactic hymn that we shall take up (42:15—43:33)[19] shows a decided advance in the direction of praise over polemic. It appears that Sirach himself has begun to sense the utter futility of his earlier rational arguments and has turned more and more to the celebration of God's majesty as manifest in the grandeur of the created order. We do not imply that this hymn completely loses sight of the antagonists; on the contrary, their objections are very much in the poet's mind (42:18, 20, 23–25). But the mood is decidedly different; Sirach is painfully conscious of his inability to proclaim God's praises in an appropriate manner (42:17; 43:27–33). Moving indeed is the religious fervor of Sirach in this hymnic attempt to praise him who is greater than all his works. While one can agree with Norbert Peters that understanding plays for Sirach a greater role than feeling and fantasy,[20] on the basis of this hymn we must credit the author with exceptional powers of poetic description. We refer to such images as that of snow freezing into pointed thorns and of water putting on ice like a breastplate (43:19–20). Rarely does Sirach achieve such exquisite poetry,[21] and his achievement is not entirely unrelated to the grandeur of the subject matter. It is no accident that the words *kābôd*, *niplā'ôt*, and *nôrā'* stand out in this hymn (42:16–17, 25; 43:2, 8, 29). The depth of Sirach's piety and the crisis of faith in his day pervade even his prayers, in one of which Sirach utters the poignant plea: "Show signs anew, and work further wonders; make thy hand and thy right arm glorious" (36:6). This text alone is sufficient testimony that the author realized the inadequacy of his arguments for divine justice. The tension between a confession of divine benevolence in the past and a recognition of his inactivity at the moment was felt by Sirach most keenly; but he chose to silence those doubting voices in a mighty crescendo of praise.

The universal decree "You must die" stands in considerable tension with Sirach's understanding of death as punitive. Thus we come to still another attempt on his part to grapple with his opponents' attack on divine justice. In these texts we move beyond hymnic materials in demonstrating that Sirach never entirely freed himself from the necessity of responding to his antagonists. We refer to his argument that the true character of a man cannot be determined until the moment of his death.

> Call no one happy before his death;
> a man will be known through his children.   11:28

Again and again Sirach lays stress upon a divine visitation *at the end*, presumably at the moment of death.

> With him who fears the Lord it will go well *at the end* (*ep' eschatōn* = *'aḥᵃrît*); on the day of his death he will be blessed.
>   1:13

> A stubborn mind will be afflicted *at the end* (*'aḥᵃrît*), and whoever loves danger will perish by it.
>   3:26

> Do not envy the honors of a sinner, for you do not know what *his end* (*yômô*) will be.
>   9:11

The same sense is communicated without the use of a word for "end", by reference either to a sudden shift in the situation or to God's time.

> Do not wonder at the works of a sinner ... , for it is easy in the sight of the Lord to enrich a poor man *quickly* (*bᵉpetaʿ*) and suddenly (*pitʾōm*).
>   11:21; cf. 11:26

> Do your work before the appointed time, and *in God's time* (*bᵉʿittô*) he will give you your reward.
>   .51:30

Such passages could easily be multiplied; these suffice, however, to suggest another direction in which Sirach moved in his futile search for a convincing answer to the issue of theodicy. This argument conceals an admission that things are not what they should be *at the moment*, since external circumstances do not always correctly mirror the inner character of a man. A theological motive for this delay in reward and punishment was easy to come by: God's mercy is equal to his wrath (16:12; 17:15–32). Nevertheless, Sirach's passion for justice expresses itself in the not very convincing affirmation that wrath does not delay (7:16; cf. 33:1). Unfortunately, such a claim ignores the presupposition of the assertions that retribution will eventually come, which implies a painful delay of punishment or reward. In truth, it is difficult to avoid the suspicion that Sirach realized in one way or another the utter futility of his efforts at theodicy. If this is correct, perhaps he took renewed strength in his conviction that one must "strive even to death for the truth, and the Lord God will fight for you" (4:28).

The Rich Tradition to Which Sirach Was Heir

Sirach was by no means the first Israelite to wrestle with the problem of evil; the fruits of this intellectual and religious pilgrimage were a part of the rich religious traditions to which he was heir. One is not limited to the translator's statement that his grandfather had immersed himself in the study of the Scriptures, for there is proof on almost every page that Sirach was conscious of the prophetic theology of history, the priestly presupposition of reward for obedience, and the dogma of retribution which the sages shared with prophet and priest. The failure of historical events to accord with theological expectation, particularly that of Zion theology, and the shock occasioned by the death of Josiah[22] were familiar experiences of the past. Despite his fundamentally conservative, even proto-Sadducean, bias,[23] the failure of nerve rationally in Job and theologically in Qoheleth had not eluded his grasp, for many of the claims of the wise men had been subjected to empirical disconfirmation. Even the probationary and pedagogical theories of suffering bore within them an inherent denial that physical evil was always a retribution for sin.[24] Moreoever, the decisive shift in attitude towards piety and wealth within some psalms indicates a certain hesitancy to view wealth as conclusive proof of God's favor.[25] Even the attempt of the Chronicler, under the sway of extreme individualism, to resolve the question of divine justice was history when Sirach wrestled anew with a vocal group bent on challenging God's power or his goodness.

For Sirach the times were out of joint, since both the Davidic and the Aaronic covenants were jeopardized in his day, and Sirach even imagined himself to be the last of a long line of scribes. Such perilous times spawned pessimism and apocalypticism,[26] from the first of which Sirach was not entirely free. As a matter of fact, his emphasis upon final judgment in light of the fact that God sees everything and his divine epithets expressive of transcendentalism, particularly "the Most High,"[27] contributed to the spirit of scepticism that pervades the literature of the last two centuries before the Christian era.[28] Long before Nietzsche had noted that man can live with almost any "how" if he has a "why," the ancient

Israelites were struggling to discover a reason for living in the midst of tyranny.

In such a situation the presence of theodicies both conservative and revolutionary, i.e., discrete theodicies of the oppressor and the oppressed, the privileged and the powerless, which we have discussed elsewhere,[29] only complicated matters further. The earlier tendency to unite the ethical and eudaemonistic was giving way, and with this came an energetic reaction from those inclined to view religion pragmatically. Sirach apparently perceived that ethical monotheism stands or falls on its ability to deal with the question of the justice of God, and, like Qoheleth before him, he saw death as the decisive issue in this dilemma.[30] For him theodicy was "the attempt to make a pact with death," since he knew that "the power of religion depends, in the last resort, upon the credibility of the banners it puts in the hands of men as they stand before death, or more accurately, as they walk inevitably towards it."[31] But Sirach can be accused of neither the masochistic response of Job, so prevalent in the Judeo-Christian world, nor the mystical giving up of the problem of theodicy; on the contrary, he attempts a marriage between Hellenism and Hebraism, between Athens and Jerusalem,[32] although he saw to it that Zion wore a chastity belt, the keys of which had been entrusted to the Most High himself.

Now it is possible that we have still not discovered all the answers that Sirach threw into the laps of his critics. Let us return, for a moment, to the text with which we began this discussion. The phrase "upon sinners seven times more" (40:8) suggests that Sirach may also have ventured into the area of the psychic life as a possible response to the problem of divine injustice.[33] While one could argue conceivably that the reference is only to external calamities such as death, bloodshed, and sword, still the presence of such words as "strife" and "affliction" suggests that Sirach actually thought of *Angst* as punishment for sin. The mention of nightmares in addition to the conscious anxiety over death is especially revealing, for no one has control over the spectres of the night.[34] A limited measure of anxiety is man's common lot, Sirach contends, but the sinner has a lion's share of consternation (cf. 31:1–4). The total context (40:1–11) reinforces such an understanding of the phrase "upon sinners seven times more"; hence we conclude that Sirach viewed a disturbed mental state as punishment for sin.[35]

In sum, the problem of the justice of God was a burning issue in Sirach's day. In no sense of the word can we assume that Job and Qoheleth settled that issue once and for all. In this regard Gerhard von Rad is probably correct in his assessment of the impact of these two documents,[36] although we think that he underestimates their influence. In any event, Sirach struggles to provide a rational basis upon which to view the problem of divine justice. His answers are remarkable ones in many ways:

1 God knows everything even before it comes into being and also sees it at the moment of fruition;
2 past experience proves that God is just;
3 at the appropriate time everything will be rectified;
4 the ultimate response to the grandeur of creation is to surrender before the divine imperative of wonder;
5 from the perspective of the purpose for which all was created, the universe is a marvelous, harmonious order of complementary pairs;
6 God punishes sin by sending great anxiety upon the guilty person.

Sirach's Bold Venture

Only the last two of these solutions break new ground in the long-standing debate in ancient Israel. The argument for some sort of divine prescience is a well-known theme of Deutero-Isaiah, who never tires of emphasizing God's prior knowledge and control of all happenings. But Qoheleth, too, knew of God's unique present knowledge; this, at least, seems to be the meaning of the obscure statement that "God seeks what has been driven away" (3:15).[37] The time-worn appeal to tradition appears in both Job and Qoheleth; in each instance little if any credence is given the argument. As is well known, Qoheleth takes up the ancient Egyptian emphasis upon the appropriate time and applies it to the belief in creation (3:1–11),[38] though without reaching the conclusion that Sirach does, viz., that in *its* time all will be rectified (but see the gloss in 2:17). As for the drowning of doubting questions in the rushing crescendo of praise, Job's ultimate surrender amounts to just that.

About Sirach's fifth solution O. S. Rankin has written: "The thought which he develops upon the perfect harmony and adjustment of creation would seem to be his own contribution to theodicy."[39] Gerhard von Rad goes one step further: "Even the wholly direct intervention of God in the world of men is regarded by men as marked by that ambivalence. This attempt to tackle the problem of theodicy is new."[40] With one stroke Sirach has freed man from the odious task of interpreting God's power in comprehensive terms on the basis of a fixed norm. It is precisely at this point, von Rad thinks, that Sirach makes his mark in the theodicy debate. If this is where Sirach takes his stand, however, it is a slippery one.

In reality, the emphasis of the text lies elsewhere than on the problem of divine intervention as such, although von Rad is probably correct in drawing the conclusion that the passage also implies the further understanding of God's intervention in human affairs as ambivalent. Nevertheless, the essential point Sirach wishes to make is that *in the creative act* God brought into being a universe that encourages virtue and punishes vice.

To recapitulate, Sirach was faced with a painful dilemma: on the one hand, he courageously refused to accept Hellenism's "easy" solution to the problem of evil,[41] viz., a final resolution in the afterlife; on the other hand, he tenaciously held onto the traditional dogma of retribution in spite of Job and Qoheleth. The challenge presented by these two books prompted Sirach to search for other options. His discoveries represent a flight from reality into the realms of metaphysics and psychology. His own twofold solution was the affirmation that the universe is wondrously made as to encourage virtue and punish wickedness, and the claim that the wicked are victims of great *Angst*, of nightmares, and of conscious worry and grief.

This flight into psychology and metaphysics was an effective answer to the vexing problem of empirical disconfirmation, for it was akin to the earlier retreat of eschatologists and messianists (as well as the later escape of millenarists) into realms not subject to objective verification. Neither the hellenistic answer nor the dualistc alternative, nor anything akin to the doctrine of karma,[42] is thought worthy of Sirach's allegiance. On the contrary, "again and again Sirach returns to (the idea of) divine retribution, which unfailingly punishes the evil deed and rewards the good deed."[43] In truth "the idea of retribution stands entirely in the center of Sirach's belief about God."[44] What is unique, however, is his belief that retribution manifests itself in the inner life and in the metaphysical realm.

In his flight to areas free from empirical verification, Sirach has ceased to walk in the steps of former sages for whom experience was the ground of all knowledge. Instead, he has allied himself with the dogmatic tradition of prophet, priest, and historian (both deuteronomistic and chronistic). Small wonder that we confront in Sirach for the first time a sage who has made peace with the sacral traditions of a revealed religion.[45] Perhaps we should speak of more than "making peace," for cultic interests dominate the "hymn" in praise of great men (44—50). How revealing in this regard such a text as 33:3 comes to be:

A man of understanding will trust in the law; for him the law is as dependable as an inquiry by means of Urim.

130

What a world-view rests behind this innocent-sounding statement! At the very least we are permitted to see the sacred lot as a symbol for the ultimate in dependability. If we are correct in this interpretation of the texts, it follows that we must part company with von Rad, who would mimimize cultic interests in Sirach.[46]

In short, refusing to posit a universe in disharmony and groping desperately for a *nomos*, a "bright 'dayside' of life tenuously held onto against the sinister shadows of the 'night',"[47] Sirach contends that the marginal situations of life, particularly sleep, fantasy, and death, become occasions of divine vengeance. In his unwillingness to subject his theory to empirical verification, Sirach approaches bad faith, for the inner dialogue between conviction and reality is silenced once and for all.

The Impact of Sirach's Answers

We do not possess the necessary data to evaluate the impact of Sirach's answers upon the doubters who stimulated the discussion in the first place. Perhaps we can assume that the multitude of attempts to solve the nagging problem of the delay in retribution indicates that Sirach was never quite happy with any of his solutions. On the other hand, we can discern the impact of Sirach's views upon subsequent Jewish literature of the pre-Christian period. We shall limit ourselves to the Wisdom of Solomon.

The author of the Wisdom of Solomon both picks up distinctive views of Sirach and develops them significantly. Here for the first time we have a detailed midrash[48] on the Exodus-event understood in terms of Sirach's theory of nightmares for the wicked. The Egyptians are said to have been "prisoners of long night . . . terribly alarmed, and appalled by specters," although thinking themselves hidden from divine scrutiny (17:2–3). In their inner chamber they were not protected from that enemy who can scale any wall, fear.

> Nothing was shining through to them
> except a dreadful, self-kindled fire,
> and in terror they deemed the things which they saw
> to be worse than that unseen appearance.

> 17:6

Even magical resources were powerless to overcome this terrible state.

But throughout the night . . . they all slept the same sleep, and now were driven by monstrous specters, and now were paralyzed by their souls'

131

surrender, for sudden and unexpected fear overwhelmed them. And whoever was there fell down, and thus was kept shut up in a prison not made of iron.

17:14–16

In such a chain of darkness even melodious tunes struck terror into the hearts of the Egyptians, for over them spread primordial darkness (17:21). On the other hand, God's holy ones walked under a great light, either in the shape of a pillar of fire that functioned as a compass to guide Israel to the promised inheritance or in the form of a harmless sun.

This author moves even a step beyond Sirach, for he views the nightmarish dreams as God's forewarning "that they might not perish without knowing why they suffered" (18:19). The reason behind this observation is, of course, the desire to exalt God even more by emphasizing not only his justice but also his willingness to communicate a knowledge of that justice to the sinner upon whom his oppressive hand falls in wrath.

Sirach's theory about the harmony of the created order likewise receives enthusiastic endorsement in the Wisdom of Solomon.

> For the creation, serving thee who hast made it,
> exerts itself to punish (*epiteinetai eis kolasin*) the unrighteous,
> and in kindness relaxes (*anietai eis euergesian*) on behalf of those who
> trust in thee.
>
> 16:24

Here, too, this author moves far beyond Sirach's theory. The Wisdom of Solomon speaks of miraculous transformations or happenings.

> For—most incredible of all—in the water, which quenches all things, the fire had still greater effect, for the universe defends the righteous (16:17). Snow and ice withstood fire without melting, ... whereas the fire, in order that the righteous might be fed, even forgot its native power.
>
> 16:22a, 23

In short, creation punishes the sinner in a way that is appropriate to the sin and rewards the good man in wondrous fashion.

Sirach's appeal to a decisive act of retribution at the end of one's life is also taken over by the Wisdom of Solomon.

> Let us see if his words are true,
> and let us test what will happen at the end of his life (*en ekbasei autou*).
>
> 2:17

In the time of their visitation (*en kairō episkopēs*) they will shine forth and will run like sparks through the stubble.

3:7

... therefore no one who utters unrighteous things will escape notice,
and justice, when it punishes (*elenchousa*),
will not pass him by.

1:8; cf. 4:6, 20

Inasmuch as the author of the Wisdom of Solomon believes in the immortality of the soul[49] and retribution in the future life, it is difficult to ascertain whether or not any of these texts refers to a divine visitation in this life. It may be that the two notions of retribution stand in tension, having been incompletely reconciled in the mind of the author.[50]

Conclusion

In struggling with the problem of theodicy, Sirach came up with a number of answers, two of which were new at the time. Both were taken up by the author of the Wisdom of Solomon and developed far beyond Sirach's fondest dreams. Neither solution was open to empirical verification, representing as they did an escape into psychology or metaphysics. In light of comparable Greek discussions of Sirach's day,[51] it may be concluded that these answers spoke to the times remarkably well. But, one might ask, how permanently valid are Sirach's solutions to the problem of evil?

David Bakan's recent study of telic decentralization,[52] if accurate, suggests that there may be some truth in Sirach's conviction that wicked men experience excessive nightmares. Of course, it has long been thought that "your cheating heart will tell on you." However, this maxim presupposes an established *nomos* that imposes upon the violator of this norm an intense sense of guilt. Given such a context, the disruptive power of duplicity is astonishing. Sirach's contemporaries may have felt the yoke of conformity more keenly than most earlier Israelites precisely because of the strong temptation to ape Greek ways. In any case, Hellenism had made decisive inroads upon Judaism at the time.[53] The danger implicit in such an argument, however, is the hidden assumption that Jews in Sirach's day were enslaved by a doctrine of righteousness on the basis of works and guilt-ridden because of their inability to achieve perfection. Otto Kaiser[54] has certainly provided a much-needed corrective to Dieter Michaelis's treatment of this subject.[55] Kaiser is absolutely right in his positive assessment of Sirach's idea of the fear of God, which rules out any talk about a righteousness that is intrinsic to works.[56] Furthermore, even Bakan's theory of telic decentralization leaves room for the recognition that mental and physical wholeness affect one's sleep or lack of it more powerfully than does one's spiritual condition.

Sirach's flight into metaphysics fares even less well. Leibniz's response to Voltaire suffices to indicate the tenuous nature of any appeal to the harmony of nature in responding favorably to the righteous person and reacting oppressively against the sinner. In our day when nature is itself the tragic victim of human rape in every conceivable way and place, there can be no talk about nature exerting itself in wrath against the sinner and relaxing in compassion towards the good man.[57] Even the effect of the dominical saying that the sun shines upon the just and the unjust has been terribly blunted for a world that can hardly see the sun for pollution. Sirach's further assumption that divine intervention falls into the category of ambivalence thus strikes a responsive chord in hearts devoid of a *nomos* and bereft of hope. The believer today, who has no "bright dayside" and is without hope, can therefore grasp something of the pathos of Sirach's necrophilia. Perhaps his sole recourse is to a kind of gallows-humor,[58] an honest self-assessment that may render him a lonely man of faith[59] in the modern religious marketplace. Perhaps some day he can again join Sirach in the mighty crescendo of praise, and by harnessing his pessimism "to the triumphal chariot of religious faith"[60] he can *live* again.[61] Until that day, the ache within his soul, which unites him with Sirach at the deepest level of human existence, bears living testimony to his ultimate concern and cries out that he has not given God up, though he has lost him.

NOTES

1   I have attempted to analyze prophetic literature from the standpoint of controversy-literature. See J. L. Crenshaw, *Prophetic Conflict* (BZAW 124; Berlin/New York: Walter de Gruyter, 1971). The present study is an attempt along similar lines to penetrate beneath the surface of the text of Sirach to the religious controversy calling forth Sirach's remarks.

2   N. Habel, "Appeal to Ancient Tradition as a Literary Form," *SBL Seminar Papers* 1 (1973) 34–54.

3   T. H. Weber ("Sirach", *JBC* § 33:38 p. 546) writes that 15:11, 15 have the "typical form used to answer an objection in the *bēt midrāš*, 'school' (51:23)." If this is correct, the form has a long history. For discussion-literature in ancient Egypt, see especially the informative study by E. Otto, "Der Vorwurf an Gott (Zur Entstehung der ägyptischen Auseinandersetzungsliter-

atur)," *Vorträge der Orientalistischen Tagung in Marburg: Fachgruppe Ägyptologie, 1950* (Marburg: Universitäts-Verlag, 1951) 1–15.

4 The passages from 'Onchsheshonqy are taken from B. Gemser, "The Instructions of 'Onchsheshonqy and Biblical Wisdom Literature," *Congress Volume, Oxford 1959* VTSup 7:102–28 (esp. 116, 118).

5 The debate-form occurs twice in Proverbs (20:22; 24:29). In both passages there is a warning against taking vengeance upon an offender. "*Do not say*: 'I will repay evil'; wait for the Lord, and he will help you" gives a theological motive lacking in "*Do not say*: 'I will do to him as he has done to me; I will pay the man back for what he has done.'" Both differ from the usual debate-form in that they do not employ the particle *kî*. Perhaps one should also note Prov. 20:9; 24:12; 30:9, each of which refers to a hypothetical statement (who can say, if you say, lest I say). The formal differences, however, between these texts and those in which the debate-form appears are great. Consequently, we shall not use these three passages in drawing conclusions about the debate-form.

6 The Egyptian examples make sporadic use of the third component known from Israelite literature, viz., the refutation introduced by *kî* or its equivalent. Actually, the Egyptian form does not deem it necessary to specify the ground upon which the authority of the statement stands.

7 For the textual tradition of these verses, see H. P. Rüger, *Text und Textform im hebräischen Sirach* (BZAW 112; Berlin/New York: Walter de Gruyter, 1970) 75–76.

8 The textual variants are given in Rüger, *Text und Textform*, 13, 35–37. A. A. Di Lella (*The Hebrew Text of Sirach* [The Hague: Mouton, 1966] 108–15) discusses 5:4–6 as a select example of retroversion (retranslation from Syriac into Hebrew).

9 The debate-form also occurs in 7:9 and 31:12 in altered form. "*Do not say*: 'He will consider the multitude of my gifts, and when I make an offering to the Most High God he will accept it.'" "Are you seated at the table of a great man? Do not be greedy at it, and *do not say*, 'There is certainly much upon it!'" In 23:18–19 the debate-form appears to have been transformed into an autobiographical narrative. This passage discusses the self-deceit of the adulterer in terms of an imaginary monologue. It may be, however, that this text, like 20:16 and 36:10, has more in common with the imaginary speeches in the psalms and prophetic literature than with the debate-form being discussed. We shall, therefore, leave all of them out of the present analysis. We have discussed the transformation of a proverb into descriptive narration in "Wisdom," *Old Testament Form Criticism* (Trinity University Monograph 2; ed. J. H. Hayes; San Antonio, Tex.: Trinity University Press 1974) 256–58.

10 In 15:12 the unusual *pen tōʾmar* occurs at the beginning of the sentence.

11 W. Baumgartner ("Die literarischen Gattungen in der Weisheit des Jesus Sirach," *ZAW* 34 [1914] 170–71) discusses 42:15—43:33 under the category of independent hymns. The other two texts, 16:26—17:24 and 39:12–35, are thought by him to contain hymnic motifs (176, 171–72). He writes that "der Inhalt [of 39:12–35) ist in der Hauptsache nicht hymnisch sondern lehrhaft.... Es ist ein didaktrisches Lied, aber wohl mit Absicht in hymnischer Form gekleidet ..." (171–72).

12   J. Marböck, *Weisheit im Wandel* (BBB 37; Bonn: Hanstein, 1971; see our review, *JBL* 91 [1972] 543–44). Marböck's influence on the following discussion of hymnic materials is readily discernible to the knowledgeable reader.

13   B. Mack, "Wisdom Myth and Mytho-logy: An Essay in Understanding a Theological Tradition," *Int* 24 (1970) 46–60. We are inclined to agree with Mack's judgment about the importance of theodicy to the postexilic community. However, we do not accept a late dating of every instance in which the theme of refusing to heed God's warning appears. On one such text, see J. L. Crenshaw, "A Liturgy of Wasted Opportunity (Amos 4:6–12; Isa. 9:7—10:4; 5:25–29," *Semitics* 1 (1970) 27–37. The mild tone of many passages used by Mack to support his thesis does not seem sufficiently serious to bear the burden of such a burning issue as theodicy. For that reason we hesitate to endorse Mack's thesis wholeheartedly.

14   Marböck writes: "Diese Ordnung ist für Ben Sira allerdings nie bloss abstraktes Prinzip, sondern Ausdruck und Offenbarung des lebendigen Gottes. Darum kann und soll sie auch hinführen zu Gottesfurcht und zum lebendigen Ausdruck im Gotteslob (17, 8; vgl. 39, 14cd. 15.35)" (*Weisheit im Wandel*, 138).

15   For a recent discussion of the meaning of this idea, see J. M. Miller, "In the 'Image' and 'Likeness' of God," *JBL* 91 (1972) 289–304.

16   G. von Rad, *Wisdom in Israel* (Nashville: Abingdon Press; London: SCM, 1972) 253. This essay on Sirach first appeared in *EvT* 29 (1969) 113–33. This same ambivalence characterizes Sirach's discussion of the educational tactics of Dame Wisdom. At first she comes with heavy tests, and her yoke appears to be chains and fetters. But he who penetrates *beyond appearance to reality* soon discovers that wisdom's yoke is a golden ornament (4:17–19; 6:18–31; 21:19–21).

17   Marböck (*Weisheit im Wandel*, 152–54) makes much of this idea of opposites.

18   G. von Rad (*Wisdom in Israel*, 254) draws this conclusion about the hymn in 39:12–35.

19   On this hymn, see the translation and notes in Y. Yadin, *The Ben Sira Scroll from Masada* (Jerusalem: Israel Exploration Society and Shrine of the Book, 1965) 27–34, 45–48.

20   N. Peters, *Das Buch Jesus Sirach oder Ecclesiasticus* (EHAT 25; Münster: Aschendorff, 1913) xlviii. Peters writes: "Das Buch ist eben in der Hauptsache die Frucht des diskursiven Denkens des inspirierten Schriftgelehrten, nicht der genialen Intuition des Dichters von Gottes Gnaden. Der Verstand ist mehr an der Arbeit, als das Gefühl und die Phantasie."

21   To these metaphors one could add the description of the frustration of affliction in terms of a eunuch who embraces a maiden and groans (30:20) and the simile about an arrow stuck in the thigh, which is compared to a word inside a fool (19:12).

22   S. B. Frost, "The Death of Josiah: A Conspiracy of Silence," *JBL* 87 (1968) 369–82.

23   A. A. Di Lella, "Conservative and Progressive Theology: Sirach and Wisdom," *CBQ* 38 (1966) 139–46. G. von Rad (*Wisdom in Israel*, 258 n. 24) has rightly called attention to the fact that *conservative* in Jerusalem does not mean the same as *conservative* in Alexandria, but this fact detracts little from Di Lella's insight.

24 O. S. Rankin, *Israel's Wisdom Literature* (New York: Schocken Books, 1969; Edinburgh: Clark, 1936) 20.

25 A. S. Kapelrud ("New Ideas in Amos," VTSup 15 [1966] 193–206) argues for an eighth-century dating of this decisive shift in viewpoint. He sees the change in perspective towards the rich and poor as a distinctive contribution of the prophet Amos.

26 For a suggestive treatment of the context and mood of apocalypticism, see L. H. Silberman, "The Human Deed in a Time of Despair: The Ethics of Apocalyptic," in *Essays in Old Testament Ethics: J. Philip Hyatt – In Memoriam* (ed. J. L. Crenshaw and J. T. Willis; New York: KTAV, 1974) 191–202.

27 According to E. Bickerman (*From Ezra to the Last of the Maccabees* [New York: Schocken Books, 1962] 67), the epithet occurs forty-eight times.

28 J. Pedersen, "Scepticisme israélite," *RHPR* 10 (1930) 317–70.

29 J. L. Crenshaw, "Popular Questioning of the Justice of God in Ancient Israel," *ZAW* 82 (1970) 380–95.

30 For my understanding of Qoheleth's view of God, see J. L. Crenshaw, "The Eternal Gospel (Eccl. 3:11)," in *Essays in Old Testament Ethics*, 23–55.

31 P. Berger, *The Sacred Canopy* (Garden City, N.Y.: Doubleday & Co., 1967) 51. Berger's discussion of theodicy has been particularly helpful in our attempt to come to grips with the difficult issue on a broader scale than that represented by ancient Near Eastern literature.

32 See especially Marböck, *Weisheit im Wandel*; M. Hengel, *Judentum und Hellenismus* (WUNT 10; Tübingen: Mohr, 1969) 241–75; and T. Middendorp, *Die Stellung Jesu ben Siras zwischen Judentum und Hellenismus* (Leiden: Brill, 1973).

33 Such an understanding of dreams is not entirely new to wisdom literature. In Job 7:14 nightmares are said to be a terrible weapon in God's arsenal, while 33:14–18 speaks of them as God's means of bringing a wicked man to his senses. Elihu's discussion of nightmares in the context of revelation has a parallel in Sir. 34:1–8. Here Sirach strikes out against those who make free use of dreams in order to predict the future. The cogency of his claim that dreams give wings to fools (34:1) is greatly weakened by the further admission that dreams may be "sent from the Most High as a visitation" (34:6). Of course, there was no way of discerning whether a dream was caused by God, by gluttony (31:19–20), or by any number of factors.

34 L. Oppenheim (*The Interpretation of Dreams in the Ancient Near East* [Philadelphia: American Philosophical Society, 1956] 197) writes that nightmares were "symptoms of a specific state of mind due to mental stress, disease or malevolent magical activities." Of all the dreams discussed by Oppenheim the most pertinent to this theme are those of Enkidu and Tammuz. Enkidu's well-known dream and awakening scream (which Oppenheim compares to *Richard III*, where the Duke of Clarence dreams he is in hell and foul fiends howled in his ears "such hideous cries that, with the very noise, I trembling wak'd and for a season after could not believe but that I was in hell …") portend ill for him, although nightmares do not always foretell tragedy. Oppenheim notes that good dreams sometimes announce terrible happenings, whereas bad dreams on occasion proclaim fortune (229). The dream of Tammuz, like that of Enkidu,

spells disaster for him. The literary device of a dream with evil content by means of which the author emphasizes the courage of the hero or the inevitability of fate is amply illustrated in the Bible; we refer to Judg. 7:13 (the dream of the frightened Midianites who face Gideon in battle) and the dream of Pilate's wife.

35 Precursors to Sirach's view that mental anxiety was a sign of divine displeasure are certainly present in the OT. We refer to the Saul narrative, which depicts the tragedy of one whom God has driven to madness (cf. also Job 3:25–26 and Prov 10:24). We have discussed the idea of the divine hardening of human hearts in *Prophetic Conflict* (77–90), while the "tragic" dimension is treated in "The Samson Saga: Filial Devotion or Erotic Attachment?" *ZAW* 86 (1974) 470–504.

36 von Rad, *Wisdom in Israel*, 237–39.

37 That is, God looks again for what he has already seen once. See the discussion of this verse in R. Gordis, *Koheleth – The Man and His World* (New York: Schocken Books, 1968) 233–34; and O. Loretz, *Qohelet und der Alte Orient* (Freiburg: Herder, 1964) 200 n. 288. Both Job (10:6) and the author of Psalm 39 interpret God's constant vigilance as cause for *dismay*; the latter urges God to look away from him so that he can know gladness (39:13).

38 "In essence the goal of wisdom instruction was the recognition of the right time, the right place and the right degree of human conduct" (H. H. Schmid, *Wesen und Geschichte der Weisheit* [BZAW 101; Berlin/New York: Walter de Gruyter, 1966] 190).

39 Rankin, *Israel's Wisdom Literature*, 35. W. O. E. Oesterley (in *APOT*, I. 310) thinks Sirach's unique contribution is the idea that God can cause a man's last hours to be so terrible that all former enjoyment of life is obliterated entirely.

40 von Rad, *Wisdom in Israel*, 254.

41 The author of 2 Esdras introduces us to the agony caused by Hellenism's answer to the problem of theodicy. Again and again this sensitive soul chafes at the thought of the eternal damnation awaiting the masses of humanity. Ezra can derive little comfort from reflection upon his own elect state; instead the powerful negative role of the belief in life after death enables him to discern the dark, shadowy side of God that dominates his relationships with mankind. To this ominous character of God Ezra objects most vigorously. For him a congruence between this world and the next was absolutely essential. Therefore, Ezra could not countenance the discernible deep gulf between the present and future ages. For this anxiety on Ezra's part, see 3:1—9:25.

42 Rankin (*Israel's Wisdom Literature*, 121–23) notes that Judaism eventually found room for such concepts. Evidence for this claim is based on the ideas of *Darkê Tᵉšûbāh* and *Gilgûl*.

43 R. Smend, *Die Weisheit des Jesus erklärt* (Berlin: G. Reimer, 1906) xxv.

44 A. Bertholet, *Die jüdische Religion von der Zeit Esras bis zum Zeitalter Christi* (1911) 189.

45 J. Fichtner, "Zum Problem Glaube und Geschichte in der israelitisch-jüdischen Weisheitsliteratur," *TLZ 76* (1951) 145–50 (also in *Gottes*

Weisheit [Stuttgart: Calwer, 1965] 9–17). For a discussion of the difficult task of recognizing wisdom influence upon non-wisdom texts, see J. L. Crenshaw, "Method in Determining Wisdom Influence upon 'Historical' Literature," *JBL* 88 (1969) 129–42.

46 von Rad, *Wisdom in Israel*, 260 n. 28.

47 Berger (*The Sacred Canopy*, 23) uses this language in discussing marginal situations and the need for *nomos*.

48 For a discussion of this terminology and the context within which the Wisdom of Solomon was written, see J. M. Reese, *Hellenistic Influence on the Book of Wisdom and its Consequences* (AnBib 41; Rome: Biblical Institute, 1970); on midrash, see esp. 91–98. J. A. Sanders ("The Ethic of Election in Luke's Great Banquet Parable," in *Essays in Old Testament Ethics*, 247–71) has some pertinent remarks about midrash with particular reference to M. P. Miller, "Targum, Midrash and the Use of the Old Testament in the New Testament," *JSJ* 2 (1971) 29–81.

49 von Rad (*Wisdom in Israel*, 262) even thinks that some passages in Sirach are amenable to a belief in retribution after death (1:13; 2:3; 7:36; 9:11; 11:26–28; 16:12; 17:23; 18:24). However, he recognizes the question posed to such a view by V. Hamp's study, *Zukunft und Jenseits im Buche Sirach* (BBB 1; Bonn: Hanstein, 1950).

50 The same tension is observable in Sirach's understanding of the physician whose profession is put under a cloud of suspicion by the belief in sickness as punishment for sin. On this, see Marböck, *Weisheit im Wandel*, 154–60.

51 Hengel, *Judentum und Hellenismus*, 241–75.

52 D. Bakan, *Disease, Pain and Sacrifice* (Chicago: University of Chicago Press, 1968).

53 Bickerman, *From Ezra to the Last of the Maccabees*, 53. R. T. Siebeneck ("May Their Bones Return to Life – Sirach's Praise of the Fathers," *CBQ* 21 [1959] 411–28) emphasizes the hellenistic threat as the primary concern of Sirach. The pedagogy of examples (44:1—50:24) is interpreted against the backdrop of a militant hellenizing movement. Opinions vary as to the role of 44:1—50:24. C. Spicq (*L'Ecclésiastique* [La Sainte Bible, ed. L. Pirot and A. Clamer, 2d ed.; Paris: Letouzey et Ané, 1946]) calls the passage a type of concluding doxology, while B. Vawter (*The Book of Sirach with a Commentary* [Glen Rock, NJ: Paulist Press, 1962]) calls it the heart of the book.

54 O. Kaiser "Die Begründung der Sittlichkeit im Buche Jesus Sirach," *ZTK* 55 (1958) 51–63. The phrase "tote Werkheiligkeit" that Kaiser challenges is taken from L. Couard, *Die religiösen und sittlichen Ausschauungen der alttestamentlichen Apokryphen und Pseudepigraphen* (Gütersloh: Bertelsmann, 1907) 139–42.

55 D. Michaelis, "Das Buch Jesus Sirach als typischer Ausdruck für das Gottesverhältnis des nachalttestamentlichen Menschen," *TLZ* 83 (1958) 601–8. Michaelis accuses Sirach of humanism and a type of religiosity that is apostasy ("Das Buch Jesus Sirach ist eins der ersten grossen literarischen Zeugnisse jenes Abfalls," col. 608). This theme has recently been taken up again by H. D. Preuss, "Erwägungen zum theologischen Ort alttestamentlicher Weisheitsliteratur," *EvT* 30 (1970) 393–417. Preuss applies Michaelis's judgment to the entire corpus of wisdom literature, which is understood as

Israel's attempt to be like her neighbors; hence it is called paganism. From the other direction W. Brueggemann (*In Man We Trust* [Atlanta: John Knox Press, 1972]) adds a much-needed corrective to an understanding of man that robs him of the dignity bestowed upon him at creation. Brueggemann celebrates the "humanism" in wisdom literature. While we readily agree with him that wisdom literature includes such optimism, we prefer to focus upon the sage's mighty cry *in tormentis*, which has seldom been heard in all its pathos.

56 Kaiser writes: "Das Gesetz ist der Kompass, der dem Menschen den Weg durch die Stürme des Lebens zeigt, der ihm in aller augenscheinlichen Sinnlosigkeit des Weltgeschehens zu der im Verborgenen waltenden richtenden und segnenden Ordnung Gottes führt" ("Die Begründung," 57). On the fear of God in Sirach, see J. Haspecker, *Gottesfurcht bei Jesus Sirach* (AnBib 30; Rome: Biblical Institute, 1967).

57 Unless, of course, we surrender to the overwhelming apocalyptic voices that proclaim a holocaust or a privation. But only the punitive side of Sirach's voice is heard in such a message of doom for the good and the bad.

58 The term is taken from H. Hesse, who likewise manifests a fascination with the idea of death (see especially *Narcissus and Goldmund*, but also *Demian*, *Steppenwolf* and *Siddhartha*).

59 This is the language of J. B. Solovietchek in a marvelous essay, "The Lonely Man of Faith," *Tradition* 7 (1965) 5–67.

60 C. Zhitlowsky ("Job and Faust," *Two Studies in Yiddish Culture* [ET and ed., P. Matenko; Leiden: Brill, 1968] 98) uses this language to describe Job's response to the Divine Presence. Zhitlowsky asks whether Job lost all courage when the gate of mystery burst open. As Job stands face to face with God, he writes, "The clouds of darkness are dispersed; a feeling of infinite confidence in the world and its Divine Leader arises in his soul and he laughs at the thousand questions, the hungry wolves with burning eyes, and they disappear from his soul" (152).

61 We refer to the biblical exhortation to choose the Lord and live (Deut. 30:19–20; cf. Amos 5:6a).

8

*The Crisis of Wisdom in Koheleth**

HARTMUT GESE

Analyses and descriptions of the wisdom of Koheleth [= Ecclesiastes] may be divided into two sorts. There are those which emphasize the more negative facets, that is, the more pessimistic and destructive aspects (referring to the destruction of the views of life which previously had a more or less religious significance). Then there are those concerned to let Koheleth appear more theologically positive – to be the one who indeed takes a critical position in relationship to the previous views but who does not find himself in crisis.[1] It is very much a matter of one's analysis of Koheleth's wisdom as far as where the stresses which give weight to the individual elements of the teaching are placed.

Interpretation can be greatly facilitated if a few parallels from ancient Oriental wisdom literature are brought in to serve for comparison. (Because it is almost international in character, Oriental wisdom literature was able to have a strong influence on the Israelite.) Strictly speaking, pessimistic voices were always to be heard among the sages so that there is much material with which to compare Koheleth.[2] But one should never fail to appreciate that statements which sound similar can have completely different meanings in the context of fundamentally different outlooks. Early wisdom was always conscious that the order present in the world into which it inquired was not accessible to humankind. It is directly from this presupposition about the inaccessibility of the world order that statements concerning the restraint and moderation of the sage, so characteristic of wisdom from the very first, are derived. Thus, for the sages the world order in the final analysis remained impenetrable.[3] This results in maxims in the proverb literature which

---

*First published in *Les sagesses du Proche-Orient ancien* (1963) 139–51. Translated by Lester L. Grabbe.

could be designated as "pessimistic," especially when the meaningless nature of human events – particularly the absence of well-being (*Heil*) in which the sage should have a part because of his pious (*heilvolles*) behavior – was felt to be oppressive. The result seems to be the appearance of darker themes in the wisdom literature of Egypt after the First Intermediate Period and of Mesopotamia in the Cassite Period. Nevertheless, one must ask whether this greater emphasis upon the impenetrability of the divine order has altered the essential structure or fundamentals of wisdom. Is it not simply a shift in nuance? For an answer we go immediately to an Israelite example in Job 4:19–21. From Job's three friends who may be taken as excellent representatives of the early wisdom we occasionally hear rather pessimistic statements, but Job in his "pessimism" is separated from these "orthodox" individuals by a deep chasm. So Eliphaz – authorized by a secret revelation – can speak as follows:

> ... and much more (the people), the inhabitants of clay dwellings
>> which have their foundations in the earth[4]:
> they are crushed as if they were moths,
>> from morning to evening they are broken in pieces,
> unnoticed they go to the ground forever,
>> their tent peg is summarily[5] yanked out,
>> they die there without wisdom.[6]

This statement does not contradict early wisdom. The hierarchical arrangement of the cosmos, with the "dwellers in houses of clay" standing at the bottom, is certainly an expression of the over-all governing order. It is to this understanding that wisdom leads (in this case it was actually revealed to the sage). The poet brings the paradox to expression in a very impressive way by means of the climactic phrase, "without wisdom" (*bĕlō' ḥokmǎ*).[7] Declarations characterized as pessimistic, however pointed they may be, can in this way be completely reconciled with the structure of early wisdom so often referred to in brief as "optimistic." By means of an analysis of Koheleth's wisdom one will be able to work out the underlying structure and compare it with the earlier Israelite wisdom or, alternatively, to trace it back and if necessary to describe any structural changes. In this way one can counter an incorrect, subjective distribution of emphasis on the individual elements of the teaching.

It is time to advance my thesis: the wisdom of Koheleth shows a mutation of structure in comparison with the earlier Israelite wisdom. This may be described as the distancing of the person –

of the "I" – from the event with which he appears to be associated, as the detachment and self-removal of the observing subject. According to Koheleth, the essence of the person is determined not only in that one perceives oneself as an individual but also in that one sets oneself against world affairs as a stranger to the world. This concept will be elaborated in what follows.

The order presupposed in the early conception of wisdom lies in the assumption that the person walks in a definite area of piety (*heilvoll*) or impiety with everything done or omitted. The individual exists in a state of being "righteous" (*ṣedek*) or "wicked" (*reša'*), in which one experiences either well-being or its opposite; thus, by one's deeds a person gains a part in one or the other. The person both does *and* experiences evil (*rā'â*); it is both evil and misfortune. Such an inner unity exists between act and personal situation (*Ergehen*) that the two can be differentiated only outwardly. There is no cause which leads to an effect; on the contrary, these are only two aspects of a *single* thing.[8] The concept of an act/situation unity presupposes the identity of a person with one's acts and one's personal situation as well as with one's reputation which that very person enjoys because of the first two. Thus, a person's social position depends on one's situation and calling. A person is in a condition of either well-being or misfortune. Koheleth, however, recognizes no relationship between act, situation, and reputation, having rejected any connection between a person and that individual's acts or state.

In early wisdom, wealth and acquired goods were the sign of one's pious (*heilvoll*) actions whereas Koheleth emphasizes that after the death of the possessor laboriously acquired goods fall into the hands of one who has not worked for them, nor does one know whether that person will be wise or foolish (2:18–19). The goods gained by wisdom do not remain in the possession of the wise (2:20–23). But it is not only death which draws the curtain on possession; even in life the frugally saved wealth can be lost unutilized (5:13–17) or, even worse, the wealthy person has to be a spectator while a stranger consumes the former's wealth (6:1–6).[9] The profit of human endeavor is, therefore, not the real possession of the person; here labor and profit do not correspond to one another. However, for Koheleth it also means that one's personal situation almost never corresponds to one's conduct in life and therefore bears little relation to it. The righteous meet what the unrighteous would meet, and vice versa (8:14). This imbalance is dominant not only temporarily but even continues into the death of the one who suffered under it or unrighteously profited from it (8:10). Indeed, the delay of retribution is accompanied by the spread of evil actions among humankind (8:11–12).

Whatever happens to a person thus does not relate to one's essential being, is not a product of oneself. For Koheleth this is expressed most strongly in the death of the individual since death is the same for all, "for the righteous and unrighteous, for the clean and unclean, for the one who gives offerings and the one who does not give offerings" (9:2). "This is the worst[10] of all that takes place under the sun, that a *single* fate overtakes all" (9:3; cf. 2:14). The word *miqreh*, which Koheleth always uses to express the "fate of death,"[11] in older Hebrew does not refer to that which one experiences because of one's conduct and actions but rather to that which has no relationship to them or at least appears to have none. For example, in 1 Sam. 6:9 the Philistine priests concluded that, if the ark of Yahweh did not return to Israelite territory on the wagon, then their experiences were not due to the hand of Yahweh. That is, there would be no connection between the plague and the capture of the ark of Yahweh, and thus it would be *miqreh*.[12] Here one could perhaps translate this lack of relationship with the word "chance." And for Koheleth especially that which befalls the individual without respect to one's conduct is death, to which the wise as well as the foolish inexorably hasten (2:15). One expects that the problem of death would move more to the fore in the later wisdom represented by Koheleth than in earlier wisdom. More importantly, however, the problem is experienced not so much in that individual existence comes to an end but rather in the lack of a connection between cause and effect (*Beziehungslosigkeit*) in a person's life.

In the earlier wisdom the position which the person enjoyed in one's own circle (shown in the height of esteem accorded) belonged to one's very essence. By this esteem the state of well-being is most obviously brought to expression; I would like to call to mind in this regard the magnificent representation of the righteous sage in Job 29.[13] Scorn, ridicule, notoriety, and secret curse are thus all dangerous attacks against the person; they are evidence that the person attacked is no longer in a state of divine favor (*Heil*). But for Koheleth, reputation ought to be unimportant since it no longer bears any relationship to the essence of the individual. He advises, "Pay no attention to all that is said, lest it should come to your ears that your servant has cursed you" (7:21), knowing how often oneself has shared in malicious gossip about others (7:22). It is axiomatic for Koheleth that the poor and needy sage who could save a whole city by one's insight would still be only scorned (9:13–16).

The separation of the person from all that is characteristic of one-self according to early wisdom goes even further in Koheleth. The direct expression of one's personal being – the very product of the person – formulated in Koheleth through the merismus of love, desire-but-not-love, desire-not (= hate), is withheld from human understanding (9:1). Also the most inherent feeling is not for human possession. Following from this are two consequences according to Koheleth: One is the concept of predestination of the person (6:10). In Koheleth it is clearly derived not from reflection on the order present in the world but from understanding of the subject's estrangement from all that happens to and around oneself. Predestination is the deepest expression of this estrangement. The consequence is the breakdown of the old concept of "righteousness" (*ṣĕdāqâ*). It is impossible for one to remain in the sphere of *ṣĕdāqâ* – to be a righteous person (*ṣaddîq*) – for one will always have a share in unrighteousness (7:20). In early wisdom the sharp distinction between the two domains of "righteous" (*ṣedeq*) and "wicked" (*rešaʿ*) was not that of a black and white picture but the foundation of a real possibility for decision and living. This compartmentalization – this thinking in mental spheres—is not possible for Koheleth because of a lack of a connection between cause and effect (*Beziehungslosigkeit*) among human beings.

The notion of an act-situation relationship is certainly not what Koheleth obtains at first glance. When he wishes to express a connection between act and personal situation, he sets in place of the automatic act-consequence relationship the model of God's judicial recompense (3:17; 8:12–13; 11:9) and speaks of the "sentence" (the Persian–Aramaic word *pitgām*) which will be passed upon the wicked deed (8:11).[14] This teaching about retribution is not, however, just a substitute for the notion of an act-situation relationship so that a new correlation of act and situation arises. For this retribution is not centered primarily on the person but is a regulation of world events and is tied up with activity at a particular time (3:17). Retribution does not enter the picture immediately – indeed, sometimes only after the death of the perpetrators who are then beyond reach (8:11 combined with 8:10). The effects of such retribution, as far as they are noticed in the world, are thus inconsequential. No new relationship of person and event is being presented!

Now it might be thought that Koheleth replaces such a correlation with that of recompense in the transcendental sphere after the death of the individual. In the late development of wisdom literature one can certainly observe the tendency to recover the order not exhibited in life by adoption of a post-mortem judgment. And without doubt this adoption meant a substantial shift in the older conceptions about order. The notion of an act-situation relationship in early wisdom stands in gross contradiction to such a doctrine of retribution. Thus it happens that thoughts about a judgment of the dead occur only allusively in wisdom texts of the Old Kingdom and first emerge in the instructions of Merikare. But even here and in the Instructions of Amenemope it is only a question of accepting an additional idea which remains completely marginal and does not interfere with the one of an act-situation relationship.[15] We can conclude from 3:19–21 that in Koheleth's time the idea existed that the human spirit rose into the godly sphere after death. In this way it would even have a part in the order which was hidden during its earthly existence and which remained without any effects observable to humankind. The same sort of concept,[16] even though difficult to reconcile with early wisdom, must have become even more significant the more wisdom took on a dualistic structure. Nevertheless, Koheleth did not take this alternative. He objected to such ideas (3:19–21)[17] and stressed the finality of death and the lack of connection between the dead and their earthly life (9:4–6).[18] Koheleth does not offer any way to overcome the alienation of humanity in the world.

Koheleth's opposition to early wisdom has also distilled itself out into a few precepts which represent an objection to the special viewpoints of early wisdom. It is especially in ch. 4 that one finds such statements, which are followed in 5:1–7 by maxims opposing views from the sphere of the cult. Koheleth 4:1–3 teaches that the oppression and violation of humanity can take forms which make life appear no longer worth living. Koheleth pronounces the dead and the unborn fortunate in comparison with the sufferers. Yet it was this call-to-life which was, for the ancients, the sign of God's desire for well-being. Thus, in the laments of individuals[19] or salvation oracles[20] reference to birth as an expression of confidence appears to be a stereotype. But Job's curse of the day of his birth at the beginning of his lament (Job 3:2ff) and Jeremiah's at the end of his monologue (Jer. 20:14ff) must have looked just as heretical as Koheleth's praise of the dead and unborn.

Koheleth 4:4 states that in every task (*'āmāl*) and achievement (*kišrôn*) jealousy – competition with one's neighbor – is a given. This is true whether the accomplished work arouses envy or whether it is aimed at one's neighbor out of jealousy or ambition. Completely contrary to early wisdom which saw piety in the success of work, Koheleth sees only the negation of one's neighbor in all positive activity.

In 4:7–12 Koheleth declares that the consequence of a deed is dependent on the number of doers: two united can produce more than a simple doubling whereas one alone is lost. How then can work and achievement, deed and situation, correspond to one another? For early wisdom, on the contrary, the individual in his *ṣedeq*-activity was part of a community from the beginning.

By means of a school example Koheleth in 4:13–16 teaches that the present condition of apparent divine favor (*heilvoller-Zustand*) in which a king finds himself has a highly restricted significance: one who is still a captive now can replace the king in short order.[21] So if the usurper also might be hailed so enthusiastically, this condition of favor (*Heilszustand*) is turned to nothing. The present reality has a diminished significance. There is certainly no reference to one who can guarantee this reality for a definite period of time. More decisive than the reality is the potentiality; however, this immediately removes any personal decision. According to early wisdom the entire future arises out of the present whereas Koheleth would like to judge the present only from the perspective of the future. For him the end is more important than the beginning (the essence of the statements in 7:1–8); therefore, any judgment of the present is impossible.

Consequently, we come closer and closer to Koheleth's fundamental statements on the order in world events, to his representation of the world order. It is above all significant that such a representation is found which disregards all conduct of the individual person. Early wisdom had never considered the world order without taking account of human conduct; rather, for it this order was directly realized in the conduct of the person. This was strongly implied in the maxims and proverbs but could not be described "in itself." According to Koheleth, if a person disengaged oneself from the happenings around – if one saw oneself in an absolute way – only then could that person describe the absolute, objective order.

What does this order look like? We have two passages concerning it: 1:3–11 and 3:1–15.[22] In 1:3–11 the eternal sameness of the world is described and supported by a doctrine of circularity. All changeable elements – sun (light), wind (air), rivers (water) – return to their place. And just as everything in this eternal circular movement in space works and produces,[23] so humankind does not cease from speaking, from seeing, and from hearing – and people speak and see and hear continually the same thing because being and doing repeat themselves eternally. The contemplative person must perceive oneself as a foreigner in relation to this world. The eternal sameness makes the world appear to be a closed and static entity, nature, which is essentially foreign to humanity. Also, the human being in his scenario appears to be the same as nature, as if the order could otherwise have been grasped "in itself." Nature and history have now parted company.

This teaching of an eternal sameness finds its counterpart in that of an eternal fluxation of the right time (3:1–15). For every type of doing and being and for its opposite (the merismus shows the entirety is meant) there is a "time" (a Greek *kairos* = Hebrew *'ēt*). Whenever there is a time, there is a specific activity suited to it, and every doing is beautiful in its own time (v.11a). But it finds its meaning only in the passage of time (*'ôlām*) for which God has created everything (v. 14aα). And this passage of time – this arrangement of individual right moments – is hidden from humanity which sees neither beginning nor end (v. 11bβ) and can neither add to it nor subtract from it (v. 14aβγ). Thus, divine action is hidden from the person even though God has given humans the aspiration of perceiving the order of events (v. 11bα). This lack of insight into the succession of time leads to an opaqueness with regard to life because one's destiny is "time and chance" (*'ēt wāpega'*), the particular moment which overtakes a person (9:11). Thus, fate – the happenstance of "time" – breaks in on one from the outside just as a net and trap capture animals (9:12). The wise can at the most understand the moment (8:5) while the universe remains closed to them because eternity (*'ôlām*) is closed to them (8:6–8). World events are unintelligible; all understanding is illusion (8:16–17).

It is important, however, to understand that despite this humanity-world discrepancy, Koheleth comes neither to a dualism which separates completely between an outer and an inner sphere nor to one which sees a unity of the two spheres by means of analogy. Later wisdom took this spiritualizing or transcendental route, but Koheleth on the contrary held fast to a *single* world in which God accomplishes and orders all things. He does not elevate human difficulty to the postulate of a sphere of being, even though he dogs its trail so radically and fundamentally, but charges the individual to abandon this experienced estrangement. In both aspects – the monistic structure of the world view and the requirement of human subordination[24] – Koheleth is a true student of early wisdom. It is only humans who deal with distancing from world events, who must deal with it because it is a part of their nature. They have been created upright (7:29), but God has put in them his quest after knowledge – after an understanding of "eternity" (*'ôlām*, 3:11) – which cannot be fulfilled. According to Koheleth, this human state of estrangement has the purpose of making one fear God (3:14). The concept of "fear of God" (*yir'at hā 'ĕlōhîm*) seems to occupy the central place here in Koheleth, and on it he develops his doctrine of "the right time." It is also in this place that he apparently takes "righteousness" (*ṣĕdāqâ*, the chief "virtue" of early wisdom) to absurdity (7:15–18 + 20). The "fear of God" takes the place of the earlier "righteousness." The concept of godly fear appears prominently in 8:12b–13 inside the complex of 8:9–14 which shows the equation of act-situation to be invalid. Also here the pronouncement is ventured that everyone who truly fears God[25] will experience good as a result. It remains open as to how far this "good" (*ṭôb*) is tangible apart from the subjective sphere of godly fear. The author of the epilogue (12:13–14) has correctly placed the requirement of godly fear at the top of his "summation."

If one abandons this distancing through godly fear, that person will replace a state of estrangement with one of openness towards the right time. One will accept the good times with thankfulness while in the bad one will understand that this time was also planned by God,[26] that it is only one's own limitations which prevent one from comprehending eternity (*'ôlām*, 7:10 + 13–14). Such persons will not place confidence in a pre-existent situation and desire to show their own strength in it (11:1–5) but in their actions will let God prevail (11:6). Above all, Koheleth cannot get enough of exhorting to enjoy the good and the beautiful in life. Continually present in his work is the urge to be happy and to enjoy (2:24–26; 3:12–13, 22; 5:17–19; 8:15; 9:7–10; 11:7–10). This is something quite different from a cheap hedonism coming out of the gloomy backdrop of doubts about existence.[27] On the contrary, God shows himself as one who also provides prosperity to persons in their limited state. Such a circumstance of well-being is "from the hand of God" (2:24), is "a gift of God" (3:13; 5:18), is "one's portion or lot" (*ḥēleq*, 3:22; 5:17, 9:9). At the acceptance of this gift "God has pleasure" (*rāṣâ!* 9:7). One could speak of a doctrine of the presence of divine favor (*Heilspräsenz*) which Koheleth develops in numerous passages. In early wisdom the state of well-being (*Heil*) was the direct result of one's standing in a "condition of righteousness" (*ṣĕdāqâ*). Such an "automatic" cause-and-effect is no longer possible for Koheleth. For him well-being must be a direct judicial gift of God to the individual.

At the beginning and end of Koheleth's wisdom stand the words, "Vanity of vanities, all is vanity" (*hăbēl hăbālîm hakkōl hebel*). These words are deceptive if one wants to read into them the content of Koheleth's wisdom. They merely show the way which leads to the right fear of God.

NOTES

1 Representatives of the latter sort tend to emphasize those passages in Koheleth in which the older "orthodox" conceptions of wisdom have found expression. In such cases, too little attention has been paid to two considerations: (1) the possibility of glosses with an "orthodox" point of view so as to weaken the revolutionary opinions of Koheleth and, more importantly, (2) the cumulative nature of wisdom literature. In these collections many elements of teaching of the traditional type could be included even while little weight was assigned to them in the overall conceptualization. One may note the following examples: above all, 9:17—20 [*sic!* 9:17—10:20?]; in second place are the traditional elements inserted by the author in 5:10–12, 20; 6:11–12 (6:19 is secondary [*sic!* 6:10?]); various individual details in 7:1–8; 7:9, 26; 8:2–4. The proverbs cited by Koheleth are to be looked upon in a different light; their *double entendre* formulation, beloved of wise sayings from old, permits an intentional concealment; examples are 1:15, 18; 4:5–6; 7:13b (parallel to 1:15a). Representations of the first sort occasionally assign certain of Koheleth's terms too negative a sense so that the late character of the language, in which much of precise meaning has worn away, has not been sufficiently considered: the verb '*ml* in Koheleth no longer means "to toil (with pain)," and '*āmāl* no longer "drudgery," but "to work," "take pains over," "acquire," and "work," "acquisitions," respectively as in later Hebrew and Aramaic. The specification "pain" has almost completely vanished. The root '*nh* (1:13; 3:10; 5:19) corresponds to the Aramaic '*n* "busy oneself (industriously) with" (cf. also the Arabic '*ny*) from which comes the frequent late Hebrew word '*inyān* "occupation," "business." The meaning "toil" has completely fallen away. In Koheleth *hebel* is primarily "nothingness" in the sense of "transience," then also "non-essentiality," "uselessness," "meaninglessness." Granted, the concept of self-deception is present in the word but not the active one of lies and deception which comes to expression in the Latin root *vanitas* (English "vanity"). The word *ra'* occasionally weakens to "bad," "adverse," disagreeable," "hard," "painful" in Koheleth and thus no longer has the concept of active, progressive evil or mischief.

2 Here one could cite the Egyptian wisdom texts of the Middle Kingdom and different Sumerian proverb collections, above all the so-called pessimistic wisdom and the acrostic dialogue (theodicy) of the Cassite period. But one should bypass the Egyptian "Man Tired of Life," which is concerned with the value and requirement of funeral rituals, and the so-called "Pessimistic Dialogue" which actually belongs to the genre of satire (E. A. Speiser, *JCS* 8 [1954] 98–105; F. M. T. Böhl, Supplements to *Numen* 2 47–48; W. G. Lambert, *Babylonian Wisdom Literature* [Oxford; Clarendon Press, 1960] 139–40).

3 For evidence, cf. H. Gese, *Lehre und Wirklichkeit in der alten Weisheit* (Tübingen: Mohr/Siebeck, 1958) 17–19, 38–41, 68.

4 As opposed to the heavenly inhabitants who are accused by God because of their sin.

5 Read bayyôm; cf. F. Horst, *Hiob* (BKAT 16; Neukirchen-Vluyn; Neukirchener, 1968) 61, on the passage.

6 Job 4:19–21; cf. 15:17ff. For Bildad, cf. ch. 25; for Zophar, 11:5ff.

7 The underlying meaning is this: The sage, even though he should at some point be destroyed like the moth, still knows he will die in accordance with an overall governing order despite the fact that this order is impenetrable by him.

8 Cf. J. Pedersen, *Israel* (Oxford, 1926) 1/11, 336ff; K. Fahlgren, *Ṣedaqa nahestehende und entgegengesetzte Begriffe im Alten Testament* (1932) passim; K. Koch, *ZTK* 52 (1955) 1–42; Gese, *Lehre und Wirklichkeit*, 42–5.

9 5:10–6:9 represents a larger composition concerning property and the struggle to obtain property (greed for gain = *nepeš*). After an introductory re-iteration of three traditional maxims over property, he deals with case # 1 in 5:13–17 and case # 2 in 6:1–6. In between has been inserted the teaching about the presence of well-being (see p. 149) whose first part (5:18) corresponds to case # 1 and the second part (5:19–20) to case # 2. In 6:7–9 the point is sum-marized: a person should live without greed for gain (*nepeš*). In this light 6:8b has a message for the sage (the *mah* "what" in v. 8b repeats the *mah* in v. 8a). The negative answer expected from Koheleth in such questions as 6:8a makes possible the following translation: "So what advantage does a wise man have over a foolish one, which the poor man does not have who knows how to live (correctly) in life?" The reference to *nepeš* (= "greed, desire" in 6:7–9) makes it impossible to understand the meaning "throat" for *nepeš* in 6:2 (that is, the description of an affliction of the neck; cf. K. Galling, *Der Prediger* [HAT; Tübingen: Mohr/Siebeck, 1969] 103). One notices especially the formulation at 6:3 (cf. also 5:10).

10 Read *hārāʿ* "the (most) evil."

11 2:14–15; 3:19; 9:2–3.

12 Cf. Ruth 2:3; 1 Sam. 20:26. Naturally, the verb, with its meaning of "occur, happen to someone," does not exclude a connection between the experience and the conduct of someone, but the meaning which comes to the fore is that of meeting something "accidentally" which is unexplainable at first sight because unexpected.

13 Typical is the formulation of 29:14. On the popularity of the sage in Egyptian wisdom literature, cf. Gese, *Lehre und Wirklichkeit*, 15, 22, 25, 36.

14 At least, 3:17 and 8:11 seem to me not to be glosses. In 8:12–13 "good" (*ṭôb*) can relate to a subjective personal situation, outwardly unconfirmed but determined by "fear" (*yārēʾ*), a word so conspicuously repeated. Perhaps the phrase, "he extends his days like a shadow" (*yaʾărîk yāmîm kaṣṣēl*), a spiritualized picture of the impious person who is heading for darkness, has been inserted at a later time under influence of v. 12 (because of syntax!). A secondary interpolation of "and not" (*wēlōʾ*) before this phrase is understand-able. The acceptance of the doctrine of retribution as a fundamental rule of life, independent of whatever should happen later, is thoroughly believeable to Koheleth (11:9).

15 G. Fecht, *Der Habgierige und die Maat in der Lehre des Ptahhotep* (maxims 5 and 19), has recently shown that already in Ptahhotep the opinion of judgment after death was inserted into the allusions (pp. 90–93) which thus would have existed from Merikare on (pp. 312–15).

16 Cf. Pss. 49; 73; Dan. 12, especially v. 3.

17 12:7b stands in contradiction to 3:21. If the formulation also refers to Gen. 3:19, this concept (which contains a return of the individual spirit to God) certainly could not be presupposed in Gen. 3:19. Thus, 12:7 is to be judged secondary along with 12:6. The allegory on old age in 12:2–5 is the highly poetic execution of 12:1b and reaches its resolution in 12:5b. A further use of the metaphor would be superfluous; therefore, it follows that the non-allegorical imagery in v. 6 is anti-climactic after the artistic allegory of vv. 3–5a.

18 In 9:6 he also turns against the view of the older wisdom that posthumous reputation is essentially united with the dead. Cf. 1:11; 2:16; 9:5.

19 Pss. 22:9–10; 71:6; 143:5. The motif is changed to its opposite in the spiritualizing Psalm 51 (v. 5), which indeed shows other formal differences (lack of the lament with acknowledgement of sin in its place, corresponding to a request for forgiveness without a request for removal of a tangible danger; repudiation of sacrifice and the offer of oneself as a sacrifice in the section pertaining to the vow).

20 Isa. 44:2, 24; 46:3.

21 The climax of v. 14b intends to say that the usurper was delivered helpless to him so that he could easily have been controlled. On the other hand, v. 14a expresses only the social difference between captive and king and thus not that the future usurper was the king's own prisoner (which would make the example incredible).

22 The fact that these passages stand out from the other units of the book is due to the composition: After the heading in 1:1 and the basic thesis in 1:2 (= 12:8 at the end of the book), 1:3–11 introduces the first part of the introduction, found in 1:12—2:11. It is in this introduction that the basic thesis is brought to bear on works (1:12–15) and wisdom (1:16–18) in which cryptic but clear traditional wisdom statements (1:15, 18) sometimes stand in place of a foundation (cf., Galling, *Prediger*, 88), while on the practical side a necessarily detailed autobiographical representation of the best life possible in general undergirds the basic thesis in 2:1–11. The second part of the introduction (2:12–26) establishes the correctness of the fundamental thesis for wisdom (2:12–17) and works (2:18–23) in an order now reversed. The ethical summary statement of the presence of divine favor (*Heilspräsenz*) is joined to 2:12–23 which closes the second part of the introduction. Beginning at 3:16 Koheleth turns his attention to the individual statements, and a systematic order is hard to prove. Therefore, 3:1–15 represents the beginning of the body of Koheleth. Furthermore, the meaning of 3:1–15 comes from the fact that this passage is repeatedly referred to: 3:17; 8:5–6, 9; 9:11–12.

23 The word *yāgaʿe* should not be translated as "weary" (so Galling, *Prediger*, 85) since the sun, wind, and rivers are never weary in their circular movement and cannot be "all things" (*kol-haddēbārîm*). All the things in question occur in a cyclical movement, so which are not included? In late Hebrew *ygʿ* has practically excluded the meaning of "weary oneself, take pains, work hard." Thus, 1:8 was originally not a riddle; the three human activities do not appear to be unconnected to the three "elements" (speech corresponding to rivers; sight to sun; hearing to wind). That human speech is not meant by "all things" (*kol-haddēbārîm*, 1:8aα; as, for example, by H. W.

Hertzberg, *Der Prediger* [KAT 17.4; Gütersloh: Mohn, 1963] 72; and W. Zimmerli, *Prediger* [ATD 16; Göttingen: Vandenhoeck & Ruprecht, 1962] 148) is suggested by two things: (a) formally, from the similar division in the beginning, v 8aβ-v 8bα-v 8bβ in comparison with v. 5-v 6-v 7); (b) stylistically, from the predicate *yĕgēʿîm*, highly poetic in a case such as this where one would have expected it in a climactic position at the end. Verse 8aα is well suited to be a culmination of, and a generalization against, vv. 5–7; it is also an introduction to v. 8aβb (a person sets up no exceptions!).

24 On subordination in early wisdom, see Gese, *Lehre und Wirklichkeit*, 15–17, 35–36, 75.

25 Note the pleonasm; cf. note 14 above.

26 Cf. the word play, *rĕʾēh-rāʿâ*.

27 Already, 2:1–11 should have guarded against this view.

Bibliography

Bailey, L. R., Sr. *Biblical Perspectives on Death*. OBT. Philadelphia: Fortress Press, 1979.

Balla, E. "Das Problem des Leides in der israelitisch-jüdischen Religion." In *Eucharistērion, Hermann Gunkel zum 60. Geburtstage*, Part 1., ed. Hans Schmidt, 214–60. Göttingen: Vandenhoeck & Ruprecht, 1923.

Barta, W. "Das Gespräch des Ipuwer mit dem Schöpfergott." *SÄK* 1 (1974) 19–23.

Becker, E. *The Denial of Death*. New York: Free Press, 1973.

Berger, P. L. *The Sacred Canopy*, 53–80. Garden City, N.Y.: Doubleday & Co., 1969.

Blank, S. H. "The Confessions of Jeremiah and the Meaning of Prayer." *HUCA* 21 (1949) 331–54.

Bloch, E. *Atheism in Christianity*. New York: Herder and Herder, 1972.

Bowker, J. *Problems of Suffering in Religions of the World*. New York and Cambridge: Cambridge University Press, 1970.

Buber, M. *The Eclipse of God: Studies in the Relation Between Religion and Philosophy*. New York: Harper & Row, Torchbooks, 1952.

Buccellati, G. "Tre saggi sulla sapienza mesopotamica," *Oriens Antiquus* 11 (1972) 161–78.

Crenshaw, J. L. *Old Testament Wisdom*. Atlanta: John Knox Press, 1981.

—"The Shadow of Death in Ecclesiastes." In *Israelite Wisdom: Theological and Literary Essays in Honor of Samuel Terrien*, ed. J. G. Gammie et al., 205–16. Missoula, Mont.: Scholars Press, 1978.

—"In Search of Divine Presence: Some Remarks Preliminary to a Theology of Wisdom." *RevExp* 74 (1977) 353–69.

—"The Human Dilemma and Literature of Dissent." In *Tradition and Theology in the Old Testament*, ed. D. A. Knight, 235–58. Philadelphia: Fortress Press, 1977.

—"Prolegomenon." In *Studies in Ancient Israelite Wisdom*, 1–45. New York: KTAV, 1976.

—"Popular Questioning of the Justice of God in Ancient Israel," *ZAW* 82 (1970) 380–95 [= *Studies in Ancient Israelite Wisdom*, 289–304. New York: KTAV, 1976].

—*Hymnic Affirmation of Divine Justice*. SBLDS 24. Missoula, Mont.: Scholars Press, 1975.

—S. V. "Theodicy." IDB Sup.

—*Prophetic Conflict.* BZAW 124. Berlin & New York: Walter de Gruyter, 1971.

—and S. Sandmel, ed. *The Divine Helmsman: Studies on God's Control of Human Events, Presented to Lou H. Silberman.* New York: KTAV, 1980.

—*A Whirlpool of Torment: The Oppressive Presence of God in Ancient Israel.* OBT. Philadelphia: Fortress (forthcoming).

Crook, M. B. *The Cruel God.* Boston: Beacon Press, 1959.

Curatorium of C. G. Jung Institute, ed. *Evil.* Evanston Ill.: Northwestern University Press, 1967.

Davis, S. T., ed. *Encountering Evil: Live Options in Theodicy.* Atlanta: John Knox Press, 1981.

Dickerson, G. F., ed., *Theodicy, Suffering, Good and Evil.* ATLA Religion Index. Chicago: ATLA, 1981.

Eichrodt, W. *Theology of the Old Testament*, II: 167–85. OTL. Philadelphia: Westminster Press; London: SCM Press, 1967.

Fohrer, G. *Das Buch Hiob.* KAT 16. Gütersloh: Gerd Mohn, 1963.

Fretheim, T. E. "Jonah and Theodicy." *ZAW* 90 (1978) 227–37.

Frost, S. B. "The Death of Josiah: A Conspiracy of Silence." *JBL* 87 (1968) 369–82.

Gerstenberger, E., and W. Schrage. *Leiden.* Stuttgart: Kohlhammer, 1977; ET: *Suffering.* Nashville: Abingdon Press, 1980.

Gese, H. *Zur biblischen Theologie: Alttestamentliche Vorträge*, 31–54. Münich: Chr. Kaiser, 1977; ET: *Essays on Biblical Theology*, 34–59. Minneapolis: Augsburg Pub. House, 1981.

Gilbert, M. *La critique des dieux dans le Livre de la Sagesse (Sg 13–15).* AnBib 53. Rome: Biblical Institute Press, 1973.

Gladson, J. A. "Retributive Paradoxes in Proverbs 10–29." Ph.D. diss., Vanderbilt University, 1978.

Glatzer, N., ed., *The Dimensions of Job*, 194–224. New York: Schocken Books, 1969.

Gordis, R. "A Cruel God or None – Is There No Other Choice?," *Judaism* 21 (1972) 277–84.

—*The Book of God and Man.* Chicago: University of Chicago Press, 1965.

Gowan, D. E. *The Triumph of Faith in Habakkuk.* Atlanta: John Knox Press, 1976.

Harrelson, W. "Ezra Among the Wicked in 2 Esdras 3—10." In *The Divine Helmsman: Studies on God's Control of Human Events, Presented to Lou H. Silberman*, ed. J. L. Crenshaw and S. Sandmel, 21–40. New York: KTAV, 1980.

Hempel, J. "Das theologische Problem des Hiob." In *Apoxysmata*, 114–73. BZAW 81. Berlin: Töpelmann, 1961.

Herrmann, S. "Die Auseinandersetzung mit dem Schöpfergott." In *Fragen an die altägyptische Literatur*, ed. J. Assmann, 257–73. Wiesbaden: Harrassowitz, 1977.

Heschel, A. *Man is not Alone*. New York: Harper & Row, 1951.

—*The Prophets*. New York: Harper & Row, 1962.

Hick, J. *Evil and the God of Love*. London and Toronto: Macmillan, 1966.

Jäger, A. "Theodizee und Anthropodizee bei Karl Marx." *SchTU* 37 (1967) 14–23.

Jung, C. G. *Answer to Job*. Cleveland & New York: World Pub. Co., 1960.

Koch, K., ed. *Um das Prinzip der Vergeltung in Religion und Recht des Alten Testaments*. WdF 125. Darmstadt: Wissenschaftliche Buchgesellschaft, 1972.

Kraeling, E. G. "A Theodicy—and More." In *The Dimensions of Job*, ed. N. Glatzer, 205–14. New York: Schocken Books, 1969.

Küscheke, A. "Altbabylonische Texte zum Thema 'Der leidende Gerechte.'" *TLZ* 81 (1956) 69–76.

Kushner, H. S. *When Bad Things Happen to Good People*. New York: Schocken Books, 1981.

Labuschagne, C. J. *The Incomparability of Yahweh in the Old Testament*. Leiden: Brill, 1966.

Lambert, W. G. *Babylonian Wisdom Literature*. Oxford: Clarendon Press, 1960.

Lamm, Norman, *Faith and Doubt: Studies in Traditional Jewish Thought*. New York: KTAV, 1971.

Levêque, J. "Le Thème du juste souffrant dans la littérature assyrobabylonienne." In *Job et son Dieu*, 1:13–36 Paris: Gabalda, 1970.

Mack, B. L. *Logos und Sophia: Untersuchungen zur Weisheitstheologie im hellenistischen Judentum*. SUNT 10. Göttingen: Vandenhoeck & Ruprecht, 1973.

—"Wisdom Myth and Mytho-logy: An Essay in Understanding a Theological Tradition." *Int* 24 (1970) 46–60.

Martin-Achard, R. *From Death to Life: A Study of the Development of the Doctrine of the Resurrection in the Old Testament*. Edinburgh & London: Oliver & Boyd, 1960.

Miller, P. D., Jr. *Sin and Judgment in the Prophets*. SBLMS 27. Chico, Calif.: Scholars Press, 1982.

Miskotte, K. H. *When the Gods are Silent*. New York: Harper & Row, 1967.

Müller, D. "Der gute Hirte: Ein Beitrag zur Geschichte ägyptischer Bildrede." *ZÄS* 94 (1967) 126–44.

Murphy, R. E. "Biblical Insights into Suffering: Pathos and Compassion." In *Whither Creativity, Freedom, Suffering?: Humanity, Cosmos, God*, ed.

F. A. Eigo, 53–75. Proceedings of the Theology Institute of Villanova University 13. Villanova, Pa.: The University Press, 1981.

Nougayrol, J. "Le version ancienne de 'juste souffrant'." *RB* 59 (1952) 239–50.

Otto, E. "Der Vorwurf an Gott (Zur Entstehung der ägyptischen Auseinandersetzungsliteratur)." In *Vorträge der Orientalistischen Tagung in Marburg: Fachgruppe Ägyptologie, 1950*, 1–15. Marburg: Universitäts-Verlag, 1951.

Paulus, J. "Le thème du Juste Souffrant dans la pensée grecque et hébraique." *RHR* 121–122 (1940) 18–66.

Peake, A. S. *The Problem of Suffering in the Old Testament.* London: Robert Bryant & C. H. Kelly, 1904.

Perdue, L. G. *Wisdom and Cult.* SBLDS 30. Missoula, Mont.: Scholars Press, 1977.

Pope, M. H. *Job.* Anchor Bible. Garden City, N.J.: Doubleday & Co., 1973.

Porter, F. C. "The Yeser Hara: A Study in the Jewish Doctrine of Sin." In *Biblical and Semitic Studies*, 93–156. New York: Charles Scribner's Sons, 1901.

Prato, G. L. *Il problema della teodicea in Ben Sira.* AnBib 65. Rome: Pontifical Institute Press, 1975.

Procksch, O. "Die Theodizee im Buch Hiob." In *Allg. evg. luth. Kirchenzeitung* 58 (1925) 722–24, 734–42, 763–65.

Rad, G. von., *Wisdom in Israel.* Nashville: Abingdon Press; London: SCM Press, 1972.

Raitt, T. M. *A Theology of Exile*, 83–105. Philadelphia: Fortress Press, 1977.

Rankin, O. S. *Israel's Wisdom Literature: Its Bearing on Theology and the History of Religion.* New York: Schocken Books, 1969; Edinburgh: T. & T. Clark, 1936.

Raphael, D. D. "Tragedy and Religion." In *Twentieth Century Interpretations of the Book of Job*, ed. P. S. Sanders, 46–55. Englewood Cliffs, N.J.: Prentice Hall, 1968.

Ricoeur, P. *The Symbolism of Evil.* Boston: Beacon Press, 1969.

Ruppert, L. *Der leidende Gerechte.* FzB 5. Würzburg: Echter, 1972.

Sanders, J. A. *Suffering as Divine Discipline in the Old Testament and Post-Biblical Judaism.* Rochester, N.Y.: Colgate Rochester Divinity School, 1955.

Sanders, P. S. *Twentieth Century Interpretations of the Book of Job.* Englewood Cliffs, N.J.: Prentice Hall, 1968.

Sandmel, S. "Some Comments on Providence in Philo." In *The Divine Helmsman*, ed. J. L. Crenshaw and S. Sandmel, 79–85. New York: KTAV, 1980.

Schmid, H. H. *Wesen und Geschichte der Weisheit*. BZAW 101. Berlin: Töpelmann, 1966.

Schmidt, L. *"De Deo."* BZAW 143. Berlin & New York: Walter de Gruyter, 1976.

Simian-Yofre, H. "La teodicea del Deuteroisaias." *Bib* 62 (1981) 55–72.

Soden, W. von. "Die Frage nach der Gerechtigkeit Gottes im Alten Orient." *MDOG* 96 (1965) 41–59.

Stamm, J. J. *Das Leiden des Unschuldigen in Babylon und Israel*. ATANT 10. Zurich: Zwingli Verlag, 1946.

—"Die Theodizee in Babylon und Israel." *JEOL* 9 (1944) 99–107.

Terrien, S. *The Elusive Presence: Toward a New Biblical Theology*. New York: Harper & Row, 1978.

Thompson, A. L. *Responsibiltiy for Evil in the Theodicy of IV Ezra*. SBLDS 29. Missoula, Mont.: Scholars Press, 1977.

Towner, W. S. *How God Deals with Evil*. Philadelphia: Westminster Press, 1976.

Tsevat, M. *The Meaning of the Book of Job and Other Biblical Studies*. New York: KTAV, 1980.

Urbach, E. E. *The Sages*, 255–85. Jerusalem: Magnes Press, 1975.

Weber, M. *Ancient Judaism*, 297–335. New York: Free Press, 1952.

Weiser, A. "Das Problem der sittlichen Weltordnung im Buche Hiob." In *Glaube und Geschichte im Alten Testament*, 9–19. Göttingen: Vandenhoeck & Ruprecht, 1961.

Würthwein, E. "Gott und Mensch in Dialog und Gottesreden des Buches Hiob." In *Wort und Existenz: Studien zum Alten Testament*, 217–92. Göttingen: Vandenhoeck & Ruprecht, 1970.

Zhitlowsky, C. "Job and Faust." *Two Studies in Yiddish Culture*, ET and ed. Percy Matenko, 90–162. Leiden: Brill, 1968.

Index of Ancient Sources

OLD TESTAMENT

159

APOCRYPHAL AND OTHER WRITINGS

NEW TESTAMENT

Enfant volée

Marsha Forchuk Skrypuch

Texte français de Martine Faubert

Éditions
SCHOLASTIC

Catalogage avant publication de Bibliothèque et Archives Canada

Skrypuch, Marsha Forchuk, 1954-
[Stolen child. Français]
Enfant volée / Marsha Forchuk Skrypuch ;
texte français de Martine Faubert.

Traduction de: Stolen child.
Pour les 9-12 ans.

ISBN 978-1-4431-0391-6

1. Guerre mondiale, 1939-1945–Enfants–Pologne–Romans, nouvelles, etc.
pour la jeunesse. 2. Lebensborn e.V. (Allemagne)–Romans, nouvelles, etc.
pour la jeunesse. I. Faubert, Martine II. Titre.
III. Titre: Stolen child. Français.

PS8587.K79S814 2010   jC813'.54   C2010-903209-8

Photo de la page couverture : gracieuseté de Lauren Shear

Édition publiée par les Éditions Scholastic,
604, rue King Ouest, Toronto (Ontario) M5V 1E1.

7 6 5 4 3   Imprimé au Canada   140   18 19 20 21 22

À la mémoire de Lidia

Table des matières

Chapitre un

1950 – L'arrivée au Canada

La femme qui disait être ma mère était si malade sur le bateau que nous avions pris pour quitter l'Europe qu'elle avait presque tout le temps un sac à vomir accroché autour du cou. Celui que j'appelais mon père avait fait la traversée un an auparavant. Il avait travaillé un peu partout au Canada, à la recherche d'un endroit où nous pourrions nous établir. Il nous avait finalement écrit qu'il avait décidé de s'installer à Brantford, en Ontario, à cause de ses arbres et de ses deux églises ukrainiennes. Et aussi parce qu'il y avait trouvé du travail dans une fonderie. Autrement dit, il y aurait aussi de la nourriture sur la table.

À cause du mal de mer, Marusia avait fait presque toute la traversée à l'intérieur du bateau. Comme je n'aimais pas me sentir enfermée, je la laissais dormir en paix. J'étais très souvent livrée à moi-même, et je ne m'en plaignais pas. Je me dépêchais de monter sur le plus haut pont et je me penchais par-dessus le bastingage pour regarder les remous que faisait le bateau dans l'eau, tout en bas. Un jour, j'ai grimpé sur le bastingage et je me suis assise sur la rampe, en laissant mes jambes se balancer dans le vide et en respirant l'air pur à pleins poumons. J'étais là depuis moins d'une minute quand un matelot m'a attrapée par la taille et m'a déposée sur le pont. Il criait dans une langue qui n'était ni de l'ukrainien ni du yiddish ni de l'allemand ni du russe. Ce n'était pas de l'anglais non plus. Je suppose qu'il me disait que j'étais folle de faire cela. Pourtant, je ne me sentais pas l'esprit dérangé. Enfin, je me retrouvais seule, face à un espace infini et, pendant un bref instant, je m'étais sentie totalement libre.

Quand le bateau a accosté dans le port d'Halifax, j'ai descendu la passerelle avec Marusia. J'étais si habituée aux mouvements du bateau en mer que, quand j'ai posé le pied sur le sol canadien, j'ai cru que ça tanguait encore. J'ai dû m'accrocher à un poteau pour ne pas tomber par terre. Marusia aussi marchait d'un pas mal assuré. Comme elle transportait notre valise, elle ne pouvait pas attraper le poteau. J'ai donc saisi sa main libre et je l'ai aidée à retrouver son équilibre; puis nous avons fait la queue au bout de l'immense file que formaient les immigrants.

En tête se tenait un agent en uniforme, qui interrogeait individuellement chaque nouvel arrivant. J'en étais muette de peur. Qu'allait-il me demander? Que devrais-je répondre?

Marusia m'a serré la main afin de me rassurer et

m'a dit :

— N'oublie pas de m'appeler Mama.

Notre tour venu, l'agent a examiné nos papiers, puis s'est accroupi de façon à avoir le visage à la hauteur de mes yeux. Il avait les traits comme taillés au couteau, mais l'air gentil, même si j'étais terrifiée par son uniforme. Il m'a alors dit en ukrainien :

— Bienvenue au Canada, Nadia. Es-tu contente d'être ici?

Comme je n'aime pas mentir, je ne lui ai rien répondu, me contentant de le fixer à travers mes larmes. J'étais contente d'être enfin sortie de cet affreux camp de personnes déplacées où nous étions restés pendant cinq ans. D'une certaine façon, j'étais contente d'être au Canada parce que c'était très loin de mon ancienne vie. Toutefois, certaines choses de cette époque me manquaient terriblement.

L'agent d'immigration a tiré sur une de mes tresses, puis s'est relevé. Je l'ai écouté poser des questions à Marusia : Où vivions-nous avant la guerre? Que faisions-nous durant la guerre? J'étais toujours surprise de voir avec quelle aisance Marusia pouvait mentir.

L'agent a demandé les billets de train que nous avaient fournis les représentants des Nations unies. Marusia les lui a tendus, sans vouloir les lâcher, mais il les a pris quand même et les a soigneusement examinés. Une fois satisfait, il a estampillé nos papiers, puis nous les a rendus avec les billets. Marusia les a repliés en tremblant et les a vite glissés sous son corsage bien repassé, puis dans son soutien-gorge. L'agent lui a remis un billet de banque.

— Voici cinq dollars canadiens pour acheter à manger, a-t-il dit.

Le port était bondé de gens comme nous, devenus sans patrie pendant la guerre. Les petits marchands se faisaient concurrence, criant à tue-tête :

— Lait!

— Pommes!

— Pain!

Marusia s'était débrouillée pour apprendre un peu d'anglais au camp des personnes déplacées, et moi aussi. Nous arrivions donc à comprendre quelques mots.

Marusia voulait des sandwichs à la viande et une bouteille de lait, mais elle ne connaissait pas le mot sandwich. Quand elle a finalement réussi à se faire comprendre d'un marchand, il lui demandait trop cher. Il nous fallait ménager le peu d'argent que nous avions. J'avais faim et soif, et je mourais de chaleur. Mais au moins, nous étions en sécurité.

— Je crois que c'est un magasin d'alimentation, ai-je dit en montrant du doigt une vitrine décorée d'une pyramide de boîtes de conserve.

La porte du magasin s'est ouverte et un client est sorti en tenant ce qui semblait être une miche de pain.

— Entrons voir, a dit Marusia en me poussant vers le magasin.

Nous avons ouvert la porte et sommes entrées; il

faisait encore plus chaud dedans que dehors. Un homme chauve au visage rougeaud et au ventre rebondi nous a souri.

— Manger…? a dit Marusia en lui montrant le billet de cinq dollars.

— Il ne me reste pas grand-chose, a répliqué le marchand en gesticulant pour nous aider à comprendre.

Nous avons regardé autour de nous. Il avait raison. Les étiquettes des boîtes de conserve de la vitrine montraient différentes sortes de légumes. Il y avait des poches de farine et de riz, mais ni petits pains, ni fromages, ni saucisses, ni rien d'autre qui aurait pu se manger sans préparation.

— Pain? a demandé Marusia.

Le marchand a secoué la tête, l'air désolé.

Nous allions partir quand soudain il nous a souri. De son doigt, il nous a fait signe de le suivre au fond du magasin. Là, il a ouvert une espèce de grand coffre, et une grosse bouffée d'air très froid nous a enveloppées. Il en a sorti un truc qui ressemblait à une grosse brique de carton blanc.

— Crème glacée, a-t-il dit avec un sourire.

— Crème lacée? Comme des chaussures? a dit Marusia, l'air perplexe.

— Non! Non! a répondu le marchand.

J'étais aussi perplexe que Marusia. Qu'est-ce que des lacets avaient à voir avec du pain?

Le marchand a pris la brique de carton et l'a

déposée sur le comptoir à l'avant du magasin, puis il s'est mis à fouiller dans une boîte sous la caisse enregistreuse. Il fronçait les sourcils. Ensuite, en nous souriant, il nous a tendu deux petites cuillères de bois.

— Je vous montre, a-t-il dit en retirant la feuille de papier qui recouvrait la brique.

Un parfum de vanille est venu nous chatouiller les narines.

— Crème… glacée… a-t-il dit.

Puis il a pris une des petites cuillères et en a raclé la surface de la brique gelée. Une boule s'est formée. Il l'a soulevée avec la petite cuillère et me l'a tendue :

— Goûte!

J'ai serré les lèvres.

— Je vais y goûter, a dit Marusia, hésitante.

L'homme a approché la cuillère de bois de la bouche grande ouverte de Marusia et a laissé tomber la boule de glace sur sa langue, comme une maman oiseau qui donne la becquée à son petit. Marusia a écarquillé les yeux de surprise. J'étais bien contente de ne pas avoir été la première à essayer. Puis elle a souri et s'est exclamée :

— Bon! Bon!

Elle en a pris avec l'autre cuillère et me l'a offerte. J'y ai goûté du bout de la langue, et j'ai pensé à une boule de neige. Puis j'ai pris toute la cuillerée dans ma bouche et j'ai eu un frisson en savourant ce délice froid, sucré et onctueux. Ce n'était pas seulement le goût délicieux, mais aussi la sensation du froid par cette lourde journée d'été. C'était divin!

— Cinq dollars, a dit le marchand.

Marusia a blêmi. Cinq dollars pour cet aliment inconnu? Elle a fait signe que non de la tête.

— C'est mangé, c'est vendu, a-t-il dit, imperturbable.

Marusia lui a tendu à regret notre billet de cinq dollars.

— Mais c'est tout ce que nous avons! s'est-elle écriée.

Le marchand le lui a arraché des mains.

— Je vous en prie, a-t-elle dit, les larmes aux yeux.

Le marchand nous a regardées et a eu l'air de nous prendre en pitié. Il a plongé la main dans sa caisse et en a ressorti un billet d'un dollar. Marusia l'a pris.

Nous sommes sorties du magasin. Marusia pressait contre elle notre précieuse crème glacée. Nous étions rendues à peine quelques portes plus loin quand elle a crié :

— Oh non! Regarde!

Son corsage était couvert d'un liquide visqueux et blanchâtre.

— Tiens, m'a-t-elle dit en me mettant le carton dans les mains.

Elle a glissé sa main entre deux boutons de son corsage, puis dans son soutien-gorge, et en a ressorti nos précieux documents d'immigration et billets de train. Le coin d'un des formulaires était mouillé, et une partie du tampon officiel était devenu illisible.

Les billets de train étaient humides, mais pas endommagés. Elle les a secoués en l'air pour les faire sécher tandis que je regardais nos quatre dollars de crème glacée fondre au soleil. Alors, elle a soigneusement replié les documents et les billets, puis les a glissés sous la ceinture de sa jupe.

— Allons nous asseoir, a-t-elle dit en me prenant par le coude pour m'emmener jusqu'à un banc public.

Nous nous sommes assises et elle m'a aussitôt tendu une petite cuillère de bois. Nous avons englouti notre crème glacée à toute vitesse. Nous avions les mains et le visage tout collants, mais cela ne me dérangeait pas. Je n'avais rien mangé d'aussi bon depuis des siècles. Nous nous sommes lavées à une fontaine publique. Le corsage de Marusia n'avait plus tout à fait l'air fraîchement repassé.

Je ne me rappelle plus très bien tous les détails des jours qui ont suivi. Mais nous avons trouvé comment nous rendre à la gare. Je savais que nous roulions vers l'ouest, et je me rappelle que nous avons changé de train à Québec. Puis nous nous sommes arrêtées à Montréal, assez longtemps pour chercher un magasin d'alimentation. Il ne nous restait qu'un dollar. La crème glacée avait été un délice, mais elle nous avait coûté très cher!

Une immigrante qui voyageait avec nous dans le train nous a suggéré d'acheter du pain Wonder.

— Ce n'est pas cher du tout, nous a-t-elle dit. Avec votre dollar, vous pourrez en acheter trois.

Nous sommes donc entrées dans une épicerie et nous avons demandé à la caissière, qui avait du rouge à lèvres rouge, où se trouvait le pain Wonder.

— Au bout de cette rangée, a-t-elle répondu d'une voix blasée, en montrant l'endroit de son grand ongle peint en rouge.

Il y avait toute une tablette remplie de miches de pain blanc moelleuses, emballées dans du papier ciré en couleurs. Marusia en a pris deux. Nous n'avons pas osé acheter à boire et, de toute façon, il y avait une fontaine publique dehors. La caissière nous a rendu quelques pièces de monnaie.

Une fois revenues dans le train, Marusia a ouvert un des emballages de pain et en a retiré quelques tranches. C'était du pain parfaitement blanc, avec une croûte dorée plutôt mince. J'ai appuyé une tranche contre mon nez pour le sentir : ça ne sentait rien! J'en ai pris une bouchée : ça n'avait aucun goût! J'ai regardé Marusia : elle mastiquait lentement, l'air éberluée.

— Je me demande pourquoi ça s'appelle du pain, a-t-elle dit, profondément déçue.

J'avais envie de pleurer. Est-ce que c'était tout ce qu'on pouvait trouver comme pain au Canada?

Marusia m'a tapoté la main.

— Je vais en faire moi-même, du vrai, quand nous serons arrivées dans notre nouvelle maison, m'a-t-elle dit.

Puis, avec le bercement du train et ma faim un peu

calmée par le pain Wonder, j'ai glissé dans le sommeil en rêvant à du vrai pain.

Nous avons traversé Ottawa à petite vitesse, puis nous avons changé de train à Toronto. J'étais impressionnée par la débrouillardise de Marusia : à chaque arrêt, elle montrait nos billets au contrôleur afin de s'assurer que nous étions dans le bon train. Nous voyagions dans des wagons fermés, avec des fauteuils confortables et de grandes fenêtres : rien à voir avec les wagons plats, en Allemagne! Par la fenêtre, je regardais les villes que nous traversions, surprise de ne pas apercevoir des immeubles bombardés ou des quartiers complètement incendiés. La guerre n'avait-elle pas traversé l'océan? Ce n'était donc pas une guerre mondiale, finalement.

À l'approche de Brantford, nous avions terminé nos deux miches de pain Wonder, et j'en avais assez de cette substance. À l'entrée en gare, j'ai aperçu Ivan (je suis censée l'appeler papa) qui nous attendait dehors. Il avait le visage fraîchement rasé, et ses cheveux encore mouillés étaient bien dégagés de son front. Il avait les deux mains enfouies dans les poches d'un vieux pantalon gris soigneusement repassé.

Quand nous sommes descendues du train, il nous a fait un grand sourire. Nous avions fait à peine quelques pas dans sa direction quand il a serré Marusia dans ses bras et lui a donné un gros baiser, devant tout le monde!

Je faisais semblant de ne pas les connaître, mais il

m'a soulevée dans ses bras et m'a serrée très fort. J'ai tenté de me dégager en le repoussant de mes deux mains, mais il me tenait trop fort.

— Tu es maintenant en sécurité, Nadia, m'a-t-il chuchoté à l'oreille. Avec nous, jamais plus personne ne te fera du mal.

Plutôt que de lui entourer le cou de mes bras, je les ai laissés pendre mollement. Je ne voulais pas d'une autre démonstration d'affection en public.

Ivan a soulevé la vieille valise toute cabossée de Marusia et l'a déposée dans le coffre de sa grosse voiture noire. Je n'avais pas de bagage : il y avait assez de place pour mes quelques vêtements dans la valise de Marusia. Nous sommes montés dans la voiture, comme si nous avions été une vraie famille. Je n'étais pas montée dans une auto depuis très longtemps. Je me suis bien calée sur la banquette arrière, me laissant envelopper par l'odeur du cuir et de l'essence…

Une grosse voiture noire conduite par un militaire en uniforme…

— Nadia, ouvre un peu la fenêtre pour te rafraîchir, a dit Marusia qui était assise à l'avant.

Puis, elle s'est retournée vers Ivan et lui a demandé :

— Est-ce que tu as acheté cette auto, Ivashko?

— Non, a-t-il répondu. C'est celle de mon patron. Il me l'a prêtée pour la journée, en l'honneur de votre arrivée dans notre nouvelle maison.

Plissant les yeux de plaisir, Marusia a caressé la joue de son mari du revers de la main.

— Quelle délicate attention! a-t-elle dit. Ça me rappelle le jour de notre mariage.

Moi aussi, je m'en souvenais. C'était quand nous vivions au camp des personnes déplacées. La cérémonie n'avait pas eu lieu dans le camp même, mais dans une église autrichienne située à proximité. Le prêtre autrichien avait laissé un prêtre ukrainien de notre camp bénir leur union. Ensuite nous étions rentrés tous ensemble en taxi. La voiture était petite et vieille, avec le cuir des sièges tout craquelé.

Je m'attendais à faire un long trajet, mais au bout de quelques minutes, Ivan a tourné dans une rue bordée de vieilles maisons de briques avec, ici et là, de petites maisons de bois. Il a garé la voiture devant l'une d'elles, qui avait l'air récente.

— Tu as acheté une maison, Ivashko? lui a demandé Marusia, tout étonnée.

— J'ai acheté un bout de terrain, Marusia, a-t-il répondu. Et je construis la maison.

Marusia et Ivan sont descendus de voiture. Je suis restée assise à l'arrière. Que m'arrivait-il? Depuis le début, j'avais hâte que ce voyage s'achève. Je voulais être chez moi. Mais étais-je vraiment arrivée chez moi?

Ivan a ouvert la portière arrière de la voiture et m'a tendu la main.

— Nadia, je t'ai installé une balançoire dans la cour, a-t-il dit.

À 12 ans, on est trop grande pour les balançoires, je

le sais bien. Je lui ai quand même souri. C'est l'intention qui compte, et Ivan faisait tout ce qu'il pouvait pour moi. Je suis descendue de voiture. Ivan a retiré la valise de Marusia du coffre, et nous avons marché tous les trois jusqu'à la porte d'entrée.

Ivan a ouvert la porte, a déposé la valise à l'intérieur, puis s'est retourné vers Marusia en lui faisant un grand sourire. Il l'a prise dans ses bras comme une enfant et lui a fait passer le seuil de la porte.

— Qu'est-ce qui te prend? a-t-elle crié. Dépose-moi par terre!

— C'est une coutume canadienne, a expliqué Ivan. C'est censé porter chance.

Il l'a déposée par terre à l'intérieur, et je les ai suivis, soulagée qu'il ne m'ait pas fait passer le seuil dans ses bras.

De dehors, la maison avait l'air finie, mais dedans, des planches de bois (Ivan a dit que ça s'appelait des madriers) se dressaient là où il aurait dû y avoir des murs. Le plancher était de bois nu, comme dans une bonne grange. Il n'y avait pas de meubles.

— Laissez-moi le plaisir de vous faire faire le tour du propriétaire, a dit Ivan en nous prenant toutes les deux par la main, tout excité.

Marusia a fait un sourire forcé, ses yeux trahissant la gêne que je ressentais moi aussi.

— Voici le salon, a-t-il dit en nous tenant toujours par la main.

Il nous a fait passer dans un cadre de porte et a

ajouté :

— Et voici la chambre à coucher.

Une maison avec une seule chambre? Toute petite, en plus. À peine assez grande pour les deux matelas posés par terre, avec des draps et des couvertures soigneusement empilés sur chacun. S'il n'y avait qu'une seule chambre, ce devait être celle de Marusia et d'Ivan.

— Alors, où vais-je dormir? Dans le salon? ai-je demandé.

Cela ne me dérangeait pas. C'était plus grand et mieux aéré que cette petite chambre.

L'espace d'un instant, Ivan a eu l'air gêné.

— Quand la maison sera terminée, tu auras ta propre chambre dans le grenier, a-t-il répondu en montrant du doigt une trappe au plafond. Et tu pourras choisir toi-même la couleur de la peinture.

Comment allais-je faire pour respirer dans un espace si petit? Dieu merci, la construction n'était pas finie. Entre-temps, on pourrait sans doute y apporter quelques changements.

— Alors, où vais-je dormir d'ici là?

— Dans la cour, avec nous, a répondu Ivan.

Dehors, donc. Je préférais cela, et de beaucoup!

— Poursuivons notre visite, a suggéré Ivan.

Il n'y avait pas grand-chose d'autre à voir. En plus du salon et de la chambre à moitié construits, il y avait une cuisine, une salle de bain et c'est tout. La salle de bain était équipée d'un évier, d'une toilette avec chasse d'eau et d'une vieille baignoire de tôle décorée de jolies fleurs peintes sur le pourtour.

— Je l'ai récupérée à la décharge publique, a dit Ivan, tout fier de lui. Quelqu'un l'avait mise aux rebuts. Incroyable, non?

Au fond, un gros éclat dans l'émail laissait voir une entaille dans la tôle toute rouillée. Sinon, la baignoire était tout à fait utilisable. Au camp des personnes déplacées, j'aurais donné ma chemise pour avoir une baignoire comme celle-là.

—Facile à réparer, a affirmé Ivan en me voyant fixer des yeux l'éclat dans l'émail. Quand la maison sera terminée.

Il nous a fait traverser la cuisine, et nous avons admiré la cuisinière électrique à deux ronds, achetée usagée, et une glacière fraîchement repeinte en bleu pâle. Sur le couvercle de celle-ci trônaient trois assiettes ébréchées et trois tasses dépareillées. Il y avait aussi un poêlon en fonte, et un couteau, une fourchette et une cuillère pour chacun de nous. Ivan était particulièrement fier de l'énorme évier de cuisine, avec ses robinets d'eau chaude et froide.

— On peut s'en servir aussi pour la lessive, a-t-il dit. Mais attendez de voir la cour.

Ivan a lâché ma main juste le temps d'ouvrir la porte arrière. Nous avons descendu un escalier temporaire fait de blocs de béton empilés. Au milieu de la petite cour se dressait un énorme chêne. Une balançoire faite d'un siège de bois et de deux grosses cordes était suspendue à la plus grosse branche.

— Pour toi, Nadia, a dit Ivan.

J'aurais voulu ne pas être contente, mais c'était plus fort que moi.

— Merci! ai-je dit à Ivan en lui sautant au cou.

À ma grande surprise, j'étais sincère. J'ai couru jusqu'à la balançoire, pour l'examiner de près. Le siège de bois était doux comme du velours. Ivan l'avait si bien poncé qu'il était impossible que j'aie une seule écharde.

Marusia et Ivan se tenaient par la main, sur le perron de blocs de ciment.

— Essaie-la, s'est écriée Marusia.

J'adorais la caresse du vent sur mes joues tandis que je balançais mes jambes d'avant en arrière pour monter toujours plus haut. Je me sentais presque libre. Au plus haut de la course de la balançoire, je pouvais voir dans les cours des voisins. Deux cours plus loin, il y avait une autre balançoire accrochée à un arbre. Au moins un autre enfant vivait dans cette rue, et c'était très bien. Peut-être que cet endroit pourrait être vraiment chez moi.

Chapitre deux

Brantford, mon vrai chez moi?

Ce soir-là, le premier que nous passions dans notre maison, des gens sont venus nous offrir des présents. Il y avait toutes sortes de choses à manger : du bon pain de seigle, des cigares au chou et de la saucisse. Marusia a reçu des pots de betteraves marinées, de confiture de fraises, de miel, ainsi que des œufs et une poche de farine. Une dame avait apporté un rouleau de tissu bleu pâle, et Ivan a reçu une bouteille de vodka. Le prêtre m'a donné un livre de prières, et une dame anglaise avec un grain de beauté sur la joue m'a offert des crayons de couleur. Au moment où presque tout le monde s'en allait, un couple est arrivé avec un petit garçon aux cheveux bruns, qui avait l'air fâché.

— Je te présente Mychailo, m'a dit la dame en poussant le garçon vers moi. Il va à l'école Centrale.

Ses parents sont entrés et l'ont laissé avec moi dans la cour.

— Qu'est-ce que c'est, l'école Centrale? lui ai-je demandé.

— Tu vas y aller en septembre, a-t-il dit. Tu vas détester ça.

— Pourquoi?

— Ils vont se moquer de toi parce que tu n'es pas canadienne.

— Est-ce qu'ils se moquent de toi? ai-je demandé.

— Plus maintenant, a-t-il dit en montrant les poings. S'ils recommencent, je leur casse la figure.

Je me suis dit que ça ne marcherait jamais pour moi. Peut-être que Mychailo pourrait se battre à ma place si nous devenions amis.

Quand tout le monde a été parti, Ivan m'a prise par la main et m'a dit :

— J'ai une autre surprise pour toi.

Puis il m'a entraînée vers les arbustes qui servaient de clôture avec nos voisins et a ajouté :

— As-tu remarqué ce que c'est?

Les arbustes n'étaient pas en fleurs. Ils avaient l'air d'avoir été plantés récemment. Mais j'ai reconnu la forme des feuilles.

— Des lilas! me suis-je écriée.

— Je les ai plantés exprès pour toi. Ils vont fleurir au printemps prochain et, le matin, leur parfum te réveillera.

J'étais si émue que j'avais du mal à articuler en lui disant merci.

— Tu es chez toi, Nadia, m'a-t-il dit en me serrant la main doucement. Nous voulons que tu sois heureuse ici.

Nous avons sorti les matelas dehors et nous nous sommes couchés dans la cour, à la belle étoile. L'air frais me faisait du bien, et j'étais ravie d'être dans un grand espace. J'étais étonnée d'entendre des chants d'oiseaux en pleine nuit, mais Ivan m'a expliqué qu'il s'agissait des grenouilles. Il en a même trouvé une petite qu'il m'a montrée. Il y avait des grenouilles chez nous, autrefois, mais je ne me rappelais même plus quand j'en avais vu une pour la dernière fois. Le chant des grenouilles est si différent du bruit des mines, des tirs d'artillerie et des bombes! Combien de fois j'avais essayé de dormir la nuit, pendant toutes ces années de guerre, malgré ces bruits infernaux? Pendant les années au camp des personnes déplacées, nous ne subissions pas le vacarme de la guerre, mais nous étions entassés les uns sur les autres et tout ce que j'entendais, c'étaient des ronflements, des grognements et des sanglots.

Couchée là, à regarder les étoiles et à écouter le chant des grenouilles, je me suis détendue. Juste un peu. Peut-être que tout irait bien. J'ai respiré à pleins poumons l'air frais de la nuit et j'ai fermé les yeux, mais le sommeil ne venait pas. Marusia s'est retournée sur son matelas. Elle me faisait face et s'est mise à chanter une berceuse que je connaissais depuis toujours :

Kolyson'ko, kolyson'ko
Kolyshy nam dytynon'ku

A shchob spalo, ne plakalo
A shchob roslo, ne bolilo
Ni holovka, ni vse tilo

En entendant ces mots, je sentais la peur quitter mon être. J'étais apaisée par le confort du matelas, des oreillers et des couvertures, et la présence de ces deux personnes qui prenaient soin de moi maintenant.

Je me suis endormie avec le sentiment d'être aimée et en sécurité.

Je suis entourée des gens que j'aime le plus au monde, blottie sous un édredon dans une chambre confortable. Soudain, on frappe à la porte. J'essaie de réveiller les gens qui dorment à mes côtés, mais ils ont disparu. Je suis seule. Mon cœur bat à tout rompre. La porte s'ouvre brusquement, mais je n'arrive pas à voir qui est là.

Je me suis réveillée en battant l'air et en criant :

— Lâchez-moi!

Des mains fortes m'ont rassise sur le matelas. J'ai ouvert les yeux. J'étais à Brantford, chez moi, dans la cour. Marusia était assise à côté de moi. J'étais en sécurité. Malgré l'obscurité, je voyais ses sourcils froncés et je lisais son inquiétude sur son visage. Ivan était là lui aussi, agenouillé près de moi.

— As-tu fait un cauchemar? m'a demandé Marusia.

La scène m'avait semblé si réelle… mais oui, ce devait plutôt être un cauchemar. J'ai hoché la tête.

—Veux-tu nous en parler?

— Non.

Marusia s'est blottie contre moi, sur le matelas, et a chanté la berceuse tout doucement dans mon oreille. Les mots m'ont un peu réconfortée, et j'ai senti le rythme de mon cœur s'apaiser.

Je voulais dormir, mais je ne voulais plus faire de rêves. Ma respiration devenue lente et régulière a facilement convaincu Marusia que tout allait bien. Ivan et elle avaient besoin de dormir.

Marusia est retournée s'installer sur son matelas. Je suis restée éveillée, à écouter le chant des grenouilles et les ronflements d'Ivan. Quand j'ai été sûre que Marusia était profondément endormie, je me suis rassise. J'ai respiré à pleins poumons l'air frais de la nuit afin de m'éclaircir les idées. Pourquoi avais-je fait ce rêve? Qui frappait à la porte?

J'ai entouré mes genoux avec mes bras et je me suis mise à me balancer d'avant en arrière, en me consolant comme autrefois quelqu'un m'avait consolée. J'ai chanté la berceuse à mi-voix : je me sentais aimée et en sécurité. J'ai cherché à retrouver dans ma mémoire la dernière fois où je m'étais sentie totalement en sécurité. C'était avant le camp. J'avais une chambre à moi toute seule. Il y avait un plafond très haut et de grandes fenêtres. La nourriture était abondante et je ne manquais pas de vêtements. Mais est-ce que je me sentais en sécurité? Non. Qui aurait pu l'être, au beau milieu de la guerre?

Chapitre trois

Mlle MacIntosh

Après ce cauchemar, j'ai essayé de rester éveillée, mais la fatigue a probablement eu raison de moi, car j'ai fini par m'endormir. Quand j'ai ouvert les yeux le lendemain matin, j'étais trempée de rosée et j'avais mal au cou. Mais j'étais contente d'être dehors, au grand air. Je me suis assise et étirée, puis j'ai regardé l'autre matelas. Marusia dormait, mais Ivan n'était plus là.

Puis Marusia a ouvert les yeux et a répondu avant même que je ne pose de questions :

— Il est parti travailler. Et je dois me trouver un travail moi aussi.

— Qu'est-ce que je vais faire?

— L'école ne commence pas avant deux mois, a-t-elle répondu. La dame qui t'a offert les crayons de couleur s'est proposée pour t'aider à apprendre l'anglais.

Nous nous sommes assises sur les blocs de ciment et nous avons posé nos assiettes d'œufs, de jambon et de pain de seigle en équilibre sur nos genoux. Nous avons fait notre toilette à l'eau chaude dans la salle de bain, et Marusia a démêlé mes cheveux avec un peigne et a refait mes deux tresses bien serrées. Ensuite elle m'a conduite à deux maisons de chez nous, là où il y avait une balançoire dans la cour. Elle a frappé à la porte, et nous avons attendu qu'on vienne nous ouvrir.

— Bonjour Nadia, a dit la dame en anglais, lentement et en articulant bien. Je suis Mlle MacIntosh.

— Bonjour, Mlle MacIntosh, ai-je répondu du mieux que je le pouvais.

Puis elle s'est tournée vers Marusia et, à ma grande surprise, dans un très bon ukrainien, lui a dit :

— Bonjour Marusia. J'espère que vous avez bien dormi en cette première nuit dans votre maison.

Pendant qu'elles bavardaient sur le pas de la porte, j'ai passé la tête à l'intérieur pour voir, mais les rideaux étaient fermés et la pièce était plongée dans l'ombre. Un léger parfum de citron et de je ne sais quoi d'autre flottait dans l'air.

Marusia a mentionné qu'elle allait chercher du travail.

— Que faisiez-vous en Europe? a demandé Mlle MacIntosh.

— Vous voulez dire pendant la guerre? a répondu Marusia, nerveuse.

— Non, avant ça, a répliqué Mlle MacIntosh.

— J'étudiais pour devenir pharmacienne. Mais je suis prête à prendre n'importe quel emploi.

— Ce ne sera pas facile pour vous, a dit Mlle MacIntosh en ukrainien. Nadia sera bien ici, pendant la journée.

Quoi? Je savais que Marusia allait chercher du travail et que je devais apprendre l'anglais avec cette dame. Mais toute la journée? J'ai tiré Marusia par la main et lui ai jeté un regard suppliant.

— Nadia, a dit Marusia, Ivan dit que Mlle MacIntosh a déjà enseigné l'anglais à bon nombre d'enfants. Tout ira bien, je t'assure.

Puis, avec une détermination qui m'a fâchée, elle a lâché ma main et s'est éloignée de quelques pas.

— Fais-moi confiance, Nadia, m'a-t-elle dit.

Puis elle est partie.

Si j'avais été plus petite, j'aurais couru à sa poursuite, mais je ne voulais pas faire d'histoires. J'ai respiré profondément et j'ai ravalé mes larmes. J'avais survécu à la guerre. Je pouvais endurer de passer toute la journée avec Mlle MacIntosh.

Quand mes yeux ont été habitués à la pénombre du salon, j'ai vu que le plancher était en bois, comme chez nous, sauf qu'il était presque entièrement recouvert par un tapis de catalogne multicolore. Ce qu'on pouvait encore voir du plancher de bois avait été verni et ciré, et brillait comme un miroir. La pièce était aussi petite que la nôtre, et je m'étonnais de voir tous les meubles qui y tenaient. À côté de la porte qui donnait dans la cuisine, il y avait une grande bibliothèque pleine de livres. Sur l'autre mur se trouvait une cheminée avec des dizaines de photos posées sur le manteau. Au centre trônait un cadre argenté contenant la photo d'un soldat au regard triste, en uniforme.

— Entre et viens t'asseoir, a dit Mlle MacIntosh en posant sa main doucement sur mon épaule pour me conduire jusqu'à un canapé bien rembourré.

Je me suis assise sur le bout des fesses. Mlle MacIntosh a pris un livre dans sa bibliothèque et s'est assise à côté de moi. Sur la couverture du livre était peint le portrait d'une fillette aux tresses blondes, exactement comme les miennes.

— Ceci est un imagier, a-t-elle dit.

J'adore les livres! Au camp, il y en avait parfois dans les colis de l'aide humanitaire, mais rarement pour enfants. J'avais vraiment envie de prendre ce livre dans mes mains, de plonger mon nez dans ses pages ouvertes et de sentir son odeur. Pourtant, je suis restée immobile sur le canapé à côté de Mlle MacIntosh. Elle a ouvert le livre à une page qu'elle avait marquée. Il y avait le dessin d'un *yabluko*.

— Pomme, a dit Mlle MacIntosh, en pointant chaque lettre à mesure qu'elle les prononçait.

— Pomme, ai-je répété.

Elle est passée à une autre page marquée, où l'on voyait le dessin d'une *aftomobile*.

— Automobile, a-t-elle dit en me souriant. Presque le même mot qu'en ukrainien!

Elle m'a appris six mots, puis elle est revenue à

« pomme », et nous les avons tous revus. Nous avons lu encore quelques nouveaux mots, puis elle a tout repris depuis le début. Je savais que je n'apprenais pas vraiment à parler l'anglais. J'apprenais juste des mots qui désignaient des choses. Mais c'était amusant de le faire avec des images.

Quand Mlle MacIntosh a conclu que je connaissais assez bien ces premiers mots, nous en avons lu six de plus, puis encore six autres. Je ne sais pas combien de temps nous sommes restées ainsi assises. Probablement pendant des heures, car j'en avais mal aux fesses.

J'ai tourné les pages et je suis tombée sur un *pes* à l'air féroce. J'ai pris une grande inspiration, puis j'ai pointé les lettres sous l'image :

— Chien, ai-je dit.

— Très bien, a dit Mlle MacIntosh.

Je voyais bien qu'elle avait compris que l'image m'avait fait très peur.

— Faisons une pause, a dit Mlle MacIntosh en se relevant du canapé.

Elle a continué en ukrainien :

— Aimerais-tu manger une bouchée?

— Oui, avec plaisir! ai-je répondu dans mon plus bel anglais, en me levant du canapé et en m'étirant.

Je ne savais pas depuis combien de temps nous étions assises là, mais le temps avait passé très vite.

Pendant que Mlle MacIntosh était occupée à la cuisine, j'ai pris la photo du soldat dans le cadre argenté qui était sur le manteau de la cheminée. Il avait l'air assez jeune. Son uniforme était de couleur foncée, et il avait une casquette sur la tête, qui penchait vers la droite...

Une autre cheminée... un autre uniforme. Foncé, celui-là aussi...

Quand j'ai remis la photo à sa place, une image fugitive m'a traversé l'esprit. Puis je me suis dirigée vers la bibliothèque. Les livres de Mlle MacIntosh avaient des dos de toutes les couleurs et ils étaient tous en anglais. J'avais envie d'en prendre un pour le regarder, mais je voulais d'abord demander la permission. Je l'ai donc rejointe à la cuisine et je l'ai regardée s'affairer.

— Viens t'asseoir ici, a-t-elle dit en désignant une des chaises.

Elle a déposé sur la table deux verres de lait, deux bols à soupe et deux assiettes. Elle a ouvert l'armoire et a pris une boîte de conserve avec une étiquette rouge et blanche. Elle l'a ouverte et a laissé glisser son contenu gélatineux dans une casserole. Puis elle a rempli la boîte de conserve avec de l'eau et l'a versée dans la casserole.

Mlle MacIntosh n'avait pas une glacière comme chez nous, mais un réfrigérateur. Quand elle l'a ouvert pour en retirer une sorte de bloc de couleur orangée, un souffle d'air froid m'a caressé le visage.

Mlle MacIntosh a coupé des tranches dans le bloc orangé et les a déposées sur des tranches de pain...

Wonder! Je pensais que j'en avais fini avec le pain Wonder, erreur!

— Dites-moi, s'il vous plaît, qu'est-ce que c'est? ai-je demandé en anglais, en montrant du doigt le bloc orangé.

— Du Velveeta, a répondu Mlle MacIntosh.

— Du Velveeta, ai-je répété, en prononçant doucement ce nouveau mot.

— C'est une sorte de fromage, a dit Mlle MacIntosh en ukrainien.

— Oh!

Elle a déposé les tranches de pain Wonder garnies de fromage Velveeta sur une plaque à pâtisserie, puis elle a mis le tout au four. La soupe fumait.

— C'est prêt, a-t-elle annoncé.

Elle a retiré la plaque du four, l'a apportée à la table et a fait glisser une tartine avec du fromage fondu dans chacune de nos assiettes. Puis je l'ai regardée remplir mon bol d'un liquide rouge à l'aide d'une louche.

Je n'avais jamais vu une soupe de la sorte. Au camp, la soupe était tout ce que nous avions à manger. Généralement, elle était faite d'eau claire avec du chou et des pommes de terre et, à l'occasion, un peu de viande. Cette soupe-ci était épaisse comme une sauce. J'en ai pris une petite cuillerée et l'ai mise dans ma bouche : un goût de tomates, acide et un peu sucré. Pas mal, mais pas vraiment de la soupe.

J'ai souri à Mlle MacIntosh :

— Bon! lui ai-je dit.

Elle a hoché la tête.

Pour la tartine, c'était une autre histoire. Je n'avais jamais vu de ma vie un fromage d'une couleur pareille, et le fait qu'il soit sur du pain Wonder n'arrangeait rien. J'ai saisi la tartine du bout de mes doigts et j'en ai pris une petite bouchée. Le pain avait grillé dans le four, et le fromage fondu avait un goût pas trop désagréable. Mlle MacIntosh me regardait, attendant ma réaction. J'ai avalé ma bouchée, reconnaissante, comme toujours, chaque fois qu'on me donnait à manger...

Marusia et moi sommes étendues sur un wagon plat, au plus profond d'une nuit sans lune. D'autres fugitifs sont avec nous, retenant leur souffle tandis que le train roule à une vitesse alarmante. Puis il ralentit et s'arrête. Je me rassois et, horrifiée, je regarde Marusia sauter du train et courir dans le champ d'un fermier. À mains nues, elle creuse le sol desséché. Je l'entends pousser un cri de joie. Elle revient en courant et remonte sur la plateforme du wagon.

— Des pommes de terre, dit-elle. Deux belles pommes de terre!

Un des fugitifs sort une casserole de son sac usé jusqu'à la corde et un autre, avec quelques branchettes, fait un petit feu au centre de la plateforme. Un troisième, qui était parti en courant dans le champ, revient avec son chapeau rempli d'une eau boueuse. Il la vide dans la casserole. Marusia y jette ses pommes de terre.

L'odeur des pommes de terre qui cuisent fait gargouiller mon estomac. Je n'ai rien mangé depuis des jours.

C'est le premier arrêt du train depuis que nous nous sommes réfugiées sur le wagon plat. Les pommes de terre ne sont pas tout à fait cuites, mais nous sommes incapables d'attendre plus longtemps. Nous ne savons pas combien de temps le train restera immobilisé et nous craignons que l'odeur du feu n'alerte des soldats.

Un homme sort une cuillère du fond de la poche de son manteau en loques. Il la brandit solennellement, la plonge dans la soupe et me donne la première cuillerée, à moi, la seule enfant du groupe. C'est la meilleure soupe que j'aie jamais mangée. La cuillère passe de main à en main, comme si elle était l'instrument d'un rite sacré. En quelques minutes la soupe est bue jusqu'à la dernière goutte. Le train se remet en branle tandis que nous finissons...

J'ai alors senti une main se poser sur mon épaule et je suis brusquement revenue dans le présent. Mlle MacIntosh me regardait, l'air inquiet.

Les larmes me sont montées aux yeux. Je les ai essuyées du revers de la main en évitant le regard insistant de Mlle MacIntosh.

Ces visions qui m'arrivaient sans crier gare me troublaient et me fâchaient aussi.

Mlle MacIntosh a fini sa soupe et sa tartine, puis j'ai empilé les assiettes et les couverts pour aller les déposer dans l'évier.

— Tu n'as pas à faire ça, a dit Mlle MacIntosh en me prenant la pile des mains.

— Mais je veux bien vous aider, ai-je dit, sachant que Marusia ne s'attendrait à rien de moins.

Et puis le travail m'aidait à faire disparaître ces souvenirs qui venaient parfois me hanter. Je me tenais debout à côté de Mlle MacIntosh tandis qu'elle remplissait l'évier d'eau chaude avec du savon.

— D'accord, a-t-elle dit en me tendant un linge à vaisselle. Tu peux essuyer.

J'ai pris les assiettes une à une et, au fur et à mesure qu'elle les déposait sur l'égouttoir, je les ai bien essuyées et rangées dans l'armoire tout en admirant les jolis dessins de roses. Elles étaient légères et satinées au toucher. Pas du tout comme les tasses et les assiettes dépareillées qu'Ivan nous avait trouvées.

Mlle MacIntosh a vidé l'évier et a essuyé le comptoir.

— Voilà qui est fait! a-t-elle dit. Maintenant, une petite gâterie.

Elle a disposé sur une assiette de petits biscuits bruns.

— Des biscuits au gingembre, a-t-elle dit en faisant signe de me rasseoir à table.

Ils ressemblaient à des *medvinyky* : des biscuits au miel. J'en ai pris un et je l'ai senti. Il ne sentait pas le miel. Il avait ce parfum que j'avais remarqué quand je suis arrivée chez Mlle MacIntosh, ce matin. J'en ai pris une petite bouchée. C'était croquant comme un biscuit au miel, mais son goût a fait remonter d'autres souvenirs…

La dame blonde a fait faire des biscuits par sa servante. Ils ont un goût qui pique un peu la langue. Ils ont la forme d'un bonhomme : des bonshommes de pain d'épices. Je croque la tête et l'avale, puis un bras et une jambe. Je regarde mon biscuit à moitié mangé et j'ai mal au cœur.

— Mange, me dit la dame blonde.

Le biscuit au gingembre était resté collé au fond de ma bouche. J'ai levé les yeux. Encore une fois, Mlle MacIntosh me regardait intensément. J'ai essayé d'avaler, mais j'ai failli m'étouffer. J'ai bu une gorgée de lait, et le biscuit a fini par glisser dans mon estomac.

— Bon! ai-je dit d'une petite voix.

Mlle MacIntosh m'a souri.

On frappait à la porte de la cuisine. Marusia avait-elle laissé tomber sa recherche d'emploi et venait-elle me reprendre?

Mlle MacIntosh a ouvert la porte. Ce n'était pas Marusia. C'était le garçon d'hier soir : Mychailo.

Son regard s'est arrêté sur Mlle MacIntosh, puis sur moi. Il a froncé les sourcils.

— Entre, a dit Mlle MacIntosh. J'ai fait des biscuits.

Mychailo est entré, puis s'est assis sur la seule chaise qui restait dans la cuisine.

— Est-ce qu'elle a déjà commencé à t'enseigner l'anglais? m'a-t-il demandé en ukrainien.

— Demande-le-lui plutôt en anglais, Mychailo, a dit Mlle MacIntosh.

Mychailo a levé les yeux au ciel, puis a pris un biscuit. Il l'a mis tout entier dans sa bouche et l'a avalé presque aussitôt. Il m'a regardée et m'a dit, dans un anglais inutilement lent et fort :

— Est-ce que tu apprends à parler l'anglais, Nadia?

— *Tak.*

Mlle MacIntosh m'a regardée sévèrement.

— Oui, ai-je dit, j'apprends à parler l'anglais.

Mlle MacIntosh a hoché la tête en signe d'approbation.

— Quand vous aurez terminé votre goûter, vous pourrez aller jouer dans la cour un petit moment.

Je ne savais pas si j'avais envie de jouer avec Mychailo. Ce que j'avais vraiment envie de faire, c'était de retourner dans le salon de Mlle MacIntosh pour regarder ses livres.

Mychailo a bu son verre de lait d'un seul trait, puis m'a jeté un regard.

—Allons-y, a-t-il dit en anglais, en montrant la porte arrière.

La balançoire de Mlle MacIntosh était identique à la mienne, mais le siège de bois était plus foncé et usé. Est-ce qu'elle se balançait dessus? Comme ce serait drôle, de voir une adulte se balancer sur une balançoire!

Elle était restée sur le pas de la porte, à nous observer. Mychailo m'a donc dit, en soignant son anglais :

— Nadia, assieds-toi, et je vais te pousser.

Mlle MacIntosh a hoché la tête en signe d'approbation, puis est rentrée. Je me suis assise sur la balançoire et j'ai balancé les jambes pour démarrer, puis Mychailo m'a poussée si fort que j'en ai eu le souffle coupé.

— Doucement! ai-je dit en ukrainien.

— Tu n'apprendras jamais si tu n'arrêtes pas de parler ukrainien! a répliqué Mychailo en imitant la voix de Mlle MacIntosh.

— Tu me fais mal!

Soit il ne comprenait pas mon anglais, soit il se fichait de moi. Chaque fois que la balançoire revenait de son côté, il me poussait fort dans le dos. La balançoire est montée si haut que j'ai eu peur de faire le Grand Soleil ou de rester accrochée dans les branches. Mais, à chaque poussée, je sentais le vent sur mon visage et je me sentais libre de voler dans les airs.

— ARRÊTE! ai-je crié.

— Comme tu voudras! a dit Mychailo en s'éloignant de la balançoire.

Il s'est vautré sur la pelouse et s'est amusé à peigner le gazon avec ses doigts, en m'ignorant complètement.

J'ai laissé traîner mes pieds sur le sol pour ralentir la balançoire, mais elle allait trop vite et j'ai perdu une chaussure. Paniquée, j'ai sauté et je suis tombée face contre terre, sur la pelouse.

— Tu es stupide, a maugréé Mychailo en continuant de peigner le gazon avec ses doigts tandis que, de la main, je secouais la poussière de mes vêtements.

La porte de la cuisine s'est ouverte et, depuis le seuil, Mlle MacIntosh a lancé :

— La leçon recommence dans dix minutes.

Je me suis allongée sur le gazon, à côté de Mychailo.

— Tu prends des leçons d'anglais toi aussi? ai-je demandé.

— Oui, a-t-il répondu. Je viens ici tous les après-midi.

— Mais tu parles déjà très bien l'anglais.

— Mes parents veulent que je vienne ici, et Mlle MacIntosh est gentille, alors ça me va. De plus, elle fait de bons biscuits.

J'ai ruminé cela dans ma tête. Est-ce que ça voulait dire que moi aussi, je viendrais ici tous les jours? Et si j'apprenais vite, est-ce que je viendrais seulement l'après-midi? En plus, je n'étais pas certaine de vouloir passer autant de temps avec Mychailo.

— Où habitais-tu avant la guerre? a demandé celui-ci.

Sa question m'a prise au dépourvu et j'ai bafouillé :
— À... À... Zolochiv.

Mychailo a levé les yeux au ciel et s'est exclamé :
— Ce que tu mens mal!

Il avait raison. Je mentais. Mais il ignorait que

j'avais vécu si longtemps dans le mensonge que je ne me rappelais même plus d'où je venais vraiment. Ce mensonge me venait tout naturellement quand j'étais au camp. Si je ne l'avais pas fait, on m'aurait aussitôt séparée de Marusia. Mais depuis que nous étions au Canada, il se passait quelque chose de bizarre. Des images du passé me revenaient, comme aujourd'hui, et elles étaient comme des pièces de casse-tête qui n'allaient pas ensemble.

— Qu'est-ce qui te fait croire que je mens? lui ai-je demandé.

— Parce que tu as un drôle d'accent en ukrainien, a-t-il dit. Mes parents sont nés à Zolochiv, Ivan vient de Zolochiv. Alors, je suis convaincu que tu viens d'ailleurs.

J'étais effrayée de constater que ce garçon en connaissait plus sur mon passé que moi-même.

— Est-ce qu'Ivan… je veux dire… mon père… est un ami de tes parents? ai-je demandé.

— Mon père était dans la résistance avec Ivan, a dit Mychailo. Ils combattaient ensemble les nazis.

Il s'est tu pendant un moment et s'est concentré sur le gazon qu'il peignait avec ses doigts.

— C'est à ça que tu me fais penser, a-t-il dit.

— À quoi? ai-je demandé.

— Avec les cheveux et les yeux que tu as? À une nazie.

Puis, sans me regarder, il s'est relevé et il est retourné à l'intérieur.

Chapitre quatre

Suis-je une nazie?

Pendant le reste de l'après-midi que je passais avec Mychailo, je me sentais bizarre, après sa remarque sur les nazis. Je n'arrêtais pas de me poser des questions. Au camp des personnes déplacées, la plupart des gens pouvaient parler plusieurs langues, mais personne n'avait le même accent que moi. À notre arrivée, des gens ont fait la remarque que je n'avais pas le même accent que ma mère et que nous ne nous ressemblions pas. Marusia les faisait taire.

Mlle MacIntosh a fait faire une rédaction à Mychailo, à la table de la cuisine, et elle a continué à regarder l'imagier avec moi. J'étais contente de ne pas être assise à côté de lui pour ma leçon.

À chaque pause, je regardais la photo du soldat sur la cheminée de Mlle MacIntosh. Une fois, elle a suivi mon regard et elle a soupiré.

— Je devais me marier avec lui, a-t-elle dit. Il est mort en France, en combattant les nazis.

Qu'est-ce que Mlle MacIntosh pouvait penser de moi, avec mes cheveux blonds, mes yeux bleus et mon drôle d'accent : que j'étais une nazie moi aussi? Que j'étais responsable de la mort de son fiancé? J'avais une boule dans la gorge et envie de pleurer.

Marusia pensait que ce serait bon pour moi d'essayer de me rappeler le plus de chose possible de ma vie avant de la rencontrer. Elle insistait toujours en disant que je n'avais aucune raison d'avoir honte. J'essayais, mais les souvenirs ne me revenaient que par bribes, et tout était confus. C'était très troublant. J'ai levé les yeux vers Mlle MacIntosh, une si gentille dame, et lui ai dit :

— Je suis désolée qu'il soit mort.

La guerre ne s'était pas rendue jusqu'au Canada, mais le fiancé de Mlle MacIntosh était parti se battre en Europe. J'imagine que c'est pour ça qu'on la qualifie de mondiale, cette guerre.

L'après-midi a passé très vite. J'étais si absorbée par l'étude du nouveau vocabulaire que j'ai sursauté quand on a frappé à la porte d'entrée. Mlle MacIntosh a ouvert, et Marusia était là, l'air triste et fatiguée.

Mlle MacIntosh m'a permis d'apporter l'imagier à la maison; ainsi Marusia, Ivan et moi pourrions pratiquer notre anglais ensemble. J'ai glissé ma main dans celle de Marusia, et nous sommes parties. En cours de route, je lui ai serré la main quelques secondes. Elle m'a regardée, l'air étonnée. Les larmes lui sont montées aux yeux, mais elle a quand même souri.

— Ne t'inquiète pas, je vais trouver du travail, a-t-elle dit.

Ça m'a fait sourire. Du plus loin que je me souvenais, j'avais toujours vécu au jour le jour. J'avais appris à ne pas m'en faire. J'avais aussi appris à ne plus rien espérer.

Tandis que nous marchions, main dans la main, Marusia m'a regardée et m'a demandé :

— Que se passe-t-il, Nadia?

Je n'ai rien dit pendant quelques secondes. Nous avions déjà eu cette discussion. Soudain j'ai explosé :

— Je suis une nazie, n'est-ce pas?

Marusia s'est arrêtée. Elle s'est tournée vers moi et m'a regardée droit dans les yeux :

— Non, *Sonechko*, tu *n'es pas* une nazie.

— Est-ce que je suis allemande, alors?

Marusia a fait non de la tête.

— Alors pourquoi ai-je les traits d'une nazie? ai-je demandé. Au camp des personnes déplacées, les autres enfants ne me ressemblaient pas et n'avaient pas le même accent que moi. Mychailo n'a pas le même accent que moi. Et toi non plus.

Marusia avait les larmes aux yeux.

— Mychailo t'a-t-il dit quelque chose?

Je n'aime pas moucharder ni mentir.

— Lui et moi, nous parlons différemment, ai-je répondu.

— Tu n'es pas une nazie et tu n'es pas allemande, a-t-elle affirmé.

— Mais je me rappelle l'endroit où tu m'as volée!

ai-je dit.

Marusia a posé une main sur sa hanche, et de l'autre, elle m'a montrée du doigt :

— Est-ce que je t'ai déjà maltraitée?

— Non.

— Est-ce que je t'ai toujours traitée comme si tu étais la chair de ma chair?

— Oui.

— Alors, tu dois me croire quand je te dis que je ne t'ai pas volée et que tu n'es pas une nazie.

Elle m'a tendu la main, mais j'ai gardé la mienne derrière mon dos. J'étais furieuse contre elle, sans trop savoir pourquoi. Nous avons fait le reste du chemin jusqu'à la maison sans desserrer les dents.

À notre arrivée, nous avons vu un camion rempli de panneaux de contreplaqué, stationné devant chez nous. Deux hommes que je connaissais pour les avoir vus la veille au soir (l'un d'eux était le père de Mychailo) déchargeaient les panneaux à l'arrière du camion. Un troisième maintenait la porte de notre maison grande ouverte.

— Viens! Allons voir ce qu'ils font! ai-je dit à Marusia.

Nous les avons suivis dans le salon. Je n'en croyais pas mes yeux! Pas plus tard qu'hier, cet espace n'était encore qu'une forêt de madriers alors que maintenant, avec les panneaux cloués à la charpente, c'était une pièce fermée. Je suis entrée dans la chambre. Ivan avait retiré sa chemise et son dos ruisselait de sueur.

Agenouillé dans un coin, il enfonçait des petits clous sur un côté du contreplaqué qu'un autre maintenait en place. Trois des murs de la chambre étaient déjà montés.

Avant que les murs soient installés, la maison avait l'air vaste et aérée. J'aurais aimé qu'elle reste ainsi. Mais j'ai pris une grande bouffée d'air qui sentait la sciure de bois et je me suis forcée à sourire à Ivan.

En entendant nos pas, il a levé la tête.

— Ah! Voici mes filles! a-t-il dit en souriant.

— Tu travailles si vite! s'est exclamée Marusia.

— Je voulais terminer les murs avant votre arrivée à Brantford, a répliqué Ivan. Mais j'ai fait beaucoup d'heures supplémentaires à mon travail, ces dernières semaines, et le temps m'a manqué.

Il a montré du doigt les trois autres hommes.

— Je n'y serais jamais arrivé sans mes chers amis, a-t-il dit.

— Vous devez avoir faim, a répondu Marusia. Nous allons vous préparer à manger.

Le bruit des marteaux résonnait jusque dans la cuisine tandis que j'aidais Marusia à préparer un repas vite fait. Après avoir mangé et terminé leur travail, les trois amis sont partis, en promettant de revenir le lendemain.

Puis Ivan et Marusia se sont assis sur les blocs de ciment pour boire un thé. Je me suis assise sur ma balançoire et j'ai écouté leur conversation.

— Quand prends-tu le temps de dormir, Ivashko? a

demandé Marusia en lui caressant le front du revers de la main. Hier soir, tu venais à peine de fermer l'œil quand l'heure de te lever a sonné.

— Je dormirai quand la maison sera terminée, a répondu Ivan.

— Pourquoi ne pas te reposer un peu maintenant? a dit Marusia. Pourquoi ne viendrais-tu pas t'étendre sur le matelas?

— Il fait encore clair, a-t-il protesté. J'ai encore un peu de temps pour travailler sur la maison.

— Allons, viens! a dit Marusia. Nous allons nous étendre tous les deux quelques minutes. Juste pour nous reposer les yeux.

Je voulais leur laisser un peu de temps à eux tout seuls. Après tout, ils n'étaient pas mariés depuis bien longtemps et ils avaient vécu séparés pendant toute une année. Je suis descendue de la balançoire et je me suis dirigée vers l'avant de la maison.

— Où vas-tu? a crié Marusia.

— Explorer les environs, ai-je crié en faisant un effort pour avoir l'air gaie.

— Ne t'éloigne pas trop, a-t-elle dit. Et reviens avant la nuit.

Ça m'a fait sourire. Marusia pensait-elle vraiment que je pouvais aller très loin? Je me suis assise sur les marches à l'avant pendant un petit moment et j'ai scruté la rue, à droite et à gauche. Je pourrais peut-être rester assise là pendant une heure? Au loin, j'entendais des enfants qui jouaient, et une ou deux voitures sont passées. Un homme en costume, une boîte à repas à la main, est passé aussi. Il m'a saluée en levant son chapeau et, en retour, je lui ai souri. Je me suis sentie en sécurité. Je ne sais pas pourquoi. Peut-être que cette nouvelle vie que nous nous étions inventée serait bien, après tout.

Mychailo m'avait dit que l'école Centrale était à l'autre bout de notre rue. Ça ne devait pas être très loin. J'ai respiré à fond et je me suis levée. Je suis une jeune Canadienne maintenant, me suis-je dit en moi-même. Et les jeunes Canadiennes marchent dans la rue toutes seules, sans avoir peur.

Je me suis donc forcée à m'éloigner de la maison et à marcher dans la rue. J'avais un peu peur, mais j'étais très fière de moi. La petite brise qui me caressait les joues était très agréable. Je suis passée devant chez Mlle MacIntosh, puis je suis arrivée à la rue George. J'ai vu ce qui ne pouvait être qu'une école : un énorme bâtiment de brique ocre, ayant deux étages et demi et, à l'avant, une grande pelouse et une entrée circulaire.

Il ne restait que peu d'immeubles de cette grosseur qui soient encore debout en Allemagne. Je me sentais étrangement en sécurité, à marcher seule dans cet endroit qui ne m'était pas familier. Il n'y avait ni bombes, ni soldats en uniforme, ni bâtiments incendiés, ni barbelés.

Je me suis rendue près d'une fenêtre et j'ai jeté un coup d'œil à l'intérieur. C'était une classe avec des rangées de pupitres et toutes sortes d'affiches accrochées aux murs. En haut du tableau noir, il y avait un portrait du roi George. Je l'ai reconnu parce que je l'avais déjà vu sur des pièces de monnaie.

Quels chefs d'État y avait-il sur les murs de mes salles de classe? J'avais un trou de mémoire complet. Je me suis assise dans l'herbe, le dos appuyé contre le mur de l'école. Ce n'était pas encore l'heure de rentrer à la maison. Alors, j'ai marché encore un petit peu plus loin. À trois rues de là, il y avait un parc magnifique, une église et, en face, de beaux bâtiments.

Le bâtiment à côté de l'église a attiré mon attention. Il avait quatre colonnes de marbre et un escalier aux marches toutes blanches qui menaient devant une belle grande porte double, à hauteur du premier étage. J'ai gravi l'escalier, puis je me suis mise sur la pointe des pieds pour jeter un coup d'œil par le carreau. J'ai vu un hall en marbre et, de l'autre côté, une pièce pleine de livres. J'aurais tant aimé pouvoir toucher ces livres. Sentir leur parfum…

— C'est la bibliothèque, a dit une voix familière dans mon dos.

— Pourquoi m'as-tu suivie jusqu'ici? ai-je dit en me retournant pour faire face à Mychailo.

Il me regardait d'un air idiot.

— Je ne t'ai pas suivie, a-t-il dit. C'est toi qui ne m'as pas entendu arriver.

Je l'ai dévisagé pour le remettre à sa place, mais

soudain j'ai remarqué qu'il tenait un gros livre.

— As-tu pris ce livre ici? ai-je demandé.

— C'est une bibliothèque, alors d'après toi? a-t-il répondu.

— Combien ça coûte?

— C'est gratuit pour moi, a-t-il dit. À condition de le rapporter.

— Qui peut se servir de la bibliothèque alors?

— Tout le monde. Tu n'as qu'à remplir un formulaire, et on te donne ta carte de bibliothèque. Puis tu peux emprunter des livres tant que tu veux, à condition de toujours les rapporter quand tu as fini de les lire.

— Qui décide quels sont les livres que tu peux lire ou ne pas lire?

— Ce n'est pas comme ça au Canada, a dit Mychailo. Tu peux lire tous les livres de la section des enfants, à condition d'avoir ta carte de lectrice.

— Est-ce que je peux y aller maintenant?

— Ça vient juste de fermer, a-t-il dit. Mais voudrais-tu revenir demain, après notre leçon chez Mlle MacIntosh?

Je commençais à apprécier Mychailo. Il pouvait être brusque et dur avec moi, comme tous les garçons. Toutefois, il aimait les livres.

Chapitre cinq

Eva

J'aurais aimé dormir encore à la belle étoile, mais de gros nuages menaçants avaient envahi le ciel à l'heure du coucher du soleil. Nous avons donc balayé la sciure de bois dans le salon, et Ivan a installé un matelas au milieu de la pièce.

— C'est presque comme si tu étais dehors. La pièce est grande. Et si tu as besoin de nous, nous sommes juste à côté, a dit Marusia en montrant la chambre.

À voir son regard, je savais qu'elle était épuisée et je savais aussi qu'Ivan l'était encore plus. J'ai donc souri et dit que c'était très bien ainsi.

J'ai apporté le livre de Mlle MacIntosh dans mon lit et j'ai regardé les images en essayant de prononcer les mots jusqu'à ce qu'il fasse noir.

Le tambourinement de la pluie sur le toit couvrait le chant des grenouilles. Peut-être qu'elles se mettaient à l'abri et dormaient quand il pleuvait? La pluie était apaisante, mais les grondements du tonnerre, au loin, me rappelaient le bruit des bombes.

Les fenêtres n'avaient pas de rideaux, alors quand

une auto passait, d'étranges ombres glissaient sur les murs. J'ai fermé les yeux et je me suis concentrée pour ralentir ma respiration, en espérant m'endormir rapidement.

Je suis confortablement couchée sous un édredon, entourée de gens qui m'aiment. On frappe à la porte. J'essaie de me cacher en me recroquevillant derrière les autres, mais ils ont disparu. Je suis toute seule. On frappe encore à la porte. Une voix d'enfant me demande d'ouvrir. Qui est-ce? Et pourquoi suis-je terrifiée par cette voix?

Je me suis assise brusquement. Où étais-je? Une grenouille a chanté. J'ai regardé autour de moi, dans le noir, et j'ai vu ma fenêtre baignée par la lumière de la lune. La pluie tambourinait encore sur le toit. J'étais dans la maison d'Ivan, à Brantford. La pièce où je me trouvais n'était pas meublée et sentait le bois fraîchement poncé. J'étais en sécurité ici. J'ai entouré mes genoux avec mes bras et je me suis mise à me bercer d'avant en arrière. J'avais envie de crier, mais je ne savais pas pourquoi. J'ai fermé les yeux et j'ai fredonné la *kolysanka*.

Qui était la fillette de mon rêve? Je ne voulais pas retourner me coucher et je ne voulais pas réveiller Ivan et Marusia. J'ai donc marché sur la pointe des pieds jusque dans la cuisine et je me suis servi un verre d'eau. Je me suis assise à la table et j'ai regardé la pluie tomber. Je voulais me rappeler cette époque. Si j'arrivais à mettre en place les pièces du casse-tête, peut-être que mes cauchemars cesseraient? Marusia avait dit que je n'avais aucune raison d'avoir honte. Mais comment pouvait-elle en être absolument sûre? J'ai encore une fois regardé par la fenêtre, en pensant à cette fillette…

Je suis dans la chambre au plafond haut. Des gouttes de pluie ruissellent dehors sur la vitre de la fenêtre habillée de rideaux roses, et je vois les premières lueurs du jour apparaître. On frappe à la porte.

Elle s'ouvre brusquement. Eva se précipite vers moi, grimpe dans mon lit et s'écrie :

Ma chère sœur, tu devrais déjà être debout! Tu vas mettre ta nouvelle robe rose, ainsi nous serons assorties.

Je regarde ses pieds potelés tandis qu'elle descend du lit et retourne vers la porte. À nous voir ensemble, jamais personne ne croira que nous sommes bien assorties, même habillées toutes les deux en rose. Je reste encore un peu au lit. Pourquoi est-ce que je ne me sens pas en sécurité dans cette chambre? Elle a tout ce dont une fillette peut rêver, avec ses rideaux roses à volants et son beau lit à baldaquin. Dans un coin, un coffre en bois déborde de jouets. Sur le mur en face du lit, une étagère est garnie de poupées toutes blondes aux yeux bleus. Des cadeaux de Vater. Je ne les aime pas.

En descendant du lit, un de mes pieds atterrit sur le coin d'un livre. Je me penche pour le ramasser : Der Giftpiltz, c'est-à-dire « Le champignon vénéneux ». Encore un présent de Vater, que je n'aime pas. Le livre me glisse des mains et tombe par terre. D'une main, je

lisse les plis de ma chemise de nuit, puis je me rends
pieds nus dans la salle de bain. Il y fait humide, et le
miroir est couvert de buée. Mutter vient probablement
de terminer sa toilette et de s'habiller. Elle doit nous
attendre, Eva et moi, dans la salle à manger.

Je prends ma brosse à dents, je la couvre de dentifrice
et je me brosse rapidement les dents. Je m'asperge le
visage d'eau en prenant soin de mouiller ma savonnette
pour qu'elle ait l'air d'avoir été utilisée, puis je m'essuie
avec une serviette de bain rose où sont brodées les
initiales GH, comme sur toutes mes serviettes.

Un coup de tonnerre m'a ramenée brusquement
dans le temps présent. L'espace d'une seconde, à
cause de la foudre, il faisait clair comme en plein jour
dans la cuisine. L'image dans ma tête était si réelle
que je sentais presque la texture du dentifrice sur ma
langue. Lentement, j'ai pris une gorgée d'eau dans le
verre qui se trouvait sur la table et j'ai essayé d'aller
plus loin dans mes souvenirs, mais la vision était
passée. Cette fille, Eva, était-elle ma sœur? Pourquoi
est-ce que je ne l'aimais pas?

Il n'y avait rien dans ce souvenir qui puisse faire
peur, alors pourquoi m'avait-il tant effrayée? Et que
signifiaient les initiales GH? Comme je ne voulais pas
retourner me coucher, je suis restée assise à la table, à
regarder la pluie et les éclairs par la fenêtre de la
cuisine. Autrefois, j'avais de quoi manger et de beaux
vêtements. J'avais Mutter, Vater et Eva. Alors pourquoi
n'étais-je pas heureuse?

Il faisait encore noir quand j'ai entendu le plancher craquer sous des pas et la porte de la salle de bain qui s'ouvrait : Ivan se préparait à partir travailler. Par la fenêtre de la cuisine, on voyait maintenant la lumière crue du soleil levant. Je distinguais la balançoire, trempée par la pluie. Je me rappelais qu'Ivan était si heureux quand je m'étais balancée. Je pourrais peut-être lui faire une surprise à mon tour? Je suis allée à l'évier et j'ai rempli la bouilloire d'eau pour le thé. Je l'ai mise sur le feu, puis j'ai sorti un poêlon et je l'ai déposé sur l'autre feu. J'ai sorti du bacon de la glacière et je l'ai mis dans le poêlon. À côté du bacon qui grillait, j'ai cassé deux œufs.

Quand la porte de la salle de bain s'est rouverte, le petit déjeuner attendait Ivan, à sa place, à table.

Il est entré dans la cuisine vêtu de sa chemise et de son pantalon de travail. Il fleurait bon le savon. Il avait les cheveux mouillés et peignés vers l'arrière.

— Nadia, a-t-il dit en posant son regard d'abord sur moi, puis sur l'assiette toute pleine. Quelle belle surprise!

À voir l'expression de ses yeux, je savais qu'il avait mille questions en tête.

— Je n'arrivais pas à dormir, lui ai-je expliqué. Et je voulais te faire plaisir.

Ivan a marché jusque derrière ma chaise, m'a entouré les épaules de ses bras et a déposé un baiser sur le dessus de ma tête.

— Tu es si gentille! Merci!

— Mange, lui ai-je dit en ravalant mes larmes. Sinon ça va refroidir.

Ivan a mangé à toute vitesse et a bu son thé d'un seul trait. Je savais qu'il ne voulait pas être en retard au travail. Après son départ, j'ai lavé la vaisselle et j'ai préparé le déjeuner pour Marusia et moi.

Après le déjeuner, j'ai pris l'imagier avec moi, et Marusia m'a déposée chez Mlle MacIntosh. Nous avons répété des phrases et elle m'a appris de nouveaux mots. Mychailo est arrivé après le dîner, comme la veille. Il avait l'air plus avenant. Il s'est assis à la table de la cuisine avec un cahier d'exercices tandis que j'étais dans le salon avec Mlle MacIntosh. Je n'ai pas vu le temps passer.

— Tu apprends si vite, Nadia, a-t-elle dit en me souriant.

Elle a pris l'imagier sur mes genoux, puis elle l'a refermé et déposé sur la table à café.

— Aimerais-tu rapporter l'imagier chez toi aujourd'hui aussi?

— Oui, volontiers, ai-je dit.

— Elle pourrait venir à la bibliothèque avec moi aujourd'hui, a dit Mychailo, depuis la cuisine. Comme ça, elle pourrait apprendre l'anglais avec d'autres livres.

— Quelle bonne idée, Mychailo! s'est exclamée Mlle MacIntosh, radieuse. Si Marusia revient avant que vous en ayez terminé à la bibliothèque, je lui dirai où vous êtes.

Mychailo ne m'a pas amenée directement à la bibliothèque. Nous sommes plutôt allés marcher un peu dans le centre-ville. Il m'a montré le cinéma, la place du marché et l'hôtel de ville. Une grande voiture grise était garée devant l'hôtel de ville.

— Je crois que c'est la voiture du maire, a dit Mychailo.

Puis nous sommes arrivés à la bibliothèque. Nous avons gravi le grand escalier blanc, et nous avons ouvert les grandes portes vitrées. Un parfum d'air frais, de livres et de meubles bien cirés m'a enveloppée.

— La section des enfants est par ici, a dit Mychailo en m'entraînant vers un escalier qui allait au sous-sol.

Nous nous sommes présentés devant un long comptoir au centre de la grande salle. Pour une bibliothèque, cette salle était étonnamment peu fournie en livres. Les murs étaient lambrissés, sans aucun rayonnage.

— Est-ce qu'on peut aller là? ai-je demandé en désignant une salle vers la gauche, qui était pleine de livres.

— Il faut d'abord trouver Mlle Barry, a dit Mychailo. Il te faut une carte de bibliothèque.

Une jolie dame est aussitôt arrivée. Elle avait les cheveux blonds et bouclés, et portait des lunettes à monture bleue.

— Contente de te voir, Mychailo, a-t-elle dit. Tu nous as amené une amie, à ce que je vois.

— Je vous présente Nadia.

— Bonjour, mademoiselle Barry, ai-je répondu poliment.

— Nadia a besoin d'une carte de bibliothèque, a poursuivi Mychailo. Je peux l'aider à remplir le formulaire.

Mlle Barry est passée derrière le comptoir et a fouillé dans ses tiroirs. Elle m'a tendu un crayon et une feuille de papier avec des questions et des lignes.

— Il me faut un numéro de téléphone et une adresse.

— Nous n'avons pas le téléphone, ai-je dit, prise d'inquiétude. Alors, je ne pourrai pas avoir ma carte de bibliothèque?

Mychailo a pris le formulaire de mes mains.

— Je vais le remplir, a-t-il dit. Et je vais inscrire le numéro de téléphone de la fonderie où travaille ton père. Mon père y travaille aussi, alors je connais le numéro.

— Merci mille fois, Mychailo!

Il m'a emmenée dans la salle à gauche.

— Ces livres sont parfaits pour commencer à lire en anglais.

J'étais béate d'admiration en entrant dans la salle. Les quatre murs étaient couverts de rayonnages remplis de livres, et il y avait aussi des rangées au centre...

Il y a très longtemps... une pièce remplie de livres, mais je n'ai pas le droit de les toucher...

— Ce livre serait parfait pour toi, a déclaré Mychailo.

Il m'a tendu un album en me lisant le titre à voix haute : *Petit train va loin.*

— Je vais dans l'autre salle. Si tu t'ennuies, viens me rejoindre.

J'ai approché le livre de mon visage et j'ai humé son merveilleux parfum d'encre et de colle. J'avais du mal à croire que je pourrais apporter chez moi un livre de cette bibliothèque. J'ai ouvert le livre. Les images réveillaient des souvenirs en moi. Un train en marche... des coffres à jouets... une poupée blonde aux yeux bleus... Ce n'était peut-être pas un bon livre pour moi. Je l'ai remis à sa place et j'en ai pris un autre dont la couverture représentait trois chatons. En me servant des images pour décoder le texte, j'ai lu tout en restant debout... chatons, mitaines, sanglots.

Et je faisais la même chose avec chaque livre que je prenais. Je n'arriverais pas à choisir! Je les ai tous remis sur l'étagère et je me suis rendue dans l'autre salle. Les livres y étaient plus gros et contenaient beaucoup moins d'illustrations. J'ai trouvé Mychailo assis dans un coin, avec des livres tout autour de lui.

— Lequel vas-tu emprunter? lui ai-je demandé.

Il a levé son regard vers moi, puis il a regardé les livres éparpillés par terre.

— Je crois que je vais prendre *Tom Sawyer* aujourd'hui, a-t-il dit. Tu n'en as pas pris un?

— Je n'arrive pas à choisir.

— Je vais te montrer ceux que j'ai bien aimés quand je suis arrivé à Brantford.

Il a ramassé les livres par terre et les a déposés sur un chariot. Avec *Tom Sawyer* calé sous le bras, il s'est dirigé vers la salle des albums illustrés. Je lui collais aux talons.

— En voici un très bon, a-t-il dit en prenant un très grand livre sur une étagère au fond de la salle. Il va t'aider à apprendre les nombres en anglais.

C'était un livre sur les nombres, très semblable à l'imagier de Mlle MacIntosh.

— Merci Mychailo, ai-je dit. C'est parfait!

Quand je suis rentrée, Ivan était étendu à plat ventre dans le salon et il clouait des petites baguettes de bois sur le pourtour de la pièce, au bas des murs.

— Puis-je t'aider? lui ai-je demandé.

Il a tourné la tête vers moi et m'a souri.

— J'aimerais bien un peu d'eau.

Je suis allée à la cuisine et j'ai déposé mon livre. J'ai rempli un verre au robinet et je l'ai apporté à Ivan dans le salon. Il l'a bu d'un seul trait et m'a rendu le verre vide.

Je l'ai rapporté à la cuisine et je me suis arrêtée un instant devant la fenêtre pour regarder dehors. J'y voyais mon reflet. Mon visage, mes yeux, mes tresses...

Je porte une robe rose. La regarder me fait horreur.

Quand je descends, Mutter est assise dans la salle à

manger. La cuisinière lui a servi son gruau, et Eva a déjà avalé la moitié du sien. Le centre de la table est occupé par un grand compotier de cristal rempli de pommes, de raisins et de petits fruits.

La cuisinière dépose un bol devant moi. Le gruau est saupoudré de cannelle et de sucre. Même apprêté de cette façon, je déteste le gruau.

— Le rassemblement est dans moins d'une heure, dit Mutter, les yeux pétillants d'excitation. Dépêchez-vous.

Eva avale les dernières cuillerées de son gruau. Elle dépose sa cuillère avec brusquerie, se lève vite de table et annonce :

— J'ai fini!

— Va chercher ta brosse à cheveux, dit Mutter. Je vais te coiffer dès que ta sœur et moi aurons terminé notre déjeuner.

J'engloutis mes céréales sans me préoccuper du goût. Je veux en finir au plus vite. Eva revient avec des rubans roses, une brosse et un miroir à main.

Mutter démêle les cheveux blond cendré d'Eva jusqu'à ce qu'ils tombent parfaitement bien dans son dos. De ses mains expertes, elle lui fait deux tresses qu'elle termine par une boucle de ruban rose.

Quand vient mon tour, elle tire sur mes cheveux et les tresse plus serré que nécessaire.

— Voilà, me dit-elle d'un ton un peu cassant en me tendant le miroir. Tu es jolie, non?

Le visage que me renvoie le miroir est le même que d'habitude. Je ne me suis jamais trouvée jolie.

Quand nous sortons, une longue voiture noire nous attend devant la porte. Un petit drapeau affichant le svastika est placé de chaque côté du coffre. Un soldat en uniforme ouvre la portière arrière. Mutter monte la première, puis Eva et finalement moi. La banquette est recouverte d'un luxueux cuir noir qui brille tant il a été bien astiqué. La portière se referme avec un bruit sec, et nous partons à toute vitesse.

Nous roulons pendant une demi-heure à toute allure pour nous rendre en ville. Les rues sont étroites. Notre chauffeur ralentit pour nous donner le temps de saluer la foule en liesse qui borde les rues sur des kilomètres.

Quand nous arrivons près de l'estrade, la voiture s'arrête. Des soldats repoussent la foule afin de nous laisser descendre, puis nous emmènent au pied de l'escalier qui mène à l'estrade. La plupart des places sont occupées par des officiers nazis, mais il y a aussi quelques mères avec leurs enfants. Nous prenons nos places dans la première rangée, derrière le podium.

La foule rugit tandis qu'une autre longue voiture noire approche. Quand le Führer sort de la voiture, la foule est en délire. Vater en descend aussi, suivant le Führer de près.

La foule scande « Heil Hitler! Heil Hitler! » tandis que le Führer gravit l'escalier qui mène à l'estrade, mais on dirait qu'il ne s'en aperçoit même pas. Il marche jusque devant moi, s'accroupit et me regarde dans les yeux. Il est si près de moi que je peux voir les poils de son nez et sentir le parfum légèrement musqué de sa *pommade capillaire.*

— Tu es la représentation parfaite de notre jeunesse aryenne, ma chérie, me dit-il en me pinçant la joue.

Je souris. Que faire d'autre? Debout derrière le Führer, Vater rayonne de fierté, mais Eva semble au bord des larmes, et Mutter pince les lèvres si fort qu'elles en sont toutes blanches. Vater s'assoit entre Eva et Mutter. Il prend la main de Mutter et y dépose un baiser.

Le Führer se rend au podium et commence…

— Nadia, que fais-tu?

J'ai sursauté en entendant la voix de Marusia. J'ai failli échapper le verre d'eau vide. J'ai cligné deux fois des yeux. Je me trouvais devant la fenêtre de la cuisine, à Brantford.

Je me suis tournée vers Marusia. Elle se tenait près de la table, et Ivan était à son côté, le marteau à la main et l'air vraiment inquiet.

J'ai secoué la tête dans l'espoir de chasser de ma tête l'image d'Hitler. Si j'ai rencontré Hitler, Hitler en personne, alors je dois être une nazie. Quel secret me concernant Marusia refusait-elle de me révéler? Qui étais-je vraiment?

Mes joues étaient baignées de larmes, mais je ne me rappelais pas avoir pleuré. Mes genoux se sont mis à trembler, alors j'ai déposé le verre à côté de l'évier et je me suis assise à la table.

Marusia est venue se placer derrière moi. Elle m'a entourée de ses bras protecteurs et a appuyé son front contre ma nuque.

Ivan s'est agenouillé à côté de nous.

— Est-ce que ça va? a-t-il demandé avec effroi.

— Je réfléchissais, ai-je répondu.

— Tu criais *Heil Hitler*, a dit Ivan, le regard troublé.

— À quoi pensais-tu? a continué Marusia.

— À la ferme et à cette famille, ai-je répondu. Mais il y avait autre chose.

— Aimerais-tu nous en parler? a-t-elle demandé.

— Non! me suis-je écriée.

Pourquoi ne voulait-elle pas comprendre que j'étais si honteuse? Marusia affirmait dur comme fer que je n'étais pas une nazie, mais ce n'était pas ce que ma mémoire me disait. J'aurais tant voulu pouvoir chasser à tout jamais cet horrible passé!

— Tu dois laisser ces souvenirs remonter à la surface, Nadia, a dit Ivan. Tant que tu ne te rappelleras pas absolument tout, tu auras des cauchemars.

Ivan disait-il vrai? Peut-être qu'il…

— Peut-être que ça t'aiderait si je te racontais ce que j'ai vécu pendant la guerre, a-t-il dit.

Il s'est assis à califourchon sur la chaise en face de moi et m'a regardée dans les yeux.

La proposition d'Ivan me surprenait. Il ne parlait jamais de son passé.

— J'aimerais bien savoir ce qu'il t'est arrivé pendant la guerre, lui ai-je répondu.

Pendant un instant, il n'a rien dit. Puis les larmes lui sont montées aux yeux avec les souvenirs qui lui revenaient à la mémoire. Il a essuyé ses larmes et a respiré profondément.

— Mon histoire est celle de bien d'autres comme moi. Les soviets ont tué mon père et mon frère en 1941. Ils ont ainsi tué des milliers d'hommes, et même des femmes et des enfants. Je n'ai pas été arrêté avec eux. Sur le coup, je me suis dit que j'avais de la chance. Mais ensuite, les nazis sont arrivés.

Ivan a croisé mon regard, et je l'ai vu rougir de honte. Il a levé les yeux vers Marusia, qui se tenait toujours debout dans mon dos, m'entourant de ses bras. Ivan a poussé un long soupir et a poursuivi :

— Je croyais que rien ne pouvait se comparer aux soviets, mais je me trompais. Les nazis étaient aussi mauvais. Ma sœur a été enlevée lors d'une rafle effectuée par les nazis pour les travaux forcés. Ma mère a été envoyée dans un camp de concentration. J'étais le seul membre de notre famille qui restait. Alors, je me suis joint à la résistance. Nous combattions tantôt les nazis, tantôt les Soviétiques. Tout dépendait du front qui était le plus près de nous. À la fin de la guerre, je me suis réfugié dans un camp de personnes déplacées.

Tant de malheurs en si peu de mots!

— Je suis désolée, Ivan.

Je sentais les larmes ruisseler sur mes joues.

— J'avais besoin de le dire tout haut, a confié Ivan. Toi aussi, tu devrais nous parler de ce que tu te rappelles, a-t-il ajouté en me serrant très très fort dans ses bras.

Il avait peut-être raison, mais je ne me sentais pas prête à en parler à ce moment-là.

Nous sommes restés sans rien dire pendant un bon moment, perdus tous les trois dans nos pensées. J'étais assise et j'essayais de mettre bout à bout les bribes de souvenirs de mon passé. La belle grande ferme et la chambre pleine de jouets. La robe rose que je détestais. Pourquoi tant la détester? Les initiales GH brodées sur les serviettes de bain. Que représentaient-elles? Est-ce que Mutter, Vater et Eva étaient ma vraie famille? La scène de la rencontre face à face avec Hitler était gravée dans ma mémoire. J'aurais aimé pouvoir la chasser à tout jamais, mais mon souvenir était si précis que je me rappelais même les odeurs.

Ivan détestait les nazis. Après ce qu'ils avaient fait à sa mère et à sa sœur... Si j'étais une nazie, alors comment Ivan pourrait-il m'aimer? Comment pourrait-on m'aimer?

Mais à quoi bon m'interroger sur ces bribes de souvenirs? Mon prénom n'était pas vraiment Nadia, mais un autre qui commençait par G. La ferme, la longue voiture noire et Hitler : ces images étaient comme des photographies imprimées dans mon cerveau.

Je savais avec quelle facilité Marusia pouvait mentir. Me mentait-elle à propos de mon passé?

Chapitre six

Les lilas

L'été a passé très vite. Marusia s'est trouvé une place de cueilleuse de fraises. Quand la saison des fraises a été finie, le même fermier l'a gardée pour travailler à d'autres récoltes. J'occupais mes journées à suivre mes leçons chez Mlle MacIntosh et à aller à la bibliothèque avec Mychailo. Mlle Barry nous accueillait toujours avec un grand sourire. Elle nous laissait regarder les nouveautés et nous indiquait des livres qui, selon elle, allaient nous plaire. Ces activités routinières semblaient me calmer un peu les esprits. Les souvenirs et les cauchemars avaient cessé, peut-être pour de bon.

Le samedi soir, si Ivan n'était pas trop fatigué, Marusia et moi nous rendions à la salle communautaire de la rue Dundas. L'immeuble était loué par tous les Ukrainiens de la ville, qui en partageaient les frais, orthodoxes et catholiques sans distinction. Marusia adorait ces sorties. Pour le travail à la ferme, elle portait de vieilles salopettes d'homme, tout usées, et quand elle rentrait à la maison, elle enfilait une robe ordinaire, achetée usagée. Mais pour ces samedis soirs, elle mettait une jupe et une jolie blouse.

À l'occasion, les gens réunis dans la salle recrutaient un orchestre et dansaient. D'autres fois, ils s'asseyaient à des tables et discutaient. Marusia se joignait généralement à un groupe qui écrivait des lettres afin d'aider un peu les organismes qui tentaient de retrouver des personnes disparues. Ils discutaient des progrès de leurs recherches et comparaient leurs notes.

J'aimais m'y rendre parce que j'y rencontrais d'autres enfants qui parlaient ukrainien. Mychailo s'y trouvait souvent. J'ai été désespérée d'apprendre que, à part Mychailo, aucun autre enfant ukrainien ne fréquenterait l'école Centrale. Nous étions peu nombreux et dispersés dans toute la ville. Il y avait deux sœurs, nées au Canada, qui ne parlaient pas très bien l'ukrainien. Elles allaient à l'école Grandview. Un garçon très grand, qui portait des lunettes et parlait l'ukrainien avec un accent polonais, était inscrit à l'école Saint-Basile.

Tous les dimanches, tôt le matin, nous nous rhabillions avec nos belles tenues et nous nous rendions à pied à l'église catholique ukrainienne de la rue Terrace Hill, c'est-à-dire une rue avant celle de la salle communautaire. L'église était petite, et il y avait tant de gens qui y venaient que nous devions arriver très tôt pour avoir des places. Cette église était le seul endroit où je me sentais totalement en sécurité. Les paroissiens sachant chanter juste étaient peu nombreux, mais je n'en faisais pas de cas. J'adorais me laisser bercer par le rythme des cantiques et sentir le parfum de l'encens. Assise dans cette église, je me sentais protégée.

Ivan travaillait sur la maison tous les jours après son travail, et la dernière semaine d'août, il l'avait terminée. Tous les matins, un camion venait chercher Marusia et l'emmenait à la ferme de Burford. Nous avions besoin de l'argent qu'elle gagnait, mais ses mains étaient enflées à cause des longues heures de travail passées aux champs.

Toutefois, je savais qu'il y avait autre chose qui la tracassait. Chaque fois que le facteur apportait le courrier, elle examinait aussitôt chaque enveloppe, cherchant quelque chose qui ne semblait jamais venir. Un jour, je lui en ai parlé et les larmes lui sont montées aux yeux.

— Je ne peux rien te dire pour le moment, m'a-t-elle simplement répondu.

Je croyais qu'elle attendait des nouvelles de la Croix-Rouge concernant un membre de sa famille. À la salle communautaire, quand quelqu'un recevait une de ces lettres, tout le monde se rapprochait pour en écouter la lecture. Parfois les nouvelles étaient mauvaises, mais quand elles étaient bonnes, nous criions tous de joie.

Autrefois, Marusia avait commencé des études en pharmacie, mais pendant la guerre, elle devait travailler dans une usine à cause des travaux forcés. Par la suite, elle a été contrainte de travailler comme cuisinière dans la ferme allemande où nous nous sommes connues. Ce devait être affreux pour elle de devoir faire encore une fois des travaux pénibles, même si elle était censée être libre. De temps en temps, je voyais comme un voile de tristesse sur son visage. Quand je lui demandais ce qui n'allait pas, elle se forçait à sourire et disait :

— Ce n'est rien, Nadia. Je réfléchissais.

Dès que nous le pouvions, nous nous installions tous les trois sur les marches en blocs de ciment de la cour, avec les livres de la bibliothèque et ceux de Mlle MacIntosh. Marusia rêvait de connaître l'anglais suffisamment bien pour pouvoir décrocher un travail dans un magasin ou peut-être même dans une pharmacie. Ivan parlait assez bien l'anglais, mais il n'avait pas l'occasion d'apprendre à l'écrire. Je crois qu'il avait hâte que je commence l'école parce que je pourrais ensuite lui montrer tout ce que j'avais appris.

La semaine avant la rentrée des classes, Ivan est venu m'accueillir à notre porte au moment où je rentrais de chez Mlle MacIntosh. Il avait un sourire jusqu'aux oreilles.

— C'est le grand jour! Tu dois choisir la couleur de ta chambre, m'a-t-il fièrement annoncé.

Non, non, non. Je m'étais habituée à dormir dans le

salon quand il faisait froid ou qu'il pleuvait, et dehors quand il faisait chaud.

— Je n'ai pas besoin d'une chambre à coucher, ai-je dit. Pourquoi je ne dormirais pas dans le salon pour toujours?

Il m'a regardée d'un air interrogateur.

— Alors tu pourrais utiliser cette pièce dans le grenier pour ranger tes affaires. Nadia, il te faut une chambre à toi, a-t-il dit en secouant la tête.

Je n'ai rien dit. Ivan m'a prise par la main et m'a entraînée dehors.

— Tu verras, a-t-il dit. Avec le temps, tu voudras avoir ta propre chambre.

La quincaillerie se trouvait dans la rue Colborne, à deux pâtés de maisons de la bibliothèque. Ivan a tenu la porte ouverte d'une main et de l'autre, il a fait un grand geste m'invitant à entrer. Une fois à l'intérieur, l'odeur de la peinture fraîche est venue chatouiller ma mémoire, mais heureusement, aucune image nette ne s'est formée dans ma tête.

Il y avait des pots de peinture en métal brillant empilés près des murs et dans les allées. Je m'attendais à voir mille couleurs, mais la plupart des pots étaient recouverts d'une étiquette blanche. Sur un présentoir près de la caisse, il y avait un catalogue d'échantillons de couleurs. Ivan m'a emmenée devant, puis l'a ouvert au hasard, à une page de jaunes et d'ocres. Il m'a regardée, attendant ma réaction, mais je me suis contentée de secouer la tête. Jaune, c'était le soleil, et j'adorais le soleil, mais le jaune me rendait triste…

Je suis dans la longue voiture noire, seule avec Vater et le chauffeur. Nous arrivons devant un groupe de bâtiments entourés de barbelés. Sur l'enseigne à l'entrée, on peut lire : Le travail libère l'homme. Les grilles s'ouvrent, et la voiture pénètre dans l'enceinte. Je ne me sens pas bien. Vater me prend par la main et me fait descendre avec lui.

Nous passons devant une longue file de femmes et d'enfants émaciés au regard dévoré par la faim. Certains sont habillés pour l'hiver et d'autres, pour l'été, mais ils ont tous une chose en commun : une étoile jaune cousue sur leurs vêtements. Une fille de mon âge porte une robe jaune toute défraîchie. Sa mère pensait peut-être qu'une étoile jaune cousue sur une robe jaune ne se verrait pas. Quand nous passons devant elle, elle me regarde droit dans les yeux.

— Ne les regarde pas, dit Vater en me tirant par la main.

Nous entrons dans un genre d'entrepôt situé à la tête de la file de gens. Des cartons et des caissons de bois débordent de vêtements et d'accessoires de luxe : des fourrures, des mules de satin bleu, un diadème. Il y a même une robe de mariée toute neuve, me semble-t-il. Un soldat au ventre bien rebondi est assis derrière un bureau. Il ne prend pas la peine de se lever quand nous entrons, mais il fait un signe de la tête pour montrer qu'il est averti de notre visite. J'ai peur, et mon cœur bat à tout rompre. Vater est-il en colère contre moi? Va-t-il m'abandonner là? Je n'ai pas d'étoile jaune.

Le soldat me sourit tout en m'examinant de la tête aux pieds. Il a les dents jaunes, et le col de son uniforme est si serré que les replis de son cou en débordent.

— *Tu dois être Gretchen, me dit-il.*

Je suis trop effrayée pour parler.

— *Tu as besoin de vêtements plus beaux que ceux que tu portes, dit-il en regardant ma tunique bleue et mon chemisier blanc.*

 Il se tourne vers Vater et lui dit :

— *Je vais lui trouver quelque chose de bien.*

Nous ressortons et nous repassons devant les femmes et les enfants avec des étoiles jaunes. Je peux sentir des dizaines de regards rivés sur mon dos...

— Que dis-tu de celle-ci? a dit Ivan.

Gretchen...

J'ai cligné des yeux.

Gretchen Himmel. GH. Je m'appelais Gretchen Himmel.

J'ai encore cligné des yeux. J'étais revenue dans le magasin, avec Ivan.

J'ai baissé le regard sur la couleur qu'il m'indiquait. Un jaune léger, de la couleur du beurre frais.

— Non, ai-je dit brusquement.

Jaune, c'était la mort. Je ne pourrais jamais dormir dans une chambre jaune. J'ai tourné la page si brusquement que j'ai failli la déchirer.

—Attention! a répliqué Ivan en écrasant de sa main

le faux pli qui s'était formé dans la feuille de papier glacé.

Mon esprit oscillait encore entre le passé et le présent. Je me suis agrippée au comptoir, de peur de m'écraser par terre.

Ivan me regardait d'un drôle d'air.

— Qu'est-ce qui ne va pas, Nadia?

J'ai respiré profondément, en essayant de me calmer.

— Rien, ça va, ça va! ai-je dit pour qu'on en finisse au plus vite. Regardons d'autres teintes.

Il y avait toutes les nuances de rose et de ·rouge, depuis le rose délicat de la robe de brocart d'autrefois, jusqu'au rouge violent du sang. Non, non, non!

Puis il y avait les pages de bleus. Ma main a comme décidé pour moi d'indiquer une teinte de mauve très léger. Un doux parfum est venu chatouiller le fond de ma mémoire : des lilas dans un jardin que j'adorais.

— Tu veux cette couleur pour ta chambre? a demandé Ivan.

À ma grande surprise, j'ai dit oui. Oui, je voulais cette couleur. Je me sentirais en sécurité dans une chambre couleur lilas. Je n'étais toujours pas ravie de devoir passer la nuit dans une petite chambre fermée, mais cette couleur me réconforterait. Et je pourrais peut-être convaincre Ivan de ne pas installer de porte.

Il a tendu une pastille de couleur lilas au commis et en a commandé un gallon. Nous sommes rentrés à pied, avec le pot de peinture qui se balançait entre nous deux.

Ivan et moi avons peint la chambre ensemble. C'était vite fait, la chambre étant si petite. J'ai continué de dormir dans le salon pendant quelques jours, le temps de laisser sécher la peinture.

Le premier soir où j'ai dormi dans ma chambre, j'étais très tendue. Ivan avait acheté une lampe usagée et l'avait installée sur le caisson de bois qui me servait de table de chevet.

— Si tu as peur, tu allumes, m'a-t-il chuchoté à l'oreille.

Il s'est assis au bord de mon matelas et a chanté la *kolysanka* jusqu'à ce que je m'endorme. J'ai rêvé de lilas, par une journée venteuse et ensoleillée...

Chapitre sept

L'école

Au cours de ces dernières semaines d'été, je n'ai pas vu Marusia bien souvent. Certains jours, elle travaillait si longtemps à la ferme qu'elle rentrait après l'heure du souper. La tâche de préparer le repas m'était revenue, mais ça m'allait. Je m'amusais à composer des menus avec tous les produits de la ferme que Marusia nous rapportait et qui variaient tout le temps, selon les jours ou les semaines : salades, concombres, maïs, tomates, pêches, oignons. Au camp, nous mangions du riz, encore du riz et toujours du riz. Maintenant nos repas se composaient d'une grosse salade ou de maïs, avec des pommes de terre bouillies et, parfois, un peu de saucisse.

Le matin de ma rentrée à l'école, Marusia m'a réveillée très tôt.

— J'ai une surprise pour toi, m'a-t-elle dit.

Quand et comment avait-elle trouvé le temps de faire cela? Je l'ignore. Elle m'avait confectionné une blouse et une jupe bleues avec le rouleau de tissu qu'une dame avait apporté le jour de notre arrivée.

Elle avait brodé de petites marguerites blanches tout le tour du col et, avec le fer à repasser, elle avait formé de beaux plis creux dans la jupe. J'ai levé les yeux et je l'ai regardée à travers mes larmes.

— Habille-toi, *Sonechko*. Tu ne veux sûrement pas être en retard pour ta première journée.

J'ai glissé mes bras dans les manches et attaché les petits boutons blancs; chaque boutonnière était délicatement brodée de fil blanc. La jupe m'allait parfaitement. Marusia m'a donné une nouvelle paire de bas blancs. Puis, en me souriant, elle a sorti d'un sac en papier des chaussures de cuir verni noir. J'ai remonté mes bas jusqu'aux genoux et j'ai glissé mes pieds dans les chaussures.

— Elles sont presque neuves, a dit Marusia. J'espère qu'elles te plaisent.

En général, j'essaie de me montrer réservée à l'égard de Marusia; elle n'est pas ma mère, après tout. Mais je sentais tout l'amour qu'elle avait mis dans la confection des plis de ma jupe et toute l'affection que représentait chaque point du chemisier. J'ai regardé son chemisier soigneusement repassé, mais montrant des signes d'usure, et ses yeux qui me souriaient même s'ils étaient cernés de fatigue. J'ai grimpé sur ses genoux et je l'ai serrée très très fort dans mes bras. Je sentais mes larmes couler sur mes joues.

— Nadia, ma Nadia! a dit Marusia en les essuyant du revers de la main. Je voulais te faire plaisir.

J'ai voulu lui répondre, mais aucun son n'est sorti

de ma bouche. J'ai donc hoché la tête, en espérant qu'elle comprendrait que j'appréciais énormément tout ce qu'elle faisait pour moi. Je me suis aspergé le visage avec de l'eau fraîche afin de soulager mes yeux rougis, puis Marusia a tressé mes cheveux.

Au lieu de les arranger comme d'habitude, elle a remonté mes tresses en couronne sur ma tête et y a ajouté une grosse boucle de ruban blanc. Je me suis regardée dans le miroir, et j'ai vu une autre moi dans un autre miroir. J'étais plus jeune, je portais une robe rose, mes yeux étaient rouges d'avoir pleuré…

— On dirait que tu as vu un fantôme, a dit Marusia.

J'ai cligné des yeux. L'autre moi plus jeune s'était envolée en fumée.

Marusia m'a accompagnée à pied jusqu'à l'école Centrale. Nous étions les premières arrivées.

Elle a ouvert la porte, et nous avons traversé le couloir qui était vide.

— Ta classe est là-bas, a-t-elle dit en me tirant par la main.

Puis elle a tourné et a pris un couloir sur la gauche. Elle a frappé à une porte et, quand on nous a répondu, elle a tourné la poignée. La porte s'est ouverte.

— Bonne chance, a-t-elle dit.

Elle a mis ses doigts en travers de ses lèvres, m'a soufflé un baiser et est ressortie de l'école. Après son départ, je me suis rendu compte qu'en venant me conduire à l'école, elle avait manqué son transport jusqu'à son travail.

Je suis entrée dans la classe vide. C'était celle que j'avais regardée par le carreau quand je m'étais aventurée dans le voisinage. À l'avant, il y avait un grand tableau noir et un gros bureau. Le reste de la salle était occupé par des rangées de pupitres. Lequel devais-je prendre? L'institutrice serait-elle choquée si, en arrivant, elle me trouvait assise à la mauvaise place? J'ai décidé d'en prendre le risque et je me suis installée à un pupitre dans un coin, au fond. Puis j'ai attendu que les autres arrivent.

Au camp, un monsieur qui avait été professeur avant la guerre enseignait l'histoire aux quelques enfants un peu plus âgés, et une dame qui connaissait l'anglais donnait des leçons aux adultes comme aux enfants. Nous nous asseyions sur des bancs, et nos genoux nous servaient de pupitre. Sur le mur, il y avait une affiche représentant Taras Shevchenko, le plus grand poète ukrainien. Je ne sais pas d'où venait cette affiche. Sûrement pas d'un pauvre réfugié! Peut-être d'un colis de l'aide humanitaire en provenance du Canada ou des États-Unis? Je me suis aussi vaguement souvenue de leçons en allemand, données par une dame à l'air sévère, dans une petite école de campagne. Mais je ne me rappelais pas quand c'était exactement.

J'ai baissé les yeux pour regarder la belle tenue que Marusia m'avait confectionnée. J'ai passé les doigts sur le tissu, heureuse de savoir que chaque point avait été fait exprès pour moi…

Vater est dans le grand salon. Il en impose, dans son uniforme noir. Je vois que ses grandes bottes de cuir sont couvertes de boue. Peu importe! Il y a des forçats pour nettoyer derrière lui. Il dépose un paquet sur la table et s'assoit. Mutter s'assoit sur le canapé en face de lui, le dos bien droit et souriant d'un air pincé. Elle tapote la place à côté d'elle. Eva s'y assoit. Je m'assois à côté d'Eva.

— *C'est pour toi, Gretchen, dit-il.*

Pour commencer, je suis excitée. Je me penche et je touche le papier brun du bout d'un doigt.

— *Ouvre-le! dit Eva.*

Je la regarde et je vois qu'elle brûle d'impatience.

Je prends le paquet, le dépose sur mes genoux et déchire l'emballage. Une magnifique robe de brocart rose. Je n'ai jamais rien eu de semblable de toute ma vie. Je sais que je suis censée être contente, mais la vue de cette robe me rend malade. Je lève les yeux vers Vater et me force à sourire.

— *Merci, dis-je.*

Vater sourit et répond :

— *Maintenant, toute la famille Himmel va bien paraître lors des rassemblements.*

J'emporte la robe dans ma chambre. Je la tiens à hauteur de mes épaules et me tourne vers le miroir. J'ai l'air de quelqu'un d'autre.

Ce soir-là, je ne peux pas dormir. J'allume ma lampe de chevet et je prends la robe. Elle sent la lessive fraîche, avec un relent d'autre chose. De la sueur? Je la retourne dans tous les sens, cherchant des indices. Je remarque un petit bout de galon cousu à l'intérieur, le long de la fermeture éclair du dos. Je retourne le galon. Une étiquette avec un nom. De petites lettres brodées : Rachel Goldstein.

Je revois brusquement cette fillette dans la file de gens, celle qui avait une robe jaune.

Je lance la robe le plus loin possible de moi.

Des voix d'enfants m'arrivant par les fenêtres de la classe, pleines de rires et d'excitation, m'ont ramenée dans le présent. Les larmes me sont montées aux yeux. J'ai respiré profondément pour tenter de me calmer.

Puis les bruits se sont rapprochés, mais aucun enfant n'est entré dans la classe où j'étais. J'aurais peut-être dû attendre dehors plutôt que d'entrer dans cette salle. À ce moment précis, une dame aux cheveux coupés au carré est entrée. J'étais prise au piège.

Elle m'a souri, puis elle a dit :

— Tu dois être notre nouvelle élève, Natalie Kraftchuk.

J'ai bondi sur mes pieds, je l'ai saluée de la tête et, dans mon meilleur anglais, j'ai dit :

— Bonjour, madame l'institutrice. Je m'appelle Nadia Kravchuk.

Elle m'a tendu la main.

— Je suis Mlle Ferris. Les autres enfants vont bientôt arriver.

Je lui ai serré la main. Elle s'est retournée et a quitté la classe. Je me suis donc rassise.

J'ai entendu une grosse cloche et j'ai sursauté si fort que j'ai failli tomber de ma chaise. Quelques minutes plus tard, les couloirs résonnaient des voix des enfants. Mlle Ferris est entrée dans la classe, suivie d'une file d'élèves.

Chapitre huit

L'humiliation

Un grand garçon dégingandé est entré le premier. Il a parcouru la classe des yeux, puis s'est arrêté sur moi. Je sentais la gêne m'envahir tandis qu'il examinait mes chaussures, mes vêtements et la boucle dans mes cheveux. Puis il a ri. Je me serais cachée sous mon pupitre si j'avais pu. En me montrant du doigt, il a donné un coup de coude au garçon qui le suivait. Celui-ci a souri. Ensuite venait une fille. Elle portait une jupe et un chemisier, rien de sophistiqué. Ses cheveux bouclés tombaient sur ses épaules. Pas de ruban. Pas de tresses. Elle a regardé dans ma direction et a aussitôt détourné les yeux, faisant comme si elle ne m'avait pas vue. Elle s'est assise le plus loin possible de moi. D'autres élèves sont entrés. Aucun ne m'a saluée, et ils se sont tous bousculés pour prendre un pupitre loin de moi.

La dernière qui est entrée dans la classe était une fille au teint basané avec une tresse d'un noir brillant qui lui tombait jusqu'à la taille. Il ne restait qu'une place, à côté de moi. Elle l'a donc prise. Elle s'est tournée vers moi et m'a souri. Elle avait un espace entre les deux dents de devant, et elle me regardait gentiment.

— Bonjour, a-t-elle dit. Je m'appelle Linda. Et toi?

Linda. Quel beau prénom! J'aurais voulu pleurer de soulagement.

— Nadia, ai-je balbutié.

Je voulais lui demander si elle habitait dans les environs, mais j'étais si énervée que je ne trouvais pas mes mots en anglais. Alors, je lui ai simplement souri.

— Les enfants! a dit Mlle Ferris en tapant dans ses mains, debout devant la classe. Nous avons deux nouveaux élèves cette année. Natalie et Bob, s'il vous plaît, levez-vous.

Pourquoi m'appelait-elle Natalie? Je me suis levée avec maladresse. À l'autre bout de la classe, un garçon s'est levé aussi. Il était si gêné que ses oreilles commençaient à rougir.

— Les enfants! Nous accueillons aujourd'hui Natalie Kravchuk et Bob Landry.

— Bienvenue à l'école Centrale, Natalie et Bob, ont ânonné les élèves à l'unisson.

Nous nous sommes rassis. Bob avait maintenant les oreilles toutes rouges, et le visage aussi. Je suis sûre que j'étais aussi rouge que lui. Mlle Ferris a pris les présences, puis nous a distribué des cahiers d'exercices neufs et de crayons à mine. Elle nous a fait lever à tour de rôle pour que chacun raconte au reste de la classe ce qu'il avait fait pendant l'été.

Comme j'étais au fond, mon tour était en dernier. J'avais donc le temps de me préparer, mais aussi de m'énerver. Je ne savais pas trop comment je pouvais expliquer ce que j'avais fait durant l'été. J'aurais pu le raconter en ukrainien, en russe, en yiddish ou en allemand... mais en anglais? Finalement, mon tour est venu. Je me suis levée.

— Je m'appelle Nadia Kravchuk. Je suis arrivée au Canada cet été, ai-je dit lentement en articulant bien.

Il y a eu des murmures et des ricanements autour de moi. J'allais m'asseoir quand Mlle Ferris m'a demandé :

— Qu'as-tu fait, une fois rendue ici, Natal... Nadia?

— J'ai appris l'anglais.

Un garçon qui était assis à l'avant de la classe a éclaté de rire.

— Pas très bien, a-t-il lancé.

— Ouais, a renchéri un autre. Elle a l'air d'une nazie.

Je me suis sentie rougir de honte. Je m'étais déjà appelée Himmel. J'avais une sœur qui s'appelait Eva. J'appelais mes parents *Mutter* et *Vater*. J'étais donc une nazie?

Marusia m'avait cent fois répété que non. Mais alors, pourquoi ces souvenirs? Ce qu'elle disait et mes souvenirs ne concordaient pas.

Mlle Ferris a donné des coups de règle sur son bureau et a crié :

— Silence!

Puis elle a montré du doigt les deux garçons et a

ajouté :

— David et Éric, au bureau du directeur. Immédiatement!

Je me suis rassise. J'aurais voulu être ailleurs. J'étais déjà embarrassée d'avoir l'air différente des autres, de porter des vêtements différents aussi, et voilà que je me faisais remarquer avec mon accent en anglais!

Je ne me souviens plus exactement de ce qu'elle nous a enseigné ce matin-là. Tout ce que j'avais en tête, c'était de rentrer à la maison pour me changer et défaire mes cheveux. J'aurais tant voulu pouvoir changer d'accent aussi!

J'ai soigneusement recopié ce que Mlle Ferris écrivait au tableau et je l'ai remerciée intérieurement de ne pas me demander de prendre la parole. Après un temps interminable, la cloche a sonné. J'ai regardé les autres ranger leurs cahiers. Dieu merci, ma torture était terminée!

J'ai refermé mes livres, je les ai glissés à l'intérieur du pupitre et j'ai suivi les autres élèves qui sortaient de la classe. Linda, l'élève gentille, me suivait de près. Dehors, dès que l'air frais a balayé mon visage, je me suis sentie soulagée. J'avais l'impression d'être en prison, là-dedans. Je suis sortie de la cour et j'ai commencé à marcher en direction de chez nous. Linda a couru me rejoindre et m'a prise par le bras.

— Tu ne peux pas quitter l'école comme ça!

Je me suis tournée vers elle, perplexe. La cloche avait sonné, me semblait-il.

— Mais la cloche… ai-je commencé.

Elle a fait un large sourire dévoilant l'espace entre ses deux dents et s'est exclamée :

— C'était la cloche de la récréation! Tu ne peux pas retourner chez toi avant l'heure du dîner!

— Je ne peux pas rester ici.

— Ils vont envoyer quelqu'un te chercher chez toi!

— Qui donc? ai-je demandé.

— Un policier. Tu ne peux pas rester chez toi durant les heures de classe.

Même l'idée de la police ne m'a pas empêchée de partir. Linda est restée à l'entrée de la cour, l'air ahurie. J'ai continué mon chemin; plus je m'éloignais de l'école, plus j'accélérais. Les jolies chaussures me faisaient mal aux talons, mais je n'ai pas ralenti le pas pour autant. Quand je suis arrivée chez nous, j'avais un point de côté. J'ai soulevé le paillasson devant la porte. J'ai pris la clé qui était dessous, j'ai ouvert la porte et je me suis précipitée à l'intérieur.

Je m'étais rarement retrouvée seule à la maison. J'étais frappée par le silence inhabituel qui y régnait. J'avais presque l'impression que la maison me regardait dans un silence désapprobateur. J'ai lancé mes chaussures dans un coin et j'ai grimpé l'escalier quatre à quatre. Le bruit de mes pieds sur les marches de bois me réconfortait. Je me suis jetée sur mon lit et j'ai donné des coups de poing dans mon oreiller, tant j'étais en colère. Comment allais-je faire pour retourner dans cette école? Les autres enfants me détestaient.

J'ai hurlé le plus fort que je pouvais, et ça m'a fait du bien parce qu'il n'y avait que la maison pour m'entendre et que je pouvais me laisser aller à ma tristesse. Quand je me suis mise à pleurer, je ne pouvais plus m'arrêter. Je pleurais sur mon triste sort d'élève nouvelle à l'école. Je pleurais de rage de me sentir si impuissante. Mais surtout, je pleurais de honte à cause de la petite fille que j'avais été par le passé. Étais-je vraiment chez moi ici? Étais-je une nazie? Je ne méritais peut-être pas de survivre. Où était-ce, chez moi?

Je ne sais pas combien de temps j'ai pleuré, mais mes yeux étaient si bouffis que j'avais du mal à les ouvrir. J'ai regardé la belle tenue que Marusia avait cousue pour moi : elle était toute mouillée et froissée. Comme j'étais méchante! Comme j'étais ingrate! Comment Marusia allait-elle réagir? Allait-elle me renvoyer dans cette autre famille, celle dont j'essayais de chasser le souvenir de ma mémoire?

J'ai déboutonné le chemisier et j'ai essayé de le défroisser. Je l'ai mis sur un cintre et je l'ai suspendu au crochet derrière ma porte. J'ai retiré la jupe en faisant bien attention de ne pas l'abîmer davantage. Je l'ai pliée, j'ai lissé les plis avec mes mains et je l'ai remise dans le premier tiroir de ma commode. J'ai sorti une jupe et un chemisier, les plus vieux que j'avais, pour me rhabiller.

— Voilà tout ce que tu mérites, petite ingrate! me

suis-je dit à voix haute.

J'avais l'impression d'avoir déjà entendu cette réprimande, il y a très longtemps. J'ai essayé de défaire mes tresses. J'ai réussi à enlever les élastiques qui les attachaient au bout, mais je ne suis pas arrivée à défaire la couronne que Marusia avait montée sur ma tête parce qu'elle l'avait attachée très serré avec le ruban blanc. J'avais mal aux bras à force d'essayer. Alors, je me suis étendue sur le dos, dans mon lit. Je voulais dormir, mais je n'y arrivais pas; alors j'ai fixé le plafond.

Puis un événement du passé m'est revenu à l'esprit...

Les hommes étaient séparés des femmes. J'étais dressée sur la pointe des pieds pour voir où on les emmenait, mais il y avait trop de monde. J'ai pensé à cette fillette avec la robe jaune et l'étoile jaune cousue dessus, qui faisait la queue exactement comme ces gens.

— Retirez tous vos vêtements, a ordonné une femme en uniforme, d'une voix blasée.

Apeurée, je me suis tournée vers Marusia, mais elle était déjà en train de déboutonner son chemisier sale et tout usé. Elle l'a lancé sur la pile de vêtements en train de brûler. Elle a enlevé sa jupe et l'a jetée aussi dans le feu.

— Vite, Nadia, a-t-elle dit.

La robe que je portais avait été une belle robe rose, mais maintenant elle était noire de crasse et de transpiration. Combien de wagons plats avions-nous pris et dans combien de fossés nous étions-nous cachées avant d'arriver dans cet endroit? Les jours s'emmêlaient tous dans ma mémoire. J'ai essayé de défaire ma ceinture de satin, mais elle était si effilochée que je n'arrivais pas à défaire le nœud. Et je n'étais pas capable d'atteindre la fermeture éclair dans mon dos.

Marusia a saisi ma robe par le col et, d'un seul geste, elle l'a déchirée de haut en bas. Elle l'a lancée dans le feu.

— Les sous-vêtements aussi, a beuglé la femme.

Nous avons tout lancé dans les flammes, puis nous avons rejoint la file suivante.

Une femme a coupé mes tresses avec de gros ciseaux, puis ce qui me restait de cheveux si près de la tête qu'on voyait mon cuir chevelu. J'ai regardé mes cheveux sales tomber en grosses touffes sur le sol.

Marusia n'a pas bronché pendant qu'on lui coupait les cheveux. Avec les autres réfugiés, nous avons fait la queue aux douches. À la porte, une femme nous a aspergées avec un truc horrible. J'ai hurlé.

— Ne crains rien, a dit Marusia. C'est pour tuer les poux.

Nous étions entassées dans une pièce couverte de carreaux blancs, sous des jets d'eau bouillante. Je regardais les rigoles noires, pleines de crasse et de poux, s'engouffrer dans l'orifice d'écoulement d'eau au centre du plancher.

J'étais contente d'être débarrassée de la robe rose et de tout ce qu'elle représentait. On nous a donné des draps pour nous couvrir en sortant des douches. Il y avait des poux dans les draps, mais nous nous sommes quand même enroulées dedans.

Ensuite il y avait l'entrevue. Nous avons encore fait la queue, trempées et grelottant de froid, mais plus propres que jamais depuis notre fuite. Je me suis mise sur la pointe des pieds pour voir ce qui se passait à la tête de la file. Un homme en uniforme était assis à une table et prenait des notes. Il estampillait un document, puis envoyait le réfugié dans une direction ou dans l'autre.

Marusia s'est penchée et m'a chuchoté à l'oreille :

— Dis-leur que tu es ma fille, que tu t'appelles Nadia et que tu es née à Lviv…

Je savais que si les Soviétiques découvraient d'où je venais vraiment, ils me garderaient, et je serais envoyée en Sibérie. Mais d'où venais-je vraiment? Je l'ignorais. Marusia le savait-elle?

J'ai été brusquement ramenée dans le présent par des coups frappés très fort à notre porte. Linda avait dit qu'il était illégal de partir de l'école. La police venait-elle me chercher? J'étais paralysée par la peur.

D'autres coups.

— Nadia! a crié une voix de femme que je connaissais.

J'ai jeté un coup d'œil par le coin de ma fenêtre. C'était Mlle MacIntosh. Et si je faisais semblant de ne pas être là? À l'instant même où je me faisais cette réflexion, elle m'a aperçue.

— Ouvre! a-t-elle ordonné

Elle n'avait pas l'air très contente.

J'ai descendu les escaliers, mais je n'ai pas ouvert la porte tout de suite. J'ai couru dans la salle de bain pour me regarder dans le miroir. J'avais les yeux rouges et enflés, et le visage bouffi. Qu'allait penser Mlle MacIntosh? J'ai passé un linge sous l'eau froide et je l'ai appliqué sur mon visage. La fraîcheur de l'eau m'a fait du bien, mais quand ensuite je me suis regardée dans le miroir, j'avais toujours les yeux enflés. Il n'y avait rien à faire.

Les coups sur la porte sont devenus plus insistants.

— Nadia! a crié Mlle MacIntosh. Je sais que tu es là.

J'ai ouvert la porte d'entrée. L'expression de Mlle MacIntosh est aussitôt passée de l'impatience à l'inquiétude. Elle est entrée et a refermé la porte derrière elle.

— Qu'est-ce qui t'arrive?

J'ai baissé les yeux, sans lui répondre. J'avais peur que, en essayant de parler, il ne sorte de ma bouche que des sanglots.

Soudain, j'ai senti les bras de Mlle MacIntosh autour de mon corps. Elle m'a soulevée comme si je n'avais été qu'un tout petit bébé. Elle m'a serrée très fort contre son cœur, et j'ai senti que je devenais toute molle. Je ne sais pas si c'était de soulagement ou de résignation. Elle m'a transportée jusque dans la cuisine et s'est assise sur une chaise, en me tenant toujours dans ses bras. Elle m'a bercée sur ses genoux, même si mes jambes étaient presque aussi longues que les siennes et que mes pieds pouvaient toucher par terre. Elle a murmuré :

— Ça va aller, Nadia.

J'ai failli me remettre à pleurer, mais une petite voix au fond de moi m'a dit que ça suffisait. Alors j'ai inspiré profondément, puis j'ai expiré lentement. Je me suis dégagée doucement des bras de Mlle MacIntosh et me suis remise debout.

— Pourquoi êtes-vous ici? ai-je demandé.

— Tu es partie de l'école, a-t-elle dit. Il faut que tu y retournes.

— Je ne peux pas, ai-je dit en croisant les bras et en essayant de la défier.

— Tu n'as pas le choix, a répliqué Mlle MacIntosh. C'est illégal de quitter l'école.

Linda avait donc dit vrai. La police allait-elle venir maintenant?

Mlle MacIntosh a dû lire la panique sur mon visage. Elle a poursuivi :

— Si tu reviens cet après-midi, il n'y aura pas de problème.

— Mais je ne peux pas y retourner avec la tête que j'ai!

— Il faut te montrer courageuse, Nadia, a dit Mlle MacIntosh d'un ton sévère. Je ne devrais même pas être ici en ce moment. Je suis censée surveiller les enfants dans la cour de l'école. Quand Linda m'a dit que tu t'étais sauvée, il fallait que je vienne te voir.

Elle s'est levée et a ouvert notre glacière. Elle en a ressorti deux pommes.

— Presse-les contre tes yeux, ça aidera à les faire désenfler.

C'est ce que j'ai fait. Je l'entendais s'affairer dans la cuisine. Elle tranchait du pain, faisait cuire des œufs. L'arôme du beurre et des œufs qui cuisaient dans le poêlon a fait gargouiller mon estomac. Puis j'ai entendu le bruit d'une assiette qu'elle déposait sur la table.

— C'est prêt! a-t-elle annoncé.

J'ai dégagé un de mes yeux. Elle était assise en face de moi et mangeait un œuf posé sur une tranche de pain, avec un couteau et une fourchette. J'ai déposé les deux pommes et j'ai dévoré mon repas. J'étais surprise d'avoir si faim.

Le repas terminé, j'ai rapporté les deux assiettes et je les ai rincées à l'évier.

— Il faut partir dans 15 minutes, a dit Mlle MacIntosh. Avant, je vais te recoiffer.

Nous nous sommes rendues ensemble dans la salle de bain, et j'ai regardé dans le miroir pendant que Mlle MacIntosh défaisait soigneusement les tresses compliquées que Marusia avait montées sur ma tête.

— C'était une coiffure magnifique, a-t-elle commenté. Mais elle ne convient pas pour l'école.

Tandis qu'elle peignait mes cheveux, son visage a soudain pris une drôle d'expression.

— Tu as une marque noire ici, a-t-elle dit. À la lisière de tes cheveux.

J'ai eu le souffle coupé pendant quelques secondes. Mon tatouage. J'ai tourné ma main gauche, paume vers le haut, et j'ai regardé l'intérieur de mon poignet qui portait la même marque. Puis je l'ai vite retournée avant que Mlle MacIntosh ne la voie. Les deux tatouages étaient si discrets que la plupart des gens ne les remarquaient pas.

— Ce doit être un grain de beauté, ai-je menti.

J'ai regardé le visage de Mlle MacIntosh dans le miroir. Elle allait dire quelque chose, puis s'est ravisée. Je me suis demandé si elle en savait plus que moi-même sur mon passé. Elle a continué à défaire délicatement les nœuds dans mes cheveux. Les coups de peigne me rappelaient une autre femme qui me démêlait les cheveux, mais en tirant rageusement dessus, sans me ménager. L'image fugitive de la robe de brocart rose m'a alors traversé l'esprit...

Mlle MacIntosh ne m'a pas accompagnée jusqu'à l'école, et je lui en étais reconnaissante. Elle a dû deviner qu'il était déjà très humiliant pour moi d'y retourner et que, si je me faisais accompagnée d'une institutrice, ce serait encore pire.

Quand je suis arrivée à l'école, j'avais encore les yeux rouges d'avoir pleuré. La première cloche avait déjà sonné, et les élèves se mettaient en rangs. Des enfants de ma classe m'ont regardée et se sont aussitôt détournés de moi. Mlle Ferris leur avait peut-être parlé. Puis j'ai entendu Éric marmonner :

— La fille d'Hitler est de retour.

Je me suis placée derrière Linda.

— Contente de te revoir! m'a-t-elle murmuré.

Je me suis assise au même pupitre et j'ai essayé de faire comme si de rien n'était. Tandis que Mlle Ferris débitait sa leçon, j'essayais de mettre de l'ordre dans les souvenirs qui m'étaient revenus récemment à la mémoire. Pourquoi me revenaient-ils justement maintenant? Quand nous étions au camp des personnes déplacées, j'arrivais à chasser toutes ces pensées de mon esprit. J'avais essayé de faire de même à bord du bateau, et j'y étais presque parvenue. Mais quand je suis arrivée à Brantford, les cauchemars ont commencé et les souvenirs me sont revenus. Pourquoi ne pouvais-je pas me débarrasser de toute cette tristesse?

Quand nous avons été tous installés, mon regard s'est arrêté sur la tête d'Éric qui se trouvait assis à quelques rangées devant moi. Pourquoi m'avait-il traitée de fille d'Hitler? C'était si méchant! Puis j'ai remarqué qu'il avait la nuque et les oreilles bien dégagées et que ses cheveux étaient un peu plus longs sur le dessus de la tête. Il ne les avait probablement pas repeignés depuis le matin et, pourtant, ils étaient parfaitement coiffés. J'étais certaine qu'un barbier les avait coupés, et pas un soldat. S'était-il déjà fait couper les cheveux à grands coups de ciseaux à cause des poux? Pouvait-il seulement imaginer une telle chose? Comment osait-il me juger!

J'ai parcouru du regard les rangées d'enfants qui se trouvaient devant moi. Tous les garçons et toutes les filles avaient l'air propres et bien nourris. Personne ne portait de haillons. Ils avaient probablement tous leurs parents. J'étais morte de jalousie. J'aurais tellement voulu avoir une vie toute simple, qui n'aurait jamais été bouleversée par la guerre.

Chapitre neuf

Mychailo

Je savais que Mychailo était le seul élève ukrainien de l'école Centrale. Finalement, je l'ai vu à la récréation de l'après-midi. Il jouait à pile ou face avec d'autres garçons, près d'un mur, et m'a aperçue du coin de l'œil. Il m'a fait un petit signe de tête et est retourné à son jeu.

Je l'ai revu plus tard, à la sortie de l'école. Il marchait à une rue de distance derrière moi. Je l'ai attendu, mais il était avec d'autres garçons. Il est passé devant moi en faisant semblant de ne pas me connaître. J'ai donc fait le reste du chemin toute seule.

Comme j'étais la première rentrée à la maison, j'ai commencé à peler des pommes de terre pour le souper. Je venais de remplir une casserole d'eau quand on a frappé à la porte d'entrée. C'était Mychailo, avec un air penaud.

— Tiens! Tu me reconnais maintenant! ai-je lancé.

— Allons! a-t-il dit en se dandinant sur ses pieds. Tu ne t'attendais tout de même pas à ce que je te parle alors que j'étais avec une bande de copains?

— Je ne vois pas ce que ça change.

J'ai laissé la porte ouverte et je suis retournée à mon évier. Il m'a suivie à l'intérieur et s'est assis sur une chaise dans la cuisine. Il m'a regardée peler les pommes de terre.

— Aimerais-tu aller à la bibliothèque? m'a-t-il demandé.

J'avais vraiment envie d'y aller, mais j'étais encore fâchée, alors je n'ai rien dit.

— Vas-tu les mettre à feu doux pendant que nous serons partis?

J'ai fait signe que non de la tête, sans prononcer un mot.

Ça me plaisait. Il semblait être dans ses petits souliers! J'ai fini de peler la dernière pomme de terre. Puis je les ai toutes rincées et je les ai mises dans la casserole avec de l'eau. Mais je n'ai pas allumé la cuisinière. Marusia m'avait prévenue de ne jamais le faire.

— Je peux aller à la bibliothèque, mais pas trop longtemps, ai-je dit. Je ferai bouillir les pommes de terre à mon retour.

Mychailo est resté sans rien dire pendant les premières minutes du trajet, puis il a dit :

— Désolé de ne pas t'avoir parlé avant.

Je ne lui ai rien répondu. Je savais pourquoi il ne m'avait pas parlé. Il ne voulait pas se faire harceler. Mais j'étais mortifiée qu'il m'ait traitée comme une inconnue.

En arrivant à la bibliothèque, Mychailo s'est tout de suite dirigé vers un chariot de livres qui étaient posés là en attendant d'être reclassés.

— J'ai fait une découverte il y a quelques jours, a-t-il dit. Les meilleurs livres sont toujours ici, sur ce chariot.

Il a pris un roman à la couverture fatiguée, qui s'intitulait *Prince Noir*.

— Tu vas l'aimer, a-t-il dit, les yeux pétillants de plaisir. Je l'ai lu l'an dernier.

Je le lui ai pris des mains et je l'ai feuilleté. Que du texte, sans aucune illustration. Et en petits caractères.

— Je ne peux pas lire ça, ai-je répliqué.

Il aurait dû le savoir. Je n'empruntais que des albums illustrés.

— Il te faudra du temps, a-t-il dit. Mais je pense que tu vas aimer cette histoire.

Puis il m'a souri en ajoutant :

— C'est un livre de filles.

— Mais tu l'as aimé!

Il a rougi un peu, puis a rétorqué :

— Il y a quand même beaucoup d'action dedans.

Il a farfouillé parmi les autres livres et en a trouvé un sur le hockey, un autre sur les roches et un troisième qui était un roman.

— Qu'est-ce que c'est comme roman? ai-je demandé en lui prenant le livre des mains.

Il m'a fallu un moment pour déchiffrer le titre, et même là, je ne comprenais pas. J'ai ajouté :

— *Freddy va en Floride?* Qu'est-ce que ça veut dire, *Freddy?*

— C'est un prénom, comme Mychailo ou Nadia, a-t-il répondu. Ce Freddy-là est un cochon qui parle.

— Un cochon qui parle? (Ça ne se pouvait pas.) Et qu'est-ce que c'est *la Floride?*

— C'est une région, a-t-il dit, l'air de ne pas comprendre ma confusion.

— Ça ne tient pas debout! ai-je répliqué. Les cochons ne parlent pas et ne se déplacent pas d'un endroit à un autre, à moins d'être conduits par des humains.

Mychailo a levé les yeux au ciel.

— Tu devrais peut-être lire un des livres de la collection, a-t-il suggéré. Alors tu comprendras. Ils sont tordants. *Freddy va en Floride* est le premier titre. J'essayais de mettre la main dessus depuis un bon bout de temps.

— Je parie que tu n'apportes pas ce genre de livres à l'école.

— Tu as raison, a-t-il avoué. Le livre de hockey, c'est pour l'école.

J'ai déposé *Prince Noir* sur le chariot. Il y avait trop de mots.

— Est-ce que je peux prendre un autre livre de Freddy?

— Bien sûr, a-t-il répondu. Allons voir ce qu'il y a sur les rayons.

Il en restait quelques-uns, alors Mychailo a pris un

exemplaire de *Freddy détective*.

— C'est le premier que j'ai lu, a-t-il précisé. C'est vraiment très bien.

Je l'ai feuilleté. Même si le livre était plus épais que *Prince Noir*, les caractères étaient gros et il y avait des illustrations. Pas autant que dans un album illustré, mais pas austère comme *Prince Noir*. J'ai humé le merveilleux parfum d'encre et de papier et j'ai caressé une page de la main. Même toucher ce livre me rendait heureuse…

Je suis dans mon lit à baldaquin, dans la ferme allemande. Je devrais dormir, mais j'ai été réveillée par des éclats de voix en bas. Je me lève. Grelottant de froid dans ma chemise de nuit légère, les pieds nus, je descends doucement l'escalier pour voir d'où viennent ces voix. La double porte de la bibliothèque est grande ouverte. Vater est assis, un ballon d'eau-de-vie à la main. D'autres hommes, la veste de leur uniforme déboutonnée, sont assis autour de la table. Ils se racontent des histoires et rient. Ce sont des soldats SS. Je le sais parce qu'ils portent sur leur veste le même écusson que Vater.

Mais ce n'est pas ce qui accroche mon regard. Je les ai vus si souvent, lors de rassemblements en ville ou de grands dîners ici. Ce qui m'intéresse, c'est la pièce où ils se trouvent. D'habitude, les portes sont fermées. Elle est tapissée de livres du plancher jusqu'au plafond. La plupart sont en allemand, mais il y en a dans d'autres langues. Il y en a des gros, des petits et certains sont même ornés de lettres dorées sur la reliure. J'adore les livres. J'aimerais tant les tenir dans mes mains. Mais je n'ai pas le droit d'y toucher.

Je retourne dans ma chambre et je prends sous mon lit le seul livre que Vater m'autorise à lire : Der Giftpiltz. *Je tourne les pages. Les illustrations ont de belles couleurs, et les lettres sont grandes et bien nettes. Je voudrais aimer ce livre, mais je n'y arrive pas. On y parle des Juifs; on dit qu'ils sont comme des champignons vénéneux, tandis que les Allemands sont comme des champignons comestibles. Une petite voix au fond de moi me dit que c'est faux. Je pense à cette fillette qui portait une étoile jaune et j'ai un pincement au cœur. Je referme le livre et je le remets sous mon lit.*

— Il faudrait y aller, dit Mychailo. Tu as un souper à faire, non?

Soudain j'étais revenue dans la bibliothèque au Canada. À Brantford. J'ai regardé Mychailo, puis l'horloge murale. Nous étions à la bibliothèque depuis une heure.

Nous nous sommes présentés au comptoir, lui avec ses trois livres et moi avec mon roman. Je me sentais un peu comme dans un rêve.

Un garçon plus vieux, qu'il me semblait avoir vu à la récréation aujourd'hui, faisait la queue devant nous. Il s'est retourné, a croisé le regard de Mychailo et l'a salué d'un signe de tête. Il n'avait pas l'air de m'avoir remarquée, mais cela ne me dérangeait pas. D'autres personnes faisaient la queue derrière nous. Je ne les connaissais pas, sauf Linda. Elle était avec une fille qui lui ressemblait beaucoup, mais qui était plus âgée. Ce devait être sa sœur. Une fois mon livre estampillé, j'ai attendu que Linda et sa sœur aient fait enregistrer les leurs.

Mychailo m'a tirée par la manche.

— Allons, a-t-il dit. Je croyais que tu avais des pommes de terre à faire cuire.

— Laisse-moi une minute!

Je savais qu'il ne voulait pas qu'on le voie avec moi. Mais là, il ne s'agissait pas d'un garçon, mais de deux filles de l'école, alors je ne voyais pas où était le problème. Il se tenait à côté de moi, trépignant d'impatience, tandis que Linda et sa sœur faisaient estampiller leurs livres.

— Bonjour Nadia! a dit Linda.

Elle a regardé Mychailo, puis elle est revenue à moi et a ajouté :

— Je vous présente ma sœur, Grace.

Grace était plus grande que Linda, mais elle avait les mêmes yeux noisette et les mêmes cheveux noirs comme le jais.

— Tu dois donc être Nadia, a-t-elle dit en me tendant la main. Enchantée de faire ta connaissance.

Elle a souri à Mychailo, puis a penché la tête afin de lire les titres sur le dos des livres que nous avions à la main.

— Je ne savais pas que tu aimais les livres de Freddy, Mychailo.

— Vous vous connaissez? ai-je dit, surprise.

— Grace et moi sommes dans la même classe, a expliqué Mychailo.

Grace a remarqué l'exemplaire de *Freddy détective* dans mes mains.

— Tu arrives à lire ça? a-t-elle demandé.

Je l'ai regardée, étonnée. Qu'est-ce que Linda avait pu dire à sa sœur à mon sujet? Je savais que mon anglais était loin d'être parfait, mais me prenait-elle pour une imbécile?

— Oui, mais lentement, ai-je dit en me forçant à sourire.

Nous sommes restés à bavarder encore quelques minutes.

— Il faut que je rentre. Je dois faire cuire les pommes de terre avant le retour de Marusia, ai-je dit.

Nous avons remonté l'escalier ensemble et nous sommes sortis par la porte de la section des enfants. Linda et Grace ont marché avec nous jusqu'à la rue Sheridan, puis Mychailo et moi avons continué de notre côté. Mychailo a déposé ses livres de bibliothèque chez lui, puis nous nous sommes rendus ensemble chez moi.

Une fois rentrés, j'ai allumé le feu sous les pommes de terre. Puis nous sommes ressortis dans la cour et nous nous sommes assis sur les blocs de ciment.

— Tu ne dois jamais oublier d'appeler Marusia et Ivan maman et papa quand tu parles à des gens qui ne sont pas ukrainiens, a dit Mychailo.

J'ai eu un coup au cœur.

— Je les appelle toujours maman et papa.

Mychailo a levé les yeux au ciel.

— Tu es si stupide que tu ne sais même pas ce que tu dis.

J'allais lui répondre en criant, mais je me suis retenue. Il avait raison. Je venais de dire « Marusia », en parlant à Linda et à Grace. J'aurais dû faire plus attention.

— Personne ne peut être parfait comme toi, Monsieur-je-sais-tout, ai-je rétorqué.

— Je parle sérieusement, a dit Mychailo. Je ne sais pas d'où tu viens vraiment, mais si tu veux rester au Canada, tu as intérêt à toujours t'adresser à Marusia et à Ivan en les appelant maman et papa.

Je n'avais rien à répondre à ça. Je savais qu'il avait raison et j'étais surprise de ma bourde. Au camp des personnes déplacées, je restais toujours sur mes gardes. Mais maintenant que nous étions en sécurité au Canada, mon passé voulait constamment resurgir dans ma mémoire, et j'avais l'esprit tout embrouillé.

C'est alors que nous avons entendu un camion s'arrêter devant chez nous et Marusia qui saluait les autres travailleurs agricoles.

— Je devrais rentrer, a dit Mychailo. Ne me salue pas à l'école, d'accord?

J'ai haussé les épaules plutôt que de lui répondre. Peut-être que j'allais le saluer quand même, histoire de l'embêter.

Un instant plus tard, Marusia était dans la cour. Elle portait un gros sac de papier. Je suis allée la rejoindre et je lui ai pris le sac des mains, puis nous sommes rentrées ensemble.

À l'intérieur, elle m'a repris le sac et a renversé son contenu sur la table : quelques tomates géantes, des oignons, un petit chou et des poivrons verts. Au fond, il y avait une demi-douzaine de belles grosses pommes.

— Je vais faire des trottoirs aux pommes pour le dessert, a-t-elle dit, les yeux pétillants de plaisir.

Puis elle a remarqué ce que je portais.

— Tu t'es changée, a-t-elle dit.

Elle a regardé mes cheveux qui n'étaient plus tressés.

— Et tu as défait ta coiffure.

En silence, nous avons rangé les légumes et une partie des pommes, puis, avec une fourchette, Marusia a piqué les pommes de terre pour voir si elles étaient prêtes.

— Comment s'est passée ta première journée à l'école? a-t-elle demandé.

J'ai respiré profondément, puis j'ai retenu ma respiration. Il fallait que je lui dise tout de suite ce qui s'était passé. Pour alléger l'atmosphère et ne pas la blesser. Mais je n'arrivais pas à trouver les bons mots.

Marusia a froncé les sourcils, puis a pris un couteau dans le tiroir et s'est mise à peler une pomme. Je regardais la pelure qui se déroulait. Je l'avais déjà vue peler une pomme d'un seul trait, sans jamais couper la pelure. Ivan n'était pas capable d'en faire autant. Moi non plus.

Le silence devenait lourd entre nous. J'ai pris le torchon et j'ai essuyé le comptoir. Je suis allée chercher le balai et j'ai balayé le plancher même s'il était propre.

Marusia a brisé le silence.

— Aujourd'hui, j'ai raconté aux filles à la ferme que je t'avais confectionné une belle tenue.

Je craignais ce qui allait sortir de ma bouche, alors je l'ai regardée en tentant de lui sourire.

— Elles m'ont dit que, au Canada, les filles ne s'habillent pas comme ça pour aller à l'école.

La pomme était pelée, alors elle l'a déposée sur le comptoir et a essuyé ses mains avec un torchon.

— As-tu eu des problèmes aujourd'hui à l'école?

— Je… j'ai… j'aime beaucoup ma nouvelle tenue.

J'avais les yeux baissés et j'étais incapable d'ajouter un mot de plus. J'avais la gorge serrée et les larmes me montaient aux yeux.

Marusia s'est approchée, m'a pris le balai des mains et l'a appuyé contre le mur. Elle m'a tenue dans ses bras très fort. J'ai soupiré. J'ai senti toute la tension et l'inquiétude se dissiper dans ce soupir. J'ai posé ma tête sur sa poitrine et j'ai entouré sa taille avec mes bras. J'avais l'impression de me noyer dans la chaleur de son corps et dans son parfum de pommes, de sueur et de foin. J'ai respiré profondément, mais je n'arrivais pas à prononcer un seul mot.

Elle m'a doucement bercée dans ses bras et m'a murmuré :

— Ça va, Nadia. Tout va bien. Il n'y a plus de problème, *Sonechko*.

Ses paroles m'ont réconfortée. Et elles ont fait surgir l'image d'une autre mère qui me tenait dans ses bras et me consolait. À une autre époque où je me sentais en sécurité...

Ce soir-là dans mon lit, j'ai essayé de réveiller d'autres souvenirs de cette autre époque et de cette autre mère, mais j'avais l'impression de pourchasser mon ombre. Je n'arrivais pas à m'endormir. J'ai donc rallumé ma lampe, et la lumière crue m'a fait plisser les yeux. Une fois mes yeux habitués à la clarté, j'ai pris le livre de Freddy et je me suis calée sur mon oreiller. Sur la couverture du livre, il y avait un cochon qui portait une casquette et avait une loupe à la main. Le texte de la première page commençait par : *Il faisait très chaud...* ça, j'étais capable de le lire.

J'ai essayé d'aller plus loin. L'histoire parlait, semblait-il, de deux canards accablés de chaleur, qui regardaient une maison. Ça ne tenait pas debout. Si je n'étais pas si fatiguée, peut-être que je comprendrais? J'ai déposé le livre et j'ai pris l'*Imagier des enfants* que j'avais déjà lu quatre fois au complet, et chaque fois, j'y avais quand même appris quelque chose de nouveau.

Cette fois-ci, en le feuilletant, j'ai prêté attention à quelques images qui se répétaient pour des mots différents. Par exemple, les mots *automobile,* *promenade* et *stationnement* étaient tous illustrés avec la même voiture de luxe. L'image n'était pas en couleurs, mais dans mon imagination, c'était une voiture noire. L'illustration du mot *brûler* était une maison en flammes, et la même illustration revenait pour *détruire* et *incendie.*

Dans ma mémoire, je sentais l'odeur de la fumée. Combien de fois avais-je vu des immeubles incendiés? La chose m'était si familière! Alors, qui étais-je et où étais-je quand ces événements s'étaient produits? Encore un autre morceau de casse-tête qui ne trouvait pas sa place.

J'ai refermé le livre et j'ai attendu que les battements de mon cœur ralentissent. Je n'ai pas éteint la lumière.

Je suis assise sur la banquette d'une longue voiture noire, vêtue d'une belle robe rose. Les portières sont verrouillées et les glaces remontées.

Je regarde par la fenêtre, à travers un nuage de fumée. Des femmes et des fillettes s'éloignent en courant d'un immeuble en flammes. Une des fillettes regarde de mon côté. J'ai l'impression de regarder dans un miroir. Elle me crie quelque chose, mais un homme en uniforme la bouscule. Je frappe du poing sur la glace et dans la portière. Je veux sortir! Je veux sortir!

Le livre a glissé de ma poitrine et a atterri sur le plancher en faisant un bruit sourd. Je me suis réveillée en sursaut. La lampe était toujours allumée. J'étais en sécurité, dans ma chambre au Canada. J'avais encore la tête qui tournait à cause du cauchemar. Je me suis frotté les yeux, et le souvenir s'est dissipé. J'étais en sécurité dans la voiture, et l'incendie était à l'extérieur. Pourquoi voulais-je en sortir? Et qui était cette fillette qui me ressemblait? Était-ce vraiment arrivé ou n'était-ce qu'un rêve?

Chapitre dix

Linda

Les premières semaines d'école se sont mieux passées que les premiers jours. Mlle MacIntosh enseignait dans une classe plus avancée et elle me saluait quand nous passions dans le couloir. J'étais rassurée de la savoir dans l'école. De même pour Mychailo. Aux yeux des autres, nous étions des étrangers, mais nous étions les seuls enfants issus des camps des personnes déplacées, et cela nous liait d'une façon très particulière.

Après l'école, il passait souvent me voir. Une fois, il m'a même aidée à faire mes devoirs. Si les autres garçons venaient à l'apprendre, il se ferait embêter. À la récréation, j'avais Linda pour jouer avec moi, et de jour en jour mon anglais s'améliorait. J'étais reconnaissante envers Mlle Ferris qui ne tolérait pas qu'on m'appelle « la fille d'Hitler » en sa présence. Cela n'empêchait pas Éric et David de le chuchoter dans mon dos.

Un jour, à la récréation, alors que Linda et moi faisions le tour de la cour d'école en regardant vaguement les autres élèves jouer, elle s'est tournée vers moi et m'a demandé :

— Aimerais-tu venir chez moi après l'école aujourd'hui?

J'étais ravie de son invitation, mais je devais la refuser :

— Marus... Maman ne saura pas que je suis chez toi, ai-je répondu. Peux-tu venir chez moi à la place?

Linda a souri.

— Bonne idée! Je vais le dire à Grace, et elle pourra avertir maman et papa.

J'étais contente de faire le trajet jusqu'à la maison avec quelqu'un à qui parler. Linda a adoré la balançoire qu'Ivan m'avait installée. Je lui ai fait faire le tour de la maison, aussi. En ouvrant les portes les unes après les autres, j'essayais de voir chaque pièce avec les yeux de Linda. Allait-elle croire que nous étions extrêmement pauvres? Qu'allait-elle penser de la baignoire avec son éclat d'émail et de la glacière repeinte, dans la cuisine? Elle n'avait fait aucun commentaire sur les blocs de ciment qui servaient de perron, mais j'avais remarqué son regard.

Quand nous sommes montées dans ma chambre, elle s'est assise sur le lit pour tester les ressorts.

— Pas mal! a-t-elle dit. Et j'adore la teinte lilas des murs. Tout a l'air si frais ici.

Je l'ai observée, essayant de voir si elle se moquait de moi. J'étais sûre que la plupart des élèves de l'école habitaient dans de bien plus belles maisons que la mienne, mais elle avait l'air sincère.

— Tu dois adorer ça, ici, a-t-elle dit.

Je commençais à m'habituer à ma nouvelle maison, et le Canada me plaisait de plus en plus. Est-ce que j'adorais ça? Je ne le savais pas exactement.

— L'endroit où j'habitais avant d'arriver ici était bien plus beau, ai-je dit.

Les mots m'étaient sortis de la bouche sans y penser.

— C'était où? a demandé Linda en se laissant tomber sur le lit.

— En Europe.

Mon cœur s'est mis à battre à tout rompre. Pourquoi m'étais-je lancée dans cette discussion?

— Si tu avais une plus belle maison, pourquoi es-tu venue ici alors? a-t-elle poursuivi.

Je n'ai rien répondu. J'aurais voulu n'avoir jamais dit ce que j'avais dit.

— Ça n'a pas de sens, a continué Linda.

— C'est à cause de la guerre, ai-je dit, en espérant mettre ainsi fin à la discussion.

Elle m'a regardée bizarrement.

— Si tu avais une plus belle maison, tes parents devaient être riches, non? a dit Linda.

J'ai ouvert la bouche pour répondre, puis je l'ai refermée. Pourquoi m'étais-je lancée dans cette discussion?

— C'était une blague, ai-je répondu à Linda. Ma famille était tout à fait ordinaire.

Mychailo m'avait avertie de ne jamais faire savoir à des Canadiens que Marusia et Ivan n'étaient pas mes vrais parents, sinon le gouvernement pourrait me séparer d'eux. Marusia me disait la même chose pendant toutes ces années au camp, puis à bord du bateau.

Je m'en voulais beaucoup d'avoir failli trahir notre secret. La dernière chose que je souhaitais au monde, c'était d'être séparée des deux seules personnes qui prenaient soin de moi. J'ai souri à Linda et j'ai haussé les épaules, en espérant qu'elle oublierait ce que j'avais dit.

— Nadia? Je suis là! a crié Marusia.

J'ai sursauté en entendant la porte d'entrée s'ouvrir et les pas de Marusia marteler le plancher de bois de l'entrée.

— Je suis ici, ai-je dit depuis l'étage. Avec une amie.

J'entendais Marusia qui marchait dans la cuisine, en dessous. Il y a eu un bruit de papier froissé quand elle a déposé le sac de provisions sur la table. Puis j'ai entendu ses pas dans l'escalier.

L'instant d'après, Marusia était dans l'embrasure de la porte de ma chambre.

— Ah! Te voilà, Nadia! s'est-elle exclamée.

Son regard s'est posé sur moi, puis sur Linda.

— Tu me présentes ton amie?

— Ma… Mama, je te présente Linda. Linda, voici ma mère.

Linda s'est levée et a serré la main de Marusia en

disant :

— Enchantée de faire votre connaissance, madame Kravchuk.

Marusia a serré la main de Linda.

— Venez me rejoindre en bas dans deux ou trois minutes. Je vais vous préparer de quoi vous régaler.

Elle a tourné les talons et est redescendue.

Quand nous l'avons entendue commencer à faire du bruit dans la cuisine, Linda m'a chuchoté :

— Que faisait-elle pendant la guerre?

Je ne savais pas quoi lui répondre. Pourquoi avais-je abordé ce sujet, alors que Mychailo m'avait bien avertie?

— Je t'en parlerai une autre fois. Allons prendre notre goûter, ai-je répondu en espérant qu'elle oublierait tout ça.

En bas, Marusia nous avait préparé à chacune un bol avec une pomme coupée en tranches et nappée de miel.

— Vous pouvez aller manger dehors si vous voulez, a-t-elle dit. Mais vous rapporterez vos bols quand vous aurez fini.

Le siège de la balançoire était juste assez large pour que nous y tenions toutes les deux, et Linda avait les jambes assez longues pour l'immobiliser. Nous nous sommes donc assises, serrées l'une contre l'autre, et nous avons mangé notre goûter.

— Miam! s'est exclamée Linda en dégustant sa pomme.

C'était un délice! Marusia ne nous avait jamais préparé ce dessert. Je suppose qu'elle avait voulu servir quelque chose de spécial pour mon amie. Elle faisait toujours tout pour me faire plaisir. Je me sentais coupable d'en avoir déjà trop dit à Linda.

Linda a regardé en direction de la maison et m'a chuchoté :

— Elle ne peut pas nous entendre depuis la cuisine, non?

— Je ne crois pas.

— Alors que faisait-elle pendant la guerre?

J'ai lentement avalé le morceau de pomme que j'avais dans la bouche.

— Rien de spécial, ai-je dit. Elle travaillait dans une usine.

— Et toi? a demandé Linda. Ce devait être intéressant de grandir en temps de guerre.

Intéressant? Je n'y avais jamais pensé de ce point de vue. Pour moi, c'était plutôt si terrifiant que j'en avais presque tout oublié.

— J'étais petite, ai-je répondu. C'est tout embrouillé dans ma tête.

— Raconte-moi ce dont tu te rappelles.

Alors, je lui ai raconté quand Marusia et moi nous étions enfuies, et notre arrivée au camp des personnes déplacées. Linda était bouche bée en entendant certaines parties de mon récit. Je n'ai pas parlé de la famille allemande.

La porte arrière s'est ouverte, et Marusia a passé la

tête par l'embrasure.

— Vous avez l'air bien installées, sur votre balançoire, a-t-elle dit en souriant. Finissez de manger vos pommes. Linda, nous allons t'accompagner jusque chez toi, Nadia et moi.

— Je peux rentrer toute seule, a dit Linda.

— Ça nous fera plaisir de marcher avec toi, a insisté Marusia.

Elle a lavé quelques pommes, les a essuyées, puis les a mises dans un sac de papier pour les apporter. Je n'ai pas compris tout de suite ce que Marusia avait en tête. Puis j'ai saisi : elle voulait rencontrer les parents de Linda. Les pommes, c'était pour les leur offrir.

La maison de Linda était en briques jaunes, avec un seul étage. Elle se trouvait dans la rue Usher, derrière la gare et à une rue avant d'arriver à l'église ukrainienne. J'étais déjà passée devant chez elle sans le savoir, en me rendant à l'église.

— Voulez-vous entrer? a demandé Linda.

— Ce n'est pas nécessaire, a dit Marusia. Je voulais juste être sûre que tu rentres chez toi sans problèmes.

Linda savait aussi bien que moi que la raison de cette petite promenade était de rencontrer sa famille.

— Attendez ici, a dit Linda. Je veux vous présenter ma mère.

Elle est passée devant nous et a disparu à l'intérieur. L'instant d'après, une femme semblant rongée par les soucis et qui s'essuyait les mains sur son tablier bleu est descendue du perron pour venir nous saluer. Linda nous regardait de derrière son dos.

— Je m'appelle Rita Henhawk. Je suis la mère de Linda.

— Marusia Kravchuk, et ma fille Nadia. Je vous ai apporté des pommes, a-t-elle ajouté en tendant le sac à Mme Henhawk. Je les ai cueillies aujourd'hui.

Mme Henhawk a pris le sac et lui a souri.

— Elles viennent de votre pommier?

— Non, a dit Marusia. Je travaille dans une ferme.

Mme Henhawk a hoché la tête pour montrer qu'elle comprenait.

— Voulez-vous entrer prendre une tasse de thé?

Elle a ouvert la porte toute grande. Un chat tigré a filé entre ses jambes et a couru jusque dans la rue.

J'allais partir à sa poursuite, mais la mère de Linda a dit :

— Ne t'inquiète pas. Il va revenir. Joe ne manquerait jamais son souper.

Nous sommes entrées et nous avons aussitôt été enivrées par une délicieuse odeur de cuisine.

— Excusez le désordre, a dit Mme Henhawk. Je suis en train de faire des petits pains au maïs.

Il n'y avait aucun désordre. La porte d'entrée donnait directement dans un salon peu meublé. Il y avait un vieux canapé, deux chaises à dossier droit et un coffre en bois qui servait de table à café. Il n'y avait pas d'étagères avec des livres, et le plancher de bois n'était pas recouvert d'un tapis, mais l'ensemble était coquet. Je voyais bien que les Henhawk étaient pauvres, mais tout aussi fiers que nous. Linda était donc sincère quand elle me complimentait sur notre maison. Je me sentais beaucoup mieux.

Après le salon, il y avait la cuisine avec un plancher recouvert de linoléum rouge, si fraîchement ciré qu'il en brillait encore. Un grand saladier en bois, garni d'une serviette à carreaux, était déposé à un bout de la table. La grande sœur de Linda était assise à l'autre bout, un manuel scolaire et un cahier à anneaux ouverts devant elle, et un verre de lait à moitié vide à portée de la main. Quand nous sommes entrées, Grace s'est levée, nous a rapidement saluées et a replongé le nez dans ses devoirs.

— Asseyez-vous, a dit Mme Henhawk en nous indiquant le canapé. Je vais aller faire bouillir de l'eau.

— C'est très gentil à vous, a dit Marusia.

Elle s'est assise sur le canapé et a tapoté le siège à côté d'elle. Je me suis assise.

— Et un peu de lait pour toi, jeune fille? m'a demandé Mme Henhawk.

Je n'avais pas soif, mais Marusia m'a donné un coup de coude, alors j'ai dit que ce serait très gentil. Linda est allée à la cuisine pour l'aider. Au bout de quelques minutes, elle est revenue dans le salon avec deux verres de lait et deux tasses de thé posés sur un plateau. Sa mère est sortie de la cuisine avec une assiette pleine de petits pains dorés.

J'ai pris mon pain au maïs dans mes deux mains et j'ai soufflé dessus pour le faire refroidir. Marusia a pris une bouchée du sien.

— Délicieux! a-t-elle dit en se léchant les lèvres.

J'ai pris une bouchée du mien, et j'étais bien d'accord avec elle : un délicieux mélange de beurre, de maïs et de bacon.

— C'est une vieille recette familiale, a dit Mme Henhawk. Je suis ravie que ça vous plaise.

Marusia et Mme Henhawk ont parlé de choses et d'autres tandis que Linda et moi sommes restées assises, en attendant impatiemment qu'elles en aient terminé. J'aurais aimé aller explorer les environs avec Linda. Ou au moins, visiter sa maison. Mais je savais qu'il fallait d'abord passer par cette étape. Marusia est très mère poule envers moi.

Finalement, Marusia a fini son thé et a déposé sa tasse.

— Je suis très heureuse de vous avoir rencontrée, a-t-elle dit.

Puis nous nous sommes levées.

— C'est du bon monde, a conclu Marusia sur le chemin du retour. Si tu veux, tu pourras aller chez eux à l'occasion, après l'école. Mais il faudra toujours m'avertir la veille.

Chapitre onze

Les fantômes

J'avais une amie, Linda, des parents qui m'aimaient et un toit au-dessus de la tête. Les semaines passaient et, avant le premier gel, Ivan avait fini la peinture et installé les portes à l'intérieur de la maison. Marusia et moi avions planté des bulbes de tulipes et de jonquilles devant. J'avais hâte de les voir fleurir au printemps. J'avais de la chance d'avoir Marusia et Ivan qui m'aimaient.

Mais tout n'était pas parfait. Éric continuait de m'appeler « la fille d'Hitler » chaque fois qu'il me voyait à la récréation ou en sortant de l'école. Et il s'arrangeait pour me voir souvent! Dieu merci, les autres garçons s'étaient lassés de ce petit jeu. Mes souvenirs du passé avaient cessé de surgir sans crier gare, et j'étais arrivée à remettre en place quelques pièces du casse-tête, mais il restait encore de grands vides.

Le soir du dernier dimanche d'octobre, j'étais assise entre Marusia et Ivan, sur les blocs de ciment du perron arrière. Un voisin devait faire brûler des feuilles mortes, car une odeur de fumée flottait dans l'air. Marusia avait préparé une infusion de camomille avec du miel, et nous sirotions chacun notre tisane. J'étais assise entre ces deux adultes qui avaient changé le cours de leur vie afin de me protéger. Je regardais la balançoire qu'Ivan avait faite pour moi et les lilas qu'il avait plantés pour moi aussi. Je pensais à Marusia qui m'avait protégée, au camp, et à la jupe et au chemisier qu'elle avait cousus pour moi de ses mains fatiguées par les travaux de la ferme. Je me suis mise à pleurer.

— *Sonechko*, a dit Marusia en posant sa tête sur mon épaule, qu'est-ce qui t'arrive?

J'avais un nœud dans la gorge.

— Rien… Ça va, ça va…

J'essayais de tarir mes larmes, mais elles jaillissaient malgré tout.

— As-tu eu un autre cauchemar? a demandé Ivan.

J'ai fait signe que non.

— Je suis heureuse, ai-je dit. Je ne sais pas comment vous faites pour m'aimer, mais je suis contente que vous…

— Nadia, Nadia, m'a interrompu Marusia d'un ton affectueux. Tu n'es peut-être pas née de ma chair, mais tu es la fille que mon cœur a choisie. Je t'aime et Ivan aussi.

— Mais je ne mérite pas d'être aimée, ai-je dit en sanglotant. Vous dites que je ne suis pas une nazie, mais ce n'est pas ce que me disent mes souvenirs.

Ivan a sorti un mouchoir de sa poche et a essuyé

mes larmes.

— Raconte-nous tout, Nadia. Peut-être que nous pourrons t'aider à y mettre un peu d'ordre.

Mes souvenirs se sont mis à revenir dans le désordre. J'ai parlé d'Eva, de la robe rose et d'où je pensais qu'elle venait. J'ai parlé des livres que je n'avais pas le droit de lire et de celui que j'étais obligée de lire. J'ai parlé de la rencontre avec Hitler. Marusia avait l'air d'être en partie au courant. Ivan restait assis sans rien dire, les lèvres pincées. Quand j'ai eu terminé, j'avais pleuré toutes les larmes de mon corps.

— Te rappelles-tu quand nous nous sommes connues? a demandé Marusia.

J'ai fermé les yeux et j'ai réfléchi très fort. Marusia était au cœur de ma vie, mais quand l'avais-je rencontrée *exactement?* Je n'en avais aucune idée. Je me rappelais clairement m'être enfuie avec elle à bord d'un wagon plat. Et le jour où nous étions arrivées au camp des personnes déplacées. J'avais aussi un vague souvenir de Marusia avec la famille allemande, dans la ferme à la campagne. Je ne savais pas ce qu'elle faisait là, mais elle y était, et les lilas aussi. Marusia m'était apparue à cette époque comme une chanson familière depuis longtemps oubliée.

— Veux-tu que je t'en parle? a-t-elle demandé.

Je me suis mise à trembler. J'ignorais pourquoi.

— Pas maintenant.

Marusia a caressé doucement mon avant-bras avec ses doigts.

— Je ne veux pas te bousculer, a-t-elle dit. Mais il faut que tu arrives à combler les vides dans tes souvenirs. Sinon, nous ne saurons jamais qui tu es vraiment.

C'était justement ce qui m'effrayait le plus. Est-ce que je voulais savoir qui j'étais? Et si je n'aimais pas cette personne? Je me suis endormie sur ces pensées...

Je tire la poignée de la portière, mais elle ne veut pas s'ouvrir, et les vitres non plus. Je frappe des poings contre la vitre.

— Laissez-moi sortir! Laissez-moi sortir!

Dehors, je ne vois que de la fumée. J'entends des sirènes. Je vois un visage qui ressemble au mien.

La porte d'entrée s'est ouverte doucement, puis s'est refermée. J'ai sauté en bas de mon lit et je me suis précipitée à la fenêtre. Ivan. Je savais que c'était Ivan qui partait pour la fonderie avant le lever du soleil. Pourquoi ce bruit m'avait-il fait si peur?

Je me suis frotté les yeux pour bien me réveiller et j'ai repensé à ce rêve qui me faisait encore peur. Pourquoi avais-je rêvé que je voulais m'enfuir d'une voiture où j'étais en sécurité, alors qu'un bâtiment brûlait dehors? Ce n'était pas logique. Et comment pouvais-je voir mon visage dans et hors de la voiture en même temps?

Je suis descendue sur la pointe des pieds et suis sortie sans bruit dans la cour. Dans le noir, je me suis assise sur la balançoire. L'odeur des feuilles mortes brûlées flottait encore dans l'air. Elle me rappelait un moment lointain, dont je me souvenais vraiment…

La longue voiture noire s'était arrêtée devant les ruines encore fumantes d'une usine bombardée, et Vater en est descendu.

— Je reviens tout de suite, a-t-il dit à Mutter en refermant la portière.

— Il a intérêt, a dit Mutter, en se parlant plutôt à elle-même qu'à Eva ou moi. Nous ne pouvons pas arriver en retard à ce rassemblement.

Encore un rassemblement! Il faisait chaud dans la voiture, et ma robe me grattait. Mes cheveux étaient tressés si serré que j'en avais mal à la tête. Eva avait les cheveux qui tombaient dans son dos, et elle portait une robe en mousseline rose, très légère. Elle était agitée. La boucle de sa chaussure a failli s'accrocher dans ma jupe quand elle est passée par-dessus moi pour atteindre la fenêtre. J'ai remis ma jupe en place en soupirant.

— Reste assise, Eva, a dit Mutter en passant le bras devant moi pour tirer sur la robe d'Eva.

Mais Eva ne voulait pas bouger de là.

— Il fait chaud ici, Mutti.

Eva a baissé la vitre, et l'air froid tout enfumé s'est engouffré dans la voiture.

— Nous allons sentir la fumée, a dit Mutter.

— Au moins, nous ne sentirons pas la transpiration, a répliqué Eva.

Si j'avais dit cela, j'aurais reçu une monumentale paire de claques. Je me suis tordu le cou pour essayer de voir ce qui se passait à l'usine. Je savais qu'on y fabriquait des armes et qu'elle avait été attaquée justement pour cette raison.

Une aile du bâtiment était complètement rasée par les bombes, et des volutes de fumée s'élevaient de ses ruines. Les ouvriers qui travaillaient dans cette aile devaient tous être morts.

Vater donnait des ordres à de jeunes garçons qui portaient des brassards avec le svastika. Des femmes affolées, vêtues de robes grises en lambeaux, sortaient du gros nuage de fumée. Tout était gris, sauf les traînées de sang sur les vêtements, qui avait giclé de coupures aux bras ou aux épaules causées par des fragments de briques projetés par les explosions. Il y avait aussi le sang séché dans les cheveux tout emmêlés, blonds, noirs ou châtains, là où un éclat d'obus avait déchiré le cuir chevelu.

— Pourquoi ne portent-elles pas l'étoile jaune? a demandé Eva.

Mutter s'est penchée pour mieux voir ces femmes. J'ai fait de même. Elles portaient un écusson bleu et blanc, avec les lettres OST dessus.

— Ce sont des ouvrières des pays de l'Est, a dit Mutter.

— Est-ce que ce sont des animaux comme les Juifs, Mutti?

— Oui, ma chérie. C'est pourquoi elles travaillent à l'usine d'armement. Tu ne voudrais pas que des Allemandes reçoivent des bombes sur la tête, non?

J'ai parcouru du regard la foule des ouvrières de l'Est, tristes et en haillons. Une fillette avait des cheveux presque aussi blonds que les miens. Comme si elle avait senti mon regard se poser sur elle, elle a levé les yeux. J'avais l'impression de me voir; elle était seulement un peu plus âgée. Nos regards se sont croisés et, de surprise, sa bouche s'est ouverte toute grande. Elle essayait de me crier quelque chose, mais un des garçons des Jeunesses hitlériennes s'est placé devant elle et l'a repoussée...

La porte arrière s'est ouverte en grinçant. J'ai cligné des yeux une fois, puis encore, et j'ai regardé tout autour de moi. Il faisait jour, et j'étais sur ma balançoire. Mes pieds avaient bleu de froid. J'ai regardé la porte de la cuisine, et Marusia se tenait là, serrant un peignoir de tissu léger autour de ses épaules.

— Nadia, a-t-elle dit, je me demandais où tu étais passée. Tu vas attraper froid!

En descendant de ma balançoire, j'ai titubé un peu sur mes jambes engourdies. Quand je suis entrée, Marusia m'a enveloppée dans une couverture. Elle s'est affairée devant la cuisinière, puis a déposé une tasse de chocolat chaud sur la table, devant moi. La tasse me réchauffait les doigts quand je la tenais pour prendre une gorgée. Des éléments de mon souvenir me semblaient aussi réels que cette tasse de chocolat chaud. Cette fille qui me ressemblait, je savais maintenant que ce n'était pas moi. Et cet écusson avec

OST, qu'elle portait, où l'avais-je déjà vu?

— As-tu d'autres souvenirs qui te sont revenus à la mémoire?

— Pas au sujet de notre première rencontre, ai-je dit. Mais je me suis souvenue de la voiture noire et pourquoi il y avait de la fumée.

Je lui ai parlé du bombardement et de la jeune fille qui m'avait regardée. Elle a tendu le bras et a pris une de mes mains. Elle est restée silencieuse un moment. On aurait dit qu'elle cherchait ses mots.

— Des millions d'Ukrainiens et de Polonais ont été emmenés comme *Ostarbeiters*. Des travailleurs de l'Est, ou Ost en allemand.

J'avais dans la tête une image de Marusia en vieille robe grise, avec un écusson arborant les lettres OST, cousu sur sa poitrine. J'ai déposé ma tasse de chocolat si brusquement que des gouttes ont coulé sur la table. Je me suis couvert le visage des mains, mais l'image ne voulait pas s'en aller.

— Tu étais une *Ostarbeiter* toi aussi, n'est-ce pas?

— Nadia, a dit Marusia, la mémoire te revient! Te rappelles-tu quand nous nous sommes rencontrées?

— Étais-tu à cette usine bombardée? C'est toi que j'ai vue? Mais en posant la question, je savais que ce n'était pas ça. Quand je regardais Marusia, je ne me voyais pas en plus âgée.

— Nous nous sommes connues à la ferme, Nadia. Rappelle-toi…

Des bribes de souvenir me revenaient…

Le camion de l'armée qui s'arrête dans notre allée. Un soldat qui ouvre le panneau arrière du camion et une *Ostarbeiter* qui en saute et atterrit sur le gravier de l'allée. Elle puait tellement que je savais qu'elle venait de loin. Marusia qui essaie de tenir sur ses jambes, mais qui est si affaiblie qu'elle s'effondre par terre. Elle lève les yeux et me regarde. Puis moi qui me sens coupable de porter de beaux vêtements et d'être qui je suis, et qui rentre en courant dans la maison, pour cacher ma honte.

— Je m'en souviens, Marusia, ai-je balbutié d'une toute petite voix. Je m'en souviens maintenant. D'où venais-tu?

— De Zelena, a dit Marusia. Un petit village de l'est de l'Ukraine. Les Allemands sont arrivés et ont ordonné à tous les jeunes de mon âge de se présenter sur la place publique. Ceux qui ne venaient pas étaient débusqués, puis fusillés. Ils ont fait un tri parmi nous. J'ai été embarquée à l'arrière d'un camion.

Du revers de la main, elle a essuyé une larme sur sa joue et elle a poursuivi :

— Il n'y avait pas de chauffage, et on ne nous donnait rien à manger. Certains avaient un peu de nourriture. Nous avons partagé. Nous avons voyagé ainsi pendant plusieurs jours.

— Puis on t'a emmenée à la ferme?

— Non, a dit Marusia. J'ai été envoyée à Cologne, pour travailler à l'usine Ford-Werke.

Des images fugitives de mon passé me revenaient.

L'usine d'armement bombardée...

— Heureusement que tu ne fabriquais pas des bombes, ai-je murmuré.

— On peut dire que j'ai eu cette chance, a dit Marusia. Mais c'était quand même de l'esclavage.

— Comment es-tu arrivée à la ferme? ai-je demandé.

— À l'usine d'automobiles, ils nous enfermaient dans de grands baraquements pour la nuit, a dit Marusia. Je me suis échappée. J'ai été rattrapée et on m'a ramenée à l'usine, mais ils ne voulaient plus de moi. Ils ont dit que je n'étais pas fiable. Ils m'ont envoyée dans un camp de concentration, mais je les ai convaincus que j'étais très bonne cuisinière. Ils m'ont donc donnée au général Himmel, qui m'a donnée à sa femme.

Je fixais mon chocolat chaud. L'homme que j'appelais Vater était celui que Marusia appelait le général Himmel. En pensant à ce qu'elle avait enduré, j'ai eu un haut-le-cœur.

— C'est bien que tu commences à te souvenir de tout ça, a-t-elle dit. Plus la mémoire te reviendra, plus tu comprendras que tu n'as pas à avoir honte de quoi que ce soit.

— Pourquoi ne me dis-tu pas tout ce que tu sais sur mon passé? lui ai-je demandé. Ce serait plus simple, tu ne penses pas?

— Je ne connais pas tout de ton passé, a dit Marusia. En te racontant ce que je sais, j'ai peur de fausser ta mémoire. Je crois qu'il vaut mieux que tu clarifies tout ça au fur et à mesure que tes souvenirs referont surface.

— Facile à dire pour toi, ai-je rétorqué agressivement. Tu n'as pas à vivre avec tous ces cauchemars.

Marusia est restée silencieuse un petit moment. Elle a essuyé une larme au coin de son œil, puis a tendu le bras et a posé sa main sur la mienne.

— J'ai aussi des fantômes dans ma vie, *Sonechko*.

Chapitre douze
L'encre rouge

Plus tard ce matin-là, à l'école, j'essayais de me concentrer, mais quand Mlle Ferris écrivait des notes au tableau, les mots s'embrouillaient et se mélangeaient dans ma tête. Je n'arrêtais pas de penser à cette fille qui me ressemblait, mais qui était plus âgée que moi. Qui était-elle et pourquoi apparaissait-elle dans mes cauchemars? J'étais si distraite que je n'ai pas entendu la cloche de la récréation du matin. Linda a touché mon bras, et j'ai sursauté si fort que j'ai failli tomber de ma chaise.

— Désolée, a-t-elle dit. On dirait que tu viens de voir un fantôme.

J'ai cligné des yeux à quelques reprises pour chasser les images de ma tête. Peut-être que cette fille qui me ressemblait n'était qu'une création de mon imagination.

— Sortons! ai-je dit.

Linda a couru devant moi dans le couloir et a ouvert la porte. Je la suivais, mais j'avais les jambes toutes molles.

— Tu es bizarre aujourd'hui, a dit Linda, une fois

dehors.

— Désolée, ai-je dit. Je ne me sens pas très bien.

— Le grand air te fera peut-être du bien.

Sauf que l'air n'était pas vraiment frais, avec son odeur de feuilles brûlées. Nous sommes passées devant un groupe de filles de notre classe qui bavardaient tranquillement ensemble. J'ai entendu des bribes de leur conversation. L'Halloween était demain, et elles parlaient des costumes qu'elles allaient porter pour la fête de la classe : une sorcière, un fantôme, une infirmière...

D'autres jouaient à la corde à sauter à deux avec les plus jeunes. Aucune ne nous a demandé, à Linda et à moi, de nous joindre à elles. La plupart des garçons étaient dans le champ voisin et jouaient à se lancer un ballon de football. J'aurais tant voulu être comme les autres élèves! Comme ce serait merveilleux de ne pas avoir de passé!

De retour en classe, j'ai remarqué une enveloppe qui dépassait du coin de mon cahier. J'ai eu un moment de panique. Mlle Ferris avait-elle remarqué que j'étais distraite ce matin? C'était peut-être un billet pour m'envoyer au bureau du directeur. J'ai retiré l'enveloppe de mon cahier et j'ai soupiré de soulagement. Un grand « N », dans une écriture enfantine, avait été tracé à l'encre rouge sur l'enveloppe, et ça ne ressemblait pas du tout à la petite écriture soignée de Mlle Ferris. Était-ce une invitation pour un goûter d'anniversaire ou pour l'Halloween?

J'ai jeté un coup d'œil sur le pupitre de Linda. Il n'y avait pas d'enveloppe. Il était hors de question que je me rende à une fête si elle n'était pas invitée elle aussi!

À ce moment-là, la plupart des élèves étaient retournés à leur place, mais les leçons n'avaient pas encore commencé. Mlle Ferris était assise à son bureau à l'avant de la classe et corrigeait encore des copies. J'ai posé l'enveloppe sur mes genoux pour que Mlle Ferris ne me voie pas l'ouvrir. Je l'ai déchirée en faisant le moins de bruit possible et j'en ai retiré une feuille de papier couverte de *svastikas* rouges, avec au centre le dessin grossier d'une fillette avec des tresses blondes. Dessous, on avait écrit : *Nadia la nazie, retourne au pays d'Hitler!*

— Nadia, que lis-tu? m'a demandé Mlle Ferris d'un ton sévère.

Elle était debout à l'avant de la classe, les mains sur les hanches.

— Tu sais qu'on ne doit pas se passer de billets en classe.

J'ai glissé la feuille dans mon pupitre, mais l'enveloppe est tombée par terre. Des élèves se sont retournés pour me regarder. Éric souriait, et David avait la main sur la bouche pour ne pas éclater de rire.

— R... Rien, ai-je dit. Je prenais juste mon cahier.

— Ton cahier est déjà sur ton pupitre, a dit Mlle Ferris d'un ton très sévère. Lève-toi et fais-nous profiter de ce que tu trouvais si intéressant.

Je me suis levée en trébuchant, mais je n'ai pas pris

l'affreuse feuille de papier. Je sentais mon cœur qui battait à tout rompre dans ma poitrine. J'étais incapable de lire ce billet à voix haute!

— Apporte-moi ce message, Nadia. Nous aimerions tous savoir ce qu'il dit.

Je suis restée figée sur place. Mlle Ferris a parcouru l'allée jusqu'à mon pupitre, puis s'est accroupie. Elle a pris la feuille de papier et l'a dépliée.

Son visage était de marbre.

— Assieds-toi, Nadia, a-t-elle dit en posant doucement sa main sur mon épaule.

Elle est retournée à l'avant de la classe et a brandi l'horrible dessin pour que tout le monde le voie. Il y a eu un grand silence dans la classe. Quelqu'un a ri. Je me suis faite toute petite sur ma chaise. Si seulement j'avais pu disparaître!

— Qui a fait ça? a presque crié Mlle Ferris.

Personne n'a levé la main.

— Vous allez tous rester en retenue si le ou les coupables ne se dénoncent pas d'eux-mêmes.

Là, elle avait vraiment crié. Personne n'a levé la main. Je fixais du regard la nuque d'Éric. Il était assis, raide comme un piquet, avec les mains sagement posées sur son pupitre. J'étais sûre qu'il ne souriait plus. Je ne savais pas si c'était lui ou David, le coupable. Mais c'était nécessairement un des deux. J'étais mal à l'aise et je me sentais faible.

— Les mains sur vos pupitres, tout le monde, a ordonné Mlle Ferris sévèrement. Les paumes tournées vers le haut!

Elle a parcouru une rangée de pupitres, puis une autre, en examinant les mains de tous les élèves afin de voir si elles étaient tachées d'encre rouge. En arrivant à côté du pupitre de David, elle s'est arrêtée. Elle a saisi une de ses mains et l'a retournée de tous les côtés.

— De l'encre rouge, a-t-elle dit. Vide ton pupitre. Immédiatement!

David a plongé la main dans son pupitre et en a ressorti des livres, des cahiers, des plumes et des crayons. Mlle Ferris a soigneusement examiné chaque objet afin de trouver d'autres preuves, puis les a jetés par terre.

— C'est tout ce que j'ai, a-t-il dit d'un air parfaitement innocent.

Mlle Ferris a plongé la main dans son pupitre et a fouillé dedans. Elle en a ressorti un bloc-note et un stylo-plume rempli d'encre rouge. Elle a feuilleté le bloc-note. Il y avait d'autres dessins représentant « Nadia la nazie ». Je me suis faite encore plus petite sur ma chaise.

— Debout, a dit Mlle Ferris.

Elle a attrapé David par une oreille et l'a fait sortir de la classe. La porte s'est refermée en claquant derrière eux, puis des dizaines de paires d'yeux se sont tournées vers moi pour me dévisager.

J'ai convaincu Marusia et Ivan de me permettre de

ne pas aller à l'école et de rester plutôt à la maison le jour de l'Halloween. Je n'avais aucune envie de me déguiser avec un costume stupide et de faire semblant de m'amuser le lendemain même du jour où David s'était montré si méchant. Je préférais de loin m'occuper de tâches domestiques à la maison.

—À condition de ne pas en faire une habitude! m'a avertie Marusia.

J'étais devant l'évier de la cuisine, en train de frotter des taches de gazon sur un des chemisiers de travail de Marusia, quand j'ai aperçu Mychailo à la porte arrière. Il n'était pas déguisé.

—C'est ouvert, ai-je crié par la fenêtre. Ta classe ne fait pas la fête cet après-midi?

—Bien sûr, a dit Mychailo. Je me suis mis un drap sur la tête et j'ai dit que j'étais un fantôme.

Ça m'a fait sourire.

Il a fouillé dans ses poches et en a ressorti un bonbon à la mélasse.

—Maintenant, tu ne pourras pas dire que tu n'as jamais reçu de cadeau d'un garçon.

J'ai rougi.

—Merci, ai-je dit. Pose-le sur la table.

J'avais les mains couvertes de savon. J'ai rincé le chemisier de Marusia et je l'ai essoré, puis je l'ai accroché dehors sur la corde à linge. J'ai déballé le bonbon et l'ai mis dans ma bouche.

—Vas-tu passer l'Halloween ce soir? a demandé Mychailo. Tu peux venir avec moi si tu veux.

Je n'avais pas prévu passer l'Halloween. Après l'incident à l'école hier, je n'avais tout simplement pas envie de sortir de chez nous. Toute cette histoire était si humiliante! En plus, cette tradition de l'Halloween me semblait très bizarre et un peu effrayante.

— Je n'ai pas de déguisement.

— Tu peux te déguiser en fantôme, a-t-il dit. Ou en vagabond.

Il m'a regardée et m'a dit d'un ton moqueur :

— Allons, ce sont des costumes faciles à faire. Des bonbons gratuits, ça ne te dit rien?

Je devais admettre que l'idée d'obtenir des bonbons gratuitement était tentante. Et je me sentirais en sécurité avec Mychailo.

— Je vais demander la permission à Mar… à Mama et Tato, ai-je dit.

— Parfait! a-t-il dit. Je vais revenir quand il commencera à faire noir.

Ivan était content que j'aie décidé de sortir pour passer l'Halloween et il était particulièrement heureux que j'y aille avec Mychailo.

— Tu as besoin de redevenir une enfant plus souvent, a-t-il dit.

Et il m'a aidée à me faire un costume. J'étais déguisée en épouvantail avec une chemise à carreaux d'Ivan, remplie d'herbes qui piquent, prises au fond de la cour. Je portais une salopette de travail de Marusia, si usée qu'elle était rapiécée par-dessus de vieilles pièces. Ivan a pris du rouge à lèvres pour me faire un maquillage d'épouvantail. Nous n'avions pas de bonbons à donner aux enfants, mais nous avions des pommes qui venaient de la ferme de Marusia, et elle les avait bien frottées pour les faire briller.

À voir l'expression de Marusia, je savais qu'elle n'aimait pas trop l'idée de me laisser passer l'Halloween, mais elle faisait quand même semblant d'être contente. Elle m'a serrée dans ses bras encore plus fort que d'habitude quand je suis partie avec Mychailo.

— Reste dans notre rue, a-t-elle dit. Et rentre à la maison dans une heure.

Ce qui est bien lorsqu'on habite une rue où les maisons sont très rapprochées, c'est qu'en une heure, on a le temps de ramasser beaucoup de friandises. Ma taie d'oreiller a été vite remplie de pommes au sucre d'orge, de maïs soufflé au caramel, de gomme à bulles et de cacahuètes. En rentrant, j'ai vidé ma récolte de bonbons sur la table de la cuisine. Ivan, Marusia et moi avons trop mangé de tout. En me couchant, j'avais mal au ventre. Je me suis retournée dans mon lit toute la nuit et j'ai fait un long cauchemar particulièrement effrayant. Le lendemain matin, je ne me souvenais que de quelques petits bouts.

Chapitre treize

Le manoir

J'avais pris l'habitude d'aller chez Linda le mardi, après l'école, et elle venait chez moi le jeudi. Chez elle, il n'y avait pas vraiment de place pour jouer à l'intérieur. Linda partageait une chambre avec Grace, à l'étage. Elles avaient des lits superposés et une étagère pleine de vieux romans. J'aurais bien aimé jeter un coup d'œil aux livres, mais j'avais l'impression d'étouffer dans cette chambre. Je crois que c'était en partie parce que Grace s'y trouvait tout le temps. Soit elle lisait, adossée contre un oreiller sur le lit du haut, soit elle était avec une amie et elles faisaient un travail pour l'école ou je ne sais quoi d'autre.

Dans la cour de chez Linda, il n'y avait pas beaucoup de place pour jouer non plus. C'était un petit bout de terrain en friche, situé sur une colline. Il était bordé d'arbustes sauvages de chaque côté, et une corde à linge le coupait par le milieu. Linda avait des cartes à jouer, et souvent nous jouions au Huit ou à la Mémoire sur la table de la cuisine. Un mardi, elle a apporté un jeu qui s'appelait le Monopoly.

Avec les cartes, nous pouvions jouer à des jeux différents pendant une heure ou deux. Au Monopoly, une seule partie durait beaucoup plus longtemps. Le mardi, après son travail à la ferme, Marusia passait me chercher chez Linda. Malheureusement, avec le Monopoly, la partie commençait justement à être intéressante au moment où Marusia arrivait, et je devais m'en aller.

— Peux-tu venir chez moi samedi? a demandé Linda. Maman a dit que tu pourrais rester toute la journée si la partie durait aussi longtemps.

Marusia et Ivan m'ont donné la permission. La mère de Linda a proposé que je vienne de bonne heure le samedi matin et m'a invitée à dîner. Comme Ivan avait des travaux à faire sur le terrain de l'église ukrainienne, il m'a accompagnée jusque chez Linda. Et nous avons décidé que, quand je voudrais rentrer, j'irais le rejoindre à l'église et nous rentrerions ensemble.

Quand je suis arrivée chez Linda, il était tout juste passé neuf heures du matin. Mme Henhawk préparait de la compote de pommes dans la cuisine.

— Linda va descendre dans un instant, a-t-elle dit.

Elle m'a offert une pomme, mais je venais juste de déjeuner.

— Va t'asseoir avec Georges, m'a-t-elle dit en montrant la chaise à côté de son mari. Il ne te mordra pas.

Je me suis assise. M. Henhawk a baissé son journal,

a croisé mon regard et m'a fait un clin d'œil. Il avait l'air aussi gentil que Mme Henhawk.

J'avais probablement laissé entrer une mouche avec moi, en rentrant par la porte arrière. Elle n'arrêtait pas de me tourner autour de la tête. Je la chassais de la main, mais elle revenait tout le temps. Soudain j'ai reçu un gros coup de journal sur la tempe.

J'ai cligné des yeux une fois, puis une seconde fois. Pourquoi M. Henhawk me frappait-il comme ça? J'ai à peine entendu ce qu'il me disait…

— *Ne t'empiffre pas Eva, dit Mutter en essayant de lui retirer l'assiette, mais Eva la tient à deux mains et tire dessus.*

— *C'est ce que j'aime le plus, Mutti, et tu le sais, dit Eva en se servant une énorme portion d'Eierkuchen aux pommes et en l'engloutissant d'une seule bouchée.*

Un morceau de pomme tombe sur la table. Elle le ramasse et le met dans sa bouche.

— *Si seulement celle-là pouvait manger la moitié de ce que tu manges, dit Mutter en me regardant. Si le Führer apprend que nous avons affamé sa petite chérie, nous allons tous passer un mauvais quart d'heure.*

Je regarde l'assiette devant moi et je prends mon couteau et ma fourchette. Je coupe un petit morceau d'Eierkuchen et je le porte à ma bouche, mais son odeur de gras me donne mal au cœur. Je pense aux femmes et aux enfants avec les étoiles jaunes. Comment pourrais-je manger de ce gâteau alors qu'ils n'ont probablement rien à manger? Je repousse l'assiette.

Mutter me giffle.

— Nadia, est-ce que ça va?

La voix de M. Henhawk m'a ramenée à la réalité. J'étais debout, contre la table de la cuisine des Henhawk, avec une chaise renversée à côté de moi. J'ai porté ma main à ma joue. Je sentais presque la douleur provoquée par les claques de Mutter.

— Ça va aller, leur ai-je dit.

Mais ça n'allait pas vraiment. Ces images du passé me rendaient perplexe et nauséeuse.

Linda est apparue sur le seuil de la cuisine, la boîte de Monopoly dans les mains, et m'a dit :

— Nadia, tu n'as pas l'air dans ton assiette.

Il faisait chaud et humide dans la cuisine emplie d'une forte odeur de compote de pommes. Je sentais que j'allais vomir.

— J'aimerais mieux aller jouer dehors, si ça ne te dérange pas, ai-je dit.

— Bien sûr, a répondu Linda en déposant la boîte de Monopoly sur la table. Nous serons dehors, d'accord? a-t-elle dit à ses parents.

— Ne vous éloignez pas trop! a répliqué M. Henhawk.

En sortant dans la petite cour en friche de Linda, j'ai pris une grande goulée d'air frais.

— Allons au parc, a-t-elle suggéré.

Je ne savais pas qu'il y avait un parc. Nous sommes restées du même côté de la rue Usher que la maison de Linda et nous nous sommes dirigées vers l'ouest.

Plus nous nous éloignions de chez elle, plus les maisons semblaient miteuses. La rue Usher faisait une courbe, puis se terminait sur la rue Rushton; et là, j'ai remarqué une grille de fer forgé presque complètement masquée par des arbustes. On aurait dit une image sortie d'un conte de fées. Est-ce que je rêvais ou était-ce la réalité? Je suis allée toucher la grille.

— Suis-moi. Je vais te montrer quelque chose de plus intéressant, a dit Linda en me prenant par la main.

C'était donc la réalité.

Nous avons suivi une courbe. À travers les arbustes, j'ai vu que la grille était fixée à une longue clôture bien ouvragée et également presque complètement cachée par les arbustes. Il y avait une brèche dans le feuillage. J'ai été si surprise par ce que j'ai vu que j'ai agrippé l'épaule de Linda pour ne pas tomber à la renverse. Un vieux manoir décrépi, perché au haut d'une colline. Il semblait appartenir à une autre époque ou à un autre endroit, comme sorti d'un rêve. Ou d'un cauchemar. Il avait l'air un peu lugubre, avec ses treillis à la peinture écaillée et ses rideaux défraîchis suspendus à l'intérieur des fenêtres aux carreaux cassés.

— C'est le château Yates, a dit Linda. Je crois que plus personne n'y habite, sauf peut-être quelques vagabonds.

Quelque chose de ce vieux manoir abandonné

titillait ma mémoire, mais pourquoi? Il ne ressemblait pas du tout à la grande maison bien tenue, à la ferme où j'avais vécu avec Eva, Mutter et Vater. Et, évidemment, il n'y avait pas de bâtiment semblable à celui-là au camp des personnes déplacées. Un goût amer m'est monté à la gorge et, pliée en deux, j'ai vomi.

— Nadia, est-ce que ça va? a demandé Linda.

J'ai respiré trois ou quatre fois à fond afin de me calmer. Au bout de quelques minutes, j'étais capable de tenir debout.

— Je... je vais bien, ai-je réussi à lui dire.

— Qu'est-ce qui ne va pas? Est-ce la maison qui te fait peur?

Je n'arrivais pas à lui répondre.

— Te rappelle-t-elle quelque chose de la guerre?

— Je crois, oui, ai-je répondu. Mais je ne sais pas quoi au juste.

— Allons, a-t-elle dit en me prenant par la main, partons d'ici.

En repassant devant le manoir (ou le château ou la maison hantée ou tout ce qu'on voudra), je n'arrivais pas à m'en détacher les yeux. Il était à la fois affreux et magnifique...

Quelqu'un me transporte sur son épaule. Je donne des coups de pieds et je crie.

— *Baba! Baba! Je veux ma Baba!*

Nous montons un escalier peint en blanc. On me laisse toute seule dans une pièce. J'essaie d'ouvrir la porte, mais elle est fermée à clé. Je donne des coups de poing sur la porte, jusqu'à en avoir les jointures qui saignent. Personne ne me répond.

Linda m'appelait par mon nom, mais je courais vers la rue voisine en l'entraînant à ma suite. Je ne savais pas du tout où j'allais, mais je savais que je devais m'éloigner de cette maison.

— Pas si vite! a-t-elle crié en tirant sur ma main. Je suis à bout de souffle!

Quand j'ai arrêté de courir, j'étais essoufflée et tout en sueur. J'ai senti la main de Linda prendre la mienne, puis elle m'a entraînée dans un sentier à travers un boisé. De l'autre côté, nous sommes arrivées sur une colline couverte d'une pelouse bien entretenue. Le terrain était dégagé et aéré, et n'avait rien d'effrayant. Il était difficile de croire qu'un si joli parc était caché à quelques pas de la rue Usher.

Linda m'a conduite jusqu'au milieu de la pelouse, et nous nous sommes affalées par terre. Pendant un long moment, nous sommes restées étendues côte à côte sans rien dire, à observer les nuages qui passaient.

Puis Linda m'a demandé :

— Qu'est-ce que le château Yates t'a rappelé?

Je me suis aussitôt sentie anxieuse. Je me suis assise et j'ai regardé Linda. Je lui avais déjà confié quelques détails à propos de mon autre vie. J'avais très envie de lui parler de ces images qui surgissaient dans ma tête. Mais comprendrait-elle? Et encore plus important : le répéterait-elle à d'autres? Mychailo m'avait bien

avertie de ne pas en parler à des Canadiens. Mais
Linda était ma meilleure amie, après tout! Il fallait
que je lui en raconte un petit bout.

— Tout ce dont je me rappelle, c'est d'avoir été
enfermée dans une belle maison, ai-je dit. Et que
j'étais morte de peur.

— Qui aurait pu t'enfermer? a-t-elle demandé,
perplexe.

— Je ne sais pas.

— Tes parents?

— Non! Marusia et Ivan ne m'auraient jamais fait
subir ça.

Comme je n'ai rien dit de plus, Linda a laissé
tomber le sujet. Nous avons joué à quelques jeux,
comme « J'ai vu quelque chose de rouge ». Nous nous
sommes amusées à voir des formes dans les nuages qui
passaient. Puis elle a dit qu'il fallait aller rejoindre Ivan
à l'église.

— Après la peur que tu as eue, je suis sûre que tu as
envie de rentrer chez toi.

J'ai regardé Linda d'un œil nouveau : quelle
délicatesse de sa part!

— Devons-nous repasser devant cette maison? ai-je
demandé.

— Pas nécessairement, a-t-elle dit, en pointant le
doigt en direction du haut de la colline. Voici la rue
Terrace Hill. Nous pouvons passer par là pour nous
rendre à ton église.

— Tu es certaine que tu ne seras pas déçue si nous

ne jouons pas au Monopoly?

— Nadia, a dit Linda, ce n'est pas grave. Nous jouerons au Monopoly un autre jour.

En haut de la colline, sur la rue Terrace Hill, nous avions une magnifique vue sur la gare et ses environs. On pouvait voir presque jusque chez moi. Heureusement, le château était caché par les arbres.

En suivant la rue Terrace Hill, j'ai été surprise de voir que l'église ukrainienne était si près et troublée de constater que le château Yates et l'église ukrainienne se trouvaient dos à dos. D'ailleurs, des marches et un chemin pour les voitures longeaient l'église et se rendaient jusqu'au château. J'ai eu un coup au cœur. Cette petite église était jusque-là un des rares endroits où je me sentais vraiment en sécurité. Maintenant que je la savais si près de cette maison à donner la chair de poule, je me demandais si je pourrais encore m'y sentir en sécurité.

Ivan ratissait les feuilles mortes sur la pelouse devant l'église. J'ai remarqué que Mychailo aidait son père à planter une haie le long du chemin qui menait jusqu'à la porte de l'église. Quand nous sommes arrivées, Ivan m'a regardée tout surpris :

— Vous avez déjà fini votre partie?

— Non, pas tout à fait, mais... ai-je dit en tournant la tête vers Linda.

Elle a croisé mon regard et m'a fait un petit signe de tête.

— Nous n'en avions plus envie, a-t-elle dit en

haussant les épaules. Nous jouerons une autre fois.

Ivan a regardé son tas de feuilles, puis le reste de la pelouse.

— Je n'aurai pas terminé avant au moins une bonne heure.

— Je pourrais t'aider, ai-je offert.

— Moi aussi, a ajouté Linda. Avez-vous d'autres râteaux?

Je l'ai regardée et je lui ai souri pour la remercier. Ivan a souri.

— Ce ne sera pas long, avec nous trois à la tâche.

Quand le nettoyage du terrain a été terminé, Ivan a pris ma main et m'a entraînée vers les marches qui menaient à la rue Usher en longeant le château Yates.

— C'est un bon raccourci pour aller chez Linda, a-t-il dit. Et je veux te montrer une maison intéressante.

Ivan connaissait cette maison! Évidemment, il faisait le jardinage à l'église. Il avait donc certainement remarqué le château qui se trouvait derrière celle-ci. J'étais simplement surprise de ne jamais l'avoir aperçu entre les branches.

Je suis restée sur le trottoir, sans faire un pas de plus.

— Cet endroit me fait peur, ai-je déclaré.

Ivan a haussé les sourcils de surprise. Il m'a regardée, puis a regardé Linda. Elle a haussé les épaules.

— Alors, tu ne veux pas passer par ce sentier? a-t-il demandé.

— Non.

Nous sommes passés par la rue Terrace Hill, puis par la rue Principale et nous avons laissé Linda chez elle en chemin.

Une fois seuls, marchant vers chez nous, Ivan m'a demandé :

— Cette grande maison t'a-t-elle rappelé quelque chose?

J'ai hoché la tête en signe affirmatif.

— La maison allemande à la campagne?

J'ai fait signe que non.

— Es-tu certaine de ne pas vouloir aller la regarder de près avec moi?

— Sûre et certaine.

— Tant pis, a dit Ivan. Elle est intéressante, et je pensais que ça allait te plaire de la voir de près.

J'ai frissonné rien que d' y penser.

— Elle a été construite dans les années 1800 par le propriétaire des chemins de fer, a-t-il dit. Il voulait qu'elle ressemble à...

J'ai serré la main d'Ivan si fort qu'il s'est tourné vers moi et n'a pas terminé sa phrase.

Chapitre quatorze

Les enfants volés

Un beau samedi matin, Marusia est rentrée à la maison en coup de vent, avec un sac de provisions dans les bras et un sourire jusqu'aux oreilles. J'avais passé l'avant-midi à la bibliothèque et je venais tout juste de rentrer.

— Vous ne devinerez jamais ce qui m'est arrivé aujourd'hui! a-t-elle dit en enlevant son manteau d'hiver.

— Tu as trouvé du travail? me suis-je exclamée.

Marusia a perdu son sourire. Une fois la saison des récoltes terminée, elle n'avait pas réussi à retrouver un travail à temps plein. Depuis le début de décembre, elle travaillait quatre matins par semaine à la buanderie automatique qui avait ouvert au centre-ville, mais elle gagnait beaucoup moins qu'à la ferme.

— Non, pas ça.

Elle a plongé la main dans la poche de son manteau et en a retiré trois petits bouts de carton.

— Des billets pour le cinéma, pour ce soir, a-t-elle fièrement annoncé. Un de mes clients me les a

147

donnés.

Fantastique! J'étais déjà passée devant le cinéma avec Mychailo, mais je n'aurais jamais cru pouvoir y entrer.

— Quel film allons-nous voir?

— *Cendrillon*. C'est la même histoire que *Popelyushka* en ukrainien.

Popelyushka! Ce nom semblait empreint dans ma mémoire. J'avais l'impression de connaître ce conte de fées depuis toujours.

Ivan travaillait à l'église ce jour-là. Dès qu'il est rentré, nous lui avons annoncé la bonne nouvelle. Nous avons soupé rapidement, puis nous nous sommes emmitouflés pour notre grande sortie. Le cinéma n'était qu'à quelques minutes de marche. Une queue s'était formée, mais Ivan est allé retrouver un employé qui portait un chapeau rouge et lui a montré nos billets. Il nous a fait signe de venir.

La première salle en entrant était un grand espace ouvert, avec des peintures d'un style démodé au plafond et des tentures de velours rouge. Un des murs était couvert d'affiches annonçant des vieux films. Sur celle d'un film intitulé *Autant en emporte le vent*, il y avait une femme aux cheveux bruns, avec du rouge à lèvres rouge. J'ai tiré sur la main d'Ivan et je la lui ai montrée du doigt. Il a souri. Marusia était aussi jolie qu'elle, ce soir, avec ses cheveux bien coiffés et son rouge à lèvres.

Nous sommes passés par une ouverture dans les

tentures et nous sommes entrés dans la salle des spectateurs. Les sièges se remplissaient vite. J'ai pointé la première rangée. Elle était presque vide. Nous nous sommes précipités avant que d'autres ne le remarquent et nous avons pris les trois sièges qui étaient en plein centre. Je me suis calée dans mon fauteuil et j'ai appuyé ma nuque contre le haut du dossier. De cette façon, je voyais l'écran géant tout entier, au-dessus de ma tête. *Cendrillon* commençait avec l'image d'un grand livre qui s'ouvrait, puis une voix qui disait : « Il était une fois, dans une lointaine contrée, un tout petit royaume… »

J'avais l'impression d'être entrée dans un livre de contes. Je n'avais jamais vu de film en dessin animé, au lieu d'acteurs, et je n'avais jamais vu de film en « technicolor » non plus. Les films que Vater nous emmenait voir étaient tous sur Hitler et vantaient ses qualités de héros. C'était toujours sérieux et ennuyant. *Cendrillon* n'avait rien à voir avec ça. Il y avait des chansons, de la danse et des scènes pleines de gaieté, même si l'histoire comportait des passages tristes. Au début du film, la chambre dénudée de Cendrillon dans le grand manoir m'a soulevé le cœur. Les chambres du château Yates ressemblaient-elles à celle-ci?

Après le film, il faisait nuit, et nous sommes rentrés ensemble à la maison. Ivan tenait Marusia par la taille, et je les devançais de quelques pas, les mains enfoncées dans les poches de mon manteau d'hiver.

Tout en marchant, je pensais à une chanson que chantait Cendrillon. Celle à propos d'un rêve qui représentait en fait ce qu'elle souhaitait au plus profond de son cœur. Je n'avais jamais pensé à mes rêves de cette façon. Mon cœur m'envoyait-il un message sous la forme d'un rêve? Mon rêve ne ressemblait pas tellement à un souhait, mais plutôt à de la peur.

Une fois à la maison, Marusia et Ivan se sont assis dans la cuisine pour bavarder. Je voulais leur laisser du temps ensemble, alors plutôt que de m'asseoir avec eux, je suis montée dans ma chambre. Je me suis assise sur mon lit et j'ai jeté un regard satisfait sur ma belle chambre. Elle était dans un grenier, comme celle de Cendrillon, mais elle était chaude et confortable. Les murs lilas me donnaient un sentiment de sécurité. Ma table de chevet faite d'un caisson en bois était simple, mais dedans il y avait mes livres de bibliothèque et dessus, ma lampe. De quoi d'autre aurais-je eu besoin? J'avais de la chance d'être aimée par Marusia et Ivan. J'ai pris un livre de bibliothèque et je l'ai serré contre mon cœur…

Des ombres noires dansent sur les murs blancs, tout égratignés. Il y a des marques d'ongles autour de la poignée de verre de la porte, qui ont été faites par je ne sais qui, et de petites échardes se soulèvent sur le panneau. L'unique fenêtre est trop haute pour que je puisse voir dehors. Je m'accroche aux barreaux et j'essaie de me hisser à sa hauteur. Pendant quelques secondes, toute tremblante, je regarde la neige sale, en bas. Mes bras n'en peuvent plus, et je retombe par terre. Pourquoi suis-je prisonnière dans cette maison?

J'ai mal à la gorge à force de crier, et mes ongles sont pleins de sang à force de gratter autour de la poignée de la porte. Je suis étendue sur le plancher et je regarde l'ampoule dénudée au plafond. Je n'entends rien d'autre que ma respiration saccadée. Puis j'entends des pas qui martèlent le plancher, de l'autre côté de ma porte. Quelqu'un traîne les pieds, se débat. Un enfant crie dans le couloir. Une porte se referme en claquant.

Un autre enfant volé.

Je prie pour que la porte s'ouvre. Je prie pour trouver un moyen de m'échapper.

Les heures, puis les jours passent. J'entends un bruit à ma fenêtre. Comment est-ce possible? Je suis au premier étage. Suis-je morte et est-ce un ange qui cogne ainsi à ma fenêtre? Puis je me rends compte qu'on lance des cailloux dans la vitre. Je me relève et j'agrippe les barreaux. En appuyant mes pieds nus contre le mur, je grimpe jusqu'à la fenêtre comme si je faisais de l'escalade en montagne. Je pose mes pieds sur le rebord de la fenêtre et je tire sur mes bras pour me hisser jusque-là.

Une femme. Les yeux si bouffis à force de pleurer qu'elle peut à peine les tenir ouverts. Sa tête est couverte d'un foulard aux couleurs défraîchies. Elle me voit à travers la vitre et agite la main frénétiquement, *puis se rend compte que je ne suis pas l'enfant qu'elle recherche. Combien d'enfants volés y a-t-il ici?*

— À l'aide! ai-je crié.

Je tape contre la vitre.

Un soldat repousse la femme de la pointe de son fusil.

D'une chambre plus loin dans le couloir, j'entends un enfant pleurer : « Mama! » Cet enfant aussi tape contre la vitre.

Pourquoi est-ce que je peux entendre cet enfant crier, alors que cette femme ne le peut pas? Elle se retourne et, une dernière fois, elle fait glisser son regard sur les fenêtres. Le soldat la frappe au visage avec son fusil, et elle tombe sur ses genoux.

J'entends la porte s'ouvrir dans mon dos. Une femme en blanc entre dans la chambre et m'ordonne de descendre de la fenêtre, mais je n'en bouge pas.

— À l'aide!

L'infirmière est à côté de moi maintenant, et elle passe son bras autour de ma taille. Je me débats à coups de pied et de poing. Je sens une piqûre sur mon épaule. Soudain je me sens faible. Je ne peux plus me tenir aux barreaux. Je tombe dans les bras de la femme.

Le livre de bibliothèque avait glissé de mes mains pour atterrir sur mon orteil. Je me suis frotté les yeux et j'ai regardé autour de moi. J'étais dans ma chambre aux murs lilas, dans la maison qu'Ivan avait construite sur la rue Sheridan, à Brantford. Il faisait noir dehors, mais ma lampe était allumée. Pas de barreaux à la fenêtre. La porte était ouverte. J'étais en sécurité. J'avais l'impression que mon cœur allait faire exploser ma poitrine.

Je ne voulais pas rester seule. Je me suis donc levée et j'ai descendu l'escalier. Marusia et Ivan n'étaient plus dans la cuisine. J'ai jeté un coup d'œil dans leur chambre. Ivan ronflait doucement, et Marusia dormait profondément. Nous n'avions toujours pas de meubles dans le salon. Je me suis donc assise par terre, au centre, et j'ai regardé par la fenêtre.

Jusqu'à ce moment-là, les images de mon passé avaient toujours été brèves. Mais cette dernière avait été longue et terrifiante. J'ai essayé de me souvenir d'autre chose à propos du bâtiment... La maison d'une famille riche de la ville, qui avait été transformée en un lieu horrible. Un grand escalier blanc qui donnait dans une belle grande entrée au plafond voûté. Deux escaliers qui montaient de chaque côté, vers un palier. Je me rappelais qu'on m'avait transportée comme un sac de pommes de terre jusqu'en haut de ces escaliers. Qu'on m'avait enfermée dans une chambre. D'autres étaient-ils enfermés dans les chambres voisines? Qu'avais-je fait pour mériter ce châtiment? Qu'était-il arrivé avant cet événement... et après? J'avais un trou de mémoire complet.

Une main chaleureuse était posée sur mon épaule. Il m'a fallu un moment pour me rendre compte que j'étais revenue dans le présent. Marusia était agenouillée à mon côté.

— Nadia… Nadia… Est-ce que ça va?

— D'autres souvenirs me sont revenus.

— Veux-tu en parler?

Je n'ai rien dit pendant un instant. J'essayais de respirer lentement pour calmer les battements de mon cœur.

— J'ai rêvé que j'étais enfermée dans une grande maison.

— La ferme allemande? a demandé Marusia.

— Non. Il s'agissait d'une belle demeure de la ville. Marusia a froncé les sourcils.

— Quel âge avais-tu?

— Je ne sais pas… J'étais trop petite pour pouvoir regarder par la fenêtre.

— C'est donc un souvenir d'avant l'époque où tu habitais avec les Allemands… a dit Marusia en parlant autant à elle-même qu'à moi.

— Avant que j'habite avec les Allemands? Comment ça? ai-je demandé.

Je la sentais qui tremblait à côté de moi. Je crois qu'elle pleurait dans le noir et qu'elle ne voulait pas que je m'en aperçoive.

— Je t'ai dit que tu n'étais pas allemande, a-t-elle précisé. Tu n'es pas née dans cette famille.

Si ce n'était pas ma famille d'origine, alors où étaient mes parents? Et qui étaient-ils?

Je savais que Marusia et Ivan n'étaient pas mes vrais

parents, mais je savais qu'ils m'aimaient. Il était clair que ces Allemands n'étaient pas mes parents. Mutter ne me traitait jamais aussi bien qu'Eva. Mais comment m'étais-je retrouvée chez eux et qui étaient mes vrais parents? Je n'y comprenais rien.

— Alors qui suis-je?

Marusia a secoué la tête.

— Je ne le sais pas exactement, mais tu es ukrainienne, j'en suis convaincue.

— Mais... comment peux-tu le savoir?

— À cause de petites choses que tu as faites sans t'en rendre compte, a-t-elle dit.

— Comme quoi?

— La façon de faire ton signe de croix après la prière, a-t-elle dit. Et tu te chantais à toi-même la *kolysanka* quand tu pensais que personne ne pouvait t'entendre.

— Je croyais que c'était ma chanson secrète.

— Oui, a dit Marusia en me serrant dans ses bras. Je le sais. Il y a aussi que tu ne ressemblais à personne d'autre, dans cette famille.

J'ai approuvé d'un signe de tête.

— Et tu parlais allemand avec un accent ukrainien, a-t-elle dit avec un sourire en coin.

— C'est vrai?

— Absolument vrai!

Tout s'emmêlait dans ma tête, mais je me sentais réconfortée de savoir que ces gens n'étaient pas ma famille. À l'école, chaque fois qu'un élève me harcelait en me traitant de « fille d'Hitler » ou de « Nadia la nazie », j'étais morte de honte. J'avais rencontré des Allemands gentils, tant au Canada que pendant la guerre. J'éprouvais de la pitié pour Mutter, car elle était toujours triste, mais elle n'était pas gentille avec moi. Et Vater était comme un étranger. Un étranger au cœur dur et froid. Après la guerre, quand j'ai entendu parler des horreurs d'Hitler, je me suis sentie honteuse de qui j'étais peut-être.

Mais la même question se posait toujours : qui étais-je vraiment?

Je ne voulais pas retourner dans ma chambre et j'étais trop bouleversée pour rester seule. Ivan n'avait plus que quelques heures à dormir avant de se lever pour aller travailler. Marusia est donc retournée dans leur chambre sur la pointe des pieds pour y prendre une couverture et des oreillers, et nous avons dormi par terre dans le salon, serrées l'une contre l'autre.

Je n'arrivais pas à m'endormir. Je ne voulais pas repenser à cette maison. J'ai donc pensé à Cendrillon et au don qu'elle avait de rêver à ce qu'elle souhaitait dans son cœur. Tout en m'endormant doucement, le souvenir d'une autre mère, il y a très longtemps, m'est revenu à la mémoire…

J'étais assise sur ses genoux, dans le noir, mes bras autour de sa taille, et je respirais son doux parfum de lilas. Je ne voulais pas la laisser partir. Elle chantait la kolysanka *tout doucement, dans mon oreille. Une larme toute chaude a atterri sur ma joue. J'ai levé les yeux. Malgré l'obscurité, je voyais son visage ruisselant de larmes…*

Qui était-elle donc?

Nous étions presque rendus aux vacances de Noël, et un blanc manteau de neige recouvrait les rues et les maisons. J'avais cessé d'aller chez Linda régulièrement. Nous étions encore des amies, mais je n'étais pas à l'aise à l'idée de me retrouver près du château Yates. Et ce n'était plus pareil maintenant, quand je me rendais à l'église. Le parfum de l'encens ne me réconfortait plus.

Un jour, après l'école et avant le retour d'Ivan et de Marusia, je me suis assise sur ma balançoire dans la cour, j'ai fermé les yeux et j'ai essayé de penser très fort à mon passé. Les souvenirs me revenaient si souvent sans crier gare. J'aurais tant aimé pouvoir y penser sur commande pour arriver à remettre en place toutes les pièces du casse-tête. J'entendais quelqu'un qui frappait avec un marteau au loin, et ce bruit m'a rappelé celui des tirs de mortiers. De gros flocons de neige tout légers tombaient sur ma tête et mes épaules. J'ai fermé les yeux et j'ai levé mon visage vers le ciel. Chaque fois qu'un flocon tombait dessus, j'essayais de me rappeler le passé. Puis tout à coup :

— Bouh!

J'ai crié et j'ai failli tomber de ma balançoire.

— Hé! Je t'ai vraiment fait peur, a dit Mychailo. Tu devrais voir la tête que tu as!

— Ce n'était pas très gentil de ta part, ai-je rétorqué. J'avais encore le cœur qui battait à tout rompre.

— Veux-tu aller au parc? a-t-il demandé.

— Il fait trop froid

Mychailo a levé les yeux au ciel.

— Si la neige te dérange, alors pourquoi restes-tu sur ta balançoire sous la neige?

— D'accord, allons au parc, ai-je dit.

C'était peut-être le meilleur moyen de chasser toutes ces idées de ma tête. J'ai écrit un mot pour Marusia et Ivan, et je l'ai déposé sur la glacière.

Nous nous sommes rendus au parc, mais Mychailo n'a pas voulu y rester parce que des garçons de l'école y faisaient des glissades avec une traîne sauvage.

— On peut simplement se promener, lui ai-je proposé. Ou aller à la bibliothèque.

Nous avons marché jusqu'à notre école, puis jusqu'à la bibliothèque. Nous avons traversé le parc Victoria, puis nous nous sommes rendus jusqu'à la place du marché sans nous adresser la parole. Comme ce n'était pas jour de marché, la place était vide. J'ai regardé les vitrines pleines de jouets, de parfums et de toutes sortes de choses de Noël. Il y avait une telle variété!

Mychailo m'a finalement demandé :

— À quoi penses-tu?

— À rien, ai-je répondu.

— Ce n'est pas vrai, a-t-il répliqué. Tu as l'air triste. Est-ce que tu penses à ton ancienne maison?

Je l'ai regardé, tout étonnée.

— Que veux-tu dire?

— Ce que je veux dire est très simple, a-t-il dit. Il doit sûrement t'arriver de penser à la maison que tu as quittée, non?

— C'est un tel fouillis dans ma tête, lui ai-je expliqué. Mais oui, j'y pense très souvent.

Mychailo avait probablement vécu une expérience semblable à la mienne. Il avait habité dans un camp, tout comme nous. Il avait survécu à la guerre. Mais nous n'en avions jamais parlé. Je ne savais pas si c'était parce que c'était trop douloureux pour lui ou parce que son esprit bloquait ses souvenirs, comme dans mon cas.

— De quoi te souviens-tu, du temps de la guerre? lui ai-je demandé.

— De tout, a-t-il dit en donnant un coup de pied sur un caillou. Par moments, je préférerais avoir tout oublié.

— Peux-tu me raconter ce dont tu te souviens? ai-je demandé. Cela m'aidera peut-être à retrouver la mémoire.

— Des odeurs, surtout, a-t-il répondu. La poudre à fusil, la pourriture et le sang.

Ces simples mots ont réveillé dans ma tête le souvenir de ces odeurs, et mon nez s'est plissé de dégoût.

— Ce qu'il y a de bien au Canada, c'est qu'on n'y rencontre pas ces odeurs.

Mychailo avait raison. Au Canada, tout sentait bon le propre.

Nous avons marché en silence jusqu'à la bibliothèque. Mychailo a ouvert la grosse porte de côté, qui donnait directement dans la section des enfants. En entrant, j'ai respiré profondément et j'ai savouré le parfum du plancher fraîchement ciré, du savon et des livres. Bien mieux que les odeurs de la guerre!

Quand je suis rentrée, Marusia et Ivan étaient là, mais je me sentais quand même seule. Je me suis assise sur ma balançoire, sous la neige, et j'ai repensé aux odeurs qui hantaient la mémoire de Mychailo. Je me rappelais tant de choses de mon passé, maintenant! Je me suis forcée à penser à ma fuite avec Marusia, en commençant par ce qui me revenait facilement à la mémoire, puis en pensant à ce qui s'était produit ensuite, en commençant par les jours qui avaient précédé notre arrivée au camp des personnes déplacées...

Le train s'est arrêté. Nous étions blottis les uns contre les autres sur le wagon plat, avec les autres fugitifs. Il nous pleuvait dessus. Un homme a retiré sa capote militaire râpée et a essayé de nous en couvrir tous.

Une jeep est arrivée. Des soldats soviétiques en sont descendus. Il y a eu une bataille, des coups de feu et des cris. Marusia m'a attrapée par la main tandis que nous nous enfuyions avec les autres fugitifs. Nous avons couru. Un autre coup de feu. J'ai senti une balle me frôler l'épaule. Nous avons été les seules à ne pas avoir été rattrapées.

Nous avons couru et couru. J'avais un poing de côté. Nous avons quand même continué jusqu'en pleine nuit et nous sommes arrivées dans un village déserté. Les Soviétiques étaient passés par là avant nous. Mon nez s'est pincé en reconnaissant l'odeur familière du sang et de la fumée. À l'emplacement d'une maison, il ne restait plus qu'un trou dans le sol et dedans, les restes d'un caveau à légumes. Marusia y est descendue, puis m'a prise dans ses bras pour m'y faire descendre à mon tour.

J'étais trempée et je grelottais de froid. La robe rose maintenant crasseuse et déchirée ne me tenait pas au chaud. Combien de temps Marusia et moi sommes-nous restées recroquevillées l'une contre l'autre au fond de ce caveau, au milieu des décombres? Je l'ignore. Nous avons essayé de nous couvrir avec des feuilles. Nous avons essayé de dormir.

Le lendemain matin, je me suis réveillée en sursaut quand Marusia a crié et a roulé par-dessus moi. J'avais du mal à respirer et je la poussais, mais elle refusait de bouger. J'ai entendu un sifflement, puis j'ai vu une fourche. Elle m'avait manquée de peu. Au dessus de nos têtes se tenait une petite vieille toute ratatinée. Elle a tendu la main pour reprendre la fourche par le manche, mais Marusia a pivoté et a saisi l'outil par les piques.

— Ne nous faites pas de mal! a supplié Marusia en allemand.

La femme a cligné des yeux de surprise.

— Une femme et un enfant! a-t-elle murmuré. Je croyais que c'étaient encore les soldats soviétiques.

— Nous les fuyons, justement, a dit Marusia.

— Vous êtes allemandes?

— Non, a dit Marusia. Nous sommes des travailleuses étrangères.

— Pourquoi ne partez-vous pas avec eux? a demandé la femme en montrant la direction des lignes soviétiques.

— Ils sont pires que les nazis, a dit Marusia.

— Alors, suivez-moi! a répondu la vieille en nous tournant le dos.

J'ai aidé Marusia à se remettre debout. Elle a attrapé la fourche par le manche, et nous nous sommes hissées hors du caveau à légumes.

La vieille pensait que nous la suivions docilement. Elle ne s'est même pas retournée pour vérifier. Comme il faisait jour, je pouvais voir les ruines calcinées des maisonnettes qui bordaient la rue. Nous l'avons suivie jusqu'à ce qui avait été la place du village. Tout était démoli sauf le coin d'une église. Du bois brûlé et des débris de verre formaient un tas d'un côté. À l'abri de deux murs d'angle, une jeune femme était étendue sur un drap crasseux, couverte de marques de coups et de sang. J'ai d'abord cru qu'elle était morte, puis j'ai remarqué un léger mouvement de son visage.

— Ma petite-fille a survécu, a dit la vieille. Mais de justesse. J'ai besoin de vous pour veiller sur elle pendant que je vais essayer de trouver quelque chose à manger.

Nous sommes restées là pendant quelques jours. La vieille partageait avec nous la nourriture qu'elle réussissait à dénicher. Marusia a nettoyé les plaies de sa petite-fille et les a désinfectées avec une teinture qu'elle a fabriquée avec des branchettes et des feuilles. Quand nous sommes reparties, la vieille nous a montré du doigt la direction du camp des personnes déplacées le plus près…

Ce soir-là, j'ai rêvé à l'odeur du fumier, des coups de feu, du sang et de la terre. Et des lilas.

Chapitre quinze

L'inspecteur Sutton

— Les enfants, vous allez être gentils, a dit Mlle Ferris le lendemain matin. Après la récréation, nous aurons de la visite, et je veux que vous ayez tous une conduite irréprochable.

Je me suis tournée vers Linda. Elle avait un sourcil relevé, l'air interrogateur. Quand Mlle Ferris s'est retournée pour écrire au tableau, Linda s'est penchée vers moi et m'a chuchoté :

— Ce doit être l'inspecteur.

Je ne comprenais pas. J'ai remarqué que plusieurs élèves étaient nerveux, et Mlle Ferris avait la voix un peu cassée. Même si je ne savais pas ce qu'était un inspecteur, je n'avais pas du tout hâte de le voir arriver.

Quand la cloche de la récréation a sonné, j'ai enfin pu demander à Linda qui était ce visiteur.

— C'est un patron qui vient visiter l'école deux ou trois fois par année, m'a-t-elle expliqué. Si une institutrice ne fait pas bien son travail, elle peut se faire renvoyer.

— Et les élèves? ai-je demandé.

— Un inspecteur peut causer des problèmes aux élèves aussi. Par exemple, si tu es absente ou en retard trop souvent, il peut demander à te rencontrer. Je déteste la visite des inspecteurs.

J'ai repensé à mon horrible première journée d'école, quand j'avais quitté la cour sans permission.

— Penses-tu que ma fuite lors du premier jour d'école risque de me causer des problèmes? ai-je demandé.

Elle a pris une seconde pour réfléchir.

— Je ne crois pas, ça fait des lunes de cela. S'il avait dû y avoir des conséquences, ce serait déjà arrivé.

À ces mots, je me suis sentie un peu rassurée. Mais comme tous les autres, je n'avais pas hâte de voir l'inspecteur.

À la fin de la récréation, quand la cloche a sonné, nous rentrions en rangs dans l'école lorsqu'un taxi noir est arrivé. Tout ce que je pouvais voir par la vitre arrière, c'était la tête et les épaules d'une femme.

J'ai donné un coup de coude à Linda et je lui ai chuchoté :

— Est-ce que c'est l'inspecteur?

— Je n'ai jamais vu une femme inspecteur, a-t-elle répondu d'un air incertain.

Mlle Ferris est venue nous rejoindre et nous a fait rentrer de manière bien ordonnée. Nous avons marché en rangs jusque dans la classe, puis nous avons pris nos places. Mlle Ferris a tapé avec sa règle sur son bureau pour attirer notre attention.

— L'inspecteur Sutton est ici, a-t-elle dit, l'air un peu paniquée. Quand elle entrera dans la classe, je vais taper deux fois dans mes mains, et vous direz tous ensemble : « Bonjour, inspecteur Sutton. »

Soudain la porte s'est ouverte, et une femme est entrée. Elle était grande, ne souriait pas et avait à la main un porte-documents noir. Ses cheveux gris étaient tirés en chignon sur sa nuque, et elle portait un tailleur brun avec un chemisier blanc, de style masculin. En la voyant dans le taxi, je m'étais sentie inquiète. Maintenant que je la voyais en personne, j'étais terrifiée. Je dirais même plus : terrorisée. J'avais le pressentiment terrible que cette femme allait me faire du mal. J'étais paniquée et je n'avais qu'une seule envie : sortir au plus vite de la classe. Mais l'inspecteur se tenait debout devant la seule porte de sortie. Je n'avais pas le choix : je devais rester assise à ma place. Alors, j'ai empoigné les deux côtés de mon pupitre pour m'empêcher de trembler.

Mlle Ferris aussi était nerveuse. Se sentait-elle comme moi ? En tout cas, elle était pâle comme un linge. Comme elle avait oublié de taper dans ses mains, des élèves se sont levés, mais pas tout le monde. J'étais la dernière à me lever. Quelques élèves ont alors dit d'une voix chevrotante :

— Bonjour, inspecteur Sutton.

L'inspecteur a posé son porte-documents par terre, puis a mis ses deux mains sur ses hanches :

— Vous ne pouvez pas faire mieux ?

— BONJOUR, INSPECTEUR SUTTON! avons-nous tous crié en chœur.

— Bonjour à tous et à toutes, a-t-elle dit.

Puis, en agitant les bras comme un chef d'orchestre, elle nous a fait asseoir.

— Bien! a-t-elle ajouté.

Puis elle a tourné la tête vers notre institutrice.

— Maintenant, mademoiselle Ferris, quel poème vos élèves peuvent-ils me réciter? a-t-elle demandé.

— Euh... Mademoiselle... Inspecteur Sutton... Nous n'avons pas fait de leçon de récitation récemment, a répondu Mlle Ferris qui serrait sa règle à s'en briser les jointures.

— Alors pourraient-ils me chanter une chanson?

Mlle Ferris parut soulagée.

— Ils connaissent la chanson de la feuille d'érable.

— Excellent! a dit l'inspecteur Sutton. Je vous écoute.

Mlle Ferris nous a tous fait lever, et nous avons entonné la chanson. Nous étions presque tous au diapason et nous avions à peu près le bon rythme. Mlle Ferris regardait l'inspecteur Sutton et attendait sa réaction.

— Bien, a dit l'inspecteur.

Elle est allée derrière le bureau de Mlle Ferris et a pris la chaise à deux mains, par le dossier. Elle l'a déplacée sur le côté et, nous faisant face, elle s'est assise.

—Voilà qui est mieux, a-t-elle dit.

Elle a pris des lunettes à monture métallique dans la poche de son tailleur et les a perchées sur le bout de son nez. Elle a sorti un carnet noir de son porte-documents, puis a commencé à désigner un élève, puis un autre. Elle nous a fait lever un par un, nous posait une question, puis nous faisait rasseoir. Elle prenait des notes sur chaque élève. Les questions n'étaient pas difficiles, mais nous étions quand même terrifiés. La question qu'elle m'a posée était : « Quelle est ta couleur préférée? » Quand je lui ai répondu que c'était le lilas, elle a souri et a dit que mon anglais était bon pour une nouvelle immigrante.

À la fin, l'inspecteur Sutton a replacé la chaise de Mlle Ferris derrière le bureau et s'est dirigée vers la porte. J'étais si soulagée de la voir partir! Elle n'avait pas parlé de ma fugue lors de mon premier jour d'école. Linda avait raison.

Je venais tout juste de me calmer quand l'inspecteur Sutton s'est arrêtée dans son mouvement vers la sortie, comme si elle venait de se rappeler qu'elle avait oublié quelque chose. Elle a ouvert son porte-documents et en a retiré le carnet noir. Elle s'est mise à le feuilleter en fronçant les sourcils.

— La nouvelle… Nadia? a-t-elle appelé en parcourant la classe des yeux par-dessus ses lunettes.

Je me suis levée.

— Approche, a-t-elle dit avec un sourire. Pourrais-tu prendre mon porte-documents?

L'idée de m'approcher de cette femme me rendait

malade à vomir. J'ai respiré profondément et je me suis dirigée vers elle. Elle sentait la naphtaline.

Son porte-documents était étonnamment lourd, et je devais m'y prendre à deux mains pour le transporter. Elle est sortie de la classe, et je l'ai suivie d'un pas maladroit. J'ai réussi à la rejoindre devant la classe de première année, où elle m'attendait.

— Merci, a-t-elle dit. Ce porte-documents est extrêmement lourd à porter toute la journée. Tiens, voici pour ta peine.

Elle a sorti de sa poche un bonbon clair enveloppé dans une papillote et me l'a tendu.

J'ai fixé le bonbon au creux de sa main tendue. Sans savoir pourquoi ni où je m'en allais, je suis partie en courant dans le couloir. Tout ce que je savais, c'était que je devais m'enfuir à tout prix. J'ai poussé la grande porte et, une fois dehors, j'ai continué de courir. Il faisait froid, et je n'avais pas mon manteau d'hiver ni mes bottes, mais je ne me suis pas arrêtée pour autant. L'air froid sur mon visage me donnait un sentiment de liberté.

— Nadia, reviens! a crié l'inspecteur Sutton.

Je n'ai pas arrêtée de courir, mais j'ai tourné la tête. Elle se tenait debout dans l'entrée et avait l'air sous le choc. J'étais bien contente qu'elle ne soit pas partie à ma poursuite. Quand je me suis retournée un peu plus tard, pour vérifier, elle était partie.

Je ne savais pas où j'allais, mais dans mon for intérieur je savais que je devais absolument fuir cette femme en tailleur brun. C'était une question de vie ou de mort. Je ne voulais pas rentrer chez nous. Ce serait le premier endroit où elle irait me chercher, non?

Sans que je m'en rende compte, mes jambes m'ont conduite en direction de la bibliothèque. Quand j'ai entendu une voiture venir, je me suis cachée derrière un banc de neige. Je voyais l'entrée des enfants, mais un groupe de mères avec leurs tout-petits dans des poussettes bavardaient devant la porte. J'ai grimpé l'escalier de l'entrée principale en sachant parfaitement que j'étais à la vue de tous. Heureusement, aucune des mères ne m'a remarquée. Une fois en haut, j'ai entrouvert la porte. J'ai passé la tête dans l'embrasure, et une bouffée d'air chaud m'a frappée au visage. Il n'y avait personne. Je suis donc entrée. À l'intérieur, avec la chaleur ambiante, je me suis rendu compte que j'étais gelée jusqu'aux os. Puis j'ai entendu des voix qui se dirigeaient vers la sortie de la grande salle. Je me suis glissée vers l'escalier qui menait en bas, à la salle des enfants.

C'était l'heure du conte dans la salle des albums illustrés, mais la salle des romans était vide. Je me suis assise par terre, dans le coin le plus éloigné de la porte, j'ai entouré mes jambes de mes bras et je me suis mise à me bercer d'avant en arrière en chantant la *kolysanka*. Je tremblais de tous mes membres, pas seulement parce que j'avais eu froid, mais aussi à cause de mes souvenirs. Ma tête était envahie par les images d'une femme en tailleur brun. J'essayais de penser à autre chose, mais en vain. J'étais morte de peur.

Chapitre seize
Les sœurs brunes

Je suis au pied de mon lit et je grelotte de froid. J'essaie de me réchauffer en serrant mes jambes contre moi avec mes bras. Nous empilons des couches de vêtements sur notre dos, mais le froid réussit toujours à les transpercer. Nous avons une seule couverture de laine, usée jusqu'à la trame et qui vaut si peu qu'on ne pourrait même pas la troquer contre de la nourriture. J'en ai couvert affectueusement les épaules de Baba, mais elle a encore les lèvres toutes bleues. Lida entre dans la chambre. Elle apporte un bol ébréché, rempli de ce que nous nous entêtons à appeler de la soupe alors que nous savons toutes les deux qu'elle est très peu nourrissante : de l'eau, un vague arôme de bouillon venant de vieux os mis à bouillir des douzaines de fois, des épluchures de pommes de terre ou de choux et tout ce que nous avons pu trouver à mettre dedans.

Elle dépose le bol sur la table de chevet et redresse le dos et la tête de Baba avec des oreillers. Baba cille des yeux. Elle me regarde, puis regarde Lida.

— Mes petites-filles, dit-elle, ne gaspillez pas cette nourriture pour moi. Je n'en ai plus pour longtemps en *ce bas monde.*

Lida et moi savons toutes deux que Baba a raison, mais comment pourrions-nous ne pas tenter de la sauver? Elle est la seule famille qu'il nous reste. Tato a été emmené par la police soviétique au début de l'été, comme tant d'autres Ukrainiens. Des semaines plus tard, Mama a été emmenée par la police nazie. Les vieillards et les enfants n'ont pas droit aux cartes de rationnement. Nous avons réussi à passer l'automne avec les maigres réserves de Baba. Mais maintenant que nous sommes au cœur de l'hiver, nous sommes au désespoir. Pour nous réchauffer, nous avons fait brûler presque tous nos meubles et aussi troqué nos précieux livres. Même notre cher lilas a été débité et utilisé comme bois de chauffage.

Lida est penchée au bord du lit et offre une cuillerée de soupe à Baba, mais celle-ci refuse de desserrer les lèvres. Lida soupire et lui suggère :

— Et si nous partagions la soupe?

Baba fait signe que oui de la tête.

— Vous deux en premier.

Nous nous passons la cuillère et, à tour de rôle, nous prenons une gorgée de notre soupe claire.

Une fois Baba rendormie, nous sortons pour aller mendier dans la rue. Pour commencer, nous nous asseyons devant la boulangerie. Quand Sarah et ses parents étaient encore en vie, ils trouvaient toujours quelque chose à nous donner, ne serait-ce qu'une vieille brioche toute racornie. Mais ils ont été parmi les premiers à se faire arrêter par les nazis.

La femme qui tient maintenant la boulangerie parle allemand. Elle nous renvoie à coups de balai. Alors nous allons nous asseoir sur les marches de l'église maintenant condamnée et nous nous recroquevillons l'une contre l'autre pour nous réchauffer. Je me rappelle l'époque où nous pouvions entrer dans l'église. Mama et Tato étaient encore avec nous. Le parfum de l'encens me donnait un sentiment de sécurité. Les gens ne viennent plus à l'église maintenant. De toute façon, il y a trop de mendiants et pas assez de nourriture. On ne nous donne plus rien, pas même une croûte de pain.

Je remarque qu'une longue file d'enfants vient de se former devant les grilles de ce qui était autrefois la synagogue. Quand une queue se forme, nous savons qu'il faut toujours nous y précipiter. Peu importe ce qu'on nous donnera, ce sera toujours mieux que rien.

En approchant, nous apercevons deux femmes en tailleur brun orné de manchettes et d'un col blancs.

— Ce sont peut-être des bonnes sœurs? dis-je, pleine d'espoir.

Lida me regarde, tout étonnée.

Les nazis se sont débarrassés des bonnes sœurs depuis longtemps.

Une des femmes prend des notes dans un carnet à couverture de cuir noir. L'autre plonge la main dans un grand sac de papier brun et en ressort des bonbons. À les voir, j'en ai l'estomac qui gargouille. Je n'arrive pas à me rappeler la dernière fois que j'ai mangé autre chose que du pain moisi et de la soupe à l'eau.

Je me dresse sur la pointe des pieds et je vois Sofia, qui habite dans notre rue, en train de parler avec les deux sœurs brunes. Elle pousse un petit cri de joie quand elle reçoit des bonbons. Finalement, c'est à mon tour. Lida est debout derrière moi, les mains posées sur mes épaules.

— Quels magnifiques cheveux blonds, dit la femme en allemand.

Elle s'accroupit, me regarde dans les yeux et s'exclame :

— Et ces yeux bleus!

Je souris poliment. Mes cheveux blonds sont un atout, quand je mendie auprès des Allemands.

— Êtes-vous sœurs? demande celle qui prend des notes.

— Oui, dis-je.

— Où habitez-vous? demande-t-elle.

— Dans cette maison, dis-je en montrant du doigt notre maisonnette aux murs blanchis à la chaux, à l'autre bout de la rue.

— C'est vrai? demande-t-elle à Lida en lui souriant.

— Oui.

L'autre femme plonge la main dans son sac et en ressort trois bonbons. Elle me les donne tous. Lida a la mine toute déconfite. La femme replonge la main dans son sac et en retire trois autres bonbons. Elle les met juste sous le nez de Lida.

— Dis-moi quel âge vous avez, ta petite sœur et toi.

— *Larissa a cinq ans, dit Lida. J'en ai huit.*

La femme sourit. Elle dépose les trois bonbons dans la main de Lida.

Lida referme sa main, et nous courons tout heureuses vers notre maison. Quand nous arrivons, Baba dort encore. Lida et moi déposons chacune un de nos bonbons sur sa table de nuit, puis nous allons nous asseoir ensemble, au coin de notre cheminée sans feu, et nous dégustons nos bonbons.

Nous dormons toutes les trois ensemble, dans le grand lit, pour avoir chaud. D'habitude, Baba nous entoure chacune les épaules d'un de ses bras et nous chante la kolysanka. *Comme elle est déjà endormie, Lida et moi la chantons nous-mêmes, tout doucement.*

Quand j'entends le premier coup frappé à notre porte, je pense que c'est un rêve. Je me rends compte que c'est pour de vrai quand Baba s'assoit dans le lit et nous entoure les épaules de ses bras décharnés.

— *N'ouvrez pas la porte, nous dit-elle entre ses dents.*

Nous sommes toutes les trois assises dans le noir, cramponnées ensemble et priant pour que ceux qui se trouvent de l'autre côté de notre porte s'en aillent au plus vite. Mais ils continuent de frapper. La porte s'ouvre brusquement. Un faisceau de lumière parcourt la grande pièce, puis s'arrête sur la porte de la chambre. Les silhouettes de deux soldats se dessinent dans le cadre de la porte, l'un tenant la lampe de poche et l'autre pointant son fusil sur nous. Quand mes yeux sont habitués à la lumière, je vois une troisième personne : la femme en brun qui nous a donné des bonbons.

Elle s'approche du lit et me saisit brutalement par le bras, mais Baba ne veut pas me laisser partir. La femme se tourne vers les soldats.

— Emmenez-la!

Baba me tient si fort que j'en aurai des bleus au torse pendant des jours, mais finalement, elle ne fait pas le poids contre deux hommes armés. L'un d'eux me met sur son épaule, comme un sac de pommes de terre. L'autre fait de même avec Lida.

Je crie « Baba! » de toutes mes forces tandis qu'ils nous emmènent hors de la chambre.

Baba retombe sur le lit, au milieu des draps déchirés; du sang coule sur sa joue. Ses bras sont tendus vers nous, et l'expression qu'elle a sur le visage me brise le cœur. Juste avant que les lampes de poche ne s'éteignent, je remarque que les deux bonbons sont restés sur la table de chevet.

Lida et moi sommes jetées à l'arrière d'un camion. L'odeur d'urine est affreuse. D'autres enfants s'y trouvent et pleurent. Lida et moi, nous nous retrouvons dans le noir et nous nous accrochons l'une à l'autre, toutes les deux effrayées et désespérées.

J'ai alors senti une main sur mon épaule, puis j'ai entendu une voix.

— Nadia, est-ce que ça va? a dit Mlle Barry.

Je me suis frotté les yeux, j'ai cligné deux fois, puis

j'ai regardé autour de moi. J'étais accroupie dans un coin de la salle des romans, dans la section des enfants de la bibliothèque municipale. À Brantford. J'étais en sécurité. Cette autre fillette était ma sœur. Lida. Où était-elle maintenant?

Je n'étais pas Nadia. Je n'étais pas Gretchen. Mon nom était Larissa!

J'ai senti quelque chose de chaud me recouvrir les épaules et le dos.

— Tu grelottes de froid, a dit Mlle Barry. Où est ton manteau?

Je l'ai regardée sans rien dire. J'avais la tête encore pleine des images du passé.

— Allons dans la salle réservée au personnel, a-t-elle dit. Tu pourras t'étendre sur le canapé.

Elle m'a prise doucement dans ses bras et m'a transportée dans l'autre pièce.

— Je vais appeler tes parents, l'ai-je entendu dire.

Je voyais ses lèvres bouger, mais je n'entendais rien. Mon esprit était retourné dans le passé…

Je suis dans une grande pièce blanche très éclairée. Peut-être dans un hôpital, mais les enfants qui sont avec moi ne sont pas malades : ils ont peur. Quand mon tour arrive, l'infirmière me fait retirer mes habits, sauf mes sous-vêtements. Je me sens rouge de honte. Quand elle approche un instrument de métal de mon visage, je me mets à crier.

— Tutt, tutt, tutt, fait-elle.

Et elle ajoute en allemand :

— *C'est un vernier... Pour mesurer. Pas de quoi avoir peur.*

Ses paroles ne me rassurent pas. Tandis qu'elle mesure et prend des notes, une autre femme me photographie de face, de côté et de dos.

Que font-elles? Qu'est-ce que cela signifie?

Elle me mesure le nez en trois endroits.

— *Tourne-toi, dit-elle.*

Je sens les deux barres de métal qui pressent sur les côtés de ma tête. Elle inscrit d'autres nombres dans son carnet. Elle mesure mes jambes, mes bras et ma taille. Pendant tout ce temps, je reste là sans bouger, paralysée par la peur.

Quand elle a terminé, elle retourne ma main gauche, paume vers le haut, et je la regarde, encore plus effrayée, tandis qu'elle marque mon poignet de petits points d'encre noire, de la grosseur d'une tête d'épingle. Est-ce du poison? Quand elle a fini, je lève mon poignet à la hauteur de mes yeux. On dirait un petit grain de beauté.

Elle saisit brutalement mes cheveux, et je sens qu'elle me marque aussi derrière l'oreille.

— *Voilà, dit-elle. Tu es maintenant une* Lebensborn.

Qu'est-ce que c'est, une Lebensborn*? J'ai entendu parler des enfants qui disparaissent. Un jour, ils mendient dans la rue et le lendemain, c'est comme s'ils n'avaient jamais existé. Est-ce que c'est ça, une* Lebensborn*?*

Lida est la suivante. On la mesure et on la photographie, mais on ne la marque pas à l'encre noire.

Quand tous les enfants ont été mesurés, on nous répartit en deux groupes : ceux qui sont marqués en noir et ceux qui ne le sont pas. Je suis donc d'un côté et Lida, de l'autre. Son groupe est conduit jusqu'à la porte.

Je crie :

— S'il vous plaît! Laissez-moi partir avec ma sœur!

— De vous deux, c'est toi qui as de la chance, dit la femme en blanc.

Je crie encore :

— Lida!

Lida se retourne et me regarde. Le désespoir se lit dans ses yeux. On la fait sortir en la bousculant. J'essaie d'aller la rejoindre en courant, mais on me retient.

Je perds le compte des jours. Des enfants marchent au pas. Des enfants saluent le Führer. On nous donne de petites portions de nourriture insignifiante. Au début, j'avale tout goulûment, puis je me sens coupable de ne pas en mettre de côté pour Baba et Lida. L'idée de manger cette nourriture me rend malade. Je parle en ukrainien avec un autre enfant. La femme en blanc me gifle.

— Tu es allemande! dit-elle. Parle en allemand.

La deuxième fois que je me fais prendre à parler ma langue maternelle, on m'emmène. On me donne des coups de pied, je déboule un escalier et j'atterris sur un sol de terre battue. Il fait très sombre, et tout ce que je peux distinguer ce sont les yeux des rats qui brillent dans le noir. J'entoure mes genoux avec mes bras pour tenter de me réchauffer. Quand la femme en blanc revient me chercher, je suis presque aveuglée par la lumière du jour.

Je vais à l'école avec les autres enfants. Une femme qui ne sourit jamais nous enseigne les règles de vie que nous devrons observer dorénavant. Les Ukrainiens et les Polonais sont des sous-humains. Ceux qu'on laissera vivre seront des esclaves pour les Aryens.

— Vous êtes des Aryens, nous explique-t-elle. Les gens que vous croyiez être vos parents sont des voleurs. Ils vous ont enlevés à vos parents aryens. Maintenant, nous vous rendons à vos parents.

Je sais qu'elle ment.

— Les Juifs sont des rats, continue-t-elle. Ils ne méritent pas de vivre.

Je pense à Sarah et à ses parents. Ils étaient juifs et ils ont été emmenés. La mère de Sarah trouvait toujours du pain à me donner. Son père n'aurait jamais fait mal à une mouche.

Je crie :

— Ce n'est pas vrai!

Je couvre ma bouche de ma main, mais c'est trop tard.

Les autres élèves, horrifiés, me regardent en écarquillant les yeux.

On me jette dans un camion et on m'emmène loin des autres enfants. Un soldat me met sur son épaule, comme un sac, et monte un grand escalier blanc, puis entre dans un manoir. Je le frappe dans le dos avec mes poings et je réclame ma Baba en criant. On m'enferme dans une pièce vide, toute blanche, sans rien à boire ni à manger. Je frappe à coups de poing dans la porte, mais personne ne vient. Le lendemain, j'appelle en allemand. On m'apporte de l'eau…

Soudain j'ai senti la couverture sur mes épaules. Elle dégageait un léger parfum de lavande et de poudre de talc. Je me suis blottie dedans, contente d'y être au chaud. Les souvenirs se sont estompés dans ma tête, et j'ai regardé autour de moi. J'étais étendue sur un canapé, dans une pièce, près du bureau de Mlle Barry. Elle était assise sur une chaise devant moi, tenant un verre d'eau dans ses mains. Aussitôt, le souvenir de l'inspecteur d'école m'est revenu à l'esprit.

— S'il vous plaît, ne me renvoyez pas à l'école!

— Tu es en sécurité ici, a dit Mlle Barry. J'ai appelé ton père à la fonderie. Il m'a demandé de rester auprès de toi jusqu'à son arrivée.

Elle m'a tendu le verre d'eau. Je l'ai remerciée et j'en ai bu quelques gorgées. J'avais la bouche toute sèche. J'ai fermé les yeux.

Chapitre dix-sept

Gretchen

Gretchen Himmel! Soudain, la lumière s'est faite dans ma tête : je me suis rappelé comment j'étais devenue Gretchen Himmel.

Au début, je faisais semblant d'être une Allemande. Ensuite, plus je mentais, plus tout devenait réel. J'ai commencé par parler en allemand pour ne plus me faire punir. Puis je me suis mise à penser en allemand. Je marchais en rangs avec les autres enfants. Nous récitions de longs poèmes et chantions des chansons faisant l'éloge d'Hitler et du Reich. Nous étions nés pour dominer le monde entier. J'étais fière d'être parmi les élus.

Larissa disparaissait, et Gretchen émergeait...

Gretchen sait que la femme que j'appelais Baba n'était pas ma grand-mère. Elle m'avait volée à mes parents, qui étaient de bons fermiers allemands. L'homme qui m'appelait sa fille était un bandit. La femme que j'appelais ma mère était une espionne. L'autre fille n'était pas ma sœur. C'était une esclave malfaisante, et elle essayait de me tromper. Elle a été punie pour ses crimes. Les Juifs sont des rats. Ils méritent la mort. J'ai hâte de retourner chez moi, auprès de mes vrais parents! Je m'appelle Gretchen. J'ai vu mon acte de naissance : dessus, il est écrit Gretchen Himmel. Je suis contente de sortir de toute cette confusion.

On me donne mon bain, puis on m'habille avec un chemisier blanc bien empesé, une tunique bleue et des chaussures qui me font mal aux talons. Mes cheveux sont propres, bien peignés et tressés. Je m'assois sur la banquette arrière d'une longue voiture noire et je respire le parfum du cuir qui vient d'être astiqué. La voiture s'arrête devant une énorme ferme, en pleine campagne. Les champs s'étendent tout autour à des kilomètres à la ronde. Des esclaves y travaillent. Le chauffeur est un soldat en uniforme gris. Il m'ouvre la porte avec un sourire et dit :

— Je suis sûr que tu es contente de rentrer à la maison, Gretchen.

Je descends de la voiture et je me remplis les poumons de l'air frais de la campagne. Une fillette blonde portant une robe rose pâle ouvre la porte de la maison et court à ma rencontre. Une femme blonde, au regard triste, la suit de près.

— Ma grande sœur est enfin arrivée! dit la petite.

Elle m'entoure aussitôt la taille de ses bras. Elle pleure ou rit, je ne sais pas très bien.

— Je suis si contente que tu sois revenue, dit Eva en allemand.

Suis-je chez moi? Je ne me rappelle pas cette maison. Mais je ne me souviens pas de grand-chose. Je suis soulagée d'être en sécurité, enfin « chez moi ».

Eva me tire par la main et m'entraîne vers la porte ouverte de la grande maison. La femme blonde nous suit, à quelques pas derrière nous. Elle m'a à peine saluée. Eva m'explique qu'elle est notre Mutti. Je l'observe du coin de l'œil et je vois qu'elle essuie une larme qui a roulé sur sa joue.

La porte de la maison donne sur une vaste entrée qui sent l'eau de Javel. Mon cœur bat très fort. Eva serre ma main.

Elle me conduit dans une pièce qui est de l'autre côté de l'entrée, et j'en reste bouche bée. Deux murs sont entièrement tapissés de livres, du plancher jusqu'au plafond. La plupart sont en allemand, et quelques-uns sont en d'autres langues. Je meurs d'envie de les toucher. Les livres semblent m'appeler par mon nom. Au-dessus de la cheminée, il y a un énorme portrait d'Hitler, notre chef et notre sauveur. Sur le manteau de la cheminée se trouve la photo encadrée d'un jeune homme au regard triste, portant un uniforme de couleur sombre.

— C'est notre cher Geert, dit Eva.

— Il est très beau, dis-je.

La femme qui est censée être notre mère se tient debout derrière nous et regarde la photo. Je l'entends renifler.

— Votre frère était beau, dit-elle. Et courageux. Il est

mort en se battant pour notre mère patrie.

Elle quitte la pièce. Eva et moi restons seules.

— *Mutti est si triste depuis la mort de Geert. Elle va peut-être aller mieux, maintenant que tu es là.*

Je n'ai aucun souvenir de Geert, et voilà qu'il est mort. Je me sens coupable.

— *Moi aussi je suis triste que notre frère soit mort, dis-je.*

Eva me regarde étrangement, puis cligne des yeux.

— *Tu vas te plaire ici, dit-elle. Il y a tout ce qu'on veut à manger.*

— Ton père s'en vient, dit Mlle Barry.

J'ai cligné des yeux une fois, lentement, et j'ai regardé tout autour de moi. J'étais sur le canapé, dans la salle du personnel, à la bibliothèque. J'ai baissé les yeux et j'ai vu que je tenais un verre d'eau dans mes mains. J'en ai bu une gorgée. Mlle Barry a relevé une mèche de cheveux qui me tombait dans les yeux. C'était si gentil de sa part que j'ai failli en pleurer...

Eva a raison. Il y a tout ce qu'on veut à manger. Des pommes et des champignons, des nouilles et de la sauce, de la viande et des pâtés. Mutter dépose toutes ces victuailles sur la table de la salle à manger. Mais j'avale difficilement tout ce que je mets dans ma bouche; tout me laisse un goût amer. Mutter fait du gâteau au chocolat avec du glaçage, pour m'inciter à manger. Elle fait des biscuits en forme de bonshommes au visage dessiné avec du glaçage blanc. Eva raffole de tout et s'empiffre à qui mieux mieux. Je me force à manger, même si cela me rend malade. Je veux que la souffrance disparaisse des yeux de Mutter.

J'ai ma chambre à moi, avec un gigantesque lit à baldaquin, mais je n'arrive pas à dormir. Des hommes en uniformes de couleur sombre dînent à notre table et discutent jusque tard dans la nuit. J'entends des verres tinter et des éclats de rire. Je vois rarement Vater, sauf lors de ces réunions. Eva et moi revêtons alors nos plus belles robes et descendons saluer les invités. Vater nous présente comme ses « deux fleurs offertes à la mère patrie ».

Quand je peux enfin retourner dans ma chambre, je chante une chanson aux paroles incompréhensibles afin d'enterrer leur vacarme. Mais je n'arrive pas à dormir.

Au printemps, la femme Ostarbeiter est arrivée à la ferme en camion. Elle sent mauvais, et je ne l'aime pas. Quand je la vois, la fois suivante, elle ne porte plus son écusson brodé des lettres OST et elle est propre. Mutter nous dit de l'appeler « Cuisinière ». Eva et moi jouons ensemble, dehors. Nous cueillons des lilas pour Mutter. Elle les met dans un vase et les dépose au centre de la table de la cuisine. Elle dit que la cuisinière va les aimer. Mutter préfère les fleurs achetées en boutique pour orner la salle à manger.

Nous n'avons pas le droit d'aller dans les champs où travaillent les esclaves. Je vois un esclave qui se présente à notre porte. La cuisinière met un bandage sur sa blessure. Mutter n'est pas au courant. Eva non plus. Je devrais en parler à Mutter mais, j'ignore pourquoi, je n'en fais rien.

Mutter emmène souvent Eva faire des courses avec elle et me laisse à la maison. Quand elles sont parties, j'ouvre la porte de la bibliothèque et je respire l'odeur de vieux papier. En sentant cette odeur, j'éprouve à la fois de la peine et de la joie. Je grimpe sur le bureau et je prends un livre au dos orné de lettres dorées. Le livre voisin tombe par terre, et ses pages se cornent.

J'entends des bruits de pas, et mon cœur se met à battre à tout rompre. C'est seulement la cuisinière. Elle ramasse le livre et le remet à sa place. Elle prend celui que je tiens dans mes mains et le replace aussi sur l'étagère. Elle examine les autres livres. Soudain, son visage s'illumine. Elle en prend un autre et me le tend.

— Tu peux regarder ce livre-ci jusqu'à leur retour, dit-elle.

Le titre n'est pas en allemand. Je m'exclame :

— Popelyushka! La cuisinière sourit.

Une autre fois, je suis assise sous les lilas et je chante tout bas, pour moi-même, ma chanson aux paroles incompréhensibles. La cuisinière vient me rejoindre. Je remarque ses mains rougies par le travail. Son regard est triste et fatigué. J'ai de la peine pour elle, même si elle est un animal. Je dis en allemand :

— Aimerais-tu m'entendre chanter?

De la tête, elle me fait signe que oui.

Je chante encore une fois ma chanson secrète. La cuisinière sanglote. Au deuxième couplet, la voix cassée par les larmes, elle se met à chanter avec moi. Elle chante la chanson avec moi, jusqu'à la fin.

Comment peut-elle connaître ma langue secrète?

— Tu connais ma kolysanka? *lui dis-je surprise.*

Elle veut me serrer dans ses bras, mais je la repousse. Mutter m'a dit de ne pas m'approcher des esclaves.

La cuisinière ravale ses larmes et, d'un ton très dur, me dit en allemand :

— Ce n'est pas chez toi ici.

Sous le choc, je reste sans voix.

Mais elle n'a pas encore tout dit. Elle ajoute :

— Je vais te protéger.

La sonnerie stridente du téléphone m'a ramenée soudainement à la réalité. J'ai cligné des yeux et j'ai regardé autour de moi. Ces images du passé étaient si réelles! Pourtant, j'étais ici, étendue sur le canapé dans la salle du personnel, à la bibliothèque. J'ai entendu la voix de Mlle Barry qui parlait avec quelqu'un à l'autre bout du fil. Puis sa voix s'est estompée...

Quand Mutter et Eva reviennent de leurs courses, je suis impatiente de leur rapporter ce que m'a dit la cuisinière. Elle devrait être punie pour son crime. Mais, j'ignore pourquoi, encore une fois, je n'en dis rien. Un autre jour, quand Mutter et Eva retournent faire des courses, la cuisinière m'invite à partager un repas avec elle à la cuisine. C'est de la nourriture pour les esclaves : du bouillon clair avec du pain noir. Je prends une cuillerée du bouillon clair et me mets à pleurer. J'essaie de me souvenir de ce que cette soupe me rappelle, mais ma mémoire n'est qu'un grand trou vide.

Nous allons assister à un rassemblement, et Mutter m'a demandé d'être prête quand elles reviendraient. Je mets ma robe rose, et la cuisinière me tresse les cheveux. J'attends. J'attends encore et j'attends toujours.

J'erre dans la maison et je vois que des tiroirs sont restés ouverts et que des vêtements jonchent le plancher. Je sens le sol trembler.

— Les soviets arrivent, chuchote la cuisinière. Il faut partir d'ici.

Je ne veux pas m'en aller. Je suis chez moi. La pièce remplie de livres est ici. Le lilas est ici. Mutter m'a dit de l'attendre. La cuisinière me prend dans ses bras et sort de la maison. Je crie et je lui tire les cheveux. Elle me laisse tomber par terre, et je me fais mal au dos.

— Si tu tiens à la vie, suis-moi, dit-elle en s'éloignant.

Je la suis en la suppliant de m'attendre. Je cours à travers les champs et je vois que les esclaves sont tous partis. Je le fais remarquer à la cuisinière, et elle se retourne vers moi. Rouge de colère, elle s'écrie :

— Les Slaves, pas les esclaves. Ce sont des Ukrainiens, comme toi.

Je ne la crois pas, mais ce n'est pas le moment de discuter. Elle me dit qu'elle s'appelle Marusia, et pas « la cuisinière ».

Nous nous cachons dans un fourré pendant que les Soviétiques patrouillent dans les champs, à la recherche des Slaves qui, comme moi, ont été volés. On va nous ramener en Union soviétique et nous punir pour nous être laissé emmener par les Allemands.

Nous traversons des forêts et des champs truffés de mines. Nous voyons des villages incendiés et nous entendons des bombes qui explosent. Je ne m'attends pas à sortir de là vivante.

Nous nous joignons à un groupe de survivants en haillons.

— Maintenant tu t'appelles Nadia, me dit Marusia. Tu ne seras plus jamais Gretchen.

Je lui demande :

— Mais pourquoi Nadia?

— Ce prénom signifie « espoir », dit-elle. C'était un des noms de baptême de ma petite sœur. Elle aussi a été volée par les nazis.

Chapitre dix-huit

Larissa

— Nadia… Nadia. Tu es en sécurité.

Ce parfum de pommes et de lessive… Ce ne peut être que Marusia. J'ouvre les yeux. En effet, c'est Marusia, en tenue de travail. Je cligne des yeux et regarde autour de moi, en essayant de me remettre les esprits en place. Je suis toujours dans la salle du personnel de la bibliothèque, emmitouflée dans la couverture de Mlle Barry. Un grand frisson me parcourt le corps. Je suis terriblement triste et j'ai très froid.

Je sens les bras de Marusia m'enlacer la taille.

Ivan est assis par terre, en tailleur. Il fronce les sourcils, l'air inquiet. Il n'y a personne d'autre ici. Seulement moi, Marusia et Ivan.

Dans quel pétrin m'étais-je encore mise en m'enfuyant une seconde fois de l'école? Ivan a deviné mon inquiétude.

— Nous avons dit à l'inspecteur que tu étais malade, a-t-il expliqué.

J'ai senti un gros sanglot me monter à la gorge, de

soulagement, mais aussi de culpabilité. Depuis quand étais-je là?

— Quelle heure est-il? ai-je demandé.

— Il est passé six heures du soir, a dit Ivan. Nous sommes assis ici avec toi depuis des heures.

Nous manquions toujours d'argent, et voilà qu'ils s'étaient absentés du travail à cause de moi.

J'ai éclaté en sanglots.

— Je suis vraiment désolée! ai-je dit. Je ne voulais pas vous déranger.

— Tu ne nous déranges pas, a répliqué Ivan.

Marusia n'a pas dit un mot. À entendre sa respiration saccadée, j'ai compris qu'elle pleurait. Je savais qu'elle ne pleurait pas seulement à cause de moi. Elle avait perdu une autre Nadia, sa petite sœur, il y avait plusieurs années. Tout comme j'avais perdu ma famille. Elle m'a serrée très fort contre elle et a posé sa tête sur mon épaule. Je l'ai serrée moi aussi. Ivan s'est penché et nous a entourées toutes les deux de ses bras. Nous avons pleuré ensemble.

Je ne sais pas combien de temps nous sommes restés ainsi, mais soudain je me suis aperçue que nous étions encore dans la bibliothèque.

— Pouvons-nous rentrer à la maison? ai-je demandé.

Nous avons desserré nos bras et, quand j'ai voulu me relever, j'avais les jambes si faibles que mes genoux ont lâché. Marusia aussi était chancelante.

— Allons! Je vous ramène à la maison, les filles de

ma vie, a dit Ivan.

Il a retiré la couverture de mes épaules et m'a tendu mon manteau, grand ouvert pour que je puisse glisser mes bras dans les manches. Il était probablement allé le chercher à l'école. Il m'a entouré la taille d'un de ses bras et de l'autre, celle de Marusia afin de nous soutenir en marchant.

À la maison, Marusia a réchauffé un reste de soupe qu'elle avait faite et a tranché du pain de seigle. Avant, un repas comme celui-là aurait réveillé en moi des souvenirs douloureux et déclenché des cauchemars. Maintenant que j'avais recouvré la mémoire, du moins en partie, j'étais capable de penser à ce dernier bol de soupe que j'avais partagé avec ma grand-mère et ma sœur. C'était une époque triste, mais pleine d'amour. Comme elles me manquaient toutes les deux!

Je n'avais toujours pas réussi à remettre en place dans ma mémoire toutes les bribes de souvenirs de ma vie avant que mes parents ne disparaissent. J'avais encore le cœur en peine de les avoir perdus. Je devais être très jeune quand ils ont été emmenés. Je savais maintenant qu'ils n'avaient pas été simplement emmenés. Ils étaient morts. Tato avait été tué par les Soviétiques, et Mama, par les nazis. Je claquais des dents. Pas à cause du froid, mais parce que je venais de comprendre tout ce que j'avais perdu.

J'ai croisé mes bras sur ma poitrine et je me suis mise à me bercer d'avant en arrière sur ma chaise. En avant, en arrière, en avant, en arrière… en essayant de me rappeler la dernière fois que mes parents m'avaient tenue dans leurs bras.

Je savais surtout que Mama et Tato m'avaient profondément aimée. Des bribes de souvenirs du passé me le montraient. Puis j'ai pensé très fort à Tato, et je me suis rappelé son sourire aimant et la dernière fois qu'il m'avait bordée dans mon lit… Mama, chère Mama! Que sa voix était mélodieuse quand elle chantait la *kolysanka!*

Et Baba? Comme elle était forte! Mais elle n'avait sûrement pas survécu au choc de m'avoir perdue, en même temps que Lida.

Lida…

La fillette aux cheveux blonds plus foncés que les miens et qui essayait de me prendre par la main… La fille des *Ostarbeiters* qui a croisé mon regard devant l'usine bombardée. C'était Lida. Je le savais maintenant.

Marusia a caressé doucement mon bras du bout de ses doigts et m'a demandé :

— Es-tu prête à nous en parler maintenant?

— Oui. Du moins de ce dont je me souviens.

Et c'était un tel soulagement de dire à voix haute tous les détails de mon histoire.

Au début, c'était très confus. Mais au fur et à mesure que j'avançais dans mon récit, mes souvenirs se remettaient en place. J'arrivais à replacer chaque souvenir dans la bonne époque; ceux où j'étais

Gretchen et ceux d'avant, quand j'étais encore Larissa. Je sentais mes épaules comme soulagées d'un grand poids, en étant maintenant certaine que Vater et Mutter n'étaient pas mes vrais parents. Le souvenir de Vater, plus particulièrement, me donnait la nausée. Toutefois, je m'inquiétais un peu pour Eva. Ce n'était pas ma sœur, mais ce n'était qu'une enfant. Où était-elle maintenant? Encore en vie? Lui arrivait-il de penser à moi?

Marusia hochait la tête tout en m'écoutant parler. Elle connaissait mon histoire à partir du moment où j'avais vécu à la ferme. De ma vie de l'époque précédente, elle en avait deviné une partie. Elle avait probablement raconté tout ce qu'elle savait à Ivan. Néanmoins, il m'écoutait bouche bée.

— Je me suis toujours demandé quel était ton vrai prénom, a dit Marusia. Larissa, c'est magnifique! Et tu as une sœur qui s'appelle Lida.

— Oui.

Ma sœur… Ma chère grande sœur Lida! Je me suis remise à pleurer.

— Pensez-vous qu'elle soit encore en vie? ai-je réussi à demander.

— Après ce que tu nous as raconté, nous arriverons peut-être à savoir ce qu'elle est devenue, a dit Marusia.

— Nous écrirons à la Croix-Rouge, a dit Ivan. Il ne faut jamais perdre espoir!

Note de l'auteure

J'ai entendu parler du programme *Lebensborn* pour la première fois de la bouche de ma belle-mère, la regrettée Lidia (Krawchuk) Skrypuch. Le front nazi était passé deux fois par sa ville, Zolochiv, et les soldats s'étaient emparés de leur maison. Ses parents et elle sont alors devenus prisonniers chez eux. Un jour, elle a surpris des bribes de conversation entre les officiers nazis. Il devait se passer quelque chose à son école, le lendemain. Ses parents l'ont gardée à la maison. Quand elle est retournée à l'école, toutes ses camarades de classe qui avaient les cheveux blonds et les yeux bleus avaient disparu. On lui a dit qu'elles avaient été emmenées pour le programme *Lebensborn*. Je lui ai demandé ce que c'était.

Le programme *Lebensborn*

L'assassinat de six millions de Juifs par les nazis (appelé l'Holocauste) pendant la Deuxième Guerre mondiale a été largement documenté. Toutefois, peu de gens sont au courant que les nazis avaient aussi des projets concernant d'autres populations. Hitler et les nazis croyaient que les peuples germaniques de l'Europe centrale étaient les descendants des Aryens, qu'ils considéraient comme une « race supérieure » destinée à dominer le reste du monde. Les autres groupes ethniques étaient ensuite classés en ordre décroissant, suivant la pureté du « sang aryen » coulant supposément dans leurs veines. La plupart des peuples de l'Europe du Nord, de la Grande-Bretagne, des Pays-Bas et même de certaines parties de la France étaient considérés comme principalement ou partiellement aryens. D'autres peuples, en particulier ceux du sud de l'Europe, étaient considérés comme moins purs, mais acceptables en tant que nations limitrophes ou alliées. Au dernier échelon de cette échelle humaine se trouvaient les Juifs et les Roms (les gitans). L'objectif des nazis était d'éliminer tous les Juifs et les gitans de la surface de la Terre. Les nazis avaient aussi comme projet de tuer toutes les personnes qu'ils considéraient comme inaptes mentalement ou physiquement.

La politique des nazis à l'égard des Slaves, c'est-à-dire les Russes, les Ukrainiens, les Biélorusses, les Polonais, les Tchèques et plusieurs autres peuples, était moins cohérente. Les Slaves étaient considérés comme une race inférieure, et Hitler a décrété que la plupart de leurs territoires en Europe de l'Est étaient des *Lebensraum* (des « espaces de vie ») destinés à l'expansion de la race aryenne. Contrairement à l'holocauste juif, les nazis n'ont pas lancé une opération de destruction systématique contre les Slaves. Toutefois, ils ont traité les populations civiles de l'Europe de l'Est beaucoup plus durement qu'ailleurs en Europe. Les historiens évaluent à au moins dix millions le nombre de civils slaves tués par les Allemands en Pologne et en URSS.

Les Slaves ont été déplacés massivement de chez eux dans le but de libérer ces « espaces de vie » pour les Aryens. Certains, des gens de l'est de l'Ukraine pour la plupart, ont été envoyés aux travaux forcés (c'est-à-dire en esclavage) en Allemagne. Des documents des services secrets britanniques indiquent que, par moments, les déportations en Ukraine soviétique ont atteint un rythme de 15 000 à 20 000 personnes par jour. Les villes soviétiques étaient pleines de ce que les nazis considéraient comme des « bouches superflues ». Un grand nombre de citadins sont donc morts de faim.

Hitler voulait davantage de naissances aryennes, mais le taux de natalité des Allemandes n'était pas assez élevé. En 1936, la police secrète d'Hitler, les SS, ont mis sur pied le programme *Lebensborn* (ou « fontaines de vie ») afin d'augmenter le nombre de naissances aryennes. La race supérieure pourrait ainsi peupler une plus grande partie de l'Europe. Au début, le programme *Lebensborn* visait surtout à ce qu'un plus grand nombre d'enfants aryens naissent dans les parties de l'Europe occupées par les nazis. Toutefois, de 1940 à 1942, les Allemands se sont plus particulièrement intéressés aux enfants blonds aux yeux bleus de Pologne et d'Ukraine, qui ressemblaient tout à fait aux enfants aryens. Ils se sont mis à voler ces enfants à leurs parents.

Deux méthodes ont été utilisées. La première consistait à prendre tous les enfants d'un âge donné dans des villes et des villages choisis au hasard, puis à les trier. Les uns étaient déportés puis tués, d'autres étaient envoyés aux travaux forcés et, enfin, certains étaient donnés en adoption à des familles allemandes.

La deuxième méthode consistait à avoir recours à des femmes nazies spécialement formées, dont le rôle était de trouver les enfants blonds dans un endroit donné. On les appelait les « sœurs brunes ». Un enfant à l'apparence aryenne se faisait offrir des bonbons, ce qui donnait aux sœurs brunes l'occasion de l'interroger. Puis la maison de cet enfant était assaillie en pleine nuit et l'enfant était enlevé.

Les enfants volés subissaient divers tests, dont la mesure de 62 parties de leur corps, afin de s'assurer qu'ils étaient vraiment « de bonne qualité raciale ». Le moindre petit défaut déterminait leur sort : se faire adopter, être envoyés au camp de concentration ou aller aux travaux forcés.

Les enfants sélectionnés comme étant de bonne qualité raciale étaient finalement envoyés dans des établissements spéciaux où on leur faisait subir un lavage de cerveau jusqu'à ce qu'ils se prennent pour des Allemands. Certains se faisaient dire que leurs parents étaient morts et d'autres, qu'ils étaient des espions ou des menteurs. Les jeunes enfants, de moins de huit ans, étaient ensuite placés dans leur nouvelle famille nazie. Les plus vieux étaient envoyés dans un pensionnat des Jeunesses hitlériennes ou étaient rejetés du programme.

Quand il a été clair que l'Allemagne allait perdre la guerre, les nazis ont tout fait pour détruire les documents concernant ces enfants. Il est donc très difficile de savoir combien ont été volés de cette façon. Pour la Pologne et l'Ukraine seulement, on estime le nombre à environ 250 000 enfants. Le programme des nazis a si bien fonctionné que, après la guerre, la plupart de ces enfants volés ont refusé de quitter leurs parents allemands, même quand leurs parents biologiques étaient encore vivants et qu'on pouvait les localiser.

Les *Ostarbeiters*

Les nazis ne se sont pas contentés d'enlever des enfants. Ils ont aussi obligé des millions de jeunes adultes à faire des travaux forcés. Ceux qui venaient de l'Europe de l'Est s'appelaient des *Ostarbeiters* (ou « travailleurs de l'Est »). Ils étaient traités durement, travaillant souvent jusqu'à en mourir. On les obligeait à porter un écusson arborant les lettres OST, et la plupart vivaient dans des camps entourés de barbelés. De 3 à 5,5 millions d'*Ostarbeiters* ont vécu dans l'Allemagne nazie. La plupart étaient ukrainiens. Beaucoup ont été forcés de travailler dans les usines de munitions allemandes, car les nazis avaient compris que ces usines étaient les principales cibles des bombardements effectués par les nations alliées. De nombreux *Ostarbeiters* sont donc morts lors des bombardements alliés.

L'identité ukrainienne

Avant la Deuxième guerre mondiale, le territoire habité par les Ukrainiens depuis plus de 1 000 ans était devenu une partie de la Pologne et une partie de l'Union soviétique. Depuis la guerre, les statistiques identifient les gens selon leur citoyenneté et non selon leur origine ethnique. Les Ukrainiens se sont donc retrouvés identifiés comme Polonais ou comme « Soviétiques », ces derniers étant souvent confondus à tort avec les Russes. Lors de la chute de l'Union soviétique en 1991, des documents d'archives dont la consultation était jusque-là interdite sont devenus accessibles aux chercheurs. Le grand public a aussi pris conscience des différences ethniques en Europe de l'Est et dans l'ancienne Union soviétique. De là a pu émerger un tableau plus véridique de ce qu'a vécu l'Ukraine au cours de la Deuxième Guerre mondiale. La nation ukrainienne s'est déclarée indépendante en 1991.